JOHN ASHBERY
AND AMERICAN POETRY

For Abi and Lily

JOHN ASHBERY
AND AMERICAN POETRY

David Herd

palgrave

JOHN ASHBERY AND AMERICAN POETRY

First published 2000 by Palgrave

ISBN 0-312-28931-9

Library of Congress Cataloging-in-Publication Data applied for

10 9 8 7 6 5 4 3 2 1

Typeset
by Northern Phototypesetting Co. Ltd, Bolton
Printed in Great Britain
by Bookcraft (Bath) Ltd, Midsomer Norton

Contents

[v]

Abbreviations

Acknowledgements

There are a number of people I want to thank for their help in the preparation of this book. John Ashbery very kindly answered all my questions, and twice agreed to the ordeal of an interview. I am extremely grateful to him for his time, and for permission to quote from his unpublished materials. I am grateful also to Kenneth Koch, Alex Katz and John Ash, all of whom gave of their time and understanding. David Trotter supervised the PhD thesis from which the book emerged. I could not have wished for a better supervisor and have benefited greatly from his support and criticism. Ian Sansom read the whole manuscript at a late stage, and it is a pleasure to thank him now for his rigorous criticism, his timely encouragement and many conversations on poetry and more. Geoff Ward, Robert Hampson, Peter Swaab and Jan Montefiore read and commented on all or part of the work at various stages of its development. The book is better than it might have been as a result of their attention. Its shortcomings, of course, are down to me.

My thanks go to the editors of *The Critical Review*, *Critical Quarterly* and *The Yearbook of English Studies* for their permission to use extracts from articles which formed early drafts of some of the arguments here. I am grateful also for the helpfulness and courtesy of staff at University College London library, the British Library, the John Rylands Library at the University of Manchester, the Templeman Library at the University of Kent at Canterbury, the New York Public Library and the Houghton Library, Harvard University.

The author and publisher wish to thank the following who have kindly given permission for the use of copyright material: John Ashbery, George Borchardt Inc., Carcanet Press Ltd, the University Press of New England, Penguin and Farrar, Straus & Giroux Inc. for extracts from Ashbery's work; Carcanet and Alfred A. Knopf Inc. for extracts from Kenneth Koch's poetry; Faber & Faber Ltd and Harcourt Brace Jovanovich Inc., for lines by Robert Lowell; Faber & Faber and Farrar, Straus & Giroux Inc. for lines by John Berryman and Philip Larkin; Faber & Faber and Alfred A. Knopf Inc. for lines by Wallace Stevens; Faber & Faber and Curtis Brown for lines by W.H. Auden; Princeton University Press for lines by David Lehman. Every effort has been made to trace all the copyright holders but if any have been inadvertently overlooked the publishers will be pleased to maket he necessary arrangements at the first opportunity.

[vii]

The staff at Manchester University Press were patient and insistent with me at the appropriate times. I am grateful for their encouragement and consideration.

My parents have, as always, been fully supportive of my efforts and it is a great pleasure to thank them for that here. My deepest thanks go to Abi, without whom this book could not have been written.

Introduction: John Ashbery's sense of occasion

John Ashbery lives with a paradox. 'On the one hand,' as he observed in interview in 1979, 'I am an important poet, read by younger writers, and on the other hand, nobody understands me. I am often asked to account for this state of affairs, but I can't.'[1] Twenty years later, Ashbery is the most influential poet writing in English. His presence can be felt in the work of such diverse American poets as Charles Bernstein and Mark Doty, and in British poets as different as Denise Riley and Glyn Maxwell. Not since Auden influenced both Ashbery and Larkin in the 1940s has a poet held such sway over the mainstream and the avant-garde. As this range of influence indicates, there are many ways for the young poet to learn from Ashbery; from his astonishing array of styles, voices, postures and concerns. Even so, in trying to describe how reading him has benefited their poetry, younger writers invariably find themselves saying much the same thing. The American poet Donald Revell puts it like this: 'when I remember my first reading of almost any Ashbery piece, I remember my own situation at the time intermingled with the figures and gestures of the poem.'[2] Revell's remark echoes Ashbery's description of the effect that reading John Clare has on him. As Ashbery put it in his 1989 Charles Eliot Norton lecture on Clare, 'the effect of reading Clare's poetry, on me at least, is always the same, that of re-inserting me in my present, of re-establishing now'.[3] That Clare's poetry can always have this effect is a consequence, so Ashbery's uncomplicated argument has it, of his poetry's relation to its own situation. 'The sudden surprising lack of distance', Ashbery suggests, 'between poet and reader is in proportion to the lack of distance between the poet and the poem … These poems are dispatches from the front. "I found the poems in the fields / And only wrote them down."'[4] So intimate does Clare's poetry seem with its own situation that it alerts Ashbery to his, if only by reminding him of the desirability of such intimacy; such intimacy being, as Ashbery has argued, the stuff of great poetry. Or as he develops the point in 'Litany', clearly and at length:

> Just one minute of contemporary existence
> Has so much to offer, but who
> Can evaluate it, formulate

The appropriate apothegm, show us
In a few well-chosen words of wisdom
Exactly what is taking place all about us?
Not critics, certainly, though that is precisely
What they are supposed to be doing, yet how
Often have you read any criticism
Of our society and all the people and things in it
That really makes sense, to us as human beings?
I don't mean that a lot that is clever and intelligent
Doesn't get written, both by critics
And poets and men-of-letters in general
But exactly whom are you aware of
Who can describe the exact feel
And slant of a field in such a way as to
Make you wish you were in it, or better yet
To make you realize that you actually are in it
For better or for worse, with no
Conceivable way of getting out?
That is what
Great poets of the past have done, and a few
Great critics as well.

(AWK, 32–3)

What this book argues, and what the extent of his influence on contemporary poetry indicates, is that, one way or another, Ashbery does exactly this. One way or another, that is, and in ways and, for reasons I hope to make clear, Ashbery has continually formulated the apothegm appropriate to his moment.

So how come 'nobody understands' him? How, in other words, can one begin to account for the paradoxical state of affairs Ashbery describes? To start with, one can query his despondent account of his reception. In 1979 he had recently won all three major American book awards for *Self-Portrait in a Convex Mirror* – the Pulitzer Prize, a National Book Award and the National Book Critics' Circle Award – and yet continually in interview he was being asked to comment on the 'difficulty', sometimes the 'incomprehensibility', of his poetry. Not surprisingly, his paradox felt acute. Since then the situation has altered somewhat. Boatloads of criticism have passed under the bridge, much of it freighted with insights. Consequently, even some hitherto severely sceptical critics have begun to develop ways of reading Ashbery. Barbara Everett, for instance, recently compared Larkin's poetry of 'attraction' with Ashbery's poetry of 'distraction', a terminology which, though clearly weighted against Ashbery, nonetheless constituted some kind of coming to terms with his poetic.[5] Yet while it would therefore no longer be true to say that 'nobody understands' Ashbery, still, as often as not, his poetry meets with irritable incomprehension. As the *TLS* reviewer of Ashbery's most recent volume *Wakefulness* understood it, 'This is not a poetry of the right words in the right order. An Ashbery admirer would be hard pushed to find a poem in which every every word and every line earns its keep.' These are not poems, he suggested, which 'lend themselves to traditional practical criticism'.[6] Likewise, for the *Poetry Review* reviewer

> much of the book is a desert of local, wilful ingenuity across which the poet can be heard nattering on and habitually juxtaposing until the reader finds himself abandoning equipment – rifle, boots, water-bottle – and running for the horizon as delirium sets in.[7]

Set against the passage from 'Litany', the relaxed arguing of which has been a feature of Ashbery's style since his earliest poems, these remarks seem oddly impertinent. The point is, however, that Ashbery still gets such reviews, and that his poetry therefore remains paradoxically poised: hugely important, because uniquely appropriate, to its time, and often misunderstood.

From certain perspectives this need not matter. Ashbery is held in the highest regard by some of the most influential critics of his time (Bloom, Vendler and Perloff to name but three) and is regularly lauded by committees that award prizes and grants (in 1985 he was awarded a MacArthur fellowship, the so-called 'genius' grant). So if it's true that 'no living poet ever arrived at the fullness of his fame', Ashbery has perhaps achieved as much recognition as he might reasonably hope for, and anyway there is still, perhaps, a certain avant-garde frisson to be gained by ruffling the feathers of those for whom poems should 'lend themselves to traditional practical criticism'. Why should it matter, then, if some, or even many, readers don't get Ashbery, when those who count do? It matters because Ashbery is, not least, a democratic poet; a poet who wants nothing more than to speak to his contemporaries. As he has said in interview, 'The reputation my poetry has of being something terribly private and difficult to get at is not at all what I hoped for. I'm hoping that someday people will see it that way.'[8] Or, again,

> My poetry is often criticized for a failure to communicate, but I take issue with this; my intention is to communicate and my feeling is that a poem that communicates something that's already known by the reader is not really communicating anything to him and in fact shows a lack of respect for him.[9]

Given this intention – an intention he has continually restated since at least the early 1970s – critical writing on Ashbery which did not clearly address the fact that in some quarters he meets with misunderstanding, would be failing the poetry, if for no other reason than that it would contravene a central, perhaps the central, impulse of the work.

Discussing the 'irrationality' of some reactions to Modernist art, Charles Rosen has observed the belief

> that a work we do not understand must be devoid of all meaning ... Ned Rorem, for instance, has written that nobody really likes the music of Elliott Carter; they only pretend to like it ... This ... is a characteristic expression of resentment ... for an art that one does not understand – or rather, for an art that one is unwilling to

understand. Taste is, after all, a matter of will, of moral and social decisions ... I myself, for example, do not care for the music of Messiaen ... But when I reflect that some of the finest musicians today, Peter Serkin among them, adore Messiaen, I realize that I, too, would learn to love his music if I decided to put my mind to it.[10]

Rosen's argument is compelling. One must be wary, of course, of indiscrimination, and, in a life of finite duration, demanding art must find some way of attracting and holding our attention, but, simply put, Rosen's point is that contemporary misunderstanding is a complex business. In Ashbery's case it has much to do with the status of the poet in western democratic culture, with the inescapable complexity of poetry which seriously aims to address that culture, and (for British readers at least) with the American idea of poetic understanding. These are questions which will be dealt with in the main body of this book, as, of course, will the question of how and when the poet himself can be thought to have got it wrong. Partly, however, Ashbery's paradoxical status is an effect of his critical treatment.

Ashbery glimpsed his critical destiny as long ago as 1968, when, in a lecture to the Yale Art School on 'The invisible avant-garde' he remarked that, 'To paraphrase Bernard Shaw, it is the fate of some artists, and perhaps the best ones, to pass from unacceptability to acceptance without an intervening period of appreciation' (RS, 390). This transition happened to Ashbery in 1975, *Self-Portrait in a Convex Mirror* thrusting him abruptly from the half-light of cult status into the limelight of official recognition. Until that point his poetry had received little substantial critical consideration, Harold Bloom being the significant exception. Since then it has been under constant surveillance. Mostly this has taken the form of academic articles and chapters in books, with admiring critics either teasing out an aspect of the writing or rendering it in the terms of a given theory. This is a problem. No criticism, it goes without saying, is without its intellectual prejudices. Ashbery's poetry has, however, been more prejudged than most. Noticing this problem in relation to Raymond Roussel, Ashbery has observed that Roussel's writing can, 'as the French say, be served with every kind of sauce. From Cocteau to Foucault and beyond, critics ... tend almost unconsciously to write about themselves. What can Roussel do for me?'[11] In the same way one can now have Ashbery à la Bloom, Lacan, Derrida, Bakhtin and Eve Kosofsky Sedgwick. On the one hand, this can be thought a healthy development, indicating that Ashbery's poetry is, as it would hope, Whitmanesque in its hospitality to a multiplicity of readers. If, on the other hand, the question shaping the reading is, 'What can Ashbery do for me?', then the equally Whitmanesque aspiration of a community of readers is undermined. Unfortunately, the timing of theoretical considerations of Ashbery was such that the latter has tended to be the case. As David Trotter has argued, Ashbery came to prominence just as the idea of theory was taking over the American academy. Licensed by his fame, critics experimenting with theoretical positions read Ashbery in the same way they were reading Romanticism, the poetry becoming a textual laboratory. But whereas the language of Romanticism was sufficiently familiar for interpretative distortions to be checked, for the overdetermined reading to be recognised as such, Ashbery's language wasn't and tended, as a consequence, to be obscured by the terminologies claiming to explain it. Or as 'The Other Tradition' has it,

> They all came, some wore sentiments
> Emblazoned on T-shirts, proclaiming the lateness
> Of the hour, and indeed the sun slanted its rays
> Through branches of Norfolk Island pine as though
> Politely clearing its throat, and all ideas settled
> In a fuzz of dust under trees when it's drizzling:
> The endless games of Scrabble, the boosters,
> The celebrated omelette au Cantal, and through it
> The roar of time plunging unchecked through the sluices
> Of the days, dragging every sexual moment of it
> Past the lenses: the end of something.
>
> (HD, 2)

The result of this kind of critical attention ('The endless games of Scrabble, the boosters, / The celebrated omelette au Cantal') was that, as Ashbery rightly observed,

> Very few people have ever written a serious mixed critique of my poetry. It's either dismissed as nonsense or held up as a work of genius. Few critics have ever accepted it on its own terms and pointed out how I've succeeded at certain moments and failed at others at what I was setting out to do.[12]

This state of affairs altered somewhat in 1994 with the publication of John Shoptaw's *On the Outside Looking Out: John Ashbery's Poetry*, a book which pushed Ashbery criticism firmly in the direction of the mixed critique. The book's value lies in its careful scholarship, and in Shoptaw's contextually detailed readings of individual poems. We know more about Ashbery as a result of his labour, from which this account unquestionably benefits. The weakness of Shoptaw's book was its critical idiom. While it did not repeat the mistake of importing a ready-made critical language, the terms it did arrive at never seemed quite germane to the poetry: not least because the notion from which Shoptaw developed his idea of 'misrepresentation', that of 'cryptology', was not Ashbery's own, but an interviewer's.[13] As a consequence, his story of the poetry's development left some of the more pressing questions unanswered. In what respects, the wary reader would still want to know, does Ashbery's oeuvre represent a continuous and developing body of work? How do such continuities square with the poetry's propensity for radical stylistic change? What makes for the difference between good and bad Ashbery? And why, if one hasn't read him seriously already, should one take the time to do so now? Finally, and more importantly from my perspective than from Shoptaw's, his terminology does not allow one to grasp how Ashbery's poetry relates to the American tradition, the particular Americanness of his syntax still proving the difference between Ashbery and many of his British reviewers.

The British poet Mark Ford has spoken of the difficulty, when writing about Ashbery's poetry, of arriving at a critical language equal to the medium one is attempting to describe.[14] Many readers and most critics of Ashbery will recognise this sensation. It goes with the territory. Aiming to show us 'Exactly what is taking place all about us', Ashbery's poetry extends the reader's sense of the given situation by exceeding that sense. This is hardly a new venture. As Shelley put it:

> [Poets] measure the circumference and sound the depths of human nature with a comprehensive and all penetrating spirit, and they are themselves perhaps the most sincerely astonished at its manifestations; for it is less their spirit than the spirit of the age. Poets are the hierophants of an unapprehended inspiration; the mirrors of the gigantic shadows which futurity casts upon the present; the words which express what they understand not.[15]

We should not be surprised, according to Shelley at least, if the poetry of a great contemporary tends to exceed the language by which we attempt to describe it. If it doesn't it is not telling us what is different about the situation we find ourselves in, and so is not telling us what is new, and therefore characteristic, about the present. Ashbery tempers Shelley's rhetoric, but takes him at his word when he observes that 'a poem which communicates something that's already known by the reader is not really communicating anything to him'. It is not surprising, then, as Ford suggests, that as one is writing about Ashbery one always feels oneself being outflanked, exceeded, extended by the poetry itself. This said, the poetry's object in exceeding understanding is to enhance it, and so (especially at this point in his reception history perhaps) Ashbery criticism can meet the needs of reader and poet only by beginning to develop a language flexible enough to tell the story of the poetry's development. My tentative objective here is to contribute to that process.

Ashbery himself has done much to expedite that process, becoming, as Robert Crawford has suggested, his own most instructive critic – forever indicating ways to approach his writing in poems, interviews, and meditations on writers and artists with whom he has an affinity.[16] Among Ashbery's more notable discussions of other writers was the series of Charles Eliot Norton lectures he gave at Harvard between 1989 and 1990. Introducing the series, entitled 'An other tradition', and including lectures on Clare, Thomas Lovell Beddoes, John Wheelwright, Laura Riding, Roussel and David Schubert, Ashbery explained that he 'chose the writers under discussion partly because I like them, and partly because I felt they would shed some light on my own writing for those who feel the need of it'.[17] Given the coolness of Ashbery's irony there are reasons to be wary of such gestures. By discussing minor poets on these auspicious occasions it has been argued that Ashbery sought to deflect critical attention away from those major poets – Whitman, Stevens, Auden – to whom he is more obviously indebted, and by comparison with whom he is less readily flattered. But one should be wary of over-wariness also, partly because Ashbery stood to lose as much as he might gain by the association with minor poets, but more importantly because, in telling us what he likes about these poets (not the same thing, it should be noticed, as reporting how he was influenced by them), Ashbery tells us what he would like to do in his own poetry. Thus for instance, of the difference between Clare and Beddoes, he notes that 'I find both kinds of poetry necessary. My own has swung, on its own I might add, always between the poles of Clare's lumpy poetry of mud and muck and Beddoes's perfumed and poisonous artifice.'[18] In speaking of Roussel, he remarks that 'Like Cage, Roussel is a poet who is about to be a poet. He is always bringing us face to face with the very latest moment in our thinking, the now where everything can and must happen, the locus solus where writing begins.'[19] In concluding his discussion of David Schubert's poem 'Midston House', he takes care to describe how

> one is tempted to complete the last line by making it 'to the person I want to say it to'. That's not what he's saying, however, though it is in a way since he leads us to expect it. The actual sense of the words is that the poem consists of speaking what cannot be said to the person I want to say it. In other words, the ideal situation for the poet is to have the reader speak the poem, and how nice it would be for everybody if that could be the case.[20]

Each of these aspirations – to sustain a language which is both mucky and perfumed, to bring us face to face with the now in which everything must happen, and, ideally, to have the reader speak the poem – is central to Ashbery's poetry. They combine, I argue, in the more general, and, I think, defining Ashberyan ambition, to write the poem fit for its occasion.

Speaking at an event called the 'Poetry Now Symposium' in March 1968, on the subject of, as he put it, 'something called the New York School of Poets', Ashbery disavowed the idea that he and his friends Frank O'Hara, Kenneth Koch, James Schuyler and Barbara Guest could be labelled a school. Accordingly he spent most of his talk telling the audience 'a number of things that the poetry isn't'. Only by way of conclusion did he endeavour to 'say a few things that it is', though this was hard because 'our program is the absence of any program'. 'I guess,' he suggested,

> it amounts to not planning the poem in advance but letting it take its own way: of living in a state of alert and being ready to change your mind if the occasion seems to require it. I hate to repeat Henry James' corny old advice, 'Be one of those people on whom nothing is lost,' but it is eminently practical and I see no other way to be.[21]

One wouldn't want to place too much importance on this particular statement. A photo of Ashbery at the event shows him looking bored and his remarks have an ad hoc quality, with the resort to James's corny old advice perhaps being evidence itself of an absence of planning. But precisely, perhaps, because he is going through the motions, Ashbery reaches for a term ('the occasion seems to require it') which had long been in currency among the poets of the so-called New York School.

In 1951 O'Hara wrote to Jane Freilicher in a state of high excitement. He had just read an article by Paul Goodman entitled 'Advance-guard writing 1900–1950' in which Goodman argued, after Goethe, that 'occasional poetry' is the 'highest kind', because 'it gives the most real and detailed subject-matter, it is closest in its effect on the audience, and it poses the enormous problem of being plausible to the actuality and yet creatively imagining something, finding something unlooked-for.'[22] Hardly able to contain himself, O'Hara urged Freilicher, 'if you haven't devoured its delicious message, rush to your nearest newsstand … It is really lucid about what's bothering us both beside sex, and it is so heartening to know that someone understands these things.'[23] Whether he had thought about art in precisely these terms before he read Goodman's article, O'Hara did so after, invariably reaching for them when assessing those writers and artists to whom he felt closest. Thus, introducing the dance writings of his great friend the New York poet Edwin Denby, O'Hara observed,

> Denby is as attentive to people walking in the streets or leaning against a corner, in any country he happens to be in, as he is to the more formal and exacting occasions of art and the theatre. He brings a wide range of experience to the expression of these insights: … his work as a ballet critic on the *New York Herald Tribune* … his more personal and more hermetic involvement with his poems; his constant traveling and inquisitive scholarship; all these activities contribute a wide range of reference for comparison and understanding of intricate occasions, as well as of complicated implications in occasions seemingly obvious and general.[24]

O'Hara's thinking about occasions is highly involved here. Everything in the first sentence – walking in the street, leaning against a corner, art, the theatre – is embraced by the term, which is thus for O'Hara, if not for Denby, a means of cutting across spheres of activity. And whatever kind it might happen to be, he, like Denby, is fascinated by the task of understanding occasions, of detailing their intricacy and complicated implications. The idea of the occasion, it seems fair to say, had clearly caught O'Hara's imagination.

If it sounds as if an argument about Ashbery is starting with O'Hara this might not be so inappropriate. In a review of Jane Freilicher's paintings which is in part a brief memoir of the earliest days of the New York School, Ashbery generously observed that

> The one thing lacking in our privileged little world (privileged because it was a kind of balcony overlooking the interestingly chaotic events happening in the bigger worlds outside) was the arrival of Frank O'Hara to kind of cobble everything together and tell us what we and they were doing. This happened in 1951. (RS, 241)

O'Hara's role, it should be noticed, was to tell Ashbery what he was already doing, not to tell him what to do. Whatever this meant, whatever O'Hara told him, what is certain is that the language of the occasion came to figure just as prominently in Ashbery's discussions of art as it did in O'Hara's. Take, for instance, 'The decline of the verbs', his review of one of his favourite novels (extracts from which he has himself translated), Giorgio de Chirico's

Hebdomeros. Ashbery's chief praise for de Chirico is on having 'invented for the occasion a new style and a new kind of novel which he was not to use again, but which could be of great interest to writers today who are trying to extend the novel form'. It is praise which, Ashbery is happy to observe, chimes with the novel's own language. As he puts it, quoting Chirico in order to illustrate his practice:

> Like Nietzsche and Chirico, Hebdomeros is sometimes forced to speak in 'a language that on any other occasion would have brought upon his shoulders not only the sarcasm of the crowd, which often is necessary to far-reaching minds, but also the sarcasm of the elite …'.[25]

Instances of Ashbery's critical use of the language of the occasion abound. More importantly, the term invariably has a controlling function in poems which in some sense or another have proved significant in his development. In 'The Instruction Manual' we meet a man in holiday mood:

> On his head sits a white hat
> And he wears a mostache, which has been trimmed for
> the occasion
>
> (ST,15).

'Soonest Mended' turns on the difficult realisation that

> Now there is no question even of that, but only
> Of holding on to the hard earth so as not to get thrown off,
> With an occasional dream, a vision:
>
> (DDS,17–18).

In 'Litany', a poem dispirited by the reception the poet has been receiving, we are assured that

> Some think him mean-tempered and gruff
> But actually his is an occasion for all occasions
>
> (AWK, 53)

In *Flow Chart*, a much more inclusive poem, we are reminded that

> Everybody gets such ideas on occasion, but here was the little shot-glass
> of night, all ready to drink, and you spread out in it
> even before it radiates in you. It doesn't matter whether or not
> you like the striations, because, in the time it takes to consider them,
> they will have merged, the rich man's house become a kettle, the wreath
> in the sink turned to something else, and still the potion holds,
> prominent.
>
> (FC, 16–17)

It is a term which finds its way into eccentric texts as well as central ones, the poem that occurs towards the end of the prose work *The Vermont Notebook* observing that 'In a screech the occasion has disappeared, the clamor resumed like a climate' (VN,93). Finally, it is a word which, when it crops up, gives him pause for thought. Thus as the revisions of 'Blue Sonata' (originally titled 'Sonatina') show, the last line of the poem originally read, 'To utter the speech rehearsed for that occasion', and then, 'To utter the speech that fits there', with the published version finally reading, 'To utter the speech that belongs there'[26]

What Ashbery means by the speech that 'belongs' to, or 'fits' the occasion, differs substantially from, but is significantly related to, what Goodman, and, in turn, O'Hara, had in mind with 'occasional poetry'. The handbooks define occasional poetry as poetry written for births, christenings, bar mitzvahs, birthdays, weddings, anniversaries and funerals. The purpose of the poem, in each case, is to hold the gathering together by focusing minds on the intricate complex of circumstances they have in common. Extrapolating from this, the thrust of Goodman's argument was that in the alienated society in which he was writing, America in the 1950s, the best hope for community, however exclusive, was to be found in the coteries of the avant-garde, and that such coteries were most likely to sustain themselves if they developed a form of occasional poetry. 'The community comes to exist', he suggested, 'by having its culture; the artist makes this culture.' I will return to Goodman's neglected article, but the pertinence of this argument to O'Hara will already be apparent. His is a poetry which clearly aims, among other things, to sustain a group of like-minded individuals by involving itself in their shared occasions. Hence the fact that, as legend has it, with the party going on at full tilt around him, O'Hara would sit down to type a poem.

Ashbery's writing retains a strong trace of this meaning of occasional poetry, 'marrying the world' as O'Hara famously put it. There are, however, as Ashbery has rightly observed, 'vast differences' between his poetry and O'Hara's, the difference being in part a question of scale and scope. Intensely as he admired O'Hara's poetry, he was worried about the implications of its coterie quality. As he has put it in interview, 'What is someone who doesn't know who Norman and Jean-Paul and Jean are going to think of this?'[27] This anxiety about O'Hara's poetry finds expression in the radically different meaning the idea of the occasion has for Ashbery. Ashbery's intention, in aiming to write the poem 'fit' for, or belonging to, its occasion, is to achieve a poem appropriate to the occasion of its own writing. His concern is with the time, place, situation and circumstances of the poem itself. As he has put in interview, 'the poems are setting out to characterize the bunch of circumstances that they're growing out of and a day might be said to be the basis for a poem'.[28] Wrongly interpreted, this can sound like a very narrow definition of poetry, as if it were concerned only with itself and its own progress. The reverse is in fact the case, as is best made apparent by thinking about Ashbery's debt to Pasternak.

Introducing his Harvard lectures, Ashbery mentioned Pasternak twice: as a major poet who had influenced him, and as a poet of the 'jump-start variety', someone he reads to stimulate his own poetry.[29] That Ashbery judges Pasternak to be so significant to his own writing should come as no surprise. Ashbery first read Pasternak as an undergraduate, in the translations of J.M.Cohen and Vera

Sandomirska, and later in the New Directions edition of *Safe Conduct* and an English translation of 'Aerial Routes'. He was the only writer Ashbery acknowledged by epigraph in *Some Trees*: 'The Picture of Little J.A. in a Prospect of Flowers' being prefaced by the precocious final sentence of Pasternak's outward-looking memoir *Safe Conduct*. And because, initially at least, 'The Picture of Little J.A.' was the poem in Ashbery's first book which promised to reveal most to the reader about the new poet, the choice of epigraph was telling; Ashbery indicating his willingness to be defined in part by his interest in Pasternak. It was a defining interest he shared with his poet friends: the letters Schuyler, Koch and O'Hara wrote to Ashbery in Paris in 1958 and 1959 buzzing with the brilliance of *Doctor Zhivago*. Given all this, and given everything that has been written on the question of Ashbery's influences, it is surprising that so little has been said about his reading of Pasternak. One of my intentions in this study, therefore, is to indicate how understanding of Ashbery is enhanced when one considers this aspect of his reading. And one of the things we better understand is what Ashbery means when he observes that the poems characterize the circumstances they grow out of.

What distinguishes Pasternak's hero Zhivago, both as a doctor but also as we ultimately and movingly realise as a poet, is what is called his 'immediate grasp of a situation as a whole'.[30] Pasternak's writing career can be viewed in these terms: as an ongoing but shifting attempt to understand his relation to the situation as a whole, and as a struggle to develop a form of expression through which the situation, including his relation to it, might be articulated. Alongside this task, and as a reflexive writer, Pasternak engaged in periodic attempts to express the aspiration itself. Discussing Pushkin in his diary, Zhivago notes, 'It's as if the air, the light, the noise of life, of real substantial things burst into his poetry from the street as through an open window ... burst in and [took] possession of his verse, driving out the vaguer parts of speech.'[31] Pushkin's writing is thus closer, in the distinction Pasternak famously developed in 1922 in 'Some theses', to a sponge than to a fountain. 'People', he suggested, 'nowadays imagine that art is like a fountain, whereas it is a sponge. They think art has to flow forth, whereas what it has to do is absorb and become saturated.'[32] What it is saturated by are the circumstances, the situation in which it is made, or, to put it in the terms of this study, its occasion. It thus follows for Pasternak, as he puts it in *Safe Conduct*, that 'The clearest, most memorable and important feature of art is how it arises, and in their telling of the most varied things, the finest works in the world in fact all tell us of their own birth.'[33]

There are other writers who might have helped Ashbery to this recognisably postmodern idea, Stevens for one having suggested in 'An Ordinary Evening in New Haven', that 'The poem is the cry of its occasion'.[34] But as *Doctor Zhivago* shows, no writer understood its scope as clearly as Pasternak. The novel concludes with Zhivago's poems, everything which has gone before being an account of their occasion. Quite as much as any of the lyrics that make up *My Sister Life*, therefore, Pasternak's epic novel tells the history of its own birth. But this is hardly to make it narrow, Pasternak's sense of the poetic occasion being at least national in its reach. To tell the history of the birth of Zhivago's poems, that is, was to tell the history of the revolution, the revolution being the poems' occasion.

It is this scope, I argue, that Ashbery learned from Pasternak. Like Pasternak's, Ashbery's career could be described as a perpetually changing attempt to understand the situation as a whole, and as a struggle to develop a form of expression through which the situation, including his relation to it, might be articulated. This can mean, as Ashbery has observed in interview, that an event as small as the ringing of the phone can divert the progress of the poem. Equally, at his best, and in a certain mood, when Ashbery sits down to write a poem, his sense of occasion is Pasternakian in its scope. Or, as he put it in 'Litany', he aims to be the one

> Who can describe the exact feel
> And slant of a field in such a way as to
> Make you wish you were in it, or better yet
> To make you realize that you actually are in it
> For better or for worse

If the question inevitably arising here is how – how does the individual poem at any given moment achieve this level of understanding? – the immediate familiarity of Ashbery's allusion to the wedding service points ironically towards a response. For J.L. Austin, a special occasion such as a wedding is defined by the fact that everybody present understands the proceedings and their role in those proceedings. If this is not the case – if the wrong person speaks 'For better or for worse' – then, as Austin would have it, the proceedings are rendered unhappy. It follows that the poem written for such an occasion (the occasional poem) can presuppose the conditions of understanding and devote itself to formulating an agreeable utterance. Ashbery's concern, as Harold Bloom has observed, is not with such privileged moments but with all those other moments that make up a life; when the situation, as William James puts it, is 'tangled, muddy, painful and perplexed', and when one's role in it, accordingly, is unclear.[35] He cannot, in other words, presuppose understanding of the occasion he means to address. Implicitly, then, an Ashbery poem must make a series of, as it were, pre-judgements. What constitutes the present occasion? What are its parameters, its dynamics, its defining circumstances? What are the best means of acquainting the reader with that occasion, of making 'you realize that you actually are in it'? Is it to 'put it all in'? To 'leave it all out'? Is it by cataloguing, representation, metaphor, parody, conversation, metonymy, deixis or studied neglect? And finally, after these pre-judgements have been made, what is the appropriate response?

To so abstract the questions implicit in Ashbery's poetry is, of course, to falsify a process the demands and rewards of which are very largely in the act of writing, but what this series of questions makes clear is that, given his sense of occasion, an Ashbery poem cannot proceed until it has prepared the reader for its own reception, until he or she has been brought to the brink of understanding. One can think of Ashbery, then, as he thinks of Roussel, as 'a poet who is about to be a poet … always bringing us face to face with the very latest moment in our thinking, the now where everything can and must happen, the locus solus where writing begins'. Or again, the point can be made through comparison with Pasternak. *Doctor Zhivago* is a supreme act of preparation, the prose section of the novel (the first seven of its eight chapters) bringing the reader to the point at which he or she can understand, and thereby judge the felicity of, the poems which conclude it. But if he is like both Roussel and Pasternak in this respect, the fact that Ashbery identifies this shared gesture in two such different writers is also a mark of his Americanness, the act of bringing the reader to the brink of understanding being definitive of a certain kind of American writing. Ever since Emerson urged the audience of 'The American Scholar' to leave the library, it has been axiomatic to American writing that the object of literary understanding is not the text but the world. As Whitman understood it, this entailed a seemingly conflictual textual motion, 'Song of Myself' drawing the reader into his text for just long enough to provoke him or her into an independent engagement with the scene he presents. The idea found philosophical expression in William James's *Pragmatism*, James self-consciously developing the Emerson–Whitman line in articulating an epistemology whereby ideas are *'true just in so far as they help us to get into satisfactory relation with other parts of our experience'*.[36] The only test of probable truth being 'what works best in the way of leading us, what fits every part of life best and combines with the collectivity of experience's demands, nothing being omitted'.[37] *Pragmatism* is a guidebook to American poetics before and since itself. Among modernist students of James, Stevens was fascinated by that late-Romantic, or constructivist strain in James's philosophy, which gave thought and language an active part in the truth process, and which finds expression in his poetry in his attention to the force of idiom. Gertrude Stein, on the other hand, developed the implication that there is more than one way to *'get into satisfactory relation with other parts of our experience'*, *Tender Buttons* being the prime example. It is not least among Ashbery's achievements that he has managed to combine these responses to James, enhancing the potential of Stein's gestural poetics by advancing Stevens's metaphorical resourcefulness, so developing a dazzling repertoire of means for getting us into relation with our experience.

A number of things follow from Ashbery's manifold means of bringing the reader to understanding. The first is that, as Goodman suggested, his poetry poses the enormous problem of being 'plausible to the actuality and yet creatively imagining something, finding something unlooked-for': 'plausible' as it gets the reader into satisfactory relation with his or her situation; 'creatively imagining' as it experiments with all manner of means for doing so. One result of this is that the movement of Ashbery's writing is still more difficultly balanced than Whitman's, his more extensive repertoire of linguistic means drawing the reader further into the poem while still aiming to prepare him or her more fully for the 'collectivity of experience's demands'. It is through this difficult balance that one can begin to formulate the distinction between bad and good Ashbery. Thus, one feature of Ashbery's less successful poetry is the predominance of means. *The Tennis Court Oath*, for instance, is both dismissed and acclaimed for the attention it brings to its own materials. As I argue below, such readings seem to me to misconstrue this particular volume, but such a predominance does seem to me symptomatic of, for instance, 'Fragment', parts of *As We Know* and much of *Shadow Train*.

Ashbery himself has suggested a criterion by which to judge the success of his, or anybody's, poetry. Discussing David Schubert, he observed that 'the ideal situation for the poet is to have the reader speak the poem, and how nice it would be for everybody if that could be the case'. The logic of this ideal is clear. If the reader were able to speak the poem, the poet would have brought him or her to such a state of understanding, into such a satisfactory relation to the occasion, that the utterance appropriate to that occasion had become apparent to all concerned; as apparent, perhaps, as the next line in the wedding service. Short of this ideal, the keenest pleasure in Ashbery is arriving at the poem within the poem, the poem for which everything else has been a preparation. Sometimes such moments are formally obvious: the sonnet among the fragments in 'Europe', the poems amidst the prose of 'The Recital', the double sestina emerging from the free verse of *Flow Chart*. More typically, such moments make themselves felt by a sense of dawning, by a conviction that the words now being spoken could hardly be more apt. From all of which it follows that to read Ashbery with no regard for the tradition he develops, as do too many British reviewers still, is not merely to misunderstand the poetry; it is to misunderstand the paradigm of understanding according to which his poetry makes sense.

Talk of William James re-ignites the question of 'theory'. Poetry will always have a vexed relationship with theory: poetry tending to concern itself with specificities in language and the world, theory tending to concern itself with abstractions. The relationship is especially tense in the case of new poetry because, as I have suggested of Ashbery, until readers have begun to grasp what it is the poetry means to communicate, then it can readily be made to mean whatever the critic wants it to. Understanding of Ashbery has thus been ill served by theoretical readings of the poetry. In her timely essay 'Postmodernism/Fin de siècle: defining "difference" in late twentieth-century poetics', Marjorie Perloff suggests that this is the case for postmodern art in general. Arguing for a more sinuous history of the postmodern period, Perloff contends that if anything characterises art after modernism it is a radical openness to contingency. This is broadly true, of course, Ashbery having affinities in this respect with Olson, Ginsberg, Pollock and Cage. It follows for Perloff that the seemingly appropriate gesture of bringing the resources of postmodern theory to bear on contemporary art is in fact inimical to the impulse prompting that art. '[R]ecent handbooks on postmodernism', she complains, 'reduce what was once the excitement of the Cutting Edge to a list of rules and prescriptions', the problem being 'the drive toward totalization and hence toward closure that bedevils current discussions of post-modernism'.[38] There is an undeniability about Perloff's argument, and she makes a strong case against the theoretical reading (which by her argument would amount to an act of non-reading) of the contemporary work of art. What Perloff does not establish – does not intend to – is that there should be no dialogue between poetry and theory. For Vernon Shetley such a dialogue is necessary to the health of both ways of writing. Arguing that '"theory" now occupies the place in intellectual life' that poetry once held, Shetley has suggested that 'Reconnecting poetry with the intellectual reader is an urgent matter not merely for the health of poetry but also for the health of the intellect'.[39] This argument cuts both ways. Positively he contends that poetry is good for the intellect. Defensively he argues that if poetry is to find the readership it so desperately needs, it must be shown to have some appeal for the intellectual reader for whom theory is currently the reading material of choice. In a weak sense of the term, this is a pragmatic argument for finding points of contact between Ashbery's poetry and elements of contemporary theory. But Shetley's argument also suggests a strongly pragmatic reason for doing so. If it is true, as Shetley suggests, that theory and poetry now seek to occupy the same territory, and if the value of a terminology is its capacity to bring people into contact with new areas of experience, then one would expect some interlocking between the Ashberyan poetic of the occasion and aspects of postmodern theory. Or to put it another way, if Ashbery's poetry answers a real need in contemporary culture, one would expect to find its echoes in other disciplines. And what a theoretical dimension to this argument helps to explain is how Ashbery's sense of occasion is an appropriate response to the liberal democratic culture from which it emerges.

Whenever postwar poetry criticism starts worrying about occasions the question of democracy is not far behind. Donald Davie, for whom occasions were a matter of some concern, is the prime example. What Davie disliked most about Thomas Hardy was his readiness to rise 'dutifully to public occasions' arguing that the defining quality of such 'occasional poems' is that they 'cannot give offence', and that Hardy's willingness to write them was a symptom of that 'decent liberalism' which represented 'a crucial selling short of the poetic vocation, for himself and his successors'.[40] Davie's reservation about Charles Tomlinson – a poet who, in the main, he held in the highest regard – also had to do with the question of occasions. Tomlinson has argued that 'There is no occasion too small for the poet's celebration'. For Davie this was a misguided belief 'naturally at home in a society that makes no distinction between small occasions and big ones, a society that resists any ranking of certain human and civic occasions below or above certain others', such a society being, as he observed, a 'social democracy'.[41] There was, in other words, a conflict in Davie's thinking on this matter: to write in recognition of large public occasions being to show a liberal's lack of ambition, while to honour small occasions was to acquiesce to the social democratic impulse. What his contradictory discussion of occasions really reveals in Davie is his anxiety about the relation of poetry to democracy. The question of how (and how far) poetry accommodates democracy could hardly be more central to contemporary discussions of the art. Because there was an anti-democratic strain to Davie's criticism, he thought as hard about the question as anybody. In linking it to the issue of occasions he suggested a way of approaching the subject which postwar poetry criticism is only now catching up with.

David Kennedy takes the idea up in *New Relations: The Refashioning of British Poetry 1980–1994*, observing in contemporary poetry a concern 'to justify its existence with an account of the occasions of its own making'. It is a development he takes to be 'symptomatic of a particular relationship with poetry and experience, language and imagination', the substance of that relationship being the erosion in social democratic society of 'sustaining cultural traditions'.[42] Paul Fry hits on a similar thought in his important book *A Defense of Poetry: Reflections on the Occasion of Writing*, when he argues that the great value of poetry in democratic society is that it embodies that aspect in literature which is 'merely indicial, disclosing neither the purpose nor the structure of existence but only existence itself' and which is best understood under the 'old-fashioned, serviceable name of "occasion"'. For Fry the purpose of modern poetry should be to disclose what he calls the 'hum of the occasion', the desire to do so being, as he sees it (and as I suggested in distinguishing Ashbery from O'Hara) 'not a coterie emotion at all but a radically democratic one'.[43] So what precisely have occasions got to do with democracy?

From a certain point of view, the pragmatic sense of occasion identified in Ashbery can seem at best unhelpful to, and at worst at odds with, democracy. The affinity between James's philosophy and Ashbery's poetry has to do with their shared emphasis on contingency and change. As James puts it,

> In the realm of truth-processes facts come independently and determine our beliefs provisionally. But these beliefs make us act, and as fast as they do so, they bring into sight or into existence new facts which re-determine the beliefs accordingly. So the whole ball and coil of truth, as it rolls up, is the product of a double influence.[44]

Or as Ashbery puts in 'The New Spirit',

> The change is not complete.
> The new morals have altered the original data
> Which have again outstripped the message deduced from
>   them.

(TP, 39)

One possible implication of such an emphasis on contingency is a breakdown of communication, a problem with which a certain kind of pragmatism is happy to live. Harold Rosenberg, a champion of Abstract Expressionism, is a case in point. The central objective of Rosenberg's criticism was to develop a critical language which would make the seemingly rebarbative canvases of Pollock *et al.* sympathetic to an American audience. Abstract Expressionism, he argued, was just the latest development of the frontier sensibility, the chief characteristic of that sensibility (what he called 'The Tradition of the New') being that 'For it, each situation has its own exclusive key ... Truth and beauty are ... the result of a specific encounter'.[45] This is problematic. If truth and beauty are the result of the specific encounter, how are they to be communicated? Rosenberg is clear: they can't. 'Each situation has its own exclusive key' and so an expression (painterly or linguistic) fit for the specific encounter can't be fit for anything else. Rosenberg, that is, trades the solidarity of communication for the free play of contingency. Ashbery's reputation as an incommunicative poet has much to with his association with the Abstract Expressionists, his poetry often being described as the verbal equivalent of the Abstract expressionist canvas. This is a long way from the truth. There is no doubt that he found the painters' willingness to experiment inspirational at a time when poetry had become very unadventurous. But he was also very suspicious of what he saw as the 'heroic quality' of Abstract Expressionism, a phrase which points precisely to the solitary, incommunicative, even (for all its celebration of freedom) anti-democratic temper of the art. The vast difference between Ashbery's poetry and Pollock's painting is that, responsive as the former is to the specific encounter, it is also, fundamentally, committed to communication.

Such a desire to reconcile contingency and solidarity has clearly audible echoes in recent philosophical developments of pragmatism. Richard Rorty is the most obvious case in point. In fact the linguistic turn Rorty gives pragmatism serves only to invert the problem. The crux of his argument, like Rosenberg's, is the term 'encounter'. But, whereas for Rosenberg this signified an engagement with a specific set of circumstances, for Rorty it means 'encounters between old and new vocabularies' with a 'liberal society' being 'one which is content to call "true" whatever the upshot of such encounters turns out to be'.[46] By this account, the test of an utterance is its allure, societies forming like gangs around metaphors that take their fancy. So, while Rorty undoubtedly achieves an image of solidarity, it is at the expense, as I have argued in detail elsewhere, of a real sense of contingency.[47] A more exacting unravelling of the tensions in pragmatism, and with it a clear sense of the relation of occasions to democracy, is provided by its linguistic tributary speech-act theory.

For J.L. Austin, it is axiomatic that 'the occasion of an utterance matters seriously, and that the words used are to some extent to be "explained" by the "context" in which they are designed to be or have actually been spoken in a linguistic exchange'. Or, as he refined this idea in his William James lectures, subsequently published as *How To Do Things With Words*, 'certain conditions have to be satisfied if the utterance is to be happy', or 'felicitous', the fundamental condition being that those involved in the utterance have to appreciate its force; to appreciate the force of an utterance being, for Austin, to understand the circumstances in which it is spoken. Thus the expression 'I do' carries its optimum force if everyone involved is acquainted with the conventions of the occasion on which it is felicitously uttered. The problem this leaves is how to establish that an utterance is happy if the occasion on which it is uttered has no precedent and so is not conventional. How, in other words, can communication be achieved in unconventional circumstances, when the etiquette is not clear and things are 'tangled, muddy, painful and perplexed'? Austin is blunt. 'There is no short cut to expounding simply the full complexity of the situation which does not exactly fit any common classification.'[48]

For Jürgen Habermas it is at this point, the point at which Austin's theory ends, that speech-act theory becomes interesting. The problem with Habermas for readers of poetry is the sheer ugliness of his prose. Beneath the jargon, however, his thinking about language and the occasions of language is supple, especially as it addresses the relation of contingency to solidarity. Linguistically speaking, his argument is against that tendency, 'in empiricist research traditions, to *separate* the cognitive-instrumental rationality based on the monological employment of descriptive knowledge from communicative rationality'. This needs translating. What 'cognitive instrumental rationality' means, as Habermas goes on to observe, is 'successful self-maintenance made possible by informed disposition over, and intelligent adaptation to, conditions of a contingent environment'. This is more familiar for the reader of American writing, intelligent adaptation to a contingent environment being the way of the frontier hero, the Abstract Expressionist, and so, as Rosenberg saw it, the tradition of the new. For Habermas, however, unlike for Rosenberg, such intelligence is entirely compatible with what he terms 'communicative rationality', 'communicative rationality' being, as he puts it less forbiddingly, the 'unconstrained, unifying, consensus-bringing force of argumentative speech'. Its purpose is to arrive at a view of the world which a 'community of speaking and acting subjects' can agree upon, such shared 'background knowledge' being necessary if people are to reach understanding about 'what takes place in the world or is to be effected in it'. As Habermas sees it, then, instrumental rationality fits into a 'comprehensive concept of communicative rationality' because at any given moment understanding arrived at through argument is dependent upon a shared account of the historical present (the 'situation present' as Auden called it) in which people find themselves.[49]

Such a shared sense of background is fundamental to Habermas, for whom ideal dialogue can take place only between speakers whose sense of their situation is undistorted. The definition of a reasonable conversation, in other words, is one in which all the parties share a clear sense of 'exactly what is taking place all about' them. From which it follows that the preconditions for what Habermas calls the 'ideal speech situation' amount to the preconditions for democracy. The big, overwhelming problem with this, of course, is that the world is not, as Delmore Schwartz would have had it, a wedding. On the contrary, in contemporary society a shared sense of the situation is perpetually thwarted, as Habermas is at pains to point out, both by the increased complexity of everyday life and by the erosion of tradition which is his subject in *Legitimation Crisis*.

It is at this crux in Habermas's thought that the importance of occasions to arguments about the relation of poetry to democracy becomes clear. A traditional society is a society rich in conventional occasions, in occasions when everybody knows what is going on, and so when everybody, according to Austin, can communicate without great difficulty. For Habermas 'Liberal-Capitalist' society is precisely not traditional, its rationalising logic calling into question all the 'meanings and norms previously fixed by tradition'.[50] The pressing question, then, from Austin's perspective, is, how can communication occur at all in a culture so lacking in conventional occasions? One way, of course, is to manufacture traditional occasions, which is what television – with its seemingly endless series of important 'events' – does all the time. But these spectacles aside, if communication is still to be possible in non-traditional society, then, as Austin puts it, 'There is no short cut to expounding the full complexity of the situation which does not actually fit any common classification.' The true value of Ashbery's poetry is not only that it understands the importance of this task but that it takes it seriously. It couldn't be further from the truth, in other words, to say that Ashbery's poetry doesn't communicate, because, more than any contemporary's, his poetry aims to make communication possible in liberal-democratic society; its ceaseless expounding of the full complexity of its own occasion amounting to what Habermas, taking full account of the demands of both contingency and solidarity, wants us to call universal pragmatics.

Comparable as it is to Ashbery's sense of what he called, in his lecture on David Schubert, the 'ideal situation for the poet', the purpose of this consideration of Habermas is by no means simplistically to suggest that Ashbery's poetry realises the ideal speech situation. The point, rather, is that in a society marked by the communicative difficulties born of the erosion of tradition, to appreciate Ashbery's sense of occasion is better to grasp the preconditions of contemporary understanding. Too easily characterised as conservative avant-garde, Ashbery is in fact, and as Fry suggests, radically democratic: his sense of occasion embodying a commitment to democratic communication which is a challenge to, not a legitimisation of, a society which makes it increasingly difficult. From which it follows that to read Ashbery in conjunction with Habermas is not to make an argument for the theoretical reading of poetry, but to make a theoretical argument for the activity of reading poetry. It is an argument which has its origins in Whitman, who argues in *Democratic Vistas* that

> Our fundamental want to-day in the United States, with closest, amplest reference to present conditions, and to the future, is of a class, and the clear idea of a class, of native authors, literatures, far different, far higher in grade than any yet known, sacerdotal, modern, fit to cope with our occasions[51]

Or as Ashbery, alive as ever to the implications of the Whitmanesque task for the contemporary poet, has put it:

> Suddenly the street was
> Bananas and the clangor of Japanese instruments.
> Humdrum testaments were scattered around. His head
> Locked into mine. We were a seesaw. Something

Ought to be written about how this affects
You when you write poetry:
The extreme austerity of an almost empty mind
Colliding with the lush, Rousseau-like folliage of its desire to
    communicate
Something between breaths, if only for the sake
Of others and their desire to understand you and desert you
For other centers of communication, so that understanding
May begin, and in doing so be undone.

(HD, 45–6)

This book offers an account of Ashbery's poetic career. It is not a life of the poet. The closest we have to a life of Ashbery is David Lehman's *The Last Avant-Garde*. Lehman's book is unusually valuable in that his vividly affectionate group biography of the New York School actually stirs one to read the poetry. As Lehman himself observes, however, 'Ashbery is certainly the least autobiographical of modern poets. No one's poems have less to do with the details of his life.'[52] So, while the facts of Ashbery's biography – his solitary childhood (following the death of his brother) in Rochester, his Harvard education, his life in New York and his love affair in Paris – might lead one to the poetry, they do not, on the whole, enable one to read it.

The detail of Ashbery's life that particularly interests critics is his sexuality. Shoptaw reads the poetry for what he calls its 'homotextuality', finding in it coded references to gay life and loves, while Catherine Imbriglio stages a conventionally 'queer' reading of Ashbery's evasiveness. Ashbery's sexuality is hardly unimportant to his writing, both because the marginality it results in is surely, as for Whitman, an impulse behind his inclusiveness, and, contrastingly, because Ashbery can be deliciously camp. Beyond these aspects of the writing, however, this book tends not to emphasise Ashbery's sexuality, for the reason that to do so invokes an idea of the poem he has worked hard to dispel – the poem as confession. As he has put it in interview:

> These are not autobiographical poems, they're not confessional poems. Not only because I don't feel terribly interested in my own experiences and feelings … but because I don't think they'll be of much help to a reader. They're very specific things that happen to me and which don't have any particular exemplary quality. What I'm trying to get at is a general, all-purpose experience – like those stretch socks that fit all sizes.[53]

From a queer theory perspective Ashbery's much-stated antagonism to confessional poetry might seem like an epistemology of the closet, and there is no denying that he could be read from this point of view; but only at the cost of presenting his whole poetic as an expression of denial. Ashbery is antipathetic to confessional poetry because it fetishises the individual, and in so doing denies poetry its broader social function. Accordingly Ashbery's life enters his writing only in so far as his life, like everybody else's, is shaped by 'what is taking place about us'. His poetry is a medium of communication not expression, and not to recognise it as such is severely to underestimate its scope.

Instead of a 'life', the purpose of this study is to offer an account of the development of Ashbery's poetry, of the evolution of his poetic. Necessarily a study of his career will draw on some facts of his life – that he read certain books, saw certain paintings, corresponded with certain people, collaborated, was interviewed about his poetry, won prizes for it, influenced younger writers and so on. But if accounts of the career and of the life overlap, there are also clearly differences in the two approaches. There are two strategic reasons for, and two significant problems with, offering an account of Ashbery's career. The first reason is that, while a lot is known about certain Ashbery poems and volumes, there is not yet a picture of the whole. What are the continuities? What are the differences? How has the poetry improved? How does one volume lead to, or away from, another? Like a retrospective of a painter's work, accounts of Ashbery's poetic development are necessary to understand the force of the whole achievement and the parts individual works play in it. The second reason for an account of Ashbery's career has to do with the broader understanding of postwar American poetry. Because the subject generally tends to be treated in the form of short articles and collections of discrete essays, understanding of it is likewise patchy. One way now to deepen our sense of the period is to consider how significant poets have dealt with the problems that have shaped it. In part, then, a study of Ashbery's career is an account of the period.

The first problem with a study of Ashbery's career is that the very idea is, in one sense, antithetical to a poetry of occasions. It is tension Ashbery raises in his prose poem 'The System'. A disquisition into the difficulty of living in the present, the poem considers two models of a life, that of 'the great careers' and that of 'the life-as-ritual concept'. As the poem puts it, the problem with the '"career" notion' is that it causes us 'to think of these people as separate entities, each with his development and aim to be achieved', a 'way of speaking,' the poem suggests, that 'has trapped each one us' (TP, 70). The image of life as career is thus objectionable because it fetishises individuality and denies the reality of interdependence. We are trapped in it but we are also trapped by it. The 'life-as-ritual concept' indicates the kind of egoless self Emerson envisages as an all-seeing eyeball, and Twain conceives in Huck Finn – a radically pragmatic self, changing with each new circumstance. Sympathetic as Ashbery's poetry of occasions instinctively is to the drift of this image of self, his narrator (like Melville's in 'The Masthead') is resistant to its final implication; the problem being that while it is exhilarating for such a self to be 'propelling itself forward at an ever increasing speed', the eventual effect is that 'in the end the soul cannot recognize itself and is as one lost, though it imagines it has found eternal rest' (TP, 70, 71) An account of Ashbery's career which charts his poetry's developing sense of its own occasion endeavours to steer between these equally pressing anxieties. Ashbery's poetry does alter significantly as its occasion changes. It never crosses the same river twice. But it is in its readiness to change as the occasion seems to require it, and in the quality and speed of judgement that develops through such readiness to change, that the continuity of Ashbery's poetry lies. One way of putting this is to advert to the tension in the term career, Ashbery's poetry following a continuous path through life in that it is always engaged in a breathtaking encounter with the onrush of events.

The second problem with addressing the development of Ashbery's poetic of occasions also has to do with the imposition of a false coherence. His poetry is characterised by nothing so much as the variousness of its forms, voices and postures, this variety partly explaining the breadth of its appeal. The hope here is that by thinking in terms of the occasion, the reader can get into satisfactory relation with these various aspects of Ashbery's writing without denying the fact of its diversity. Thus, that the idea of the occasion touches the momentary, circumstantial or situational quality of his writing, its feeling for simultaneity, is evident. It registers the democratic quality of his writing in various ways: recognising his interest in the ordinary not the extraordinary moments of life; and showing, through this, how he means both to communicate with his contemporaries and to develop the conditions for contemporary communication. Related to this, the idea is also sensitive to what one can call the polyphonic, multivocal or dialogical, quality of the poetry, Ashbery's consensual sense of occasion being arrived at, as I argue below, through collaboration with other voices. Obviously an idiom attentive to Ashbery's sense of occasion will pick up the sometimes celebratory tone of the poetry. It also allows one to approach the question of taste – one's sense of occasion being very much a matter of taste – and, through that, to address the related issues of influence, camp and the mix in his poetry of high and popular culture. Goodman's sense that the occasional poem must be both plausible and creatively imagined indicates how the idea can accommodate the tension in Ashbery between what he terms the muddy realism of Clare and the perfumed artifice of Beddoes. But most importantly perhaps, and as I have indicated already through Pasternak, the idea of the poem fit for, or appropriate to, its occasion offers a way of articulating what can be termed Ashbery's democratic sublime, the hum of the occasion amounting to the roar of everyday life.

But this is not all of Ashbery. In particular, his writing is neither always sublime nor always aiming at sublimity. Sometimes – as in the plays, the collaborations with Kenneth Koch, *A Nest of Ninnies* (the novel he wrote with James Schuyler), the cartoons of *The Double Dream of Spring*, *The Vermont Notebook*, the one-line poems of *As We Know*, and an increasingly high proportion of the late poetry – Ashbery's writing is explicitly not fit, meet, felicitous and appropriate, but vulgar, comic, impolite and ludicrous. Indeed, Ashbery is rare among major twentieth-century poets in being able to make the reader laugh out loud, and it would therefore be an incomplete story of the poetry which could offer no account of its irreverent sub-plot. However, as the Ashberyan joke is invariably bathetic, the guffaw in Ashbery is no less rooted in simultaneity than the gasp – the difference being that at such moments the concatenation of words and events is suddenly bizarre, humbling, humorous or just plain daft. It is precisely a consequence, in other words, of his sense of occasion that Ashbery is also acutely attuned to the inappropriate, his different degrees and species of comedy being best understood as the other side of the coin, or the back of the tapestry.

Ashbery has turned the tapestry round to both funny and strategic effect throughout his career. At times, as with such jarringly ironic poems as 'Variations, Calypso and Fugue on a theme of Ella Wheeler Wilcox' and 'Farm Implements and Rutabagas in a Landscape' the hopelessly inappropriate utterance has seemed the best means of leading the reader towards the appropriate sensibility. At other times – as in the exquisitely misjudged B-movie sentimentality of *A Nest of Ninnies*, the alienated antagonism of a number of the shorter poems in *Self-Portrait in a Convex Mirror*, and the controlled, seemingly deconstructive, disaffection of 'Litany' – he has turned the tapestry round in order to examine his own impulses and procedures. Often, however, the inappropriate has simply seemed the only appropriate gesture. The ludic collaborations with Koch written in the midst of the tranquillised 1950s are an example of this, as was 'Daffy Duck in Hollywood', its cartoonic vision pricking the overbearing seriousness with which 'Self-Portrait in a Convex Mirror' was received. So too are the poems Ashbery has been writing throughout the 1990s, his seemingly ceaseless comedy defying both the critics who would have him go quietly, and death.

In tracing Ashbery's poetic development I do not consider his writing book by book, but as it were phase by phase. Sometimes a phase coincides with a book, as in the stylistically anomalous second volume *The Tennis Court Oath*. The tendency, however, has been for the phases of his development to lengthen as a particular concern unravels through more than one book. Structurally the chapters are linked, in that in each case I try first to indicate the situation – the context, or occasion – out of which the writing arises. In order, the chapters consider: Ashbery's early reaction to the middle generation; his collaborations; his sense of the role of the avant-garde in mass democracy; his response to the conflicting pressures on American poetry in the 1960s; his disquisition, in *Three Poems*, on the absence of a contemporary spiritual discourse; his relation to the reader in his long poems of the 1970s; the anxiety of influence as his poetry begins to attract followers; and his late, which is to say his latest, writing. In the course of these discussions I hope to indicate how Ashbery's poetry of the occasion has developed, how it has dealt with the issues and problems the period has posed its major poets, and how it has faced up to and resolved tensions internal to itself. In presenting his poetry in this way I have tried to remain aware that, as Ashbery puts it in 'The Skaters', explanation, good or bad, can be 'costly stuff', but also that, as Gertrude Stein puts in 'Composition as explanation', 'it is so very much more exciting and satisfactory for everybody if one can have contemporaries, if all one's contemporaries could be one's contemporaries'.[54]

NOTES

1 Peter Stitt, 'The art of poetry XXXIII: John Ashbery', p. 399.
2 Donald Revell, 'Purists will object: some meditations on influence', p. 17.
3 At the time of writing Ashbery's Charles Eliot Norton lectures were unpublished. I heard recordings of the lectures held by the Woodberry Poetry Room in the Lamont Library, Harvard. All subsequent references are to these recordings. John Ashbery, rec. of 'John Clare's inquisitive eye'. Lamont Library, Harvard University.
4 Ibid.
5 The paper in which these terms were suggested was given at the Anglo-American Poetry Relations Conference, London University, July 1998.
6 Tim Kendall, 'Uh oh, no last words', p. 23.
7 Sean O'Brien, 'Historical sicknotes', p. 36.
8 Alfred Poulin Jnr, 'The experience of experience: a conversation wih John Ashbery', p. 251.
9 Janet Bloom and Robert Losada, 'Craft interview with John Ashbery', p. 12.
10 Charles Rosen, 'Who's afraid of the avant-garde', pp. 21–2.
11 John Ashbery, rec. of 'The bachelor machines of Raymond Roussel', Lamont Library, Harvard University.
12 Sue Gangel, 'An interview with John Ashbery', p. 14.
13 See Richard Jackson, 'The imminence of a revelation', p. 69.
14 Anglo-American Poetry Relations Conference, London University, July 1998.
15 Shelley, 'A defence of poetry', p. 59.
16 Robert Crawford, *Identifying Poets*, p. 105.
17 'John Clare's inquisitive eye'.
18 John Ashbery, rec. of 'Olives and Anchovies', Lamont Library, Harvard University.
19 'The bachelor machines of Raymond Roussel'.
20 John Ashbery, rec. of 'Schubert's Unfinished', Lamont Library, Harvard University.
21 Transcript of John Ashbery's contribution to 'Poetry Now Symposium', 5 March, 1968. John Ashbery Manuscripts, AM6, The Houghton Library, Harvard University.
22 Paul Goodman, 'Advance-guard writing 1900–1950', p. 376.
23 Cited in Brad Gooch, *City Poet*, p. 187.
24 Edwin Denby, *Dance Writings*, p. 576
25 John Ashbery, 'The decline of the verbs', p. 5.
26 John Ashbery, 'Sonatina', in John Ashbery Manuscripts, AM6, The Houghton Library, Harvard University.
27 Piotr Sommer, 'An interview in Warsaw', p. 307.
28 Janet Bloom and Robert Losada, 'Craft interview with John Ashbery', p. 20.
29 Ashbery actually describes Pasternak as a poet who 'probably' influenced him. In doing so he is indicating uncertainty not about Pasternak,but about the idea of influence. Other major poets he mentions as 'probably' influencing him include Auden, Stevens, Marianne Moore and Bishop.
30 Boris Pasternak, *Doctor Zhivago*, p. 366.
31 Ibid., p. 258.
32 Cited by Donald Davie in *Modern Judgements: Pasternak*, p. 23.
33 Boris Pasternak, *Safe Conduct: An Early Autobiography and Other Works*, p. 213.
34 Wallace Stevens, *Collected Poems*, p.473.
35 William James, *Pragmatism*, p.8

36 Ibid., p. 23.
37 Ibid., pp. 31–2.
38 Marjorie Perloff, *Poetry On and Off the Page*, pp. 15, 18.
39 Vernon Shetley, *After the Death of Poetry*, p.171.
40 Donald Davie, *Thomas Hardy and British Poetry*, pp. 36, 40.
41 Donald Davie, *Under Briggflatts*, pp. 64, 65.
42 David Kennedy, *New Relations*, pp. 60, 63.
43 Paul Fry, *A Defense of Poetry*, pp. 11, 12, 29.
44 James, *Pragmatism*, p. 87.
45 Harold Rosenberg, *The Tradition of the New*, p. 19.
46 Richard Rorty, *Contingency, Irony and Solidarity*, p. 52.
47 See David Herd, 'Occasions for solidarity: Ashbery, Riley and the tradition of the new'.
48 J.L. Austin, *How To Do Things With Words*, pp. 100, 45, 38.
49 Jürgen Habermas, *The Theory of Communicative Action, Volume 1*, pp.14, 10, 13.
50 Jürgen Habermas, *Legitimation Crisis*, p. 47.
51 Walt Whitman, *Complete Poetry and Collected Prose*, p. 932.
52 David Lehman, *The Last Avant-Garde*, p. 94.
53 Alfred Poulin Jnr, 'The experience of experience: a conversation with John Ashbery', p. 251.
54 Gertrude Stein, *Look at Me Now and Here I Am*, p. 23.

CHAPTER ONE

Two scenes: the early poetry and its backgrounds

The first poem in *Some Trees* is 'Two Scenes'.

I

We see us as we truly behave:
From every corner comes a distinctive offering.
The train comes bearing joy;
The sparks it strikes illuminate the table.
Destiny guides the water-pilot, and it is destiny.
For long we hadn't heard so much news, such noise.
The day was warm and pleasant.
"We see you in your hair,
Air resting around the tips of mountains."

II

A fine rain anoints the canal machinery.
This is perhaps a day of general honesty
Without example in the world's history
Though the fumes are not of a singular authority
And indeed are dry as poverty.
Terrific units are on an old man
In the blue shadow of some paint cans
As laughing cadets say, "In the evening
Everything has a schedule, if you can find out what it is."

(ST, 9)

'Two Scenes' is a significant poem. It was significant at the time because, as the first poem in Ashbery's first widely distributed book, it was the piece with which he chose to introduce himself to the American reading public.[1] It is significant in retrospect because it remains broadly representative, the poem displaying various qualities we would now call Ashberyan. Its organising principle, if that's the term, would seem to be parataxis: mountains following water-pilots following tables following trains with barely a by-your-leave. It is conspicuously polyphonic, each scene ending with another person's voice. It is also irreverently occasional. This is, monumentally, a day 'Without example in the world's history', and yet the young cadets are laughing, amused perhaps by the know-ingly clunky rhyming of machinery, honesty, history, authority and poverty. And because 'Two Scenes' finds Ashbery already comfortable with strategies which will figure in his mature style, it follows that we learn something important about his poetry if we can establish where the light, airy, deftly occasional lan-guage of this early poem came from. What was it reacting against? How did it mean to distinguish itself? What did it mean to say to the readers who made up its poetic environment?

Ashbery has been a quite severe critic of his own early poetry. Speaking of both his own writing and O'Hara's, he has observed how while

> Later on in the more encouraging climate of New York, we could begin to be our-selves … much of the poetry we both wrote as undergraduates now seems marred by a certain nervous preciosity, in part a reaction to the cultivated blandness around us which also impelled us to callow aesthetic pronouncements.[2]

Ashbery arrived in New York from Harvard in the early summer of 1949.[3] The 'cultivated blandness' to which he feels he and O'Hara reacted (by which they were 'impelled') thus refers to the poetry scene of the late 1940s, when, as Ash-bery observes, 'the kind of dream-like, more imaginative poetry of the thirties such as that of Delmore Schwartz, and Randall Jarrell, was replaced by their later work and by Lowell'.[4] A similar shift, he has observed, was taking place in Britain, with some of his favourite poets of the late 1930s and 1940s, notably Nicholas Moore and F.T. Prince, slipping into obscurity in the wake of the rise of Larkin.[5]

Quite how strongly the poets of the New York School felt impelled to write against what became thought of – owing to the poets' university affiliations, their friendship with the New Critics, and their preoccupation with matters of form – as the academic style of the Lowell-dominated middle generation, is nowhere more apparent than in Kenneth Koch's poem 'Fresh Air'. A sort of anti-mani-festo for the emergent poetry of the New York School, 'Fresh Air' is set in 'The Poem Society', Koch staging an argument between the resident 'professors' and the poets of 'the new poem of the twentieth century'. The poem is explicitly antagonistic, Koch observing of the professor-poets: that they 'have never smiled at the hibernation / Of bear cubs except that [they] saw in it some deep relation / To human suffering'; that they are 'physically ugly', having 'certain hideous black hairs' and a voice like the sound of 'water leaving a vaseline bathtub'; that they are 'worms'; that they are 'maker[s] of comparisons'; that they insist on pre-cision ('One more mistake and I get thrown out of the Modern Poetry / Associ-ation') while actually producing 'hideous fumes' (as opposed to the 'Fresh Air' of the new poets); and, just in case the reader hadn't already worked out who these 'abstracted dried-up boys' with their 'stale pale skunky pentameters' were, that they publish in '*Partisan, Sewanee,* and *Kenyon Review*!'.[6]

'Fresh Air' is both subtler than it seems and strategically simplistic. It is subtle in that, as it describes the gloomy circumstances out of which 'the new poem of the twentieth century' is struggling to emerge, it tells the story of its own birth – Koch imagining his own writing to be part of the 'new poem' – and so manifests a central aspect of the New York School aesthetic. It is simplistic in that, just as new generations of poets (especially avant-gardistes) habitually caricature the previous generation as a means of carving out a space, and working up an impulse, for their own writing, so always the relation between the generations is more complicated than the caricatures suggest.[7] Thus for instance, the poetry editor at *Partisan Review* was Delmore Schwartz, and both Koch and Ashbery had gone to Harvard in large part because Schwartz taught there; Ashbery subsequently describing Schwartz as one of the writers of the 1930s who 'helped to shape the poetry I was then writing' and whose work, as he sees it, has 'simply been forgotten' as a consequence of the rise of Lowell.[8] And Ashbery has generally been careful to discriminate between different phases of middle generation writing, distinguishing early Jarrell and even early Berryman from their later work. But if 'Fresh Air' simplifies things for effect, what is clear from Koch's poem and Ashbery's remarks is that the New York poets were confirmed in their repulsion for the presence of Lowell. Speaking in 1965 (and so some time after the grudge had first formed) O'Hara remarked how 'Lowell has ... a confessional manner which [lets him] get away with things that are really just plain bad but you're supposed to be interested in him because he's supposed to be so upset'.[9] Three years earlier he had taken a more direct dig, opening a reading with Lowell at Wagner College, Staten Island, with a poem ('Lana Turner has collapsed'), which, as he was delighted to inform his audience, he had written on the ferry on his way to the performance. The point of the gesture was to prick the studied manner of Lowell's writing. 'The audience loved it,' David Lehman reports, 'Lowell looked put out.'[10]

But if some of their early poems were 'callow aesthetic' responses to poetry for which they felt deep distaste, the New York poets' reaction to the Lowell-dominated middle generation was by no means entirely negative; the very absence of a poetry scene with which they could readily identify prompting them to read widely and more actively. Ashbery has remarked of O'Hara that the first four or five years of his writing life were 'a period of testing, of trying to put together a tradition to build on where none had existed', and that

> The poetry that meant the most to him when he began writing was either French – Rimbaud, Mallarmé, the Surrealists ... or Russian – Pasternak and especially Mayakovsky, from whom he picked up what James Schuyler has called the 'intimate yell'.[11]

The remark applies equally to Ashbery himself, as it does to Koch, one section of 'Fresh Air' being devoted precisely to the act of putting together a tradition upon which the new poetry might be based:

> Who are the great poets of our time, and what are their names?
> Yeats of the baleful influence, Auden of the baleful influence, Eliot of
>   the baleful influence

(Is Eliot a great poet of our time? no one knows), Hardy, Stevens, Williams, (is
    Hardy of our time?),
Hopkins (is Hopkins of our time?), Rilke (is Rilke of our time?), Lorca
    (is Lorca of our time?), who is still of our time?
Mallarmé, Valéry, Apollinaire, Éluard, Reverdy, French poets are still of
    our time,
Pasternak and Mayakovsky, is Jouve of our time?

All of which suggests that to grasp Ashbery's early poetry, and to understand
where the new language of such poems as 'Two Scenes' was coming from, it is
important to understand both what the Lowell-dominated middle generation
had come to mean for American poetry by the late 1940s, and what Ashbery was
reading to help distinguish himself from it. In itself, of course, the fact of an
antagonism between avant-garde groupings such as the New York School and
the so-called academic poetry of the middle generation is hardly breaking news,
the distinction having solidified as long ago as the early 1960s into the 'raw' and
the 'cooked'. Partly, however, because of the speed with which this convenient
distinction hardened into place (amalgamating, as it did, the very different poet-
ries of the New York School, the Beats and the Black Mountain School) and
partly because thinking about recent poetry has tended to be theoretical rather
than historical, the antagonism between the avant-gardes and the academics has
more often been assumed than detailed. Detail is warranted because, in relating
the emergence of Ashbery's new language, what one is necessarily describing is
the difficult birth of postmodern writing.

Identified with one another from the start, leading, as Lowell put it in his elegy
for Berryman, 'the same life, / the generic one / our generation offered', the
beginnings of the middle generation were decidely undynamic. Berryman and
Jarrell were first published together, both poets appearing in the 1940 New
Directions anthology *Five Young American Poets*. In the anthology each poet's
selection is prefaced by their observations on the state of contemporary poetry.
And what the prefaces demonstrate is not the youthful energy of a brave new
literary movement but a profound uncertainty, the whole volume being charac-
terised by a disorientating lack of definition. Thus, as Berryman sees it:

> None of the extant definitions of poetry is very useful; certainly none is adequate;
> and I do not propose to invent a new one. I should like to suggest what I under-
> stand the nature and the working of poetry to be by studying one of the poems in
> this selection.[12]

There is a curious play of confidence and insecurity in Berryman's remarks:
rejecting out of hand all of the 'extant definitions of poetry', but shrinking from
the task of proposing a new one. Opting, instead, to provide a careful analysis of
one of his own poems, Berryman feels his way towards a definition along the
more cautious route of practical criticism. But nothing one could call a defini-
tion emerges, Berryman risking no more than the unremarkable observation

that 'Poetry provides its readers, then, with what may be called a language of experience, an idiom, of which the unit may be an entire complicated emotion or incident. The language is not the language of prose'.[13] As the history of rallying-calls for a new generation goes, this is one of the less galvanising.

Faced with the same lack of direction that Berryman voices, Jarrell knew where to place the blame, the problem, as he told it (in no uncertain terms), being modernism. 'Modernist poetry', he contested,

> extorted its attraction because it was carrying the tendencies of romanticism to their necessary conclusions; now most of those conclusions have been arrived at; and how can the poet go any further? How can poems be written that are more violent? more disorganised? more obscure? more – the adjectives throng to me – than those that have already been written?[14]

Finding his critical style early, Jarrell's state-of-the-art account is altogether more forceful (if more broad-brushed and arguable) than Berryman's. It is all the more striking, therefore, that the keynote of his remarks is also uncertainty. Like Berryman, Jarrell can offer no new definitions, can make no predictions. Rather,

> [w]e have reached one of those points in the historical process at which the poet has the uncomfortable illusion of choice; when he too says, 'But what was it? What am I?' … So the poets repeat the old heartlessly, or make their guesses at the new.[15]

Jarrell returned to the question of what comes after modernism two years later in an article for *The Nation* entitled 'The end of the line', this time tying the modernist demand for novelty to the Romantic commitment to originality:

> Romanticism … presupposes a constant experimentalism, the indefinite attainment of originality, generation after generation, primarily by the novel extrapolation of previously exploited processes … All these romantic tendencies are exploited to their limits; and the movement which carries out this final exploitation is what we call modernism. Then, at last, romanticism is confronted with an impasse, a critical point, a genuinely novel situation that it can only meet successfully by contriving genuinely novel means – that is, means which are not romantic; the romantic means have already been exhausted.[16]

The tone is apocalyptic, but the problem is a real one – one that poets since the war, whether late-, post- or even anti-modern have had in some way to negotiate – namely, how to keep on making it new, when novelty itself has become familiar. Or as O'Hara, out-Jarrelling Jarrell, put it, 'New is an old word let's get a new one.' Seeing it as his main task to make his readers face up to their postmodern condition, Jarrell makes an announcement:

> It Is The End Of The Line. Poets can go back and repeat the ride; they can settle in attractive, atavistic colonies along the railroad; they can repudiate the whole system, à la Yvor Winters, for some neo-classical donkey caravan of their own. But Modernism As We Know It – the most successful and influential body of poetry of this century – is dead.

Criticism as forceful as this commands attention, so it is important to notice how Jarrell maps the postmodern scene here. Repetition (which would be continuation), separatism (along the lines of an artistic colony), and nostalgia (à la Yvor Winters) are all swiftly rejected: the only new directions 'the age offers to the poet' being, as Jarrell sees it, 'a fairly heartless eclecticism or a fairly solitary individuality'. The appearance of these alternative marks an important shift. In 1940 Jarrell had felt that there was only an illusion of choice, and that the poet could only guess at the new; in 1942, an opposition around which poets might begin to position themselves, by which they might redefine their task, was beginning to be formed. Jarrell's terms were insightful – postmodern poetry still divides between the sophisticated collages of LAN-GUAGE poetry at the one end, and the inward gaze of confessionalism at the other – and, while he was not himself especially attracted to either alternative, he worked hard to make the opposition stick. Writing about the New Directions anthology of 1941 (which included Nicholas Moore and F.T. Prince), he found in it 'a sort of encyclopaedic contradiction', 'a queer mediocre hodge-podge'. 'Nowadays,' he concluded, 'seeing people being consciously experimental together has the brown period smell of the Masonic ceremonies in *War and Peace*'.[17]

Jarrell worked hard to establish an opposition because his generation needed one. Strong literary movements gain much of their energy through the friction of opposing the previous generation. What the early critical writings of Jarrell, Berryman and Karl Shapiro show is that they felt no such opposition. Whether because of the war, the link between aesthetic and political fundamentalisms, the neutering of its strategies by the critical procedures that had developed to explain them, or, as Jarrell implies, sheer exhaustion, modernism, as, the poets of the middle generation saw it, was finished, and something else had to be done. But in pronouncing the death of modernism, they were not defining themselves against it, only after it, still holding, as they did, the achievements of its major writers (Eliot and Yeats in particular) in reverence. The consequence of this reverence for a movement they considered aesthetically obsolete was that if, as a generation, they were to gain impetus from opposition, then, unusually in literary history, they had to generate that opposition for themselves: witness Jarrell's criticism; Shapiro's *Essay on Rime*, with its bleak poetic alternatives of 'ennui' and 'violence'; and, most tellingly here, Berryman's decisive 1947 review, 'Lowell, Thomas, & Co.'.[18]

Focusing on *Lord Weary's Castle*, the point of Berryman's review was, as the title of a later piece had it, to distinguish between 'Lowell and others', to which end he formulated a new opposition:

> Whatever the devotion of a lesser poet, it may be put as the difference between the *occasional* and the *thematic*, between the making of a few fine poems and the conversion of a whole body of material. If the first is impressive, the second is oppressive as well, troubling, overwhelming. Now Robert Lowell seems to me not only the most powerful poet who has appeared in England or America for some years,

master of a freedom in the Catholic subject without peer since Hopkins, but also in the terms of this distinction, a thematic poet.[19] (Berryman's italics)

Lowell later described Berryman's review as 'definitive', which it was, in various respects. The central opposition itself is strict: 'theme' deriving from the Greek for deposit, and so indicating that which endures through time and resists change; *thematic*, poetry thus standing in clear contradistinction from poetry written for the occasion. And in this sense Lowell's early poetry is strictly *thematic*, his poetry being marked from the outset by the ambition to endure through time. The opening of the volume's major poem 'The Quaker Grave-yard in Nantucket' made this clear:

> A brackish reach of shoal off Madaket,-
> The sea was still breaking violently and night
> Had steamed into our North Atlantic Fleet,
> When the drowned sailor clutched the drag-net.[20]

The sailor dies and his name is inscribed in nothing more permanent than yellow chalk. But this is not to be Lowell's fate. With its historical subject, and its allusion to Captain Ahab, America's most enduring literary hero, the poem clearly has something monumental about it. It is in his carefully wrought sound, however, that Lowell most clearly signals his intention to survive: the repeated 'c's', 'k's', 't's' and 'd's', deriving as they do from the oldest names on the American map, generating a percussive, consonantal music that in its sheer hardness shows a determination to endure.

But Berryman's review was definitive also because, more so than Jarrell's, the terms of his opposition gave rise to a structure of judgement capable of shaping the contemporary poetry scene. Certainly Berryman worked them hard, modulating them only slightly in his review of 'Lowell and others' to speak of the difference between improvised and 'deliberate' poetry. Of 'improvisation' he suggests that

> you can see it best, after Auden's early books, in the beautiful work done by Delmore Schwartz at the decade's end in America – to name one line of corroboration, Blackmur hung his review of *In Dreams Begin Responsibilities* on the word 'improvised' … But Mr. Lowell's poetry is the most decisive testimony we have had, I think, of a new period, returning to the deliberate and the formal.[21]

Improvisation is not yet rejected out of hand (some of his best friends had improvised), but equally there is no doubt that the kind of poetry Berryman now values highest is the 'deliberate' and 'formal'. By 1948, however, resistance to improvisation had become axiomatic for Berryman. Reviewing the British poet Henry Reed, Berryman again asserts Lowell's value antithetically. He is not altogether unimpressed by Reed, suggesting that he is 'a poet whose slightest shift can contrive excitement'. His real value in this review, however, is, again, to act as other to Lowell. Berryman is explicit:

Strategies and strategies. Confronted equally with difficult situations, Reed *relaxed* beyond relaxation and Lowell *tightened* beyond tightening. Reed breaks metre into anapaests, feminine endings, extra-syllabled lines of all sorts, Lowell into spondees and humped smash. Lowell's work is 'difficult,' Reed's on the whole 'plain,' in extreme degrees.

In 1940, it is worth reiterating, it seemed to Berryman and Jarrell that the poetry scene lacked definition, that the age offered only the illusion of choice. By 1948, however, the territory has become so rigidly defined, the oppositional schema so well established, that even a poet whom, as Berryman says of Reed, he had not read 'till the day before yesterday' falls immediately into place. He has to be either one thing or the other, and Reed is emphatically the other, because, as Berryman suggests, 'one's strongest sense [when reading him] is of an *accepting* poetry' (Berryman's italics).[22] The problem with poetry which accepted its circumstances, as Berryman now saw it, was that in failing to transcend those circumstances it would therefore fail to survive them, with the poetry's, or rather the poet's, survival being, according to the new criteria, the be all and end all. André Breton could thus be promptly dismissed because he wrote poetry Berryman doubted would 'last two centuries'. Jane Lewis's problem was that, slight as her poetry was, it lacked the durability, even though 'handsome' to 'keep it in memory'.[23] Only the thematic poet would reach Parnassus, because by definition (as Berryman saw it) only the thematic poem could survive the ravages of time.

Jarrell, likewise, came to see things in terms of the thematic and the occasional. William Carlos Williams's poems, which previously he had admired, now seemed to him to fail because they 'do not give us a big, secure, formed, regularly rhythmed world to rest in, and we fall from one homogeneity of instant occasion into another'.[24] While confirming the speed with which a means of discrimination had hardened into a prejudice, Jarrell complained that the occasional, improvisational art of the Abstract Expressionists could have been produced by a chimpanzee.[25] Lowell's poetry, by contrast, and this was high praise indeed, was 'more at home in the Church Triumphant than in the Church of this world':

> the coiling violence of its rhetoric, the harsh and stubborn intensity that accompanies all its verbs and verbals, the clustering stresses learned from accentual verse, come from a man contracting every muscle, grinding his teeth together till his shut eyes ache.[26]

In the event, thematic poetry proved less than enduring. In part the problem was that what appeared to Berryman, and subsequently to Jarrell, as a transferable poetic strategy was actually, as Helen Vendler puts it, the 'personal *donné* that [Lowell] could not avoid treating'.[27] Lowell being a Lowell, and having a family tree that spanned and embraced the nation's history, was almost bound to concern himself with the question of survival through time, and so to write a self-consciously thematic poetry. Indeed, what the subsequent confessional turn of his poetry was to prove was that Jarrell's terms were more apposite than Berryman's, a 'solitary individuality' being the real alternative to eclectic and occasional poetry. None the less, during the ten years that followed the publication of *Lord Weary's Castle*, the seemingly thematic character of Lowell's poetry had a dramatic effect on a poetry scene that had hitherto lacked a certain shape. On those who admired him the effect was a temporarily distortive influence, with no one admiring Lowell more, or being more distorted by his presence, than Berryman himself. Determined to write his own thematic work, he produced *Homage to Mistress Bradstreet*, a poem so convinced of the need to endure time that it describes the poet's affair with a seventeenth-century woman poet. The poem went deeply against the grain, Berryman's descriptions of its writing being precisely symptomatic of a certain kind of mid-century sensibility.

> The eight-line stanza I invented here after a lifetime's study, especially of Yeats's, and in particular the one he adopted from Abraham Cowley for his elegy 'In Memory of Major Robert Gregory.' ... For four-and-a-half years, then, I accumulated materials and sketched, fleshing out the target or vehicle, still under the impression that seven or eight stanzas would see it done. There are fifty seven. My stupidity is traceable partly to an astuteness that made me as afraid as the next man of the ferocious commitment involved in a long poem and partly to the fact that, although I had my form and subject, I did not have my theme yet. This emerged, and under the triple impetus of events I won't identify, I got the poem off the ground and nearly died following it. The theme is hard to put shortly, but I will try.[28]

Written in answer to a questionnaire, this puts it politely. Writing to Allen Tate during the composition of the poem, Berryman was more frank: 'I feel like weeping all the time. What keeps me from weeping is partly my ecstasy and partly a daily necessity of the hardest, most calculated work I have ever done ... Lord have mercy on us and bless you.'[29] *Bradstreet* and Lowell out of his system, Berryman soon realised that it was the end of the line for such calculated work, his next, more viable, project being *The Dream Songs*; a series, as John Haffenden describes it, not organised around a theme, but 'constituted by multiple occasions', or, as Berryman explained, when asked what 'structural notion' he had in mind when writing *The Dream Songs*, 'it was what you might call open-ended. That is to say, Henry to some extent was in the situation that we are all in actual life – namely, he didn't know and I didn't know what the bloody fucking hell was going to happen next.'[30]

The effect of Lowell's poetic was dramatic also in that, having previously lacked the energy that comes of antagonism, once an opposition came into view the middle generation insisted on it more forcefully than ever; with the further effect that non-Lowellian poetry was also sharply outlined. Not to be Lowell was, clearly, to be eclectic, improvisational, occasional and accepting. And so the problem for a poet like Ashbery, who had been attracted to the kind of poetry Lowell had come to displace, was how to be these things without seeming simply like Lowell's negative; how to differentiate oneself from Lowell without seeming simply (and so negligibly) impelled to be his other. But somebody had to do it, because, if the value of Lowell's poetry is that it offers a critique of the worst excesses of American culture – of its violent history and its technological present – the problem is that in doing so it throws the baby (although not 'Commander Lowell') out with the bathwater. Criticising the Edenic, and so, as the poem tells it, arrogant, impulse guiding America's earliest settlers, 'The Quaker Graveyard in Nantucket' absolves itself of the sins of the poet's fathers by returning to England, consoling itself with the Eliotic timelessness of the shrine of Our Lady at Walsingham. Ashbery has described the cost of this manoeuvre, observing how

> without the contribution of poets like [Charles Olson and Allen Ginsberg] and O'Hara in particular, there probably wouldn't be a generation of young poets committed to poetry as something living rather than an academic parlor game.[31]

In saving American poetry from the parlor, Ginsberg, O'Hara and Ashbery himself were saving it period; the academic parlor (and the backward-looking habits of mind it cultivated) being the stifling environment Emerson had sought to liberate American poetry from in the first place.

The way Ashbery, along with O'Hara and Koch, solved the problem of not being Lowell was by reading widely in pursuit of alternatives, revitalising American poetry as they did so – and in the time-honoured fashion of Whitman, Eliot, Pound and Stevens – by absorbing influences from elsewhere, France and Russia in particular. Of these multiple influences, the one I want to focus on is Pasternak: partly because, in warranting an epigraph, he was the most conspicuous external source in Ashbery's poetry; partly because Ashbery has continually referred to *Safe Conduct* when seeking to explain his aesthetic; partly because Pasternak's aesthetic is, in almost every particular, the antithesis of middle generation poetics; and finally because in considering Pasternak's influence in particular one learns something general about the function of influence in Ashbery's poetry.[32]

When *Doctor Zhivago* was published in America in 1959, most readers struggled to come to terms with it. The appearance of the book, after its censorship in Russia, being trumpeted as 'an historic event', all manner of commentators clamoured to voice their opinion on it, the text, in the process (and by an irony that would not have been lost on its author), becoming confused with its context.[33] The subject of debate was not, primarily, Pasternak's writing but the Cold War, and in particular the American way of life, the arguments turning, predictably, on the status of the individual. For Isaac Deutscher, offering something like the Soviet line, Pasternak's account of a 'thoroughly "cultured" and in every respect sterile egotist', was oblivious to the fact that 'slowly yet rapidly, painfully yet hopefully, the Soviet Union has moved into a new epoch'.[34] Irving Howe, amongst others, responded to Deutscher with 'a kind of gratitude', glad that it had 'all come out into the open', finding in the novel confirmation that 'Russia is ... a party-state still in basic opposition to the values of democracy and socialism'.[35] Nicola Chiaramonte was similarly grateful that 'a Russian writer has resumed his freedom of speech in order to make "available to all" what he thinks of the history lived through and suffered by his people'.[36] One consequence of such ideologically distorting accounts was to prompt more aesthetically minded critics to mount unusually close readings of Pasternak's text, and it was in these that the question of the individual became interesting. Tracing the structures of myth and legend which he took to inform the text, Edmund Wilson claimed to find clear evidence that it had 'been influenced by *Finnegans Wake*'.[37] What this comparison actually evinces is the failure of a certain kind of modernist critical idiom to come to terms with Pasternak, Wilson confessing bafflement at the author's decision to describe 'at such length some aspect of the weather or the landscape or to concentrate upon some scene involving a set of characters whom we ... do not expect to meet again'.[38] For the British commentator Stuart Hampshire, this missed the point almost entirely. The 'endless landscape', he asserted, 'was as much part of the novel as the revolution itself, as being the constantly changing background of the central story'. He was likewise less put out than Wilson by the fact that 'none of the characters is endowed with ... rounded naturalness nor are their lives steadily unfolded before the reader'.[39] But Hampshire could not see what might be made of these effects, suggesting that Pasternak would have 'no great influence on the writing of novels in ... America', because he had been too little affected by recent literary experiments.[40] It was left to O'Hara, arguing passionately in 'About Zhivago and his Poems', to show how the foregrounding of background bled into the unsteadiness of character, and why this was important. Politically the review was poised, O'Hara remarking that Soviet society was not alone in 'seducing the poet to deliver half-truths'.[41] Critically it was far in advance of anything else being written in the West. What O'Hara understood was that for Pasternak 'The human individual is the subject of historical events, not vice versa; he is the repository of life's force'.[42] What the novel poses, then, as O'Hara saw it, was 'a question of articulation: the epic events of *Doctor Zhivago* demand from their participants articulate perception or mute surrender'.

O'Hara understood the historical value of *Doctor Zhivago* more clearly than any of its other reviewers because the poets of the New York School had been reading Pasternak since the English translation of *Safe Conduct and Other Writings* was first published in American in 1949. What they were immediately able to see in the novel, therefore, was a development on a massive scale of the Pasternakian principle, already carefully formulated, that the object of art is to foreground its own background. As he put it (and to reiterate his most compelling formulation), 'People nowadays imagine that art is like a fountain, whereas it is a sponge. They think art has to flow forth, whereas what it has to do is absorb and become saturated.'[43] What art was to absorb and become saturated by were the circumstances in which it was made, and so as Pasternak puts it in *Safe Conduct* (and again to reiterate), 'The clearest most memorable and important feature of art is how it arises, and in their telling of the most varied things, the finest works in the world in fact all tell us of their own birth.'[44]

What this desired proximity of writing to situation meant in practice for Pasternak might be likened to what Marjorie Perloff identifies as the 'Ouspensky strain' in Russian Futurism. Outlining Ouspensky's philosophy of the 'fourth dimension', in which time and space are held to intersect, Perloff quotes his observation that

> If a man climbs a mountain or goes up in a balloon he sees *simultaneously* and *at once* a great many things that it is impossible to see simultaneously and at once when on earth – the movement of two trains toward one another which must result in a head-on collision; the approach of an enemy detachment to a sleeping camp; two towns separated by a mountain ridge and so on.[45]

The ambition of thus opening his writing to the things that are going on around it (as opposed, one might notice, to the ambition articulated by 'grinding [one's] teeth together till [one's] shut eyes ache'), required Pasternak to develop certain rhetorical strategies and structural devices which find an echo in Ashbery. In the first place, Pasternak inculcates a situational sense in the reader by rehearsing an extensive vocabulary for interconnectedness which crosses registers from the mundane to the mythological. To encounter any of 'surroundings', 'contexts', 'interlocking', 'chance', 'accident', 'climate', 'weather', 'rain', 'vast', 'event', 'situation', 'destiny', or 'fate' in Pasternak's writing is to find him contemplating the substance of points of contact.

More precisely, Pasternak builds contacts into the act of writing, developing what Roman Jakobson calls a poetic of proximity. What Jakobson intends to describe here is what J.M. Cohen calls Pasternak's 'provocative image'.[46] For example, from *Safe Conduct*: 'The sun rose from behind the post office, then, settling down like a fruit jelly, it set over Neglinka. As it gilded our flat, after dinner it reached into the dining-room and the kitchen.'[47] For Andrei Sinyavsky such images are instances of Pasternak's metaphorical method, reminding us that in Pasternak 'the chief role of metaphor is to connect one thing to another'.[48] Jakobson is more precise, also attending to the principle of connection, but suggesting that 'Pasternak's lyricism, both in poetry and prose, is imbued with metonymy; in other words, it is association by proximity that predominates'.[49] This appears to be true, though metonymy in Pasternak is stretched beyond familiar limits. The fruit jelly is applied to the sun on the basis of association, but the association could hardly be said to be conventional; rather it is instantaneous, scenic, arising from the coincidence of the sundown and the after-dinner scene. By commonly depending on such extra-linguistic associations, Pasternak's writing thus points beyond itself to the circumstances in which it is made.

What Jakobson sees with brilliant clarity is that the principle of proximity embedded in his metonymy underpins those aspects of Pasternak's writing which most readily define it. Witness what Pasternak's less insightful American readers took to be the unrounded, undeveloped quality of his characterisation in

Doctor Zhivago. Zhivago himself made it abundantly clear that this was no over-sight: 'However far back you go in your memory, it is always in some external, active manifestation of yourself that you come across your identity – in the work of your hands, in your family, in other people.'[50] Thus as Jakobson puts it, in Pasternak 'images of the surrounding world function as contiguous reflections, or metonymical expressions of the poet's self'.[51] The self, in other words, in Pasternak's writing, is not lost in the background; it is found there.

Finally, the device of association by proximity engineers what might be called the spaciousness of Pasternak's writing. This is nowhere more apparent than in 'Aerial Routes', a short story of 1924 first published in America, as Ashbery recalls, soon after *Safe Conduct and Other Writings* and to which O'Hara drew attention in his review. The story turns on the kidnapping of a young son, his family's search, the arrival of the boy's illegitimate father, and the mother's next meeting, on the occasion of the son's court martial some fifteen years later, with the father, now a member of the Revolutionary Provincial Executive Commit-tee. In this story, however, action is strictly secondary to setting, Pasternak's concern being to trace the ramifications of the event. This would seem in part to be a temporal process, hence the fifteen-year hiatus between meetings. In fact time is relevant only in so far as it takes a certain period for ripples to reach their full extent – as a function, in other words, of space. It is the spatial plane that is of primary importance here, Pasternak considering how the boy's disappearance connects with things, people and events with which it overlaps, intersects, or coincides, or to which it is adjacent. The story is thus an exercise in contextual-isation, Pasternak locating the event by intertwining the process through which 'the news of the sad event' spreads, with a series of larger, more comprehensive occurrences: the coming of a storm, the arrival of a train, the progress of the rev-olution, day break. Thus

> now the world all at once began to grow lighter in a more concerted way. The gar-den filled to the brim with moist, white light, light which clung most closely to the stuccoed wall, to the gravelled paths and the trunks of those fruit trees which had been smeared with a coppery wash now whitish like lime. It was now, with a death-like an expression on her face, that the mother of the child came dragging her feet in from the fields.[52]

Brief as it is, then, 'Aerial Routes' anticipates *Doctor Zhivago*, a novel in which the particular is forever interfusing with the general (as the 'vast' event which 'was on everybody's lips' incorporates all that surrounds it) and which was therefore, for Andrei Sinyavsky, the culmination of Pasternak's intention to 'draw into the action the whole of its environment, and leave no neutral background'.[53] Cen-trally concerned with the task of absorbing its own occasion, it is hard to imag-ine a more *accepting* writing than Pasternak's – save Ashbery's.

Published in 1956, after being awarded the Yale Younger Poets prize by Auden in 1955, *Some Trees* is a self-consciously oppositional book. Consider 'The

Mythological Poet', which, as the volume's polemical centrepiece, has been a focus for critical attention ever since Auden tried to find something to say about Ashbery in his preface to the Yale edition. A two-part poem, the first presents the degraded poetry of those 'Whom we do not sustain', and to which 'the mythological poet' of the second part would appear to be the answer:

> It was the toothless murmuring
> Of ancient willows, who kept their trouble
> In a stage of music. Without tumult
> Snow-capped mountains and heart-shaped
> Cathedral windows were contained
> There, until only infinity
> Remained of beauty.

> (ST, 34)

Indubitably this describes a poetry which, if one encountered it, one would want to oppose: toothless, lacking tumult, trading in clichés long since made meaningless. The question is, who would ever write such a poetry? There is just the suggestion of a specific antagonist in the equation of 'beauty' with 'infinity', implying a poetry not much concerned with the given occasion; but broadly speaking the first part of Ashbery's polemic is the kind of generic caricature of generically bad poetry Wordsworth went in for when distinguishing the *Lyrical Ballads* from the 'gaudiness and inane phraseology of many modern writers'. Like Wordsworth's 'Advertisement', the first part of 'The Mythological Poet' paints contemporary poetry so detrimentally as to make itself the only alternative.[54]

The opposition which really informs this poem, and which, perhaps, the poet wants to distract attention from for fear of seeming simply reactive, is actually to be found in the definition which opens the second part of the poem:

> The mythological poet, his face
> Fabulous and fastidious, accepts
> Beauty before it arrives.

> (ST, 35)

Though the cluster of adjectives are the sign of a poet trying to identify himself, whether for his own benefit or the reader's, when we finally encounter the new poetry this poem is preparing us for, it is not in any significant sense either 'mythological', 'fabulous' or 'fastidious'. It does, however, accept:

> Close to the zoo, acquiescing
> To dust, candy, perverts; inserted in
> The panting forest, or openly
> Walking in the great and sullen square
> He has eloped with all music
> And does not care.

> (ST, 35)

As it watches the world go by in a public space, 'The Mythological Poem' resembles an early Berryman poem, 'The Statue', in which the poet, sitting 'near the entrance to the Park', observes how

> The statue, tolerant through years of weather,
> Spares the untidy Sunday throng its look,
> Spares shopgirls knowledge of the fatal pallor
> Under their evening colour,
> Spares homosexuals, the crippled, the alone,
> Extravagant perception of their failure[55]

The difference, of course, is that whereas Berryman's statue endures the circumstances and the people in and among which it finds itself, Ashbery's 'mythological poet' accepts them, the poem concluding with an image of child and pervert momentarily hand in hand against a background of statuesque disapproval:

> And oh beside the roaring
> Centurion of the lion's hunger
> Might not child and pervert
> Join hands, in the instant
> Of their interest, in the shadow
> Of a million boats; their hunger
> From loss grown merely a gesture?

(ST, 36)

Determined to prove itself thoroughly *'accepting'* (Berryman's italics), 'The Mythological Poet' is the antithesis not of the ill-defined murmuring of the first part of the poem but of the very clearly defined poetics of the middle generation.

Ashbery's dialogue with the language of the middle generation flickers into view elsewhere. In 'Popular Songs', the order is reversed, the wilfully digressive first paragraph ending with a disapproving voice: 'Some precision, he fumed into his soup.' This is the kind of voice Koch disapproved of in 'Fresh Air', the combination of precision and fumes criticising the poetic vagueness that comes of academic accuracy. And Ashbery distances himself from it here, the second part of 'Popular Songs' laughing at an obviously out-moded, not least because thuddingly iambic, poetic expression:

> You laugh. There is no peace in the fountain.
> The footmen smile and shift. The mountain
> Rises nightly to disappointed stands
> Dining in "The Gardens of the Moon."

(ST, 34)

The two parts of *Le livre est sur la table* likewise turn on a heavily drawn opposition between competing poetic languages. The first part ends with a most morose couple:

> But what

> Dismal scene is this? the old man pouting

At a black cloud, the woman gone
Into the house, from which the wailing starts?

(ST, 74)

The second part begins with a scene from Stevens:

The young man places a bird-house
Against the blue sea. He walks away
And it remains.

Like the jar in Tennessee, the bird-house provides a focus for, and so directs attention to, the background against which it is placed. Quite the reverse of the gloomy, domesticated, inward-looking poetry offered by the scene which precedes. 'The Mythological Poet', 'Popular Songs' and *Le livre est sur la table*, are anxious poems, Ashbery engaging in dialogue with a poetic language he cannot fully acknowledge because not confident of the new language with which he would displace it. If these poems are clearly not Lowell, they are not clearly Ashbery either, the overload of adjectives at the beginning of 'The Mythological Poet' and the too recognisable presence of Stevens in *Le livre est sur la table* marking a poetry not quite itself.

Nor are these the least self-assured pieces in *Some Trees*, a number of poems seeming so preoccupied with what they are not as to lose sight almost entirely of what it is they are aiming to become. 'The Hero', for instance, lacks even the distance of caricature:

Whose face is this
So stiff against the blue trees,

Lifted to the future
Because there is no end?

But that has faded
Like flowers, like the first days

Of good conduct. Visit
The strong man. Pinch him –

There is no end to his
Dislike, the accurate one.

(ST, 23)

As a sketch of the Lowell-like poet this is hardly to be faulted, the heroic individual being: obsessed with the future (and so unmoved by his startling environment), old-fashioned, hard, disapproving, ultimately precise. Indeed the only problem with the poem is Ashbery's own accuracy, his imitation of the language against which he is defining himself leaving him no scope to develop his own, save, perhaps, in the mischievous 'pinch'; though such high-jinking irreverence is also to be found in Stevens. The same is more or less true of 'Album Leaf', another poem which begins with its other:

The other marigolds and the cloths
Are crimes invented for history.
What can we achieve, aspiring?
And what, aspiring, can we achieve?

What can the rain that fell
All day on the grounds
And on the bingo tables?

(ST, 26)

Defending Koch against the orthodox criticism of Harry Roskolenko, O'Hara argued that

> Mr. Koch's poems have a natural voice, they are quick, alert, instinctive and, within the limited scope of his first volume, indicate a potentially impressive variety. His technique is opposed to that Academic and often turgid development by which many young poets gain praise for their 'achievement,' an achievement limited usually to the mastery of one phase of Yeats (and usually the last).[56]

The best that can be said of poems like 'Album Leaf' is probably that they 'indicate a potentially impressive variety'. Arguably they do prefigure mature Ashbery in that, like 'Fresh Air', they record their own emergence out of the dismal American poetry scene of the late 1940s and early 1950s. But in so doing they become swamped by the language of the scene, its concern with 'history', its 'achievement', its Parnassian 'aspirations'. Against this Ashbery's own language is, self-consciously probably but self-defeatingly none the less, unimpressive, the 'marigolds', 'cloths', 'bingo tables', 'receipts' and 'sweet peas' of 'Album Leaf' tending to justify the spirit of Auden's warning in a letter to O'Hara, after he had come second to Ashbery in the Yale competition, that

> I think you (and John too, for that matter) must watch what is always the great danger with any 'surrealistic' style, namely of confusing authentic non-logical relations which arouse wonder with accidental ones which arouse mere surprise and in the end fatigue.[57]

As readers of Pasternak, Ashbery and O'Hara rightly resisted Auden's advice to suppress the accidental relations in their writing, but the warning that these might issue in 'mere surprise' was pertinent, a number of early Ashbery poems being impelled to a nervous surrealism by their determination to resist the achievements of others. 'Errors' is a case in point:

Jealousy. Whispered weather reports.
In the street we found boxes
Littered with snow, to burn at home.
What flower tolling on the waters
You stupefied me. We waxed,
Carnivores, late and alight
In the beaded winter.

(ST, 47)

Expressly concerned not to be precise, 'Errors' is notable only for the sibilant consonantal music with which it distinguishes itself from the hardened sound of a certain kind of middle-generation poem, the rest, the odd conjunctions and strained relations, indicating only a 'potentially impressive variety'.

Yet where O'Hara was reserved in his review of Kenneth Koch's early poetry, he was abundant in his assessment of Ashbery's; and while a number of poems in *Some Trees* warrant only the limited praise he offered Koch (or even only the faint praise which was the best Auden could muster), the volume as a whole deserves O'Hara's description of it as 'the most beautiful first book to appear in America since Wallace Stevens' *Harmonium*'. It justifies the claim because like *Harmonium* (a debut volume itself not unmarred by preciosity) and for all a certain anxious scratching after difference, *Some Trees* not only manifests a new style, but inaugurates a new poetic, Ashbery's poetry here, as subsequently, proving never more itself than when receding into its own background.

'Some Trees', written while he was still at Harvard, is one of Ashbery's earliest poems to recede into the background. A love poem with an American accent – the title expressing not only the presence of the trees but, through an American emphasis on the word *some*, the wonder the trees inspire in the poet – the poem begins by presenting a couple so wrapped up in one another that they lose sight of themselves as separate entities, and so find themselves absorbed in their wooded surroundings.

> These are amazing: each
> Joining a neighbour, as though speech
> Were a still performance.
> Arranging by chance
>
> To meet as far this morning
> From the world as agreeing
> With it, you and I
> Are suddenly what the trees try
>
> To tell us we are:
> That their merely being there
> Means something; that soon
> We may touch, love, explain.

(ST, 51)

The poem's American accent is learned chiefly from Emerson, the couple's heightened sense of one another widening to a more general awareness of what Emerson calls 'not-I':

> And glad not to have invented
> Such comeliness, we are surrounded:
> A silence already filled with noises,
> A canvas on which emerges
>
> A chorus of smiles, a winter morning.

Placed in a puzzling light, and moving,
Our days put on such reticence
These accents seem their own defense.

(ST, 51)

Attractive and accomplished as it is, everything in this poem happens just a little too easily and quickly. The sense of 'surroundings' is uncomplicatedly natural, while the poet and his partner simply lose all sense of self, becoming, as they proceed towards the woods, ego-less Emersonian 'eye-balls'. And hurried as it is, one has the sense of a poet in flight, the Emersonian background being either a too ready alternative to the emphatic individualism of middle generation poetics or, arguably, a version of the closet, the gay couple wishing themselves as inconspicuous as possible. What is lacking in 'Some Trees' is any tug in the other direction, any sense that it is neither possible nor desirable simply to shed one's individuality in favour of an all-embracing environment; the dialectical sense that, while the self might consist in its situation, even so it is still possible to talk about the self.

In 'Some Trees' the Cheshire Cat disappears. Elsewhere, more interestingly, it is on the verge of disappearing. 'The Painter', for instance, the earliest poem in the book, addresses similar questions of self-abnegation, presenting what now reads like a critique of the abstract expressionist aesthetic:

Sitting between the sea and the buildings
He enjoyed painting the sea's portrait.
But just as children imagine a prayer
Is merely silence, he expected his subject
To rush up the sand, and, seizing a brush,
Plaster its own portrait on the canvas.

(ST, 54)

Painting against the backdrop of the sea, the painter is always on the verge of being overwhelmed. But he never actually is, 'The Painter' being a more exacting poem not only because it argues with the artist who imagines that his subject, the sea, might simply emerge on to his canvas, but because the skilfully handled sestina form reminds the reader of the presence, for all his desire to slip into the background, of the poet himself. Even so the sense of 'surroundings' the poem offers, the sea, is still uncomplicated, and it is not until three poems he wrote after reading *Safe-Conduct and Other Writings* that Ashbery begins really to resemble his mature aesthetic self; Pasternak already having a fully developed lexicon for the sense of background and occasion by which Ashbery was seeking to define himself against the poetic orthodoxy of the late 1940s.

'The Picture of Little J.A. in a Prospect of Flowers' is the prime example. While not looking like any poem Pasternak ever wrote or even, one suspects, imagined writing, 'The Picture of Little J.A. in a Prospect of Flowers' is Pasternakian at every turn, Ashbery's poetry transformed here by a reading of Pasternak which registers the full force of his principle of association. The choice of the final sentence of 'Safe Conduct' for the poem's epigraph is a measure of this reading. In concluding the memoir, the sentence also concludes the account of Mayakovsky which constitutes the final section of the work. Ashbery's quotation is thus a knowing gesture, signalling not, as one might think, that his real interest is in Mayakovsky, but rather his understanding (pre-*Zhivago*) that for Pasternak, 'it is always in some external, active manifestation of yourself that you come across your identity – in the work of your hands, in your family, in other people'.[58] The gesture is made doubly knowing by the fact that, as Ashbery's epigraph is the memoir's final sentence, the reader is obliged to read all of a different work to understand this one. The text's meaning, like Pasternak's identity, is in another.

The poem's first line – 'Darkness falls like a wet sponge' – is likewise awash with Pasternakian resonances. The comparison works by the principle of proximity Jakobson described as Pasternak's metonymy. Thus, the falling darkness is likened to a wet sponge on the same occasional basis that the sun setting over Neglinka is likened to a jelly, the sponge arising from the children's bed-time ablutions at nightfall like the jelly arises from the dinner table. More than this, though, Ashbery's opening line has its meaning in others, and so is all about absorption. The line alludes to Pasternak, of course, art being, as he insisted, more like a sponge than a fountain. But it also alludes to Nashe, or rather to Joyce alluding to Nashe: Stephen Daedalus (in *A Portrait of the Artist as a Young Man*) mis-remembering the line 'Brightness falls from the air' from Nashe's 'In Time of Pestilence' as 'Darkness falls from the air'.[59] So to a degree and with a literalness that Pasternak had probably not anticipated, 'The Picture of Little J.A' shows Ashbery's to be a thoroughly spongy poetry: the self-conscious product of the various influences that constitute its aesthetic background.

For Koch, who recalls reading 'The Picture of Little J.A.' just after it was written, the poem was a breakthrough: 'a vault over W.C. Williams and a bypass of Dylan Thomas' as he puts it in 'A time zone'.[60] The poem would have seemed a breakthrough to Koch not least for the eclecticism of a first line which alluded to Nashe, Joyce and Pasternak, eclectic tastes being crucial to New York School poetry and friendships. Recounting his first meeting with O'Hara at a cocktail party at the Mandrake Book Shop in Cambridge, Ashbery remembers O'Hara saying

> 'Let's face it, *Les Sécheresses* is greater than *Tristan*.' I knew that *Les Sécheresses* was a vocal work by Poulenc which had been performed recently at Harvard; I also knew, back in those dull and snobbish days, that nobody at Harvard took Poulenc, or any other modern composer (except Hindemith, Piston and Stravinsky), seriously, and that this assertion was in the way of a pleasant provocation. Also, I was somehow aware, it summed up a kind of aesthetic attitude which was very close to my own.[61]

O'Hara's tastes were always ahead of the game, Ashbery recalling that on their second meeting he was 'carrying a stack of books by various writers I had never heard of, including Samuel Beckett, Jean Rhys and Flann O'Brien'. Ashbery's were neither less varied nor less advanced, and it is a defining characteristic of *Some Trees* that in amongst allusions to Whitman, Stevens and Auden, it also makes reference, passing or otherwise, to, for instance, Riding, Roussel, Prince and Wheelwright among writers, and Saint-Saëns, Glazunov and Rimsky-Korsakov among composers. O'Hara, certainly, was keen to acknowledge the range of Ashbery's tastes in his review, noting 'references to other poets which are not quite parody, such as: "He" (Blaise Cendrars), "The Thinnest Shadow" (Housman), "Canzone" (Auden), "The Instruction Manual" (Whitman)'.[62] Nor was the poetry only open to influences from the reading and music of Ashbery's aesthetic hinterland. 'Popular Songs', for instance, was

> written in an attempt to conjure up the kind of impression you get from riding in the car, changing the radio station and at the same time aware of the passing landscape. In other words, a kind of confused, but insistent, impression of the culture going on around us.[63]

All of which now familiar (and recognisably postmodern) habits of mind suggest, as John Pilling has persuasively argued, that – whether in the interests of escaping the baleful influence of any single modernist poet such as Eliot, or whether to open the language of poetry, after modernism, to a democratising range of sources – no individual influence had priority in Ashbery. All are equal in the poetry because the poetry is equally in all of them. Where is the poet to be found, after all, if not in his range of tastes: in the reading, music, popular culture and people with which and whom he spends his time. Except that, *pace* Pilling, whose argument is right in every particular, all of this is very Pasternakian. Later in *Dr Zhivago* it is explicitly always in 'some external, active manifestation of yourself that you come across your identity – in the work of your hands, in your family, in other people'. But the argument is clearly there in his early writing as well, Ashbery taking it to heart in 'The Picture of Little J.A. in a Prospect of Flowers'. Thus not only are we referred to Marvell by the title, Pasternak by the epigraph, Nashe and Joyce by the first line, but when we might think finally that we are looking at Ashbery himself (in so far as that means anything) we are also looking at Wordsworth, the little J.A.'s 'head among the blazing phlox' recalling Wordsworth's 'To H.C., Six Years Old', 'H.C.' being 'A young Lamb's heart among the full-grown flocks'.[64]

Still though, as we locate Ashbery in Wordsworth, what we are really offered by the poem's conclusion is another image of Ashbery in Pasternak:

> Yet I cannot escape the picture
> Of my small self in that bank of flowers:
> My head among the blazing phlox
> Seemed a pale and gigantic fungus.
> I had a hard stare, accepting
> Everything, taking nothing,
> As though the rolled-up future might stink
> As loud as stood the sick moment

The shutter clicked. Though I was wrong,
Still, as the loveliest feelings

Must soon find words, and these, yes,
Displace them, so I am not wrong
In calling this comic version of myself
The true one. For as change is horror,
Virtue is really stubbornness

And only in the light of lost words
Can we imagine our rewards.

(ST, 28–9)

The passage communicates the general sense of a self merged with his sur-
roundings ('*in* that bank of flowers', '*among* the blazing phlox'). But there is also
a precise sense of mergence, indicated by the startling image of the boy's head as
'gigantic fungus'. A fungus is a parasite, feeding off its environment. It is also,
etymologically at least, related to the Greek *spongos*. The small self the poet
cannot escape – which is, in fact, his 'true' self – is thus intimately related to,
because saturated by, his environment; is lost, or rather found, in a Pasternakian
background.

Like Jarrell's opposition of the art of the solitary individual and the art of
eclecticism, but more so, Pasternak's distinction between art as fountain and art
as sponge allows one to map the major differences in postmodern art: the foun-
tain describing the pouring out characteristic of all forms of the confessional; the
sponge pointing to all that art, from Cage to LANGUAGE, which aims, ulti-
mately, to take account of the inescapable sense, in the postwar period, that as
O'Hara put it, 'The human individual is the subject of historical events, not vice
versa; he is the repository of life's force'. And, as 'The Picture of Little J.A.' pre-
dicts, nobody has worked harder to absorb this Pasternakian truth than Ashbery.

Two other noticeably self-assured poems in *Some Trees* have their origin in
Pasternakian dynamics. The first is 'The Instruction Manual', which, with its
promise of illumination, has, like 'The Mythological Poet' and 'The Picture of
Little J.A.', been the subject of much critical comment. Ashbery has described
'The Instruction Manual' written in 1955, and one of the latest poems in *Some
Trees*, as a 'rather paint by numbers poem' – a reader-friendly guide, as the title
suggests, to the strange new poetry being offered. Transporting himself from the
office in which he is obliged to 'write the instruction manual / on the uses of a
new metal', the speaker visits Guadalajara, guiding the reader around the 'City I
wanted most to see, and most did not see, in Mexico!', and introducing them, in
the process, to key elements of Ashbery's new poetry. We encounter his Russian
tastes: 'The band is playing *Scheherazade* by Rimsky-Korsakov' (ST, 14). We are
introduced to his sense of occasion, this being a public holiday, and the poet
noting that

First, leading the parade, is a dapper fellow
Clothed in deep blue. On his head sits a white hat

And he wears a mustache, which has been trimmed for
    the occasion.
His dear one, his wife, is young and pretty; her shawl is
    rose, pink, and white.
Her slippers are patent leather, in the American fashion,
And she carries a fan, for she is modest, and does not want
    the crowd to see her face too often.

(ST, 15)

Both the dapper fellow and his wife resemble the poet: the man suiting himself
to the needs of the occasion; the woman, in her American fashion, feeling most
comfortable when absorbed into the occasion of which she is a part. While the
Mexicans the speaker meets are, as Geoff Ward has pointed out, as hospitable to
foreign bodies as Ashbery's poetry aims to be:

An old woman in gray sits there, fanning herself with a
    palm leaf fan.
She welcomes us to her patio, and offers us a cooling drink.
"My son is in Mexico City," she says. "He would welcome
    you too."

(ST, 17)

The most conspicuous influence on style of 'The Instruction Manual' is
Roussel, the long, digressive sentences introducing the reader to a place the
writer has never visited. Structurally, however, the poem is Pasternakian. Writ-
ten out of a sense of obligation to provide a guide to his poetry, to the uses of his
new metal, Ashbery's poem absorbs its own occasion: the poem telling of its
own birth by showing a writer hard at work on an instruction manual. And in
guiding the reader through the public squares and twisting side streets of his
poetry, Ashbery is all the time indicating that the substance of his poetry is an
ever expanding sense of its own occasion, the poem broadening to include the
band, the parade, the crowd at the parade, the people who didn't make it, until
finally offering a view of the whole situation, the poem concluding with a view
of the city from a church tower:

Soon we have reached the top, and the whole network of
    the city extends before us.
There is the rich quarter, with its houses of pink and
    white, and its crumbling, leafy terraces.
There is the poorer quarter, its homes a deep blue.
There is the market, where men are selling hats and
    swatting flies,
And there is the public library, painted several shades of
    pale green and beige.

(ST, 17–18)

Opening by telling the story of its own birth, 'The Instruction Manual' charts an
ever widening sense of occasion until by the end of the poem we have the kind
of overview of the scene Pasternak developed in 'Aerial Routes'.

For Sinyavsky, such manoeuvres were central to Pasternak's writing, holding as he did that 'a poet's perception [must] be broad and entire, for its task was to recreate in verse some one single scene or atmosphere of life'.[65] It is perhaps no surprise, then, finally, that in the two scenes of 'Two Scenes', but especially the first, Ashbery is alive as ever, to Pasternakian suggestion.

> We see us as we truly behave:
> From every corner comes a distinctive offering.
> The train comes bearing joy;
> The sparks it strikes illuminate the table.
> Destiny guides the water-pilot, and it is destiny.
> For long we hadn't heard so much news, such noise.
> The day was warm and pleasant.
> "We see you in your hair,
> Air resting around the tips of mountains."
>
> (ST, 9)

Each line contains a Pasternakian element. The first line externalises identity, finding it, perhaps, in the 'work of our hands'. The second visualises a sense of intersection. The train bearing good news could come from anywhere perhaps, but few writers make more of locomotion than Pasternak, and anyway it is used to illuminate that with which it is in proximity. 'Destiny' mythologises such interconnectedness, while 'news' becoming the noise of life renders it mundane again. Finally, the shift in scale from 'hair' to 'mountains' dislocates conventional perspectives by proceeding according to the metonymy of sight. But, these Pasternakian elements notwithstanding, 'Two Scenes' is also the poem in *Some Trees* (as he surely thought by placing it first) in which Ashbery is most like himself – the Russian poet helping him to absorb the echoes of Auden and Stevens audible in the second part of the poem, and to distinguish himself from the clunky thematic language of the middle generation, by enabling him to develop a sense of occasion all his own.

O'Hara's review of *Some Trees* made three substantive points: that Ashbery's influences are many and various; that 'the poems open outward to the reader'; and that Ashbery 'establishes a relation between perception and articulateness which is non-rhetorical and specific'. These last were the terms of highest praise in O'Hara's lexicon, being the terms, as we have seen, he would later use to introduce the American reader to 'Zhivago and his Poems'.

NOTES

1 Ashbery's first collection, *Turandot and Other Poems*, was published in a small printing by the Tibor de Nagy Gallery. Part of a series designed by John Myers to display the New York School poets and some of their painter friends, Ashbery's collection included paintings by Jane Freilicher. All the poems published there were also published in *Some Trees*, except 'White' and 'Turandot'. *Some Trees* was published in the

prestigious Yale Younger Poets series, the competition for which was judged by Auden.

2 John Ashbery, 'A reminiscence', pp. 20–21.

3 Ashbery provides an account of his arrival in New York in his review 'Jane Freilicher: paintings 1953–85' (RS, 239–40).

4 David Herd, 'John Ashbery in conversation with David Herd', p. 36. Ashbery makes the same point in his 'Introduction' to Pierre Martory, *The Landscape Is Behind the Door*, p. xi.

5 Ibid., p. 33.

6 Kenneth Koch, *Selected Poems*, pp. 30–6.

7 For a theoretical formulation of this see Pierre Bourdieu, *The Field of Cultural Production*.

8 Ashbery, *The Heavy Bear: Delmore Schwartz's Life Versus His Poetry*, p. 1.

9 Edward Lucie Smith, 'An interview with Frank O'Hara', in Frank O'Hara, *Standing Still and Walking in New York*, p. 13.

10 Lehman, *The Last Avant-Garde*, p349

11 Ashbery, 'Introduction' to *The Collected Poems of Frank O'Hara*, pp. viii, vii.

12 *Five Young American Poets*, p. 45.

13 Ibid., p. 48.

14 Ibid., p. 88.

15 Ibid., p. 89. Delmore Schwartz was similarly left barely able to guess at the end of his 1941 essay, 'The isolation of modern poetry', which he concludes: 'I have also spoken as if this isolation of the poet had already reached its conclusion. Whether it has or not, and whether it would be entirely desirable that it should, may be left as unanswered … questions.' Delmore Schwartz, 'The isolation of modern poetry', *Selected Essays of Delmore Schwartz*, p. 12.

16 Randall Jarrell, *Kipling, Auden and Co.* p. 77. For a different consideration of this article and of some of the other materials in this section, see James E.B. Breslin, *From Modern to Contemporary*, pp. 1–52.

17 Ibid., pp. 81, 82, 84, 87.

18 Shapiro, *Essay on Rime*, p. 69.

19 John Berryman, 'Lowell, Thomas & Co.', p. 73.

20 Robert Lowell, *Poems 1938–1949*, p. 18.

21 Berryman, 'Lowell, Thomas & Co.', pp. 79–80.

22 Ibid. pp. 307, 308.

23 John Berryman, *The Freedom of the Poet*, pp. 294, 295.

24 Randall Jarrell, *Poetry and the Age*, p. 237.

25 Jarrell, *Kipling, Auden and Co*, pp. 287–8.

26 Jarrell, *Poetry and the Age*, p. 191.

27 Helen Vendler, *The Given and the Made,* p. xii.

28 John Berryman, 'One answer to a question', in Howard Nemerov (ed.), *Contemporary American Poetry*, p. 126.

29 Berryman, letter to Allen Tate, 6 February 1953, cited in John Haffenden, *John Berryman: A Critical Commentary*, p. 26.

30 Haffenden, *John Berryman: A Critical Commentary*, p. 6. Peter Stitt, 'An interview with John Berryman', p. 30.

31 Ashbery, *The Collected Poems of Frank O'Hara*, p. ix.

32 In an essay on Kitaj Ashbery is 'reminded of Scriabin's exhortations to the young Boris

Pasternak, cited in Pasternak's memoir *Safe Conduct*, to simplify art as much as possible' (RS, 303).

33 Nicola Chiaromonte, 'Pasternak's message', p. 232.
34 Isaac Deutscher, 'Pasternak and the calendar of the revolution', p. 258.
35 Irving Howe, 'Freedom and the ashcan of history', p. 259.
36 Chiaromonte, 'Pasternak's Message', p. 231.
37 Edmund Wilson, 'Legend and symbol in *Doctor Zhivago*', p. 47.
38 Ibid., p. 52.
39 Stuart Hampshire, '*Doctor Zhivago*. As from a lost culture', p. 4.
40 Ibid., p. 3.
41 Frank O'Hara, *Standing Still and Walking in New York*, p. 103.
42 Ibid., p. 106.
43 Cited by Donald Davie, in Davie and Livingstone (eds), *Modern Judgements: Pasternak*, p. 23.
44 Boris Pasternak, *Safe Conduct*, p. 213.
45 Marjorie Perloff, *The Futurist Moment*, p. 129.
46 J.M. Cohen, 'The poetry of Pasternak', p. 24.
47 Pasternak, *Safe Conduct*, p. 179.
48 Andrei Sinyavsky, 'Boris Pasternak', p. 164.
49 Roman Jakobson, 'The prose of the poet Pasternak', p. 141.
50 Pasternak, *Doctor Zhivago*, p. 70.
51 Jakobson, 'The prose of the poet Pasternak', p. 141.
52 Pasternak, *Safe Conduct*, p. 119.
53 Sinyavsky, 'Boris Pasternak', p. 181.
54 Wordsworth and Coleridge, *Lyrical Ballads*, p. 7.
55 John Berryman, *Collected Poems*, p. 4.
56 Frank O'Hara, *Standing Still and Walking in New York*, p. 59.
57 Letter from W.H. Auden to Frank O'Hara, 3 March 1955, cited in, *City Poet* p. 261.
58 Pasternak, *Doctor Zhivago*, p. 40.
59 James Joyce, *A Portrait of the Artist as a Young Man*, pp. 237–8.
60 Kenneth Koch, *One Train*, p. 27.
61 Ashbery, 'A reminiscence', p. 20
62 Frank O'Hara, *Standing Still and Walking in New York*, p78
63 Sue Gangel, 'An interview with John Ashbery', pp. 17–18.
64 William Wordsworth, *The Oxford Authors: William Wordsworth*, p. 247.
65 Sinyavsky, 'Boris Pasternak', p. 179.

CHAPTER TWO

The art of life: collaboration and the New York School

In 1961 Ashbery, Koch, Schuyler, O'Hara and Harry Mathews published an issue of *Locus Solus* especially devoted to collaborations. Taking its title from a novel by Raymond Roussel, *Locus Solus* was the only publishing venture to carry the poets' collective imprimatur. Part of its purpose, accordingly, and within the bounds of an aesthetic that aimed to resist all conventions of style, was to identify and distinguish the New York School. As Schuyler put it in a letter to Chester Kallman,

> I and 'others' (it is a deep secret; the other is John Ashbery) are invisibly editing an anthology-magazine … [P]art of its unstated objective is as a riposte at The New American Poetry, which has so thoroughly misrepresented so many of us – not completely, but the implications of context are rather overwhelming.

Itself a riposte against Donald Hall and Robert Pack's over-cooked, academic anthology *New Poets of England and America*, Allen's *The New American Poetry 1945–60* gathered together, but in so doing homogenised, the diverse avant-garde poetries of the Beats, the Black Mountaineers and the New York School. By way of distinguishing themselves from Ginsberg and Olson *et al.*, what the editors of *Locus Solus* were seeking, Schuyler told Kallman, were 'cheerful, serious, international kind of Paris–New York edited contents'. 'I hope,' he signed off, 'in all this camp' – the letter is very camp – 'you can discern that the "Occasional Anthology" is a serious opus.'[1] Of the five issues of the magazine, each guest-edited by either Ashbery, Schuyler or Koch, the second, the 'Special Issue of Collaborations', was the most self-conscious, Koch's careful editorial note on the issue, and the rigorously researched notes on individual works and authors, distinguishing the New Yorkers as, among other things, poets who took collaboration seriously.

Collaboration has often been important to avant-garde practice. As Cynthia Jaffee McCabe puts it in her brief history of the form, 'Camaraderie, friendship, mutual interests and ambition, the dynamism of nascent art movements, and proximity amid wartime or other disruptive conditions are all incentives toward the creation of collaborative works of art.'[2] McCabe's 'disruptive conditions' are key here. When Wordsworth and Coleridge (avant-gardistes *avant la lettre* perhaps) joined forces on *Lyrical Ballads* and when Eliot sought Pound's assistance on *The Waste Land*, the point in both cases was that conditions had recently been so radically altered by disruptive events that the language, through poetry, had to be made new. In both cases this monumental task proved more than the work of the solitary poet, and so, as Wordsworth explained the collaborative format of *Lyrical Ballads* in his 'Preface', 'from a consciousness of my own weakness I was induced to request the assistance of a friend'.[3] Or as Pound, describing his editorial contribution to *The Waste Land*, explained, so difficult was the birth of Eliot's innovative poem that the occasion called for his surgical assistance:

> If you must needs enquire
> Know diligent Reader
> That on each Occasion
> Ezra performed the caesarian Operation.[4]

Historically, then, as Pound's metaphor implies, collaboration had been vital to avant-garde practice in so far as it had been instrumental in its productions – Conrad and Ford, Eliot and Pound, the Dadaists and the Surrealists collaborating primarily because the task of bringing a new rhetoric into being required the energy and judgement of more than one writer.

In America in the early 1950s, when Ashbery first joined forces with Koch, the situation of the avant-garde was somewhat different, with their collaborations mattering not only for the productions they gave rise to but for the act itself. Or at least, so Paul Goodman implied in his brilliantly timely essay 'Advance-guard writing 1900–1950'. Writing in the summer 1951 issue of the *Kenyon Review*, Goodman set out (via a history of advance-guard writing in America in the twentieth century) to sketch directions for the contemporary experimental artist. Starting from the Wordsworthian premise that advance-guard writing arises whenever 'the mores are outmoded, anti-instinctual, or otherwise counter to the developing powers of intelligent and sensitive persons', Goodman took the ongoing objective of avant-garde writing to be the re-integration of the language (and so the people who use it) with the disruptive circumstances from which it had become estranged.[5] With this in mind, avant-garde writing, he argued, was always, of necessity, operating beyond (although preferably only just beyond) the writers' control, experimenting, as they were, towards a form of language appropriate to circumstances from which, in common with their community, they had become cut off. And the point of the article was that never in forty years had the literary atmosphere been so unconducive to such writing. Acknowledging that even to write about the avant-garde (especially, perhaps, in *The Kenyon Review*) he must seem like 'a spectre of the past oddly haunting the literary scene', Goodman took this fact as his justification.[6] The extreme academicism of the journals, he argued, was a symptom of a 'complete inability to bear anxiety of any kind, to avoid panic and collapse'. Whether because it felt threatened by external forces, or by the social ramifications of its own massive and rapid economic development, American culture was clinging to established, but hopelessly outmoded conventions, terrified that the slightest formal disruption would cause the whole fragile ideological edifice to come crashing to the floor. Arguably only a culture so anxious that it could not begin to acknowledge its own anxiety could produce the paranoid conservatism of McCarthy. At any rate the 1950s were 'tranquil-lised', to pursue Goodman's argument in Lowell's perspicacious terms, because only by sedating itself so heavily against the reality of its circumstances could American society persist in its thoroughly alienated state. If experimental writing was never less likely to succeed in America than in 1950, then by precisely the same cultural logic it had never been so important that it should.

Given this degree of alienation – of society from its reality and so, in all mean-ingful ways, of people from one another – the essential task, as Goodman saw it, of the contemporary avant-garde (of the as yet 'unnamed writer who proceeds from a remark of Goethe') was the 'physical re-establishment of community'. The writer was

> to solve the crisis of alienation in the simple way: the persons are estranged from themselves, from one another, and from their artist; he takes the initiative precisely by putting his arms around them and drawing them together. In literary terms this means: *to write for them about them personally*.

These are familiar gestures, Whitman having long ago indicated his intention to encircle the reader by writing for them personally. Goodman's qualification is that in present circumstances, given the care needed to reacquaint readers with themselves and with their circumstances,

> such personal writing about the audience itself can occur only in a small commu-nity of acquaintances, where everybody knows everybody and understands what is at stake; in our estranged society, it is objected, just such intimate community is lacking. Of course it is lacking! The point is that the advance-guard action helps create such community, starting with the artist's primary friends. The community comes to exist by having *its* culture; the artist makes this culture.

What Goodman describes here is what Habermas has come to call the ideal speech situation; ideal communication taking place precisely when everybody 'understands what is at stake'. There is, of course, a difference of scale, Good-man calling not for a universal pragmatics but for the intimate communication of the coterie. This said, his argument, clearly, was very much for a coterie which, in due course, would come to look beyond itself; the community it cre-ated starting, but by no means ending, with the group of friends. At the present moment, however, the most important thing for the avant-garde artist and his or her friends was to establish their own community, their work thus becoming, as Goodman put it,

> a genre of the highest integrated art, namely Occasional Poetry – the poetry celebrating weddings, festivals, and so forth. 'Occasional Poetry' said Goethe, 'is the highest kind' – for it gives the most real and detailed subject-matter, it is closest in its effect on the audience, and it poses the enormous problem of being

plausible to the actuality and yet creatively imagining something, finding some-thing unlooked-for.

Goodman does not detail how occasional poetry manages to be both 'plausible to the actuality and yet creatively imagining' – a high ambition, surely, for any poetry, and one that speaks forcefully to Ashbery's sense of the loose but never uncoupled relation of language to events. He does, however, indicate the effect of such poetry on its audience.

> An aim, one might almost say the chief aim, of integrated art is to heighten the everyday; to bathe the world in such a light of imagination and criticism that the persons who are living in it without meaning or feeling suddenly find that it is meaningful and exciting to live in it.[7]

Poetry which could do all this would be, in a strict sense of the term Ashbery chose to describe O'Hara's poetry in his Introduction to *The Collected Poems*, 'viable', such occasional poetry being, as Goodman puts it at the end of his arti-cle, 'the art of life'.[8]

Seeing himself, perhaps, as Goodman's 'unnamed writer', O'Hara appreci-ated the value of his article immediately, urging Jane Freilicher in a letter of 1st August 1951, 'if you haven't devoured its delicious message, rush to your near-est newsstand … It is really lucid about what's bothering us both beside sex, and it is so heartening to know that someone understands these things.'[9] And certainly nobody worked harder to establish their intimate community than O'Hara, his occasional poems frequently naming his friends precisely as a means of holding them together. Indeed, one could read O'Hara's whole career – from his hugely energetic and ceaselessly self-effacing orchestrating of the New York art world to his relative poetic decline in the years before his death – in terms of Goodman's article. He was himself inclined to, a demoralized let-ter to Ashbery in Paris enclosing his 'two latest efforts' and wondering 'where I went off onto the dirt road. It may be that remark of Goodman-Goethe: "Occasional poetry is the best kind".'[10] Accounts of O'Hara in the years before his tragically early, accidental death in 1966 describe him becoming exhausted by the expense of energy needed to continue the role in which he had cast him-self. Always there was a painter who wanted the benefit of his criticism; always a new young poet to bring into the fold; always a reading or an opening to grace. So if eventually his poetry went off on to the dirt road (and certainly by 1957, when he wrote to Ashbery, it was not there yet) it was partly because there was just too much holding together to be done. But partly also, what O'Hara's writing appears not fully to have registered was the trajectory of Goodman's argument, the article arguing for the kind of poetry necessary for a coterie, but for the kind of coterie that could come eventually to look beyond itself. Some-how, as Goodman envisaged it, the integrating art of occasional poetry had to be developed. In the main, of course, this was for the sake of the wider com-munity. But partly also, perhaps, it was for the sake of the poet (the poet like O'Hara), who, if his writing was to remain viable, had to widen his scope; the alternative being a poetry that continued to turn in the same, gradually less sustaining circles. But that's another story.

It was in the early 1950s that the poets of the New York School were at their closest. They were, as Koch remembers it, 'together all the time', becoming, as a consequence, very 'involved in each other's work'.[11] O'Hara's occasional poetry was crucial to this sense of intimate community, his constant name-dropping and willingness always to address himself to the given moment adding meaning to the time they spent together. But the poetic occasions when the poets really integrated, when they were really 'involved in each other's work' were the collaborations. Collaboration has much to do with integration: the writers integrating their words and ideas such that the final product is different from anything either poet might have achieved alone; while the practice itself, as the notes in *Locus Solus* take care to point out, has traditionally had a social function. Tenth-century Japanese linked-verse collaborations, we are told, formed 'a regular part of palace social life', while the *tensos* of the Troubadours were 'contests, like the singing matches in the Eclogues' performed for their own and their audience's amusement.[12] Rarely, though, has writing been a more sociable activity than it was for the New York School.

Put simply, when they met they wrote poetry together. O'Hara and Koch wrote 'Sky / woof woof! / harp' during O'Hara's lunch hour at the Museum of Modern Art. Ashbery and Koch wrote 'The New York Times September Eighth Nineteen Fifty-One' over coffee in Greenwich Village. Schuyler and Ashbery began *A Nest of Ninnies* in the back of car on the way back from the Hamptons. O'Hara, continuing the transport theme, wrote 'Flight 115' with Bill Berkson while on an airliner. Ashbery and Koch collaborated on some of the poems that appeared in the *Locus Solus* special issue while Koch was visiting Ashbery in Paris ('Gottlieb's Rainbow' taking its name from the pinball machine in the café where the poem was composed). O'Hara and Koch kind of collaborated on their respective long poems 'Second Avenue' and 'When The Sun Tries To Go On', reading their poems to one another (and so involving one another in their writing) over the phone every night. And so it went on, the poets appearing in one another's plays (O'Hara and Bunny Lang taking parts in Ashbery's 'The Compromise') and subsequently in their painter-friends' paintings, O'Hara and Koch collaborating with, among others, Larry Rivers, Alex Katz, Red Grooms and Fairfield Porter.

In part because of their collaborations, which are never less than playful, the New York School are often figured as poets of fun, the excesses of their writings and the jouissance of their social lives being taken as a kind of non-political protest at the puritanical conformism of the American 1950s.[13] But this is only half the story, the other half being told by the letters Ashbery received from O'Hara, Schuyler and Koch while he was in Paris. Entertaining and instructive as they gossip about friends, enthuse about new tastes, and make an art form out of the camp name, the letters are impressive not least for the quite daunting level of productivity they present: the ceaseless succession of poems, plays, novels, translations, essays and reviews they describe constituting a highly serious commitment to the creative act. If they were having fun they were working hard at it, and nowhere more so than in their collaborations, which were, as Koch recalls, 'a way to be at work and at a party at the same time'.[14] Involving themselves in one another's work and integrating, as they did so, their working with their social lives, the New York poets were, as Ashbery's obliquely nostalgic poem 'The Other Tradition' implies, latter-day 'Troubadours'; street musicians (as the title of another poem has it) who in working hard at their play were engaged in the serious business, as Goodman saw it, of having their culture.

The specific charms of the collaborative encounter for the New York School were various. For a start, as Koch observed at the beginning of his note on the collaborations issue, it was stimulating: 'The act of collaboration on a literary work is inspiring, I think, because it gives objective form to a usually concealed subjective phenomenon and therefore it jars the mind into strange new positions.'[15] With the inspiration flowing both ways – each poet both provoking the other and opening himself or herself to the other's provocation – the collaborative poem is, by definition, just beyond the writers' control, neither knowing where the other will take his or her words. The resulting tangents, digressions, non-sequiturs and juxtapositions issue in a supremely mobile writing, beautifully illustrated in the *Locus Solus* anthology in the shifting scenes of the fifteenth-century Japanese poem 'Three Poets at Minase', and nowhere more tangible than in the opening chapters of *A Nest of Ninnies*. As Ashbery and Schuyler take it in turns to write a sentence, each sentence deflecting the work anew, the effect is of a prose constantly pushing against the novel form. As its plot, in so far as it can be said to have one, develops before their eyes, so, from the reader's point of view quite as much as the writers', the overriding sensation is of writing at the edge, each sentence nudging the novel into a permanently evolving present. This effect is all the more noticeable because set against the novel's steadfastly suburban environment, the uncertainty of the collaborative form adding just a little lustre to the everyday world of the archly conventional American lives it presents.

To collaborate was also, unusually at this point in their careers, to have a reader. Koch (who, as David Lehman has pointed out, has done most to promulgate the New York School aesthetic) has observed that, at a time when they had 'just about no audience but each other', collaboration gave him 'an instantaneous perceptive audience for every move I made (word I wrote)'.[16] The effect of this instantaneous audience was variously to sharpen their writing, the collaborations, for all their playfulness, being competitive, critical environments, each poet aiming to excel the other's taste, with the question of what was and wasn't tasteful going variously to the heart of the collaborative exercise.[17] Thus if part of the point of *Locus Solus* was to display their collective talents, it was also to showcase their tastes, the anthology bringing together, among others, ninth-century Chinese poetry; Japanese poetry from the tenth to the fifteenth centuries; the Troubadours; Fletcher and Shakespeare; Donne and

Goodyere; Cowley and Crashaw; Coleridge and Southey; the Italian Futurists; the Surrealists; Ern Malley; Burroughs, Corso and a cut-up Rimbaud; Yuri Gagarin (cut-up); Ruth Krauss; Jane Freilicher and Kenward Elmslie. Likewise the works themselves were experiments in taste. In Ashbery's collaborations with Koch, for instance, each poet's line aims always to incorporate a more appropriate, more outlandish, more current or more kitsch reference than the last. The element of competition notwithstanding, their shared poems thus become the spongiest of structures, and if the New York School collaborations, like those of Wordsworth and Coleridge and Eliot and Pound, were instigating something new, it was a poetry viable in an age of widening democracy because capable of absorbing all aspects of the culture.

But if, as the New York School developed it, collaboration was a sponge for the very various sources which constituted their shared background, it is absorbent, also, in the more strictly Pasternakian sense that, above all other modes of artistic production perhaps, it has to do with the occasion of its own making. This is apparent from the scholarly apparatus supporting the *Locus Solus* anthology, which is necessary because the achievement of a collaboration makes little sense unless one knows either what rules of composition the occasion conventionally called on the poets to adhere to, or, as in modern instances, what rules the poets set themselves for the occasion. It helps to know, for instance, that 'Three Poets at Minase' was required to have verses of, alternately, 7, 5, 7 syllables and 7, 7 syllables, and that among its rules of diction was the prescription that, if one verse mentioned autumn, the following two to four verses had to make synechdocal reference to it. And in knowing this, one learns something about the proprieties and priorities of the culture from which the rules emerged, the poem thus bringing the society with which it was integrated along with it. More to the point, though, a concern with the poem's own making is more often than not apparent within the poem itself. This is as one might expect. Setting out to write a poem together, the collaborating poets must establish the common ground on which they will work, and since the most obvious common ground is the odd writing situation in which they find themselves, then the occasion of the collaboration becomes its subject. Thus 'A Letter written by Sir Henry Goodyere and John Donne: alternis vibis' is, as the notes to *Locus Solus II* quote James Zito as remarking, 'interesting ... [because] the collaboration itself becomes the controlling conceit'.[18]

This same sense of the shared occasion informed Ashbery's collaborations with Koch, the poems having had, as Ashbery puts it, no 'raison d'être other than our being in the same room together'.[19] For Koch, likewise, it was 'sort of nice just to do something for the occasion'. Accordingly, in 'A Time Zone' (his poetic history of the interlocking lives of the New York School) it is the occasions, quite as much as the poems they gave rise to, that the Koch recalls. Outside a Fifth Avenue restaurant, on a 'lunch connection' with O'Hara:

> A little hard-as-a-hat poem to the day we offer
> 'Sky / woof woof! / harp'
> This is repeated ten times
> Each word is one line so the whole poem is thirty lines
> It's a poem composed in a moment
> On the sidewalk about fifteen blocks from the Alice in Wonderland
>   Monument[20]

Likewise, meeting for coffee in Greenwich Village with Ashbery:

> Next we do a poetic compendium called The New York Times
> September Eighth Nineteen Fifty-One both with and without rhymes
> Our poems are like tracks setting out
> We have little idea where we're going or what it's about
> I enjoy these compositional duets
> Accompanied by drinking coffee and joking on Charles and Perry Streets[21]

When Koch says that he enjoyed collaborating not least because it was good to do something 'for the occasion' he means, of course, that it was pleasurable to produce something fleeting, a one-off, something that probably wouldn't endure and so could be as daring and experimentally playful as one liked. But there's something, also, just a little bit mystical about his expression, as there is in the idea of him and O'Hara offering a poem to the day. It is as if the collaboration is not just 'for the occasion' in the sense of being something passing, but 'for the occasion' in that, just as the occasion has provided the raison d'être of the poem, so the poem, in return, is offered as a gift for the occasion: a gift given, if you like, in exchange for the given of the poem.

If this is mystical, and more than a little convoluted, it is not, I think, a wholly inappropriate way to think about the collaborations of the New York School, and indeed an impressively elaborated critical literature has built up around the analogy of avant-garde poetry to gift economies. The basis for the analogy is that the coteries of the avant-garde, with their largely undesirable products, mainly operate outside the normal laws of supply and demand.[22] And at the risk of ascribing too great a self-consciousness to their socialising, one could, perhaps, pursue the analogy in the case of the New York School. Thus on the one hand, their collaborations were sometimes explicitly gifts: Ashbery, O'Hara and Koch writing 'The Coronation Murder Mystery' for Schuyler's birthday; O'Hara and Koch writing a Nina Sestina for Nina Castelli's birthday. And perhaps with this sort of thing in mind, when Ashbery alludes to the passing of the New York School in 'The Other Tradition' he seems to have something to say about their mutual generosity, about how, 'Dispersing, each of the / Troubadours had something to say about how charity / Had run its race and won' (HD, 2). On the other hand, and from the other end of the analogy, writing about the concept of the gift has much to say, as one would expect, about collaborations and occasions. In her introduction to Marcel Mauss's seminal essay on gift economies, Mary Douglas describes how in his fieldwork Mauss discovered a mechanism by which individual interests combine to make a social system, without engaging in market exchange … gift complements market insofar as it operates where the latter is absent. Like the market it supplies each individual with personal incentives for collaborating in the pattern of exchanges.[23]

Mauss himself concludes his anthropological findings by indicating their possible ramifications in his own culture. 'A considerable part of our morality and our lives are still permeated', he is pleased to observe,

> with this same atmosphere of the gift, where obligation and liberty intermingle … Things still have sentimental as well as venal value … There still remain people and classes that keep to the morality of the former times, and we almost all observe it, at least at certain times of the year on certain occasions.[24]

Tempting as the analogy is, however, it is not because it would allow one to ascribe such a political subtext to the New York School that I want to make use of the idea of the gift: that would be to spoil all the fun. What interests me rather is the connection between the way gifts and poems are judged to relate to their occasions, for which one needs not Mauss's essay on 'Gifts' but Emerson's.

Trying to explain 'the reason of the difficulty at Christmas and New Year and other times, in bestowing gifts', Emerson observes, incontrovertibly, that

> the impediment lies in the choosing. If at any time it comes into my head that a present is due from me to somebody, I am puzzled what to give, until the opportunity is gone. Flowers and fruits are always fit presents; flowers, because they are a proud assertion that a ray of beauty outvalues all the utilities of the world.[25]

Though it never actually loses sight of the act of giving which is his theme, Emerson's essay is really about the act of judgement, and more specifically (though by analogy of course) about the act of poetic judgement. Indeed, one learns something about the balance of Emerson's critical and poetical powers from the fact that, eloquent as he is on the concept of the gift, when it comes to giving he never knows what to offer until after the opportunity is passed. But then giving a gift, as he makes clear, is a very difficult business. It does not only involve judging what the recipient might like, what they might appreciate from you (the donor) in particular, and what is deemed appropriate to the particular festival – birthday, Christmas, New Year or whatever. It should also, in addition, involve an element of surprise: the surprise element being that little bit extra which might be thought to differentiate genuine from dutiful gift giving. Indeed for a gift to be truly 'fit', to use Emerson's term, involves the most supple of judgements, the best gifts showing a full and acute awareness of the occasion: of the various expectations that inform it, and of just the degree to which it is appropriate to depart from them. A gift fit for its occasion must therefore be, to use Goodman's terms, both 'plausible to the actuality' (taking into account all the salient circumstances) and 'creatively imagining something, finding something unlooked for'. To give a gift that managed all this would very much be to 'heighten the everyday; to bathe the world in such a light of imagination and criticism that the persons who are living in it without meaning or feeling suddenly find that it is meaningful and exciting to live in it'. It would do all this because it would indicate a meaningful understanding on the part of the person giving the gift of the circumstances in which the recipient finds himself or herself. And the point, of course, is that writing a collaboration, and writing a poem which has the same sort of sense of occasion as a collaboration, involves an act of judgement entirely analogous to giving an appropriate gift: the writer taking into account all the circumstances while at the same time hoping to provide that measure of surprise which is a sign of real thought. Like a gift, then, the point of the New York School collaborations was always to heighten the everyday, a lunch connection or an afternoon drinking coffee being lifted by the poem it gave rise to. It was Auden's capacity to do this, and so, ideally, to re-integrate ordinary lives, that the young Ashbery most admired in the older poet, Ashbery's final-year thesis on Auden applauding his way of 'bringing innumerable people closer to the world in which they have to live'.[26] Ashbery's poetry has a similar gift. Hence his Emersonian advice to the young poet in his self-explanatory poem 'And *Ut Pictura Poesis* Is Her Name'

> Now,
> About what to put in your poem-painting:
> Flowers are always nice, particularly delphinium.

(HD, 45)

Ashbery and Koch wrote two kinds of poem together. The first kind – six of which ('The Young Collectors', 'Crone Rhapsody', 'The Inferno', 'Gottlieb's Rainbow', 'New Year's Eve', and 'A Servant to Servants') were published in *Locus Solus* – were distantly in the tradition of Japanese linked verse and the Troubadours' *tensos*. Each line had to meet certain rules designed, as Lehman puts it, 'for the occasion'. 'Crone Rhapsody', for instance, was, according to Koch's note, 'written according to the following requirements: that every line contain the name of a flower, a tree, a fruit, a game, and a famous old lady, as well as the word *bathtub*; furthermore, the poem is a sestina and all the end-words are pieces of office furniture.'[27] One marvels at the ingenuity of the rules, let alone the poem that results and it is clear how the competitive requirement to get all of this in would help to generate a more absorbent poetry. But while the poem itself is funny, one feels that really to have enjoyed the joke one would probably have to have been there. The second kind of poem follows roughly the format of Ishmael's spoof theatre bill in the first chapter of *Moby Dick*, his own little destiny overwhelmed by (but also undermining) the larger events from which 'those stage managers the Fates' chose to exclude him:

> '*Grand Contested Election for the Presidency of the*
> *United States.*
>
> 'WHALING VOYAGE BY ONE ISHMAEL.'
> 'BLOODY BATTLE IN AFGHANISTAN.'[28]

[61]

Ashbery and Koch's poem 'New York Times, Sunday, October 25, 1953' is divided into twenty similar sections, each section beginning with a headline from the newspaper in question, the poem mentioning, among other events, Eisenhower's agricultural programme, an abandoned milk strike, the eighth anniversary of the UN, and a few import fund for Japan. The fun and judgement is in the poetic response to the headline, which, whether satirical, surreal, or archly lyrical, has the effect of putting the apparently important event in its place. For instance:

OFFICER WHO SOLVED KIDNAP QUITS; $300,000 OF RANSOM
STILL MISSING

Foreign May socked jeer curio simplicity
As Peg wager dons ultra tie muff.[29]

While such collaborative exercises should not be disregarded – the poets honing a style capable of accommodating the tabloid cadence – one would hardly want to take them too seriously, their lasting value being the much suppler currency of such mature poems as Ashbery's 'The Skaters' or 'Soonest Mended', or Koch's 'The Art of Love'.

A Nest of Ninnies is a different kettle of fish. Ashbery and Schuyler started the book, its title taken from a Jacobean jest book by Robert Armin, during a car journey from the Hamptons to New York in 1953 – Schuyler suggesting they pass the time by writing a novel – and finished it some fifteen years later, the novel finally appearing, to largely humourless reviews, in 1969. The reason for the delay was not so much the demanding requirement, eventually relaxed, that the writers write alternate sentences, but Ashbery's sojourn in Paris. As he told Bill Berkson, 'it did seem to require us being together; we once tried to do it by correspondence, but it … lacked a sort of home-made-quality'.[30] Or as he told Schuyler in a letter, 'I liked your "page" for the Nest, but somehow it seems to lack the nubbly, handwoven texture that we can probably only get by pitting our respective 'wits' against each other, which I think is the principal thing to be said in favour of the book, although no one else may ever say it.'[31]

The ninnies in question are a group of friends and neighbours living in the kind of generic American suburb Ashbery and Schuyler were passing through as they began the book. The structure of the novel is situational, the action (if one can call it that) starting in the suburb, and proceeding through various unannounced shifts of location as the ninnies and their ever widening circle of friends visit New York, Key West, Paris and Rome and various unnamed but vaguely recognisable minor French and Italian towns before ending up back in the suburbs for a gala night at the Trentino, 'as it had come to be known' (NN, 169). A conversational novel throughout – the manner of writing being itself conversational – the dialogue is flawlessly clichéd, the characters invariably speaking in the restricted tones of the B-movie.

Fabia said, 'You seem so little aware of me when I am with you, Marshall,
I wonder if you ever think of me when I'm not. I know I often muse
about you and Alice and your little house.'

'It always amazes me we are near neighbours,' Marshall replied. 'Alice and
I tend to be people who lead somewhat isolated lives because they are self-
sufficient.'

Fabia said, 'I too lead an isolated life but not for that reason.'

Marshall looked shifty. 'I hope you won't confide in me,' he said.
(NN, 14)

This is parodic, of course, but by no means aggressively so, Ashbery and
Schuyler, as they hint later with reference to Dante, delighting in exploring
the expressive resources of the American vernacular. And generally this proves a
much more accommodating language than one might think, the characters,
for all their obsessing over ice boxes and fake fur coats, filling their conversa-
tion with confident borrowings from French and Italian, and knowledgeable
references to, for instance, Keats, Dashiell Hammett, Boccaccio, 'The Masque
of the Red Death', *Roberts' Rules of Order,* 'a minor follower of Bayre', Stendhal
and Lamartine.

Even so, B-movie conversation and journalistic clichés would seem a thin
resource on which to build a novel, lacking, as they do, any potential for the kind
of emotional deepening that constitutes character development. And in fact in
general *A Nest of Ninnies* signally fails to progress as a novel should. It has, appar-
ently, no themes to speak of, a fact Dr Carlsbad draws attention to when
contemplating the eclectic items (the 'Guatamalan *rebozos*', the 'Eskimo walrus-
tooth accessories' and the 'Navajo turquoise and silver jewelry') that make up
the stock list of Victor and Alice's proposed new shop.

'Is there any central theme to all of this?' Dr. Carlsbad asked.

Victor looked sly. 'You mean the figure in the carpet? That's a poser you'll have to
solve for yourself.' (NN, 83)

Indeed in so far as the novel form is characterised by development, by the
progress and elaboration of characters and ideas through the passage of time,
then *A Nest of Ninnies* is hardly a novel at all, but, as certain episodes indicate, a
parody of the great American novel. It is a far cry, for instance, from the disas-
trous fate of the Pequod to the delayed return of some of the party from Captain
Hanson's boat-trip round a 'remote and gloomy portion of the Everglades'
(NN, 55).

But if it subverts the basic conventions of the novel (including the conven-
tion that the chapters proceed numerically, there being, here, no chapter thir-
teen) and if it parodies the picaresque form of the great American novel in
particular, *A Nest of Ninnies* is, in its own ironic, understated way concerned
throughout with the question of American identity which is the subject of such
questing works. Indeed, one would say that Americanness was the novel's
theme, were it not for the fact that it is so integrally a function of its occasional

structure. Formally speaking, the novel is nothing more (or nothing less) than a series of variously special and everyday occasions: coffee-breaks, lunches, '*giorni di festi*' (when in Rome …), dinner parties, birthdays, weddings, and gala nights. This form arises from the manner of the writing, *A Nest of Ninnies* having been written, as Lehman reports Schuyler as recalling, 'all over the place, in cars, over martinis, any place'; and so too does everything else about the novel, not least its characterisation. Thus because it was written over a long period of time, and on and about a series of discrete occasions, hosts of minor characters are introduced whom we do not expect to meet again. Similarly major characters undergo stark, comically disturbing personality shifts, as for instance in chapter eleven when 'It suddenly occurred to Marshall that a change had taken place in Alice. Her former aggressive reserve had been replaced by something else, but he could not tell what' (NN, 134). Nothing, it might be observed, escapes the ironic touch of Ashbery and Schuyler in this novel, the instability of their characterisation parodying that most sacred of their shared texts *Doctor Zhivago*, the central characters of which, as Stuart Hampshire observed, are not 'endowed with … rounded naturalness nor are their lives steadily unfolded before the reader'.

All of which instability might seem to undermine the very possibility of identity, were it not a wry affirmation of that very American sense of self that Charles Olson had in mind when, in his rather more earnest way, he suggested that 'An American / is a complex of occasions, / themselves a geometry / of spatial nature'.[32] Twain makes the point much more comically with Huck Finn, whose journey down the Mississippi does not cause him to develop (he means to light out for the territory at the end of the book as he did at the beginning) but instead sees him pass through a series of radical shifts of identity, each new necessary act of imposture amounting to a new Huck. Huck's identity, in other words, is not stable, coherent or developing. In fact it is a function not of Huck at all, but of the situation in which he finds himself. He is discernible in what he is not.

Over and above permitting the kind of occasional character shift that would make even Huck blanch, Ashbery and Schuyler's comic elaboration of this American line involves making many of the occasions the pretext for a discussion of national identity, the best example being the evening of Claire Tosti's departure for France. To mark her last night in New York, Mrs Kelso (who is a 'mine of colonial food lore' and whose interest in all things American runs to an LP of 'F.D.R.'s more cogent speeches') lays on a 'typically American' dinner party. Starting with peanuts (which, as Clare observes, are actually, as ground nuts, 'an English food'), and ending with baked Alaska (and all that suggests about fixed national identity), the *piéce de résistance* is a New England boiled dinner. As the summation of the evening's quest for the typically American, Mrs Kelso's hot-pot is ironically appropriate, the New England one-pot dish being a version not only of that most authentic of Provençal meals, the casserole, but as such of that most familiar of American tropes, the melting pot. On this occasion, in other words, as elsewhere, this generically American group of friends identify themselves most clearly by accepting what they are not. Even Mr Turpin, who as he caps the meal with an Izarra rather than the Southern Comfort he is offered, 'settle[s] himself uneasily on a Moroccan leather pouf' (NN, 78). A deadpan commentary on the central questions of major American fiction, Ashbery and Schuyler's collaborative novel is, as Auden suggested, 'a minor classic'.

In all respects, then, *A Nest of Ninnies* is characterised not by the kinds of development one expects of a novel but by the situational shifts and chance encounters one associates with the occasional sensibility. In all respects, that is, apart from the writers' sense of occasion itself. Written in the spirit of the coterie, as a means of amusing and exercising themselves during the journey from the Hamptons to New York, Ashbery and Schuyler's opening chapter is an inward affair. More than at any other point in the book one in is aware of the compositional process, the written exchanges being all but a continuation of a private conversation, the writers, barely in character, chatting away about the night before.

> 'Why don't you admit that you enjoy my unhappiness?'
> '...You didn't seem so unhappy last night.'
> 'What happened last night? You certainly can't mean that a pickup supper and a rummy game would affect my spirits.' (NN, 10)

Chapter one is aware of the occasion of its own writing in the limited sense that it reads as record of Ashbery and Schuyler being in one another's company. As they reflect on one another's words so the image of reflection comes to mind, the opening paragraph observing that 'Alice was tired. Languid, fretful, she turned to stare into her own eyes in the mirror above the mantelpiece before she spoke' (NN, 9). And as they read and respond to each other's sentences, so they also seem to reflect that they are alone in doing so, the collaborators being, as Koch observed, one another's only audience. Collaborating in part because they are sealed off from the rest of the world, the sense of being sealed off finds its way into the collaboration: '"It always amazes me we are near neighbours," Marshall replied. "Alice and I tend to be people who lead somewhat isolated lives because they are self-sufficient" (NN, 14). The sense of occasion communicated in chapter one is that of writers writing from within a coterie: the fact of their being together, and so having their culture, is what matters.

The last chapter is altogether wider in its scope. It is gala night at Alice's restaurant and most of the Ninnies' ever widening circle of friends, plus a number of characters to whom are we are only now introduced, are present. Still the occasion itself provides the subject of discussion, characters who hardly know each other finding common ground in the situation they now have in common. Explaining to Claire why it is that the restaurant's decor is so appropriate, Nadia observes,

> 'It is just right: it is so "with it" as to be invisible; one cannot see it until its time is past. More definition would crush some part of the public – make them self-conscious. As it is, all types and ages can come and rub along together.' (NN, 181)

Far from the isolation of the opening chapter, this, we are to understand, is a most democratic environment, hence the fact that towards the end of the chapter:

> It was decreed that the Carlsbad and Bridgewater tables be pushed together in such a manner as to accommodate all the friends at a single festive board, and to allow Mildred Kelso to converse with the hirsute youths who had so unexpectedly opened up new pathways in music appreciation. (NN, 183)

What really holds things together here is the affectionately ironic manner which for Susan Sontag constitutes camp, the writers rubbing along with their parodic characters by gently satirising their own accommodating aesthetic. Written over a period of some fifteen years, *A Nest of Ninnies* is the product of a coterie learning, as Goodman suggested it must, to look beyond itself.

Ashbery was as involved as any of the New Yorkers in the Collaborations Special Issue of *Locus Solus*. The issue opened with his poem 'The Waterfowl', a cento and as such a collaboration with the poetic tradition. He also featured as the translator of poems by René Char and Paul Eluard and of prose by André Breton and Paul Eluard, as the co-author with Schuyler of the first four chapters of *A Nest of Ninnies*, and with Koch of six collaborative poems. So, if part of the point of *Locus Solus*, and of the second issue in particular, was to identify the New York School, Ashbery was as fully identified with it as anyone. And yet, more than the others, Ashbery has been at pains to resist the New York School tag, and the suggestion of a group identity that goes with it. As he told the *Paris Review*:

> This label was foist upon us by a man named Bernard Myers, who ran the Tibor de Nagy Gallery and published some pamphlets of our poems ... I think the idea was that, since everybody was talking about the New York School of painting, if he created a New York School of poets then they would automatically be considered important because of the sound of the name ... I don't think we ever were a school. There are vast differences between my poetry and Koch's and O'Hara's, and Schuyler's and Guest's. We were a bunch of poets who happened to know each other; we would get together and read our poems to each other and sometimes we would write collaborations ... Somebody wrote an article about the New York School a few years ago in the *Times Book Review*, and a woman wrote in to find out how she could enrol.[33]

Koch, similarly, has observed that he, Ashbery and O'Hara were 'comfortingly various'. For all that variety, however, as Koch remembers it they were 'very very close', whereas for Ashbery they were 'a bunch of poets who happened to know each other'. More to the point, perhaps, at the time *Locus Solus* was published Ashbery had been living in Paris for some four years. There were no doubt various reasons, as David Lehman has suggested, for Ashbery's decision to leave New York and live in Paris, on and off, for the best part of ten years: his relationship with Pierre Martory, his strained relationship with his parents, his desire to get a different perspective on his culture. But one obvious effect was to detach himself from a milieu which had become 'very very close'.

Uncharitably, one would say that Ashbery's tendency over the years to distance himself from the New York School is a result of his having achieved exit velocity. His place in literary history secure, he no longer needs to draw on the critical mass of the group. But if there is some truth in this, it is fairer, and I think more true, to say that Ashbery always meant to achieve this distance, and that what he was distancing himself from, from the very beginning, was the closed society of the coterie. Thus, while O'Hara's name-dropping held the community together, and is part of the enduring fascination of his poetry, one has the unavoidable feeling, as an outsider, of peering in at a life from which one is separated. And while its vitality and grace are lessons for life, one can sometimes emerge from O'Hara's writing feeling not so much integrated with one's own circumstances as regretful that one was not party to his. Ashbery, by contrast, resisted the double-edged allure of names from the beginning, his being instead always a poetry of pronouns. As such, while it has never had quite the immediate impact of O'Hara's, it has, in the end, a much stronger appeal for the outsider, drawing him or her in not, finally, to indicate something to which they cannot have access, but rather to ready them for that to which they do.

As it does so, Ashbery's poetry unravels a tension in New York School poetics which is as apparent as anywhere in their collaborations. Thus while the collaborations were, in their absorption of all kinds of cultural reference, all about acceptance, they were also the means by which this small, unknown, secretive group held itself together. Open to influences from all corners of the culture, the collaborations were also the medium for the shibboleths and private jokes by which a group of marginalised poets must necessarily strengthen their identity. So if one learns a great deal about Ashbery's poetry by thinking about the collaborative milieu in which he came of age – his collaborations with his friends serving as much as anything to sharpen his sense of the poetic occasion – one learns a lot also by understanding how he has pushed beyond that milieu. Thus while his poetry continues to be significantly collaborative – listening to and absorbing the voices of the culture in an ongoing effort to arrive at the fit utterance – in certain crucial respects his idea of collaboration has changed. In his Charles Eliot Norton lecture on David Schubert, Ashbery, it will be recalled, commented of Schubert's poem 'Midston House', that

> one is tempted to complete the last line by making it 'to the person I want to say it to'. That's not what he's saying, however, though it is in a way since he leads us to expect it. The actual sense of the words is that the poem consists of speaking what cannot be said to the person I want to say it. In other words, the ideal situation for the poet is to have the reader speak the poem, and how nice it would be for everybody if that could be the case.

Ashbery's ideal collaborator, the person he most wants to speak the next line, is no longer a fellow poet but the reader.

NOTES

1 James Schuyler, letter to Chester Kallman, copied to John Ashbery 3 September 1960.

2 C.J. McCabe, 'Artistic collaboration in the twentieth century: the period between the wars', McCabe (ed.), *Artistic Collaboration in the Twentieth Century*, p. 15.

3 Wordsworth and Coleridge, *Lyrical Ballads,* p. 242.

4 Ezra Pound, letter to Eliot, 24 January 1921, cited in Lyndall Gordon, *Eliot's Early Years*, p. 106.

5 Paul Goodman, 'Advance-Guard Writing, 1900–1950', p. 360.

6 Ibid., p. 357.

7 Ibid., pp. 372, 375, 376, 379.

8 Ashbery, *The Collected Poems of Frank O'Hara*, p. ix.

9 Cited in Brad Gooch, *City Poet*, p. 187.

10 Frank O'Hara, letter to John Ashbery, 27 March 1957.

11 David Herd, 'Kenneth Koch in conversation', pp.28,29.

12 *Locus Solus II*, pp. 198, 194.

13 For an excellent, finely balanced account of the function of pleasure in the poetry of the New York School see Geoff Ward's *Statutes of Liberty*.

14 Kenneth Koch, *The Art of Poetry*, p. 168.

15 *Locus Solus II*, p. 193.

16 Koch, *The Art of Poetry*, pp. 170, 168.

17 For an extensive discussion of the competitive character of the New York School and its collaborations see David Lehman, *The Last Avant-Garde*, pp. 65–93.

18 *Locus Solus II*, p. 201.

19 David Herd, 'John Ashbery in conversation with David Herd', p. 44.

20 Kenneth Koch, *One Train*, p. 23.

21 Ibid., p. 27.

22 See, for instance, Pierre Bourdieu, *The Field of Cultural Production*, pp. 74–111; Jacques Derrida, *Given Time*; Simon Jarvis, 'Soteriology and recriprocity'.

23 Mary Douglas, 'Foreword' to Marcel Mauss, *The Gift*, p. xiv.

24 Marcel Mauss, *The Gift*, p. 65.

25 Ralph Waldo Emerson, *Essays*, p. 159.

26 John Ashbery, 'The Poetic medium of W.H. Auden', p. 25.

27 *Locus Solus II*, p. 196

28 Herman Melville, *Moby Dick*, p. 98.

29 John Ashbery Manuscripts, AM6.

30 Cited in David Kermani, *A Comprehensive Bibliography*, p. 23.

31 Cited in Lehman, *The Last Avant-Garde*, p. 83.

32 Charles Olson, *Selected Poems*, p. 148.

33 Peter Stitt, 'The art of poetry XXXIII: John Ashbery', pp. 395–6.

CHAPTER THREE

An American in Paris: *The Tennis Court Oath* and the poetics of exile

In September 1955 Ashbery left America for France. His means of travel was a Fulbright scholarship, the purpose of which was to study for a year at Montpellier University. Soon tiring of Montpellier, he switched to Paris the following February and managed to extend his scholarship a further year. He returned to New York in 1957, taking a Master's course in French Literature at NYU. But the object was to get back to Paris, which he did in June 1958. Save for the occasional visit (and in the last five years he didn't even make these) Ashbery did not return to America until 1965.

Why he stayed away so long is not altogether clear. He loved Paris. He was also in love in Paris, with Pierre Martory. These were good reasons to stay. Another good reason, if more prosaic, was money, Ashbery being unable to afford the fare back for the last five years of his stay. As he recalls in interview, 'I would have liked to have been able to visit America, but I didn't have enough money to do so. I was quite poor at the time I was living there. My parents were unhappy about my staying there, and would have paid my passage home, but not my return.'[1] Unhappy as they were, it was partly due to his parents that Ashbery was able to stay as long as he did; supplementing his earnings as an art reviewer for the International edition of the *New York Herald Tribune*, and as translator of French murder mysteries, with a regular allowance. Letters to Ashbery from his mother from this period – his father seems rarely to have written – are often just a little tense: his mother wondering when he might come home, while at the same time reluctantly agreeing to forward more funds. In fact Ashbery appears to have incurred just the kind of parental disapproval Victor Bridgewater suffers in *A Nest of Ninnies*. Always disappointing his permanently stern father – he can't drive a car without Dr Bridgewater correcting him – Victor drops out of college, toys with the idea of opening a shop, and finally decides to marry Nadia, a Frenchwoman. Pleasing as this might be to his suburban family – not least because for a while it seemed he would take up with his travelling companion Paul – Victor's good news meets with only qualified approval, because his intention is to stay in France:

> Mrs. Bridgewater drifted over to the window, and stood gazing at the sunlit Mediterranean. Reacting to this as though it were his cue, Dr. Bridgewater asked

in sepulchral tones, 'And what would you do in Paris?'

'I was coming to that,' Victor chuckled. 'Nadia has a friend who works on the desk at the *Herald Tribune* there. She thinks he could get me a job rewriting, at least until I learn the antique business.' (NN, 121–2)

But if love, lack of funds and, as suggested in the last chapter, the desire to flee a New York scene to which he had become stiflingly central might seem good enough reasons to have held Ashbery in Paris, the poet himself has suggested others. Introducing a review of an exhibition of the Stein collections at the Museum of Modern Art in 1971, Ashbery opened by quoting Gertrude Stein on Picasso, and by observing that 'Poets when they write about other artists always tend to write about themselves' (RS, 105). The review is largely made up of an eloquent discussion of Stein's expatriate experience.

> Why Gertrude Stein … chose to anchor herself in Paris…is not entirely clear. Certainly Paris is, or was, a very agreeable city to live in, but we tend to discount mere hedonism as a motive when dealing with an artist or an intellectual. We know her feeling that America was her country and Paris her home town; that good Americans go to France when they die; but these are typical Steinian statements rather than explanations. One feels there must be a connection between her decision to install herself in Paris … and the beginning of a period that saw the birth of *Three Lives* and *The Making of Americans* … The distance from America afforded the proper focus and even the occasion for a monumental study of the making of Americans; the foreign language that surrounded her was probably also a necessary insulation for the immense effort of concentration that this book required. (RS, 109)

Ashbery's account of Stein's Paris experience speaks directly to his own. While in Paris Ashbery was in regular correspondence with his New York School friends, his letters containing the poems of *The Tennis Court Oath* and, subsequently, *Rivers and Mountains*. These sometimes mysterious, sometimes dazzling new poems were greeted with amazement, delight and jealousy. As Koch wrote in February 1959,

> getting your poems was an experience. You always make me feel like a hairdresser to your Phidias. Your poems are so absolute; they offer one nothing but themselves, like golden apples. Then one has to live with the mysterious and troubling fact that they exist. The redeeming feature of their troublesomeness is that they radiate beauty and pleasure through the chilly air and drive me like a thunderstorm to my typewriter.[2]

Their own poetry – as their replies to Ashbery describe – squeezed between the demanding working lives and hectic social lives that shaped their New York existences, O'Hara, Koch and Schuyler developed at a steady but (inevitably given their other activities) not dramatic rate during this period. Ashbery, meanwhile – his expatriate social life streamlined and the burdens of work eased by a parental allowance – had the time and energy both to radically dismantle and to re-assemble his style, and in the process, like Stein, to reassess his relationship with his culture. It was in Paris that Ashbery became a great American poet.

The first poems Ashbery wrote while in Paris, the poems he published in 1962 in his controversial volume *The Tennis Court Oath*, were remarkably different not only from the poems he published in *Some Trees* but, as it has turned out, from almost anything else he has written. Harold Bloom and Charles Bernstein do not concur on many subjects, but they do agree that *The Tennis Court Oath* is a very singular work.[3] For Bloom it bears no relation to anything else Ashbery has written, and he cannot 'accept the notion that [it] was a necessary phase in the poet's development'.[4] For Bernstein it is Ashbery's 'best book', while more generally, as Ashbery observed in interview with John Ash, 'the LANGUAGE poets consider *The Tennis Court Oath* to be my only worthwhile book'.[5] Bloom and Bernstein are right: *The Tennis Court Oath* – whether aberration or outstanding success – is exceptional within the Ashbery oeuvre. Indeed in certain respects what it represents is the very opposite of the Ashberyan poetic. Take the opening section of the volume's third poem, 'America':

Piling upward
the fact the stars
In America the office hid
archives in his
stall …
Enormous stars on them
The cold anarchist standing
in his hat.
Arm along the rail
We were parked
Millions of us
The accident was terrible.
The way the door swept out
The stones piled up –
The ribbon – books. miracle. with moon and the stars

The pear tree
moving me
I am around and in my sigh
The gift of a the stars.
The person
Horror – the morsels of his choice
Rebuked to me I
 – in the apartment
the pebble we in the bed.
The roof –
rain – pills –
Found among the moss
Hers wouldn't longer care – I don't know why.

(TCO, 15)

The first difference from Ashbery's earliest poetry one notices here is visual. The radical brevity of the sentences invites readers to linger still longer over each and every word, and as they do so the language itself acquires a new prominence. The words, in short, stand out, thrown into relief by the blank white background of an almost empty page. Nor are the words the only things standing out here. The poem's central figures are also clearly defined. The narrative 'I' is clearly detached, being seen alone, at first, in his apartment, and then (and at most) in the company of just one other. The cold anarchist in his eye-catching hat is similarly clearly distinct; highly visible even against a background of millions of other people.

Typical of the most radically distinctive writing of *The Tennis Court Oath*, what distinguishes 'America' from anything in *Some Trees* is precisely this sense of background. Compare 'The Picture of Little J.A. in a Prospect of Flowers', the poem in which Ashbery most readily identified himself in his first volume. There the central figure was sponge-like, absorbing all that was going on around him, and in the process all but disappearing into the background amid which he was pictured. Only the grin was left. Here the figures, like the sentences, stand out: the background of the crowd and the environment of the page bringing self and word into sharp relief. What explains this shift?

In part the shift is to be expected. When people are abroad they do stand out (or feel they do), their unfamiliarity with what is going on around them distinguishing them from the crowd. From this point of view, then, *The Tennis Court Oath* is a kind of performative travel writing, the words enacting the isolation which are part and parcel of the foreigner's experience. But if it is hardly unsual for the foreign visitor to feel detached from things, it is in the nature of Ashbery's poetic that he should have been particularly struck by this. Asked whether, like Gertrude Stein, when he was in Paris he felt insulated from what was going on around him, Ashbery observed:

> I felt inhibited at first by not having my own language, by not hearing it spoken around me. Lots of my poems have their origin in what I hear people saying in the street in New York, in the American vernacular, which I guess is what American is. So I felt insulated not in a good sense, for quite a long time.[6]

Ashbery's qualification is important. The next chapter of this book considers *Rivers and Mountains*, much of which Ashbery wrote while still in Paris, but after he had grown used to being there. A breakthrough volume and a monumental achievement, *Rivers and Mountains* is explicitly the product of intense concentration, and 'The Skates' in particular is the work of a writer who had become insulated in the good sense Ashbery has in mind when he talks about Stein – the relative isolation of the expatriate experience giving him the time and space to focus great energy on his writing. *The Tennis Court Oath* is insulated 'not in a good sense'. Struggling with a language that, as he puts it, he could speak but could not use, Ashbery's relation to his immediate environment – a relation which in *Some Trees* was already becoming the core of his work – was fundamentally altered. Living in a foreign culture, and operating in a language which seemed to him 'much too clear a language for poetry', Ashbery's absorbent aesthetic was out of place.[7]

His immediate environment made inaccessible, Ashbery's thoughts turned naturally, and, it would appear, frequently towards home. When asked, subsequently, to explain the 'Americanness' of his writing, Ashbery put it down to his expatriate experience. 'Perhaps', he suggested, 'it has something to do with my having lived abroad for so long. As many expatriates, including Gertrude Stein, have pointed out, one thinks more about one's "Americanness" when one is outside of America.'[8] In terms of its titles, certainly, *The Tennis Court Oath* is a much more self-consciously American book than was *Some Trees*, '"They Dream Only of America"', 'America', and 'Idaho' serving to locate the volume's concerns. Likewise in the reviews he was writing at the time, Ashbery showed that for all his interest in twentieth-century French poetry – he read, among others, Jacob, Breton, Eluard, Reverdy and Roussel while in Paris – he was equally preoccupied by the writings of Americans abroad, Hawthorne and James cropping up in his art criticism quite as often as Baudelaire and Sarraute. Indeed, to read Ashbery's carefully researched article on American artists in Paris ('American Sanctuary in Paris'), one is left with the impression that such expatriates think only of America. Caroline Lee, one of the twelve artists Ashbery interviewed for the article, is intrigued by the question of 'where on the American horizon my work will sit, as I cannot identify anywhere else, despite my chosen exile' (RS, 90). Shirley Goldfarb likewise finds herself feeling 'intensely American, perhaps more so here than when I'm in America' (RS, 92). And Ashbery concludes his survey on just such an American note. 'This perhaps is the real reason why younger American painters take to Europe: a feeling of wanting to keep their American-ness whole, in the surroundings in which it is most likely to flourish and take root' (RS, 96–7).[9] A commonplace on the one hand – there's nobody more American than the American abroad – Ashbery's remark is also a nice teasing out of the paradoxical aesthetics of his Paris poems. Committed to a Pasternakian sense of the artist's relation to his environment, but insulated from his immediate environment by his unfamiliarity with the language, Ashbery reflects more self-consciously than ever while in Paris on his national and cultural background. Or as he said of Stein, articulating the situation in his prefered terminology, 'The distance from America afforded the proper focus and even the occasion for a monumental study of the making of Americans.'

Ashbery's reflection on Stein does not only draw attention to the subject matter of Ashbery's Paris poems; it also tells us something about their style, that while he was clearly thinking about America during this period, he was also thinking monumentally.[10] Again one can hear it in the titles. So while *Some Trees* presented nothing more immodest by way of titles than 'The Mythological Poet', and opened with the immaculately reserved 'Two Scenes', *The Tennis Court Oath* offers such conspicuously important pieces as 'A Last World', 'The New Realism', 'Faust', 'The Ascetic Sensualists', and most of all, perhaps, 'America'. And again this seeming monumentalism has its echo in the subjects and tone of Ashbery's art criticism of this period – the essay he wrote for the catalogue accompanying an exhibition of 'New Realist' art being a case in point.

[73]

The catalogue accompanied the New York showing of the exhibition in 1962, shortly after the publication of *The Tennis Court Oath*, and some months after Ashbery had first seen the exhibition in Paris. Impassioned to the point of zeal, Ashbery's essay is tonally atypical of his art criticism, which even at its most enthusiastic coolly resists foisting itself upon the reader. Conceptually also it is somewhat out of character, Ashbery's argument for the New Realism oscillating between somewhat divergent notions of the avant-garde. Thus on the one hand, it draws on the integrated, communal sense of the avant-garde articulated by Goodman in 'Advance-Guard Writing'. The everyday objects which are the stuff of the New Realism are important, Ashbery suggests, because 'They are a common ground, a neutral language understood by everybody, and therefore the ideal material with which to create experiences which transcend the objects' (RS, 82). Like the occasional poetry of the New York School, then, the New Realism bathes the everyday world in a light of imagination and criticism, so making it the ground for collective understanding. But, running against, and running through the essay, is a much more traditional conception of the avant-garde. 'The artists in this exhibition', we are told,

> are at an advanced stage of the struggle to determine the real nature of reality which began at the time of Flaubert. One could point to other examples in the arts today (elsewhere for instance the 'objective' novels of Robbe-Grillet and Sarraute …) of this continuing effort to come to grips with the emptiness of industrialized modern life. (RS, 81)

The language here – of struggle and industrialised emptiness – is, as it were, traditionally avant-garde. The essay concludes on a similar note, describing the function of artists, and their relation to society, in the following, not unfamiliar, terms:

> The unmanageable vastness of our experience, the regrettable unpredictability of our aims and tastes, have been seized on by the New Realists as the core of a continuing situation; that of man on the one side and a colorful indifferent universe on the other. There is no moral to be drawn from this, and in any case the artist's work on this as on other occasions is not preaching or even mediation, but translation and exegesis, in order to show us where the balance of power lies in the yet-once-again altered scheme of things. Today it seems to repose in the objects that surround us; that is in our perceptions of them or, simply and once again, in ourselves. (RS, 82–3)

The task described is of monumental importance, and so the image of the avant-garde is accordingly that of artist as hero – poised perpetually at the front-line of experience, and so isolated from a society which, if it only knew it, is in fact dependent on his or her perceptions. It is an image of the artist that would have pleased Rosenberg, and which Peter Bürger would come to define as the historic avant-garde: out on a limb, and alert to the new, but detached from the community the art means to affect.

It is a conception of the artist that crops up time and again in *The Tennis Court*

Oath, not least in his poem 'The New Realism', and one that various features of Ashbery's circumstances were prompting him towards during this period. His reading was one. Thus, whatever his motives for returning to Paris in 1958, his pretext was the need to research the life and writing of Raymond Roussel for the purposes of a PhD thesis. This was a pretext not a motive in that, as Ashbery said in his Charles Eliot Norton lecture on Roussel, his parents were more inclined to help him out if his reason for returning was academic. The thesis was eventually abandonded, but Ashbery took his reseach seriously, tracking down members of the writer's family in order to gain access to his papers, and publishing essays on Roussel in France and America. Speaking of Roussel's *Nouvelles Impressions d'Afrique* in an essay published in 1962, Ashbery notes that the text is made complete by the 'militant banality of the 59 illustrations which Roussel commissioned of a hack painter through the intermediary of a private detective agency'.[11] And it was Roussel's 'militancy' that at this time, if not so much subsequently, seems to have caught Ashbery's imagination. It is not without a certain gleefulness that he describes Roussel's plays as 'a "theater of cruelty" that outdid anything Artaud ever dreamed of, turning a civilized bourgeois audience into a horde of wild beasts'.[12]

There is something of the '"theater of cruelty"' in *The Tennis Court Oath*, a series of asides amid Ashbery's recalcitrant poems – 'I oppose with all the forces of my will / Your declaration', 'I detest you' – informing the reader that he or she is positively unwanted here. Partly this is on the grounds that one has to be cruel to be kind, the aggressive, often rebarbative address of Ashbery's poems meaning to shock the reader into a state of self-awareness. More to the point though, and largely undermining this aggressive objective, the antagonism was mutual. If the reader is not, here, wanted by the text, the text, Ashbery had good reason to think, was not wanted by the reader. *Some Trees* had sold badly, and with the exception of O'Hara's had received few, and predominantly underwhelming, reviews. It was not without good reason, then, that, as Ashbery told the *Paris Review*, 'I didn't expect to have a second book published, ever.'[13] *The Tennis Court Oath*, as a consequence, reads like a text without readers.

It was without readers also in that having removed himself to Paris, Ashbery had removed himself from the mutually critical environment of the New York School. He didn't, he has said, have many friends when he was first in Paris, though he did meet the American writers Harry Mathews and Elliott Stein. And although Pierre Martory was a poet, he 'wasn't used to modern American poetry' and so they didn't 'have any common roots'.[14] Such critical responses as Ashbery did receive came from home, in the letters from O'Hara, Koch and Schuyler, but, as he reports, 'I never seemed to get enough … Frank and Kenneth praised these poems, but I was never quite sure whether they were doing that just because they were pals.'[15]

Ashbery had every reason to find the historic avant-garde attractive at this time. Detached from his immediate environment, absorbed in the militancy of Roussel, abandoned by the reader, and apart from the collaborative milieu of the

New York York School: Ashbery's whole situation was propelling his writing towards heroic self-exile. But so too, crucially, was his culture, American intellectuals of every stripe, during the 1950s, calling on the avant-garde as the last line of defence against the barbarian forces of popular culture.

As the 1950s drew to a close, the debate about the character and quality of American culture that had been bubbling away in intellectual circles since the war heated up. The opinion-forming books of the 1950s and early 1960s, as Paul Breslin points out, were large-scale cultural critiques: David Riesman's *The Lonely Crowd*, Vance Packard's *The Hidden Persuaders*, C. Wright Mills's *White Collar* and, a little later, Herbert Marcuse's *One Dimensional Man*.[16] 'This period', as Norman Mailer put it in a *Partisan Review* symposium grandly and symptomatically entitled 'Our Country and Our Culture', 'smacks of healthy manifestoes'.[17] The war having altered American relations with the rest of the world, and the postwar economic boom rapidly altering its sense of itself, it was a time, so it seemed to many intellectuals, for monumental studies of America.

The great question posed by these studies was whether to affirm or dissent from American culture.[18] The impulse to affirm was directed outwards, American democracy being all but unanimously held to be preferable to Soviet totality. 'The culture we profoundly cherish', Newton Arvin observed, 'is now disastrously threatened from without; and the truer this becomes, the intenser becomes the awareness of our necessary identification with it.'[19] The trouble was that, from the point of view of the intellectual, it had never been so hard to identify with American culture. Political democracy was coming at the increasingly high price of mass market forces, and as it did so the culture Arvin wanted so profoundly to cherish showed itself much less effective at generating individualism and independent-mindedness than at producing kitsch: 'television, radio, Hollywood movies, mass-market paper-back books ... advertising, and other mass-produced goods and art'.[20] And for many intellectuals, such pure products of America posed as great a threat to the American way of life as did Stalinism. 'It will require', Reinhold Niebuhr announced, 'the most rigorous and vital kind of criticism to save our American culture from destruction by technocratic illusions.'[21] The most likely supplier of that criticism, so it seemed to many intellectuals, was the avant-garde. Thus, while he noted the typical faults of the advanced artist ('pride of caste', 'a much too solemn and devotional view of the artist's vocation', 'distortions of perspective' resulting from 'aloofness'), Philip Rahv voiced what was for many critics and intellectuals an article of faith. 'What the avant-garde actually represents historically,' he argued, 'from its very beginning in the early nineteenth century, is the effort to preserve the integrity of art and the intellect amidst the conditions of alienation brought on by the major social forces of the modern era'. It had achieved this standing, Rahv argued, by 'cultivating its own group norms and standards', and 'by resisting the bourgeois incentives to accommodation', so 'making a virtue of its separateness from the mass'.[22]

Rahv's argument is awkwardly poised: troubled by impressions of aloofness on the one hand, but arguing, on the other, for the integrated culture of the avant-garde which in itself made a 'virtue of its separateness from the mass'. Quite how that separateness was to be overcome, and a more general integration achieved, is less clear in Rahv than it was in Goodman. For C. Wright Mills, the most radical of dissenters and among the more zealous proponents of the avant-garde, the problem of separateness was very clearly outweighed by the unique contribution such art and artists were now required to make to American culture. The fundamental issue, as Mills put it, in his 1959 essay 'Culture and politics', was that

> We are at the ending of what is called The Modern Age. Just as Antiquity was followed by several centuries of Oriental ascendancy which Westerners provincially call The Dark Ages, so now The Modern Age is being succeeded by a post-modern period. Perhaps we may call it: The Fourth Epoch.

Not much given to understatement, as Mills saw it the central problem of this new period was of bringing its defining realities into view. This is the central problem of any period no doubt, but two factors in contemporary culture militated strongly against such clear sightedness. The first was that

> our basic definitions of society and self are being overtaken by new realities. I do not mean merely that we *feel* we are in an epochal transition. I mean that too many of our explanations are derived from the great historical transition from the Medieval to the Modern Age; and that when they are generalized for use today, they become unwieldy, irrelevant, not convincing.

The problem here was a problem of scale. The prevaling rhetoric of American society, the rhetoric of liberalism and democratic participation, was predicated, Mills argued, on a kind of community which simply no longer existed. 'Many classic liberals', he argued,

> especially of the Rousseauian and Jeffersonian persuasion, have assumed the predominance of rural or 'small city states,' in brief, of a small-scale community. Liberal discussion of the general will, and liberal notions of 'public opinion' usually rest on such assumptions. We no longer live in this sort of small-scale world.

The rhetoric of American public life had come seriously adrift from events, and far from describing the reality of people's lives it now served, he suggested, only as 'an excellent mask for those who do not, cannot, or will not do what would have to be done to realise its ideals'.[23] If the democratic ideals of American society were to be realised, then now more than ever a new language was necessary, bringing into view the cultural developments that were actually shaping people's lives.

But this was only the half of it, the further problem being that the very cultural developments that needed to be brought into view were, as Mills echoing Rahv saw it, inimical to clear-sightedness. As he put it in a grammar-straining sentence in 'The cultural apparatus' (also published in 1959):

> Nowadays in the overdeveloped society, everyday life and the mass arts; private
> lives and public entertainment; public affairs and the stereotypes put out about it –
> they reflect one another so closely that it is often impossible to distinguish image
> from source.

The cause of such indistinguishability was the cultural apparatus of his title (the
media and related forms of modern communication) an apparatus which had
become 'so decisive to experience itself', that 'often men do not really believe
what "they see before their very eyes" until they have been 'informed' about
it by the national broadcast, the definitive book, the close-up photograph, the
official announcement'. The deleterious effects of modern methods of mass
communication (of 'mass distraction' as he liked to call it) had for some time
been a key theme in Mills's writing. The 'ugly clamour' of the media, he had
suggested, had become 'so much part of the texture of our daily lives that we do
not truly experience it any more'. In one sense such incomplete experience was
a good thing, for, if people fully experienced the media's clamour, they would
become 'blathering idiots'. But such immunity had a price: 'Our eyes and ears
feelings and imaginations withdraw in panic lest they be shattered ... By our
trained inattention, we thus blunt our capacity for liberating experience as we
block off those experiences that would stultify us.' 'The newspaper,' as Ashbery
would put it in Europe, 'is ruining your eyes'.

The cure for this condition, for Mills, as for Rahv and Niebuhr, was to be
found in the productions of the avant-garde. Its task, he argued in 'The decline
of the left', was to 'confront the new facts of history-making of our time'. 'The
politics of truth' was, 'in this time and in America, the only realistic politics of
possible consequence', and the 'independent artist' was among

> the few remaining personalities equipped to resist and to fight the stereotyping and
> consequent death of lively things. Fresh perception now involves the capacity con-
> tinually to unmask and to smash the stereotypes of vision and intellect with which
> modern communications swamp us ... If the thinker does not relate himself to the
> value of truth in political struggle, he cannot responsibly cope with the whole of
> lived experience.[24]

Contrary to Ashbery's expectations, the poems of *The Tennis Court Oath*
did begin to secure an audience. Koch and O'Hara introduced them at readings,
and Ashbery, his mysteriousness enhanced by his absence, assumed a kind
of cult status on the American poetry circuit. So much so that, as Richard
Kostelanetz recalls, in the early 1960s 'Ashbery's work became a controversial
issue – a litmus test that ... seemed to separate advanced tastes from retro-
grade'.[25] What all this goes to suggest, then, is that it is more against the
background of the American scene than Ashbery's Parisian environment that
one should read Ashbery's controversial second volume. To do so is to get some
sense of why Ashbery's isolated words might have seemed monumentally
important.

Ashbery's 'America' is a dissenting poem: its refusal to accommodate the reader's expectations and habits of mind signalled by its dismantling of conventional syntax. The poem's recurring motif is of accumulation, the first line noting a 'Piling upward / the fact the stars'. A little later we learn that 'The stones piled up – / The ribbon – books' (TCO, 15). In the second section we observe 'The deep / additional / and more and more less deep' (TCO,15). What this adds up to, we are advised in section 4 of the poem, is that in this 'country / lined with snow / only mush was served / piling up' (TCO, 18). Whatever else is going on in 'America', more is definitely less, because what is being accumulated is what is undesired, and the result is a kind of pulpy 'mush'.

These images of self-defeating accumulation dominate the poem, thus pro-viding the backdrop against which all its other concerns and preoccupations take shape. In particular, terms and ideas central to the American way of life are called into doubt. The freedom to choose is not all it might be, the poem observing 'The person / Horror – the morsels of his choice'. Nor is liberty in general all it might be, the only aspect of American society which is any sense free being the media, hence 'Chain to fall apart in his hand / Someday liberty / to be of the press' (TCO, 15, 19). Also called frequently into question is the iconography by which America identifies itself, the razzmatazz by which it celebrates itself. In the fourth section we see 'these stars in our flag we don't want / the flag of film / waving over the sky' (TCO, 18). Later we are shown 'Some tassels first / then nothing' – all the cheerleading and parades by which Americans are encouraged to feel good about themselves being, the poem suggests, based on 'nothing'. And indeed, there is plenty in this poem not to feel good about. Every so often the reality of modern industrial life breaks through the surface, and when it does the tone becomes sinister. Briefly we glimpse 'the lathes around / the stars with priv-ilege jerks / over the country last year we were disgusted meeting / misguided' (TCO, 16). We hear 'of the arsenal / shaded in public / a hand put up / lips –' (TCO, 17). And, having seen millions of us parked in the first section, we find that by the final section an obstruction has resulted as 'Cars / blockade the streets' (TCO, 19). One has to be careful what one makes of all this, of course, the very act of reading – of making sense of the whole – being, as the poem puts it, 'on trial', but with with its ongoing accumulation, its excessive jingosim, and its sinister images of the military-industrial complex, Ashbery's 'America' is a less than great place to live.

One of the things that makes it less than great is, as the poems of *The Tennis Court Oath* seem repeatedly to insist, the inadequacy of what one might call the rhetoric of the public sphere. 'White Roses' seems to address itself quite explic-itly to that rhetoric:

The worst side of it all –
The white sunlight on the polished floor -
Pressed into service,
And then the window closed
And the night ends and begins again.

[79]

Her face goes green, her eyes are green;
In the dark corner playing 'The Stars and Stripes Forever.' I try
      to describe for you,
But you will not listen, you are like the swan.

No stars are there,
No stripes,
But a blind man's cane poking, however clumsily, into the inmost
      corners of the house.
Nothing can be harmed! Night and day are beginning again!
So put away the book,
The flowers you were keeping to give someone:
Only the white, tremendous foam of the street has any importance,
The new white flowers that are beginning to shoot up about now.

                                                              (TCO, 35)

For various reasons, this poem seems to suggest, people are getting out of touch with things. White sunlight on a polished floor is the stuff of the magazine lifestyle feature, sunshine on floorboards being a nice addition to the ideal home. The poem is suspicious of such glossy images, the occupants of such homes, so it suggests, desiring no real contact with the sun – hence the fact that their window is closed – but wanting rather to press it into service; valuing it only as it glances off the polished floorboards. A high-brow satire on middle-brow habits, one might say well say, following Philip Rahv, that this poem resists 'bourgeois incentives to accommodation'; or at least that it resists incentives to bourgeois accommodation. But the object of the poem is not simply to scoff at the middle-class apartment, the point being, rather, that such degraded contact with the natural world is symptomatic of a more widespread cultural condition.

This is apparent from his attitude to '"The Stars and Stripes Forever"': the rhetoric of which, the rhetoric by which America publicly defines and identifies itself, being, so the poem is determined to point out, out of touch with reality. Indeed the problem is not only that such public rhetoric has no basis in fact – 'No stars are there / No stripes' – but that, as the speaker tries to point this fact out, his audience is distracted by the sound of such songs: 'I try / to describe for you / But you will not listen'. The poet's descriptions fall on deafened ears, drowned out by the sound of the nation's anthems. The net result is profoundly disabling, hence the 'blind man's cane poking, however clumsily, into the inmost corners of the house'. It is extremely difficult, this poem asserts, to negotiate the world when all one has by way of a guide is the inaccurate rhetoric of patriotic songs; and all the more so when, as the poem's closing lines indicate, things are changing even as one speaks.

'White Roses' works synecdochally, the anthem 'The Stars and Stripes Forever' standing for the language of national self-definition of which it is so salient a part. The language by which America publicly describes itself is thus shown to be coming dangerously adrift from reality. 'Two Sonnets' makes the point more graphically, the government officials in the 'cream-colored' embassy failing to notice that blood is being spilled around them because they are forever playing the same old songs:

> The iodine bottle sat in the hall
> And out over the park where crawled roadsters
> The apricot and purple clouds were
> And our blood flowed down the grating
> Of the cream-colored embassy.
> Inside it they had a record of 'The St. Louis Blues'.
>
> (TCO, 20)

To listen to popular songs, with their falsely reassuring, old-fashioned values, makes it difficult, one might say, to distinguish public affairs from the stereotypes put out about them; so difficult, perhaps, that one becomes blind to bloody reality.

'White Roses' and 'Two Sonnets' have a general point to make, their emblems and icons signifying a widespread cultural condition. Elsewhere in *The Tennis Court Oath* Ashbery is more specific, with the deleterious effect of newspapers in particular being a recurring concern. In 'The New Realism' an exasperated speaker loses patience with his newspaper:

> ... Confound it
> The arboretum is bursting with jasmine and lilac
> And all I can smell here is newsprint
>
> (TCO, 60)

There is no lack of vernal activity in *The Tennis Court Oath*, the burst of 'jasmine' and 'lilac' indicating, here as elsewhere, that things are changing, that a new life is emerging. Registering such change, however, is a difficult task and certainly the print media does not seem to be up to the job. Here the newspaper fails to transmit the new and subtle perfumes of 'jasmine' and 'lilac', the only smell it gives off being its own. Likewise in 'The Tennis Court Oath', the only thing which is said to be 'easily visible' is 'the / lettering ... along the edge of the *Times*' (TCO, 11). Newsprint, in other words, does not communicate events but obscures them. It is 'the *Times*', not the times, that is made easily visible. More explicitly in 'Europe', at the heart of the poem, we are warned that 'The newspaper is ruining your eyes'. Or as Mills might have put it, so decisive has the newspaper become to experience itself that 'often men do not really believe what "they see before their very eyes"'.

If newspapers are, indeed, ruining people's eyes – distracting attention from what they purport to make clear – then one response might be simply to do away with them, an option 'The Ascetic Sensualists' would seem to argue for with its image of

> The scissors, this season, old newspaper.
> The brown suit. Hunted unsuccessfully,
> To be torn down later

The horse said.

(TCO, 51)

Cultural argument and poetic practice merge nicely here, the image telling the history of its coming into being. One of the ways Ashbery made a number of the poems in *The Tennis Court Oath* as disjointed and unaccommodating as they are was by the practice of cut-ups. Ashbery cut up various kinds of text to produce *The Tennis Court Oath*: American magazines he bought in Paris, 'things like *Esquire* and *Life*', and pulp fiction like William Le Queux's *Beryl of the Biplane* and, as Shoptaw notes, '*Soundings* ... a popular novel by A. Hamilton Gibbs, which Ashbery found in his parents' home in Sodus'.[26] As Neil Jumonville points out, magazines like *Esquire* and 'mass-market paperback books' were paradigmatic of what dissenting 1950s intellectuals termed the middle-brow, or kitsch; the problem with 'kitsch' being for Clement Greenberg that it constituted a 'vicarious experience', 'faked sensations'.[27] One way to regard Ashbery's procedure of cutting-up texts is thus as an act of very physical dissent, the poet, as the image from 'The Ascetic Sensualists' makes vivid, taking his scissors to the forms of communication which are distracting readers from the reality of their lives. Indeed, this must be true, because as the image suggests, we have it from the horse's mouth: the temporal disjunction of 'this', the present 'season', and the 'old newspaper', leading to the scissors and the decision to mutilate.

The dissenting implications of the practice of cutting up take us to the heart of Ashbery's deeply uncharacteristic poetry of this period. Popular fiction, newspapers and magazines are, in a sense, the very stuff of Ashbery's poetry, his writing absorbing their languages as a means of presenting the situation in which his readers find themselves. He had already begun to do this in his collaborations with Koch. He does it all the more substantially in passages in 'The Skaters'. Cutting up texts is, of course, a way of absorbing them, but it is a particularly hostile way of doing so, the poet not welcoming the words of popular communication, but ripping them from their conventional environment. Figuratively, then, the cut-up is another instance of the poet's temporarily tense relation with his background, the poet taking in the languages that make up that background, but only after having first demonstrated his resistance to them.

National anthems and popular fictions are, however, by no means the most important forms of expression to be shown drifing off from events in *The Tennis Court Oath*. The most important, as Mills wanted people to believe, is the language of democracy itself. The volume begins with an image of just such a linguistic failing, the title poem opening by putting the question:

> What had you been thinking about
> the face studiously bloodied
> heaven blotted region
> I go on loving you like water but
> there is a terrible breath in the way all of this

You were not elected president, yet won the race

(TCO, 11)

As in 'Two Sonnets' blood is being spilt while people are thinking about some-thing else. Here, however, the distracted thinking is tied to a failing democratic process; a process which somehow elected the person who did not win the race. Again the poem is difficult to follow, but that, of course, is part of the point. The language of the poem is not working because the language of democracy is not working, the political idiom surviving in spite of, rather than as a consequence of, events.

A similar thing happens in 'The Ascetic Sensualists', where

These times, by water, the members
Balloting, proud stain adrift
Over the glass air.
See, you must acknowledge.
For big charity ball.

(TCO, 51)

Here the problem is more explicitly put. The act of balloting has come 'adrift' in that a political gesture which should carry considerable significance is now being tied to the most insignificant objectives and decisions. Here, then, the proud members are balloting for nothing more significant than a 'big charity ball'. Such votes, it is clear, are of little consequence, as 'Landscape', also, makes abundantly clear. In this case the problem is not that the act of voting is being trivialized by misuse but that a vote simply fails to register:

It decided to vote for ink (the village).
There was surprise at the frozen ink
That was brought in and possibly rotten.
Several new lumps were revealed
Near Penalty Avenue.

(TCO, 55)

Despite the outcome of its vote, the village receives not ink but frozen ink, the democratic process thus failing to deliver to the voters what they wanted (just as it failed to deliver when 'You were not elected president, but won the race'). What is delivered is said to be 'possibly rotten', and as soon as this is noticed 'Sev-eral new lumps were revealed'. 'Landscape' is rather easier to read than most poems in *The Tennis Court Oath*, and with this image in particular one is on famil-iar metaphorical territory: the failing political process, a suspicion of rottenness and lumps breaking out all over all being symptoms of a cancerous body politic. Not only, it seems, are popular songs, glossy magazines and newspapers becom-ing seriously detached from events, but the democratic idiom itself, the language by which America was constituted, is ceasing to provide an accurate account of the way things now happen. And just as Mills suggested that the purpose of lib-eral-democratic language was no longer to describe but to mask events, so in this

[83]

poem any attempt to give an accurate picture of the changing landscape is thwarted by the terms and institutions of democracy. Thus,

> The bathers' tree
> Explained ashes. The pilot knew.
> All over the country the rapid extension meter
> Was thrown out of court ... the tomatoes ...

(TCO, 55)

'Ashes' was O'Hara's nickname for Ashbery, and so here the poet makes an appearance, this time promising some kind of explanation. The trouble, as far as he seems to sees it, is that nationwide the 'rapid extension meter' has been thrown out of court. A device for measuring, or registering rapid and considerable change, poetry, one might think, is just such a meter. We do not, however, learn what this meter might have to tell us, its findings being thrown out of court. This is, of course, a familiar complaint, Ashbery's poetic struggle with the legislature recalling Shelley's unacknowledged legislator, and so the Romantic origins of avant-garde authority.

There is an admirable critical energy to these poems, Ashbery extending the scope of his writing by responding forcefully to the state of the nation. But what the poems lack is intimacy – the kind of closeness of contact Ashbery achieved, albeit on a much smaller scale, in 'Two Scenes'. One of the defining ironies of the volume is perhaps that, as he contemplated America from a distance, Ashbery was dependent for his information on the very forms of communication with which he is so keen to argue: the newsapers and magazines by which the expatriate keeps in touch. Perhaps, even, it is this dependence on such media that makes him resent them enough to want to cut them up. But if they lack the intimacy with their surroundings that distingushes the best of Ashbery's poetry, they do present a cultural condition: a condition given most satisfying expression in the volume's most anthologised poem, '"They Dream Only of America"'.

'"They Dream Only of America"' has been much interpreted, especially by critics and poets associated with LANGUAGE poetry. For Andrew Ross the poem, and in turn the book, show 'how and why language has nothing at all to do with unmediated expression, except when it chooses to voice parodically the fallacy of such an idea'.[28] For Bruce Andrews, putting his argument in the fragmented style of the book, '"Now he cared only about signs." Well, not true, not even here, but he does care very deeply and seems suspicious of their instrumental value.'[29] The volume as a whole, as Andrews sees it, makes the argument that 'Description would be choiceless, "unintentional". Personhood might be mere transmission ... But a critique in action of the representational capacity of language seems to reaffirm personhood, as choice itself.'[30] This gets the wrong end of the stick: the wrong end, one might say, of the blind man's cane.

Certainly the poem is centrally concerned with signs, consisting, as it does, of a series of now conventional images of America: Whitman's ('To be lost among the thirteen million pillars of grass'), Twain's ('hiding from darkness in barns / They can be grown ups now'), Chandler's ('And the murderer's ash tray is more easily'), Stevens's alliterative version ('The lake a lilac cube'), and the Beats' ('We could drive hundreds of miles / At night through dandelions') (TCO, 13).[31] Ashbery cares about these signs. They are, after all, his literary background. The point of the poem is, however, to indicate what happens if such signs come to dominate. Thus whenever in the poem the speaker seems to be growing too fond of signs and symbols – at each point at which they seem in danger of preoccupying him – he receives a painful reminder that such fondness is inappropriate, dangerous even, in so far as it causes one to neglect the reality of the situation. Just at the point at which he gets carried away with Whitman's honeyed homoerotic pastoral, so at that point the honey *'burns the throat'* (TCO, 13). Likewise just as the Kerouac-like road-trip begins to exert its symbolic allure, so the driver's headache gets worse, and the travellers have to stop at a 'wire filling station' (TCO, 13). And most painfully of all, just as the speaker, seduced by the Freudian cigar, starts thinking of the wrong kind of 'key' (of the key to the detective mystery, not the key to the door he is opening), so he stumbles and breaks his leg. The experience is painful enough to influence the poet's attitude to language, and so, fond as he is of signs and the symbolic worlds they conjure, he is reminded also that language must sometimes be more matter-of-fact, hence his prosaic account of the incident, '"I would not have broken my leg if I had not fallen / Against the living room table …"' (TCO, 13). To become too attached to signs, it would seem, is to become so detached from the world of objects that one is likely to do oneself an injury. One is likely, that is, to find oneself disabled.

'"They Dream Only of America"' is one of the strongest poems in *The Tennis Court Oath*. This is partly because it is more like the poems in *Some Trees* than most of the other pieces in Ashbery's second volume. Like 'The Picture of Little J.A.', the poem absorbs its literary background, constituting itself in a series of allusions which are the history of its coming into being. It is also both a more affectionate and a more intimate account of America. Shoptaw reads the poem as a love lyric, identifying the 'They' of the title as Ashbery and Martory dreaming of a projected visit to America. This is not the whole truth of the poem, but perhaps it helps us understand what that whole truth might be. If Ashbery is, in this poem, 'dreaming of' in the sense of yearning for America, then for once he has a meaningful link with the cultural condition so many of the poems are keen to address. Mills said of this cultural condition that 'mind and reality' have become 'two separate realms'. Which is as much as to say, from the poet's point of view, that '"They dream only of America"'. The implication of Andrews's account is that this is a state of affairs *The Tennis Court Oath* means to argue for, on the grounds that a language detached from reality is free to be manipulated by the user. The truth is more like the opposite: the blind man stumbling about his room and the speaker breaking his leg on the bed being symptoms of a linguistic condition to which the poet means to offer a cure.

The cure *The Tennis Court Oath* offers, hardly surprisingly given its own zeal for experimentalism and the urgings of intellectual opinion, is the practice of the avant-garde. Invariably, among the rubble of this volume, some figure is at hand brave and well-equipped enough to perform an act of rescue, and the Poet, one suspects, if not the poet, is the hero every time. 'The New Realism' closes with just such an image of rescue:

> Hosts of bulldozers
> Wrecked the site, and she died laughing
> Because only once does prosperity let you get away
> On your doorstep she used to explain
> How if the returning merchants in the morning hitched the rim of the van
> In the evening one must be very quick to give them the slip.
> The judge knocked. The zinnias
> Had never looked better – red, yellow, and blue
> They were, and the forget-me-nots and dahlias
> At least sixty different varieties
> As the shade went up
> And the ambulance came crashing through the dust
> Of the new day

(TCO, 62)

The passage indicates the two main functions of the avant-garde artist as Ashbery then saw them. The first is to smash those structures (of thought and representation) which have become obsolete, hence the hosts of bulldozers wrecking the site at the beginning of this passage. The second is, by its daring experiments to find a way of keeping pace with changing circumstances: the bulldozer (having cleared the way for new forms) becoming a van, and the van becoming an ambulance, crashing fearlessly through the dust to provide cultural resuscitation. Those in, or rather at, the van are, the poem suggests, capable of registering the rapid change symbolised by the sudden blooming of 'sixty different varieties' of dahlia and forget-me-not.

What this suggests is that *The Tennis Court Oath* embodies the then contemporary view that the role of the 'independent artist' was to 'confront the new facts of history-making of our time', and by 'fresh perception', to 'unmask and to smash the stereotypes of vision and intellect with which modern communications swamp us'. Indeed, everywhere one looks in *The Tennis Court Oath* people are being urged to see things clearly. In 'The Suspended Life', Julian is asked,

> Do you see
> The difference between weak handshakes
> And freezing to death in a tub of ice and snow
> Called a home by some, but it lacks runners,
> Do you?

(TCO, 37)

In 'Rain', the speaker notes that 'At night / Curious – I'd seen this tall girl', following which sighting he has the confidence to assert that 'The facts have hinged on my reply' (TCO, 30). In 'Our Youth' someone, the reader perhaps, is asked, 'Do you know it? Hasn't she / Observed you too? Haven't you been observed to her?', questions which lead to a disquisition on seeing (TCO, 41). In 'The Ascetic Sensualists' the reader is urged, 'See, you must acknowledge', while later, in its closing section, the poem pays tribute to the reader's sharpened eyes: 'You see well, the perverted things you wanted gone in a group of colored lights all lucky for you' (TCO, 51, 54). And, in one of the most visual moments of the book, in 'Idaho', Carol points a telegram out to Cornelia:

'See?' She pointed to the table.
Cornelia unfolded the piece of crude blue paper that is a French telegra.
###############

(TCO, 92).

'Idaho' is full of such visual moments, the exhortation to 'see' being under-lined by what Shoptaw helpfully terms Ashbery's 'painterly punctuation'.[32] Thus:

??

(TCO, 91)

and

!!!!!!!!!!!!!!

(TCO, 93)

and again

,,,,,,,,,,,,,,,,,,,,

(TCO, 93)

These are odd moments indeed, and more than ever the reader's patience is taxed. They are not, however, insignificant gestures, but rather the most visible signs of a visual argument to which the whole book seems variously to con-tribute, and to which the practice of cutting-up gave forceful expression.

The period's other great cut-and-paste poet was William Burroughs.[33] Recall-ing why it was he first became interested in the possibilities of the technique, in Paris, as it happens, 'in the summer of 1960', Burroughs explained the procedure in terms of its optical value. Cut-ups, he suggests,

> make explicit a psychosensory process that is going on all the time anyway. Some-body is reading a newspaper, and his eye follows the column in proper Aristotelian manner, one idea and a sentence at a time. But subliminally he is reading the columns on either side and is aware of the person sitting next to him ... That's a cut-up – a juxtaposition of what's happening outside and what you're thinking of ... Most people don't see what's going on around them. That's my principal message to writers: For Godsake keep you *eyes* open. Notice what's going on around you.[34]

The point of cut-ups, as Burroughs saw it, was to open the reader's eyes to what was going on around them. It was, moreover, an optic for its time. In 'Cut-ups: a Project for Disastrous Success', Brion Gysin (the self-proclaimed first cut-up poet and the writer from whom Burroughs took the idea) observes that 'Cut-ups are Machine Age Knife-magic … Cut this page now. But copies – after all, we are in Proliferation, too – to do cut-ups and fold-ins until we can deliver the Reality Machine in commercially reasonable quantities'.[35]

Ashbery has expressed his interest in the cut-up in similar terms, approving Marianne Moore's collage poems because they are 'a necessary lesson in how to live in our world of "media", how to deal with the unwanted information that constantly accumulates around us'.[36] It was in these terms, also, that a somewhat baffled, but by no means uncomprehending, O'Hara read 'Europe', the longest poem in *The Tennis Court Oath*. Writing to Ashbery in 1960, O'Hara described his reaction to the troubling beauty of the poem, telling Ashbery that

> it is a great pleasure to find something again so intriguing, compelling and attention-demanding, and mysterious. I'm not really mentally lazy, you see, it's just that everything has gotten too easy these days and I'm a grifter. It feels right now like when I first read Pasternak, the same kind of obscure appeal which one is at the same time absolutely certain is going to prove fruitful in a completely original way.[37]

The key phrase here is 'attention-demanding', the point of the poem being, as O'Hara implies, to demand of the reader a heightened attention (attention dulled by precisely the kind of pulp-fiction 'Europe' cuts up) in order that he or she should be better equipped to face 'the new facts of history-making of our time'. Which is to say that 'Europe', like Moore's collages, can be read as 'a necessary lesson in how to live in our world of "media"', a lesson made concrete by its visual argument.

The poem opens with an image of constructive destruction, the poet deploying 'her / construction ball' (TCO, 64). The ball is like the bulldozers in 'The New Realism', brought in to wreck outdated and inadequate forms of representation. Such forms, the poet informs us in section 7, are 'absolute, unthinking / menace to our way of life' (TCO, 64). What he means by this becomes apparent in section 8 where we are presented with an unadulterated passage from *Beryl of the Biplane*, the only unadulterated passage in the poem. Such pulp fiction, the poet is indicating is a 'menace to our way of life', constituting, as has been indicated before, a degraded cultural condition. Not that this degraded condition need necessarily prove fatal, for, as the poet indicates in section 9, 'there is a cure' (TCO, 65). Whatever the cure is, however, it will involve surgery, the poet announcing in section 12 that 'that surgeon must operate' (TCO, 65). What follow are some forty-five sections of cutting and splicing, the readers being left to negotiate their own way around a text which seems to defy interpretation but which involves the kind of tax on the eyes made by a jump-cut movie-sequence.

Then, in section 57, we are finally given something we can read: a syntactically conventional, semantically orthodox poem in the form of seven unrhymed couplets It is the one section in the poem that makes anything like extended sense, its purpose being to tell us why all the other sections don't make such sense. Thus someone announces, the poet perhaps, or even a sympathetic reader, that

We are not more loved than now
The newspaper is ruining your eyes.

(TCO, 74)

All that has gone before, in other words, is a loving gesture, the poet risking the reader's wrath in the interest of trying to cure his or her culturally induced blindness. This, however, is as far as he is prepared to go by way of explanation, and there follow 57 further sections of cutting and splicing until, with section 104, we arrive at a passage which simply and concretely refuses to be read hermeneutically, and which insists on its visual status: a passage with four words, 'blaze', 'out', 'aviators', 'dastardly' contained within boxes the poet has actually drawn on to the page (TCO, 82). Baffled readers, if they have got this far, will no doubt only be more baffled. For the reader, however, who has noticed that the point of this text is not, as it were, to read it, but to see it, to acknowledge its visual impact, then this graphic section will feel like something of a climax, a conclusion to the argument. If so, he or she will further understand what is meant when, in the very next section (105), a voice reminds us that

We must be a little more wary in
    future, dear.

(TCO, 82)

If this poetic operation has worked, if, as result of all the cutting-up, we are in fact a little more wary in future, then we will, perhaps, find some way of negotiating the tricky double columns of section 107. And more to the point, perhaps, we will understand what has been achieved when, in the final section, a voice cut (one might say liberated) from its pulp fiction environment observes that 'Half an hour later',

Ronald recognised him.
They suddenly saw a beam of intense, white light,
A miniature searchlight of great brilliance,
– pierce the darkness, skyward.

They now recognised to be a acetylene,
a cylinder mounted
upon a light tripod of aluminium
with a bright reflector behind the gas jet

(TCO, 84)

O'Hara was by no means alone among Ashbery's contemporary readers in discerning that, true to its moment, *The Tennis Court Oath*, and 'Europe' in particular, meant to make a visual argument. As one reviewer, R.W. Flint, told his readers, 'this extreme disjointedness proves to have a tonal unity in no way dependent on meter or even cadence conventionally understood, but rather on a cadence of feeling-sight'.[38] But if some of the reviewers got the point, they didn't like it. Or rather, they didn't like the pointed, often antagonstic, sometimes aloof way in which it was being made. John Simon found the book 'arrogant', Paul Carroll felt 'annoyed' because the poetry made him 'feel stupid', while Mona van Duyn caught the drift of the poet's monumental intention, but simply refused to play ball:

> If a state of continuous exasperation, a continuous frustration of expectation, a continuous titillation of the imagination are sufficient response to a series of thirty-one poems, then these have been successful. But to be satisfied with such a response I must change my notion of poetry.[39]

Ashbery has taken these responses on board, subsequently distancing himself from a book which, while it has continued to have a kind of cult status, was variously – and uniquely in his oeuvre – distanced from the ordinary reader. Not that the book was inherently undemocratic. Addressing a cultural condition which it thought damaging to the reader's well-being, it was serious when it suggested to him or her that they were never 'loved more than now'. The trouble was it had a funny way of showing it.

Speaking in interview, Ashbery has remarked of his second volume that it

> presents, in a sort of concrete way, something that is unintelligible as well as some-things that are intelligible. And this was the dilemma of understanding that I was actually trying to duplicate, or rather, reproduce in the poems. I suppose if the majority of readers don't get anything out of a poem then it is ineffective … If this happens, then I have undoubtedly failed.[40]

Ashbery's tough assessment of his controversial poems is borne out by his next two books. What *Rivers and Mountains* and *The Double Dream of Spring* preserve from *The Tennis Court Oath* is the sense of reach and scope which is the most exciting feature of Ashbery's unaccommodating poems. But what they learn also, precisely from its relative failure, is the need to restore that relation of writing to background which is vital to the poetry's sense of occasion.

NOTES

1 David Herd, 'John Ashbery in conversation with David Herd', p. 34.
2 Letter from Kenneth Koch to John Ashbery, 9 February 1959.
3 For an account of the critical controversy surrounding *The Tennis Court Oath*, see John Shoptaw, *On the Outside Looking Out*, pp. 42–4.
4 Harold Bloom, *Figures of Capable Imagination*, p. 174.
5 Charles Bernstein, *Content's Dream*, p. 433. John Ash, 'John Ashbery in conversation with John Ash', p. 31.
6 Herd, 'John Ashbery in conversation', p. 34.

7 Ibid. For other discussions of the impact of Ashhery's self–exile on his poetic expression see Geoff Ward, *Statutes of Liberty*, p. 112, and Fred Moramarco, 'The lonesomeness of words: a revaluation of *The Tennis Court Oath*'.

8 Louis Osti, 'The craft of John Ashbery', p. 88.

9 'American Sanctuary in Paris' was published in 1966, just after Ashbery's return to America. It was researched, clearly, in Paris.

10 Critics have noted the monumental character of *The Tennis Court Oath*: Bruce Andrews finding the style of the book 'prophetic'; Mark Ford observing that 'the reticent de–mythologizing of self' (which for him characterises *Some Trees*) 'gives way in this next book to a larger scale, almost epic attempt to dismantle the organic symbolist lyric'. See Bruce Andrews, 'Misrepresentation', p. 528; and Mark Ford, *A Critical Study of the Poetry of John Ashbery*, p. 33.

11 John Ashbery, 'On Raymond Roussel', first published as 'Re–establishing Raymond Roussel', in *Portfolio and ARTnews Annual* no. 6 (Autumn 1962), repr. in Raymond Roussel, *How I Wrote Certain of My Books*, p. 54.

12 Ibid., p. 55. For detailed accounts of Ashbery's relation to bourgeois language see Keith Cohen, 'Ashbery's dismantling of bourgeois discourse'; Paul Breslin, *The Psycho-Political Muse* pp. 211–35.

13 Peter Stitt, 'The art of poetry XXXIII: John Ashbery', p. 411.

14 Herd, 'John Ashbery in conversation', p. 34.

15 Ibid.

16 Paul Breslin, *The Psycho-Political Muse*, p. 4.

17 'Our country and our culture: a symposium' appeared in three successive issues of *Partisan Review*: 19:3 (May–June 1952), pp. 282–326; 19:4 (July–August 1952), pp. 420–50; 19:5 (September–October 1952), pp. 562–97.

18 See Neil Jumonville, *Critical Crossings*, pp. 49–101.

19 'Our country and our culture', p. 287.

20 Jumonville, *Critical Crossings*, p. 151.

21 'Our country and our culture', p. 303.

22 Ibid.

23 C. Wright Mills, *Power, Politics and People,* pp. 236, 192, 189.

24 Ibid., pp. 407, 350, 235, 299.

25 Richard Kostelanetz, *The Old Poetries and the New,* p. 99.

26 Herd, 'John Ashbery in conversaton', p. 34; Shoptaw, *On the Outside*, p. 53.

27 Jumonville, *Critical Crossings*, pp. 151, 156.

28 Andrew Ross, 'Taking *The Tennis Court Oath*', p. 209.

29 Bruce Andrews, 'Misrepresentation', p. 523.

30 Ibid., p. 525.

31 For other useful accounts of '"They Dream Only of America"' see Geoff Ward, *Statutes of Liberty*, pp. 105–10; and Shoptaw, *On the Outside*, pp. 63–6.

32 Shoptaw, *On the Outside*, p. 54.

33 Some of Burroughs's cut-ups were published in the collaborations special issue of *Locus Solus*; pp. 148–51.

34 Cited in William S. Burroughs and Brion Gysin, *The Third Mind*, pp. 3, 5.

35 Ibid., p. 51.

36 Ashbery, 'Jerboas, pelicans and Peewee Peese', p. 8.

37 Frank O'Hara, letter to John Ashbery, 7 January 1960.

38 R.W. Flint, 'Poetry chronicle', p. 90.

39 John Simon, 'More brass than enduring', p. 457; Paul Carroll, *The Poem in its Skin*, p. 6; Mona van Duyn, 'Ways to Meaning', p. 394.

40 Janet Bloom and Robert Losada, 'The craft of John Ashbery', p. 95.

CHAPTER FOUR

Forms of action: experiment and declaration in
Rivers and Mountains and *The Double Dream of Spring*

In September 1966 Ashbery published an article called 'Frank O'Hara's question'. Written less than two months after O'Hara's tragically early death – he was killed in a car accident on a beach on Fire Island – Ashbery's article was not an obituary but a defence of O'Hara's art. It was couched, in part, in terms of prevailing poetic trends, Ashbery observing that Frank O'Hara's poetry

> has no program and therefore cannot be joined. It does not advocate sex and dope as a panacea for the ills of modern society; it does not speak out against the war in Viet Nam or in favor of civil rights; it does not paint gothic vignettes of the post-Atomic age: in a word, it does not attack the establishment. It merely ignores its right to exist, and is thus a source of annoyance for partisans of every stripe.[1]

The article itself annoyed Louis Simpson. Writing in *The Nation* some seven months later, in an essay on poetic responses to the Vietnam War, Simpson observed that with few exceptions American poets were joined in 'one common enterprise of poetry readings or protests against the war in Vietnam'. The exception, Simpson wanted his readers to believe, was Ashbery. Noting that Ashbery had 'complimented' O'Hara on 'not having written poetry about the war,' he remarked that 'it was not amusing to see a poet sneering at the conscience of other poets. Some people seem able to protest only against an act of protest by others.'[2] Ashbery replied to Simpson's 'unjust attack' with a letter to *The Nation*. He was not, he justifiably complained, sneering at anybody's conscience. Nor was he protesting against acts of protest by others. He had himself protested vigorously against the war, and, though he would have preferred not to make such facts public, he was obliged by Simpson's attack to list a series of the marches, rallies, and readings he had attended. He did, however, stand firm on the point he had been trying to make in connection with O'Hara.[3] 'All poetry', he wrote, 'is against war and in favour of life, or else it isn't poetry, and it stops being poetry when it is forced into the mold of a particular program. Poetry is poetry. Protest is protest. I believe in both forms of action.'[4]

Ashbery's words might have been weighed more carefully: to make O'Hara's decision not to write about the war seem a little less easily taken; to give the sense that, while it was contrary to the radical spirit of O'Hara's poetic to issue or subscribe to manifestos, he was aware, in this case, of the counterpressure. Even so Simpson's article was a grubby response. It makes no mention of the fact that Ashbery was writing in a state of grief, that while his words might have been slightly ill-advised there were particular circumstances to be taken into account. It is dubious, also, in the rhetorical use it makes of Ashbery's comments. Thus while, on the one hand, Simpson was keen to be seen applauding those poets who wrote in protest against the war, he also felt, like many other commentators who broached the subject, that

> The occasion has not produced much good poetry – occasions hardly ever do – but it may serve to change the poet profoundly, so that in the future their poems will be political in the way that really counts – that is by altering the angle of vision. Political poetry need not be about a political occasion; it may be about a butterfly.[5]

What, then, was Simpson's disagreement with Ashbery? Both poets argue that the strictures of politics are deleterious to poetry, and that the best way for poets to affect the world – in so far as they are able – is to alter the way the reader approaches it. As Ashbery would later put it to Piotr Sommer, explaining his sense of the relation between the action of poetry and the action of protest, 'The pleasure that you get if you love poetry, is a pleasure that's going to cause you to act, it forces you back into life.'[6] So if, in fact, they had no substantial disagreement, why was Simpson so keen to make it seem as if they did? Simpson, like a number of poets of his generation, wanted to have it both ways over this issue. He wanted to be seen to be at the frontline of poetic protest against the war. He also wanted to distance himself from some of the poetry being written in the name of protest. Perhaps it was to square this circle that he picked an argument with Ashbery: distracting the reader's attention from his own doubts about protest poetry by highlighting the doubts of another.[7]

In its accusatory tone, its wilful misconstructions, its sense of anxiety and its mood of overall confusion, Ashbery's exchange with Simpson was symptomatic of a period in which American poetry found itself motivated by sharply conflicting impulses. The first impulse was to experiment: to innovate towards new ways of seeing in order that people might better comprehend their environment. Thus, as Paul Carroll observed in 1968, his (and Ashbery's) generation of poets

> was on the high, happy adventure of creating and innovating a complex of new ways in which to view our common condition – an adventure which in its abundance, freshness and originality is, in my opinion, as interesting as any since the Olympians of 1917.[8]

The second, new and intensely felt impulse was the impulse to declare. Almost without exception, Simpson was right in saying, American poets opposed their country's involvement in Vietnam, and many felt the need to declare that opposition. On refusing a $5,000 grant from the National Foundation for the Arts and Humanities awarded to his small publishing outfit The Sixties Press, Robert Bly declared, 'Since the Administration is maiming an entire nation … it is insensitive, even indecent, for that Administration to come forward with money for poetry.'[9] Broadly speaking, then, American poets in the 1960s felt the need both to experiment with new forms of expression, and a pressure to declare themselves clearly and without misunderstanding. The result was a conflict of interests by which few, if any, serious poets were untouched – Ashbery being no exception.

Among those pressing the poet to experiment, nobody did so more concertedly than Susan Sontag. Writing in 'Against interpretation' in 1964, Sontag argued that the role of the contemporary artist was to develop the 'new sensibility' required by America's rapidly changing culture. Developing arguments made on behalf of the avant-garde in the late 1950s, Sontag called loudly and clearly for both an art and a criticism which radically privileged questions of style over questions of content. Urging her fellow critics to throw off 'means of defending and justify-ing art' which have become 'insensitive to contemporary needs and practice', Sontag identified 'content' in particular as a category which had grown obsolete: 'Whatever it may have been in the past, the idea of content is today mainly a hin-drance, a nuisance, a subtle or not so subtle philistinism.' The trouble with read-ing works of art for their content was that in doing so the surface of the work was disregarded, when in fact, in the contemporary climate, it was precisely on the surface of the work that critics should be concentrating their attention, the point being, as Sontag saw it,

> All the conditions of modern life … conjoin to dull our sensory faculties. And it is in the light of the condition of our senses, our capacities (rather than those of another age), that the task of the critic must be assessed.
>
> What is important now is to recover our senses. We must learn to see more, to hear more, to feel more.

Sontag presses a familiar case; Mills had made it a few years earlier. Her contri-bution to the argument was to tie the question of sensibility so strongly to the question of style. Style, she suggested, both constituted the artist's sense of their relation to the world, and, in the demands it made on the audience, fostered a heightened attention to things. The force of Sontag's argument was thus, in sum, that, 'In place of a hermeneutics we need an erotics of art'.[10]

Writing a year later (1965) in 'On style', Sontag nuanced her erotics. 'The great task' remaining to critical theory was to examine 'the formal function of subject-matter'. Until this function was properly explored it was 'inevitable that critics will go on treating works of art as "statements"', and to treat art in this way, though 'not wholly irrelevant', was to make the mistake of 'putting art to use', of using it 'for such purposes as inquiring into the history of ideas, diagnosing contemporary culture, or creating social solidarity'. To use art to create social solidarity need not, one might thing, be such a bad thing. So strongly, however, did Sontag feel the cultural imperative to argue for the privileging of style that anything which smacked of a statement – and so drew attention from style back to content – had to be excluded from her project. To dramatise the issue, and, as she thought, to prove the viability of this position, she turned the terms of her argument to the Nazi-implicated artist Leni Riefenstahl. 'To call Leni Riefenstahl's *The Triumph of the Will* and *The Olympiad* master pieces', she argued,

> is not to gloss over Nazi propaganda with aesthetic lenience. The Nazi propaganda is there. But something else is there, too, which we reject at our loss. Because they project the complex movements of intelligence and grace and sensuousness ... we find ourselves – to be sure, rather uncomfortably – seeing 'Hitler' and not Hitler, the '1936 Olympics' and not the 1936 Olympics. Through Riefenstahl's genius as a film maker, the 'content' has – let us even assume, against her intentions – come to play a purely formal role.

What Riefenstahl's films surely really indicate is not that content can become form, but that in certain situations form can become content; the film's 'grace and sensuousness' coming to serve an explicitly propagandistic role. That Sontag could not see this, in 1965, indicated quite how radically considerations of content had come to be excluded from thinking about art. Having pursued her aesthetic of radical stylistic experiment as far as she had (driven, it must be remembered, by real cultural changes which really did require a new sensibility), Sontag had arrived at a position whereby she could deal with political questions at best only very 'uncomfortably'. Or, as she explained in 'Notes on "camp"', 'To emphasize style is to slight content, or to introduce an attitude which is neutral with respect to content. It goes without saying that the Camp sensibility is disengaged, depoliticized – or at least apolitical.'[11]

Against Interpretation – the volume in which these essays were collected – was dated the moment it was published, and what dated it was precisely its attitude to matters of politics. There was much truth in Sontag's claim that art should be an 'instrument for modifying and educating sensibility', that such art must be 'in principle, experimental', and even that such art is 'notably apolitical and undidactic, or, rather, infra-didactic'. But had she been writing a year or two later – after President Johnson had escalated the war in Vietnam, and after the consequences of the escalation had begun to play out nightly on American television screens – it is unlikely that Sontag would have been quite so sanguine.[12]

Writing in 1968 about what he called the 'generation of 1962', Paul Carroll was less sanguine. He agreed with Sontag that experimentalism was the order of the day, believing, as has been observed, that his generation of poets was 'creating and innovating a complex of new ways in which to view our common condition'. Given the changed circumstances, however, Carroll could not admit, even if he thought it, that such poetry was therefore 'apolitical and undidactic'. Arguing that previous generations had excluded politics on the grounds that it was not 'pure' enough for poetry, he contended that 'Nothing could be more alien to this attitude than the exploration of political convictions, prejudices and indignations by many of the new poets.'[13] The problem is, Carroll readily admits, 'Not all of the political poetry of this generation ... is particularly good.'[14] Carroll practices here what was an entirely typical contemporary manoeuvre – Simpson had performed it a year before – calling on the one hand for politically committed poetry, and acknowledging on the other that most, if not all, of the poetry which declared its political commitment was, in fact, barely poetry. And how could it be, poetry worthy of the name in the 1960s generally being held to be that which was uncertain enough (of itself and its world) to experiment towards new ways of seeing? But if this argument is easy enough to make now, it was not at the time, and the critical pressure was on to find a way of speaking about poetry which could somehow articulate both impulses.

Carroll's effort centred on the idea of impurity. The present generation's incorporation of 'the impure', Carroll felt, was 'an innovation of the first order in the art of American poetry'. He introduced the idea with reference to his generation's willingness to discuss things political, but he explores it in detail in a discussion of Ginsberg. Speaking of Ginsberg's 'Message', he suggests that the impurity lies 'in the lack of organic function or justification' of the poem's images. Ginsberg's images 'are simply there'. What Carroll means to denote in speaking of the impure elements of a Ginsberg poem is the way the poet simply names things and places, for no other reason than to incorporate them into the poem, the point of the gesture being to 'open unexpected doors previously locked and allow more reality than ever to enter the poem'. But if it would seem that by being impure the poet might manage both to develop a new sensibility and to declare his political opinions, the resolution is merely terminological. The point about the impure images in Ginsberg's poem, Carroll points out, is that they stand on their 'own two or three feet', that, as he says, they 'lack', and so implicitly deny the need for, 'justification'.[15] In other words, they do not require, and in fact refute, interpretation. So, if politics is, as Carroll suggests, an impure element in the poem, it must be a different kind of impure element, because to speak politically is necessarily to invoke notions of justice and justification, notions that formal impurity seems intended to deny. In all but name Carroll's impurity was another form of Sontag's erotics.

Carroll was hardly alone in failing to reconcile the competing pressures facing the American poet in the 1960s, few if any poets having the resources to resolve dilemmas which, as critics have argued, have had a lasting impact on the state of the art.[16] In part the problem was a question of distance. Very largely driven, as Sontag among many others argued it had to be, by the need to acquaint people with the new circumstances in which they found themselves, American poetry since the war had been seeking a language of intimacy; a form of expression capable of getting close to events otherwise untouched by modern forms of communication. By sharp contrast, the war in Vietnam was a distant event, the reality of which very few poets had any real acquaintance with save through the media. And protest poetry, if it was to be at all meaningful, demanded big gestures, not nuanced utterances. As Cary Nelson puts it, 'The public life of the period … made aesthetic detachment increasingly untenable and current events began to threaten their belief in what poetry could accomplish.'[17] For Nelson, that is, the 1960s generated a double bind for poets, compelling them to engage with events in a way they were unused to, but showing them, simultaneously, that their engagement was inconsequential. It was a double bind, moreover, which went deeper than a general feeling of impotence, the presiding impulse, Nelson suggests, of postwar poetry, being thrown into serious doubt:

> As these poets move steadily toward more radically open, even dismantled, forms, their work fulfils the need repeatedly articulated in American poetry and prose for a democratically responsive and inclusive aesthetic, while largely undermining its potential for affirmation.[18]

Charles Altieri puts it more positively:

> No matter how acute one's sensibility, no matter how attentive one is to numinous energies, it is impossible to write public poetry or make poetry speak meaningfully about pressing social concerns without a return to some notion of cultural models preserving ethical ideals or images of best selves.[19]

This, for Altieri, becomes the American poet's next challenge, the conflicting impulses of the 1960s defining

> both the values and the limits of the Heraclitean desire to recover the familiar, and in so doing [making] the reader feel once again the need to reinvent Plato ... learning to live with the contradictory claims of Heraclitus and Plato has become the burden of poetry in the seventies.[20]

The effect at the time of this new burden was to divide poets. Berryman chose to subordinate political pressures to aesthetic demands, although not without qualification. Recalling a telephone conversation with Bly in interview, Berryman noted that

> he said, 'Do you mean you're not willing to read against the war?' And I said, 'No.' And he said, 'Well, I'm appalled.' And I said, 'Well, be appalled!' and hung up. I'm completely against the war – I hate everything about it. But I don't believe in works of art being used as examples.[21]

Not that Berryman didn't feel the counterpressure, immediately qualifying his remark by observing that 'I would like to write political poems but aside from "Formal Elegy," I've never been moved to do so.'[22] Kenneth Koch, who like Ashbery had marched and read against the war, tried to write a protest poem, but, discovering that he didn't have 'a talent to do that', found himself instead writing about 'The Pleasures of Peace'. For George Oppen, his Communist background notwithstanding, the issue was more clear-cut. 'If you decide to do something politically,' he told L.S. Dembo, 'you do something that has political efficacy. And if you decide to write poetry, then you write poetry, not something that you hope, or deceive yourself into believing, can save people who are suffering.'[23] Oppen's position – the implied inefficacy of which he felt very deeply – put him at odds with his friend Denise Levertov, for whom the first duty of the poet was to protest against the evil of American foreign policy. Levertov, in turn, found Robert Duncan's closely argued objections to her polemical poems pedantic to the point of immorality, and after an angry exchange of letters severed contact with him until the end of her life.[24] In his letter to *The Nation*, as has been observed, Ashbery, like Oppen, drew a distinction between the action of poetry and the action of protest, and certainly he never chose to write a protest poem. But he was acutely aware of the pressure to do so, pressure he took account of, as his prose and poetry of the period indicates, by revising his sense of the poetic occasion.

One way to view the conflicting pressures shaping and distorting American poetry in the 1960s is in terms of the period's characteristic artistic occasions. The first is the art event known as the Happening. As Susan Sontag saw it in 1962, the Happening was a conceptual art form whose function was to be understood in relation to recent art history. Happenings 'register', she suggested, 'a protest against the museum conception of art – the idea that the job of the artist is to make things to be preserved and cherished'.[25] That Happenings had this significance resulted, as Sontag saw it, from their occasional character:

> Once dismantled after a given performance or a series of performances, it is never revived, never performed again. In part, this has to do with the deliberately occasional materials which go into Happenings – paper, wooden crates, tin cans, burlap sacks, foods, walls painted for the occasion – materials which are often literally consumed, or destroyed, in the course of the performance.[26]

The significance of the Happening, as Sontag makes clear, was that in all manner of ways it would not outlast its own performance. It was an art form 'for the occasion' and was the logical conclusion of a Rosenberg-like experimentalism. The second kind of artistic occasion characteristic of the 1960s was the protest reading. Cary Nelson recalls that 'Hearing Ginsberg read "Wichita Vortex Sutra" during the war was exhilarating. In a large audience the declaration of the war's end was collectively purgative.'[27] Such exhilaration, he observes, is not easily recovered. Ginsberg's 'Pentagon Exorcism', he suggests, is 'essentially an unmodulated chant that is hardly a poem at all, retains none of the drama of its most appropriate public occasion – the 1967 march on the Pentagon.'[28] In a certain sense, Ginsberg's anti-war poetry was not unlike the Happening, being written for occasions which, in certain cases, it did not outlast. In a key respect, however, the two events are strikingly different, the difference having to do with the way the performances address their respective occasions. In the Happening, everything was always on the verge of breakdown, the passing of the period of the performance rendering the materials of the performance obsolete, and so requiring new materials – new means of communication – to be developed each time. To all intents and purposes, then, the idea of the Happening undermines communication, the audience no sooner having adjusted to the new forms of expression than new ones again are introduced. The protest poem – for all that its relevance might recede with the event for which it was written – addresses its occasion in a very different spirit; its purpose being to consolidate, to establish common ground, to hold the audience together, to communicate. To be sure, as Robert Duncan observed of Denise Levertov, such poems preach to the converted. But preaching to the converted is not all bad news. If the message of the poem is not new to anybody in the room – they are not likely to be there if it is – it can none the less perform a valuable rhetorical function: the fact of its being read (and listened to) issuing in a heightened sense of community.

It is this kind of rhetorical effect Ashbery has in mind when, much later in his career, in 'Fantasia on "The Nut-Brown Maid"' he observed that 'What I am writing to say is, the timing, not / The contents, is what matters' (HD, 85). So, while Ashbery would clearly have recognised the value of the Happening, believing strongly in the need for innovation, and while, like Duncan, he would have recoiled at the image of the protest poet trying to tell people what to think, he would have appreciated the sense of occasion implicit in the anti-war reading. For Ashbery, then, the question the conflicting impulses of the 1960s gives rise to is whether it is possible to arrive at an utterance which accommodates change, but which also, and without being preachy, manages to bring people to a shared sense of the situation in which they find themselves. One can see Ashbery turning this question over, for himself perhaps, more than his reader, in the critical prose he wrote during the 1960s.

In 'The decline of the verbs', his 1966 review of Chirico's novel *Hebdomeros* (a section of which he translated for *Art and Literature*), Ashbery observed that Chirico had 'invented for the occasion a new style and a new kind of novel which he was not to use again, but which could be of great interest to writers today who are trying to extend the novel form'.[29] In fact Ashbery would himself use Chirico's 'new style' not to extend the novel form but to break the bounds of the poem, the accelerating sentences of *Hebdomeros* informing the remarkable prose of Ashbery's *Three Poems*. Even so, there was a slight nervousness in Ashbery's voice as he justified Chirico's procedure. Using the novel to explain itself, Ashbery observes,

> Like Nietzsche and Chirico, Hebdomeros is sometimes forced to speak in 'a language that on any other occasion would have brought upon his shoulders not only the sarcasm of the crowd, which often is necessary to far-reaching minds, but also the sarcasm of the elite …'.[30]

Ashbery had himself recently incurred such sarcasm, the less friendly of reviewers referring to *The Tennis Court Oath* as just so much wreckage, and so there is an element of self-justification here. Art produced for the occasion owes its first commitment to the requirements of the occasion, and if that results in a language difficult to understand then so be it. Or as Sontag put it, 'Having one's sensorium challenged or stretched hurts.'[31] Except that Ashbery does not want to be quite so bold as Sontag. He wants to explain to both the crowd and the elite that Hebdomeros, Chirico, Nietzsche, and all those others, in fact, who sometimes adopt a difficult style, are 'forced' into it. But even then, one feels, he is not, himself, quite convinced.

That he is not quite convinced is apparent in 'Tradition and talent', a review of new books by Philip Booth, Adrienne Rich and Stanley Moss. Using Booth to define his own stance on contemporary aesthetic questions, Ashbery suggests he is an 'archetype of the conservative manner', too unwilling 'to experiment, to take risks, to believe that there can be other valuables than the established canon'.[32] Significantly though, for all his conservative manner, Booth's central failure, as Ashbery sees it, is a failure to observe the requirements of decorum. Noting that when reading Booth 'we hear a lot about people and places we do not know', Ashbery suggests that,

> Booth is here flaunting [*sic*] one of the primordial rules of social conduct by discoursing at length on topics with which his hearers are not familiar. Most of us, unfortunately, cannot gauge the rightness of 'white as / Machia after / the hayrake rain' and after a while our attention begins to wander.[33]

Ashbery, one might feel, is having it all ways. On the one hand he argues that poets should experiment, should be prepared to produce art for the occasion (even where that means alienating crowd and elite alike). On the other, he is suggesting that poets should observe the rules of social conduct. On the face of it there is a tension here, but not an unresolvable one. Critically speaking Ashbery partly resolves it in his consideration of Marianne Moore's *Tell Me, Tell Me!*, Ashbery observing that

> The subject of poetry for Miss Moore is any subject in which she might be interested. No more is necessary to establish a neutral ground where reader and writer may meet and the latter begin operations. This means remaining apparently intent on her animal or vegetable subject ... and only incidentally producing those blinding flashes of poetry that are the reward for our attentiveness.[34]

Moore's poetry is preferable to Booth's not least because, unlike him, she establishes a neutral ground on which reader and poet might meet and, as Ashbery puts it, begin operations. Moore, unlike Booth, does not flout the primordial rules of social conduct: she establishes the basis on which poet and reader can engage in communication. But what, one wonders, from Ashbery's account of the matter, are they communicating about? In her eagerness to establish common ground, Moore, Ashbery suggests, can tend to neutralise the occasion of the poem, being only 'apparently intent on her animal or vegetable subject'. The solidarity of communication is thus achieved at the cost of the contingent, of what's new.

The critical piece from this period in which this conflict came closest to resolution was 'The invisible avant-garde', Ashbery's lecture to the Yale Art School. The subject of Ashbery's lecture was the decline, or at least the transformation, of the avant-garde, and its central issue was thus the continuing validity, or otherwise, of artistic experiment. The drift of the argument was that, somewhere along the way, experimental artists had lost sight of their objectives. Opening with reference to his arrival in New York, and his first contact with Abstract Expressionism, Ashbery recalls how

> At that time I found the avant-garde very exciting, just as the young do today, but the difference was that in 1950 there was no sure proof of the existence of the avant-garde. To experiment was to have the feeling that one was poised on some outermost brink. In other words if one wanted to depart, even moderately, from the norm, one was taking one's life – one's life as an artist – into one's hands. (RS, 390)

What had made experiment worth the risk in 1950 was the felt need to develop a viable art, an art capable of re-integrating people with their surroundings. The problem as Ashbery writes in 1968 is that artistic innovation has lost its edge, experiment having become a certain kind of norm – Andy Warhol appears on the *Tonight Show* – and society dividing all too conventionally between those who do and those who don't.

> In both art and life today we are in danger of substituting one conformity for another, or, to use a French expression, of trading one's one-eyed horse for a blind one. Protests against the mediocre values of our society such as the hippie move-ment seem to imply that one's only way out is to join a parallel society whose stereotyped manners, language, speech and dress are only reverse images of the one it is trying to reject. We feel in America that we have to join something, that our lives are directionless unless we are part of a group, a clan … Is there nothing then between the extremes of Levittown and Haight-Ashbury, between an avant-garde which has become a tradition and a tradition which is no longer one? (RS, 393)

The point of the lecture is to indicate that there is something between these extremes, that all is not lost for the avant-garde artist, even if he now has to re-identify himself as a member of the post-avant-garde.

What the third way involves is not, as Ashbery makes very clear, calling for a halt to artistic experiment. It does, however, involve reconsidering the relation of the experimental artist to the general public. 'If people like what I do,' Ash-bery asks, 'am I to assume that what I do is bad, since public opinion has always begun by rejecting what is original and new?' (RS, 393). This is not a question Ashbery would have been likely to ask while he was writing *The Tennis Court Oath*, his second book aiming quite deliberately – though not irresponsibly – at unacceptability. What his lecture contemplates, by contrast, is the possibility of a publicly viable experimental art. In fact, of course, for all that it might have slipped to the back of his mind for a while in Paris, this is not a new thought for Ashbery, the collaborations of the New York School aiming precisely at integra-tion through experiment. And as he now reassesses the relation of the experi-mental artist to his or her culture, it is towards a more collaborative sense of the occasion of the utterance that he begins to turn his attention. That this is so is apparent in the poems of the period – in *Rivers and Mountains* and, more so, in *The Double Dream of Spring* – but it is apparent also in the style of his lecture.

Historically, innovative American writers have put the lecture to good use: Emerson in particular subverting the preachy expectations of Harvard's 'Divinity School Address' to prompt his audience to reflect on their situation.[35]

Ashbery did something similar at Yale. As a guest lecturer Ashbery had been given the opportunity to declare his opinions on a question of pressing concern. But he does not make a declaration; quite the opposite. 'The fact that I, a poet,' he opens,

> was invited by the Yale Art School to talk about the avant-garde, in one of a series of lectures under this general heading, is in itself such an eloquent characterization of the avant-garde today that no further comment seems necessary. (RS, 389)

Far from using the occasion to make a declaration, the occasion, Ashbery suggests, can speak for itself. He does, of course, continue to speak, because he has been contracted to do so; and because the occasion will not be complete if he is not speaking. But he plainly feels, and in some sense is right to feel, that nothing he can say can alter the fundamental force of his utterance: that twenty years ago he would not have been here because twenty years ago no one would have noticed his existence. Here, then, in the ideal speech situation of a lecture (ideal because everybody involved knows, or thinks they know, what to expect), Ashbery performs his sense of occasion. His opening gambit is curious, intriguing even. The point of Ashbery's intrigue is to invite his audience themselves to reflect on the occasion, to work out for themselves why it is that their presence combined with the poet's is so eloquent that no further characterisation is necessary. He calls on his audience to reflect on the occasion in which they too are participating, to which they too contribute, and the significance of which they too are more than capable of grasping. Ashbery, in other words, sets out to use the occasion not as an opportunity to preach to his audience – they do not need a poet telling them what to think – but to draw their attention to the occasion itself, and so to draw their attention to what they have in common. It is by just such a manoeuvre that in his strongest poetry of the 1960s Ashbery comes to handle the conflicting pressures of the period – not protesting perhaps, but bringing a public dimension to experimental poetry.

Rivers and Mountains is a lonely book. Like *The Tennis Court Oath*, it was written in Paris, the earliest poem in the collection dating from 1961 and the latest from 1965. Unlike in *The Tennis Court Oath*, however, the loneliness of *Rivers and Mountains* is not a consequence of the poet's expatriate status; not primarily at least. By the early 1960s Ashbery had successfully integrated with Parisian literary and artistic culture. He was art critic at the Paris office of the *New York Herald Tribune*. He was writing translations of American popular fiction for French publishers. He was publishing poems and essays in French magazines, most notably *Tel Quel*. The loneliness of *Rivers and Mountains* is not so much, therefore, that of the American abroad, out of touch with his new environment and the people and things he finds there. It is the loneliness, rather, of the experimental poet; the deliberate solitude of a period of intense concentration.

Not that the two states are entirely unconnected. Reflecting on this phase of his career in a review of a Jane Freilicher retrospective, Ashbery has observed that 'After the early period of absorbing influences from the art and other things going on around one comes a period when one locks the door in order to sort out what one has and to make of it what one can' (RM, 241). *Rivers and Mountains* has the air of a book written with the door locked firmly shut; the poet always at work in the 'middle class apartment' which is the explicit setting for most of the poems in the book. Paris had thus come to mean for Ashbery what he subsequently took it to mean for Stein. No longer on the outside, but not, as he would have been in New York, absolutely in the thick of things, Paris had become a good place to work. Stein, he would later observe, was probably insulated by the foreign language that surrounded her as she wrote *The Making of Americans*, but in the good sense that this was 'probably also a necessary insulation for the immense effort of concentration that this book required'. *Rivers and Mountains* is likewise the result of an immense effort of concentration, Ashbery being engaged, more self-consciously than ever, in the lonely task of developing a language equal to the rapid cultural change that had always been the premise of his writing; a language equal to the flow of its contemporary environment.

There is, however, a paradox in this. Having absorbed enough influences to set about making a language equal to its environment, and having locked the door in order to do so, the environment in which Ashbery now found himself (his apartment) was practically unchanging. In *Rivers and Mountains*, as the poems repeatedly remind us, the poet is always in his study. Arguably there is nothing exceptional about this. It is the condition, after all, of being a poet. Except to say that Ashbery, like O'Hara, had previously made a practice of writing in all manner of environments – bars, cars and Greenwich Village coffee shops – and also that Ashbery's mood during the writing of *Rivers and Mountains* is a good deal more studious than normal. So much so that the least interruption, the visit of the postman say, becomes an event of epic proportions.

> A postman is coming up the walk, a letter held in his
>   outstretched hand.
> This is his first day on the new job, and he looks warily around
> Alas not seeing the hideous bulldog bearing down on him like sixty,
>   its hellish eyes fixed on the seat of his pants, jowls a-slaver.

> (RM, 50)

One means by which Ashbery handles this paradoxical condition of his writing in *Rivers and Mountains* is to engage in an oblique (but clearly audible) dialogue with the one notably new presence in the volume, Thoreau. That Thoreau is on Ashbery's mind in *Rivers and Mountains* is evident from the natural imagery which is oddly, but unmistakably, the book's dominant currency, the rural elements of the book's title seeping into: the title of the first poem ('These Lacustrie Cities'), the fields and swamps of the title poem, the 'upland pastures' and 'swamps' of 'Civilization and its Discontents', the freezing rivers of 'Into the Dusk-Charged Air', the islands and 'Creek' of 'The Thousand Islands', the momentum of 'Clepsydra', and the icy central scene of 'The

Skaters'. Wooded, swampy, watery, icy, *Rivers and Mountains* is, in its rhetoric at least, one of the most environmental works by an American since *Walden*.

Why Ashbery should have had Thoreau in mind as he wrote *Rivers and Mountains* is apparent from the similarity of the writers' positions. Like *Walden*, Ashbery's third book is the work of a writer in retreat from society, cutting himself off in order to develop a language capable of making meaningful contact with the circumstances in which he finds himself. There is then, as Ashbery seems to see it, a fundamental similarity between his situation and Thoreau's, Thoreau being the type of the experimental writer. But there are crucial differences also, the most important being that, whereas Thoreau gladly shunned company, Ashbery conceives of his isolation in *Rivers and Mountains* as a necessary evil. For all its loneliness 'The Skaters' is not, therefore, as Charles Molesworth suggested, 'a paean to solipsism', because it is not, as this implies, an articulation of loneliness as a philosophically unavoidable condition.[36] It is the loneliness, rather, of a poet engaged in the immense effort of developing a language which will ultimately be capable of articulating a shared sense of its occasion. Cutting himself off in the interests, eventually, of communicating more effectively with his contemporaries, Ashbery endures rather than celebrates his solitude.

In *Rivers and Mountains*, as often in an Ashbery collection, the first poem serves to set the new scene. 'These Lacustrine Cities' thus opens with a densely sweeping history of people's relation to their environment: from fear and loathing, through the cultivated forms (the cities) by which they come to protect themselves from that environment, to a sense of the stifling order those forms produce, and so to a useless nostalgia for a past (and especially a past relationship with nature) that never actually existed.[37] The poet's reaction to this situation is to announce a change of tack. Hitherto, the poem observes, 'Much of your time has been occupied by creative games' (RM, 9). From now on, an Audenesque authority figure informs him, 'we have all-inclusive plans for you. / We had thought, for instance, of sending you to the middle / of the desert.' The voice is that of the poet's intention, outlining for both the reader's benefit and his own what he means to do in the present volume. His plans are 'all-inclusive' in the sense that, as 'The Skaters' in particular makes clear, his object now (and in contrast to *The Tennis Court Oath*) is to develop a language capable of absorbing its environment. In so far as 'the desert' is one possible location for such an undertaking, this task is clearly held to require isolation. Hence the poet's paradoxical condition: his newly all-inclusive writing being developed in an environment where there is little or nothing to include. This, as the ominous Audenesque voice puts it, is the 'logic / Of your situation'.

'These Lacustrine Cities' thus tells the history of its own coming into being, extending the reach of Ashbery's language even as it presents a highly elaborated image of the poet endeavouring to do so. The densely sweeping narrative with which the poem opens – knowing (and loathing) its own faintly ludicrous abstract status, but serving also to apprise the reader of the aesthetic assumptions which are part of the poet's background – will subsequently become an integral part of Ashbery's writing, *Three Poems* in particular developing his brand of mytho-history. It is a narrative mode which owes something to early Auden, an influence of which Ashbery is now able to make serious use.[38] In particular what Ashbery learns from Auden here is intrigue, the ominous voices and the beguiling images making the poem compelling reading even as its subject is the apparently dry one of the poet experimenting with his style.

This need, from both reader's and poet's point of view, to make linguistic innovation compelling reading is very much on Ashbery's mind in *Rivers and Mountains*. Witness the title poem, which is extraordinary not only for the syntactical developments it introduces into Ashbery's writing but for the interest it stimulates in that process, the poem's innovations being threaded together by snippets of plot-lines from popular-fiction:

> On the secret map the assassins
> Cloistered
>
> (RM, 10)

> Your plan was to separate the enemy into two groups
> With the razor-edged mountains between.
>
> (RM, 11)

The point of such intriguing fragments is to inveigle the reader into the poem's aesthetic manoeuvres; manoeuvres which, roughly speaking, take three forms. In the first place, the poem presents a situation not only in which has representation lost touch with its environment but in which the map has become the territory. Positioning itself at a late point in the history of American adventuring, the poem finds itself at the

>   wan ending
> Of the trail among dry, papery leaves
> Gray-brown quills like thoughts
> In the melodious but vast mass of today's
> Writing through fields and swamps
> Marked, on the map, with little bunches of weeds.
>
> (RM, 10)

The poem's response to this potentially wan ending, to this state of affairs in which people see not fields and swamps but the cartographer's inadequate representations of them, is to recall earlier American writers who have sought to re-acquaint writing with its environment. We glimpse Thoreau 'in the woods' while 'dull sleep still / Hung over the land'; Twain in 'these moonless nights spent as on a raft'; and William James in the image of the map as 'a tender but tough bark / On everything'.[39] The point of the allusions is to remind the reader of that tradition of the new in terms of which Ashbery's own experimental strategies make sense. And chief among these, as the breathlessly long sentence which makes up the whole of the second paragraph of the poem makes clear, is the mobilisation of poetic syntax. Too long to quote in full, the sentence begins:

> So going around cities
> To get to other places you found
> It all on paper but the land
> Was made of paper processed
> To look like ferns, mud or other
> Whose sea unrolled its magic
> Distances and then rolled them up
> Its secret was only a pocket
> After all but some corners are darker
> Than these moonless nights spent as on a raft ...
>
> (RM, 10)

Poetry like this is not, as in *The Tennis Court Oath*, entirely at odds with ordinary speech. But it is not entirely at one with it either. At key moments in its progress this sentence goes further than the reader expects. The conjunction in the third line, while not leading to a non-sequitur exactly, does not offer the direct reversal of sense one anticipates either. What it leads to, instead, is an invigorating digression. Likewise, with almost every clause there is an introduction of new material, the sentence coming to accommodate information which it had not foreseen at its outset. Learned, if anywhere, from the British poet F.T. Prince, but more mobile than anything to be found in Prince, such sentences are entirely characteristic of *Rivers and Mountains*: their digressive syntactical energy producing a sped of response which as much as anything has come to fit Ashbery's poetry for its postwar environment.

Not all the poems in *Rivers and Mountains* are quite so compelling, not least because at times the poet seems to be finding it hard to stick to his task. 'Civilization and Its Discontents', for instance, is a rather disconsolate exploration of the poet's lonely situation, the poem being an ingeniously extended quibble with Thoreau. The Freudian title appeals directly to the isolatoe's mindset, the discontents of civilisation providing the impulse for total withdrawal; except that, as the poem unfolds, what it actually describes is the emptiness of the self-sufficient life. The poem itself is self-sufficient from the start. Needing to get itself going, but with no external support (nothing new in its environment) to draw on, the poem reflects on beginnings: 'A people chained to aurora / I alone disarming you / Millions of facts of distributed light' (RM, 14). Familiar as she is as a figure for dawn – and thus a good place to begin for a poet who is struggling to get going – Ashbery's reference to the Roman goddess Aurora might come from, or lead him to, any number of writers. Among Americans, however, nobody was more taken with 'Aurora' than Thoreau, it being absolutely central to *Walden* to restore his reader to what he terms the morning condition. As he puts it in the context of a justification of his domestic arrangements:

> Morning work! By the blushes of Aurora and the music of Memmon, what should be man's *morning work* in this world? I had three pieces of limestone on my desk,

but I was terrified to find that they required to be dusted daily, when the furniture of my mind was all undusted still, and I threw them out the window in disgust. How, then, could I have a furnished house? I would rather sit in the open air, for no dust gathers on the grass, unless where man has broken ground.[40]

'Civilization and Its Discontents' is an act of dusting, the poem no sooner mentioning 'aurora' than it demythologises her as 'millions of facts of distributed light'. The poet thus disarms the reader of a habit of thought which distances him from the reality of his situation. That Ashbery is quibbling with Thoreau here – pointing out that Thoreau had recourse to forms of language which dulled not enlivened the mind – is indicated by the poem's shift from the act of demythologising to the act of furnishing a house: 'Helping myself with some big boxes / Up the steps, then turning to no neighbourhood' (RM, 14). Like Thoreau, Ashbery, as a self-exiled experimental poet, must help himself into his new environment. As he moves in, therefore, and as in *Walden*, there are no neighbours around to give him a hand. The difference is that for Ashbery self-reliance is not a virtue in and of itself, his defining sense of self being as something porous and so dependent on others. The poem is thus at pains to remind us how much the poet misses company: 'You must not, then, / Be very surprised if I am alone: it is all for you, / The night, and the stars, and the way we used to be' (RM, 14). 'Civilization and Its Discontents' is an elegant performance, enacting self-reliance (in that the whole piece takes its momentum from its opening image) while at the same time arguing with its implications.[41] There is, however, something thin about the result, the poem's reflexivity producing a measure of inwardness which runs against the grain of Ashbery's better instincts.

For the most part, however, in *Rivers and Mountains* Ashbery's experiments are remarkably compelling, 'Clepysdra' being a strong case in point. Ashbery's now hugely extended sentences moving on from themselves at such a pace as to render critical analysis virtually impossible, this poem's meaning is more than ever in its impact on the reader. And that impact is all but overwhelming, the relentless speed of the poem's transitions appearing to leave the reader little choice but to go with the flow. This can be exhilarating or exasperating depending on one's point of view. Either way, however, the purpose of the poem is not simply to chart the speed with which events now appear to flow towards one, but, as far as possible, to find ways of living with that flow. In the first place, then, there are moments of relief in this poem; moments when, although the flow has by no means ceased, a feeling of clarity sets in. The poem does not linger unduly over such moments, but they are here, and the beauty of the poem lies in the unexpectedness of their appearance.

> Or it was
> Like standing at the edge of a harbor early on a summer morning
> With the discreet shadows cast by the water all around
> And a feeling, again, of emptiness, but of richness in the way
> The whole thing is organized, on what a miraculous scale

(RM, 30)

Such moments are familiar – Wordsworth called them spots of time, Eliot called them still points – and Ashbery's poetry does not deny the reader the reality of their satisfactions. But the reality, also, as this poem observes, is that such moments are always slipping away, and no sooner, in fact, than they have manifested themselves. So Ashbery's poem moves on, and in moving on asks the central post-Romantic question (to which he will return in *Three Poems*) what is one to do with such moments of clarity once they have gone.

The second sense in which 'Clepsydra' lives with, rather than simply in, the flow has to do with the poet's speed of thought. Thus for all the relentlessness of its perpetual advance, 'Clepsydra' is an argumentative poem: discoursing on Romantic and modernist aesthetics even as in its practice it is moving dramatically beyond them. It is not, therefore, a poem without an organising mind. What makes its measure of organisation plausible to its reality, however, is the fact that the mind in question is almost always, though never quite, losing control. Writing in 1964, a year before Ashbery wrote 'Clepsydra', Sontag argued that 'What is important now is to recover our senses. We must learn to see more, to hear more, to feel more.' 'Clepsydra' suggests that nobody felt the force of this cultural imperative more strongly than Ashbery. So too, more importantly, does 'The Skaters'.

'The Skaters', the long poem with which Ashbery concludes *Rivers and Mountains*, is an extraordinary achievement, more than justifying the period of experimental exile, which, as it reflects on the circumstances out of which it emerges, becomes the poem's urgent, and brilliantly elaborated theme. The title, as critics have observed, recalls the skaters passage in *The Prelude*. There are, however, skaters in *Walden* also, Thoreau (himself alluding to Wordsworth, perhaps) giving extended attention to the minute operations of those water insects which inhabit the surface of his pond.[42] Ashbery's title is thus a deft allusion: Wordsworth's autobiographical poem being important background reading in so far as 'The Skaters' observes not the growth of a mind over a period of time, but the operations of mind in the time of their happening; Thoreau's prose providing a model for Ashbery's practice, the poet's intention in tracking the operations of mind being precisely to sensitise his language to the 'intensity of minor acts' (RM, 37).

Part of the achievement of 'The Skaters' is its structure, the mind-bending flow of 'Clepysdra' giving way, here, to a discernibly musical style of development. In a statement about his poetry published a year after 'The Skaters', Ashbery suggested a comparison between his poetry and music. 'What I like about music', he observed, 'is its ability of … carrying an argument through successfully to the finish, though the terms of the argument remain unknown quantities … I would like to do this in poetry.'[43] The four parts of 'The Skaters' carry Ashbery's argument in the manner of a quartet: the first part establishing the poem's subject, the second exploring that subject by introducing its background, the third deepening understanding of the subject by darkening its implications, and the fourth recapitulating the poem's argument by way of a coda.

The poem opens with an image of the poet at work, listening to what would appear to be skaters outside his window, and, as he makes clear, endeavouring to track the fluctuations of his environment: 'But the water surface ripples, the whole light changes' (RM, 34). His subject is the painful necessity of such intense attention, hence the shock of the first three lines of the poem: 'These decibels / Are a kind of flagellation, an entity of sound / Into which being enters and is apart (RM, 34). Ashbery's decibels are as the 'Sounds' of Thoreau's forest. Devoting a chapter to such 'Sounds', Thoreau picks out the calls of certain birds – the '*Hoo hoo hoo, hoorer, hoo*' of the owl, for instance – describing them as a '*tintinnabulum*'.[44] Ashbery is listening similarly hard. So hard, in fact, that the sounds with which the poem opens strike him not as the ringing of a bell but as a kind of tinnitus, a 'flagellation'. What this implies is not only the level at which the poet has come to concentrate but also the cost of such intense attention.

The cost of intense attention, as this first part of the poem sees it, is a Stevens-like imprecision. There is, the speaker observes, 'error / In so much precision. As flames are fanned, wishful / thinking arises' (RM, 38). The errors of precision are twofold. The first, simply, is that being precise about one thing means being imprecise, or negligent, about another: 'Leaving phrases unfinished, / Gestures half-sketched against woodsmoke' (RM, 37). The second, more problematically for the poet, is that in seeking to refine one's language as a means of paying better attention to things, it is one's expression, not that which is being expressed, which invariably becomes the object of one's attention. This is the central concern of 'The Skaters'. Always in this poem the consciousness is drifting away from its occasion, a word giving off an association which in turn gives rise to separate thought. Always, eventually, the poem will come back to the scene of the writing: 'It is already after lunch, the men are returning to their / positions around the cement mixer' (RM, 36). But never for long, association tugging against reference as the drift of language starts up again.

Much of the ironic beauty of 'The Skaters' lies in its willingness to follow this drift: memories, reveries, fantasies and catalogues, scrolling out into marvelously expansive metaphors, the subject of which is language itself. It is in such scrolling that the poem most clearly develops Ashbery's powers of expression, the poet learning to take in whatever comes to hand or mind, and to pursue it through the full course of its associations. But this is the poem's defining weakness also, as the poet is at pains to observe in the poem's clearest self-commentary.

> But this is an important aspect of the question
> Which I am not ready to discuss, am not at all ready to,
> This leaving-out business. On it hinges the very importance
>   of what's novel.
> Or autocratic, or dense or silly. It is as well to call attention
> To it by exaggeration, perhaps. But calling attention
> Isn't the same thing as explaining, and as I said I am not ready
> To line phrases with the costly stuff of explanation, and shall not,

Will not do so for the moment. Except to say that the carnivorous
Way of these lines is to devour their own nature, leaving
Nothing but a bitter impression of absence, which as we know
    involves presence, but still.

                                                                         (RM, 39)

This is a crucial passage – one to which Ashbery will return at various moments in his career – articulating as it does a reflexivity of language which becomes critical to his sense of the poem's relation to its occasion. The question the passage asks is how best to heighten attention. Simply to explain to the reader that his purpose was to heighten attention would be self-defeating, the autocratic pose of the explanatory poet being more likely, as Ashbery sees it, to produce a passive (and so inattentive) than an active reader. Thoreau knew this, hence the challenge of his text. What Thoreau did not observe was that simply to pay heightened attention to things through one's writing is also, invariably, self-defeating; attention to things becoming attention to language, while the environment of the utterance slips from view. The answer to this problem, as Ashbery observes, in a formulation which will characterise his practice in *The Double Dream of Spring* and which builds into his writing an altogether new scope, is to 'call attention'. Writing which the reader knows, because it knows itself, to be drifting from its occasion, never actually loses sight of that occasion. Writing, that is, which knows it calls attention to itself can, in calling attention to that fact, call attention in turn to that which it knows it is leaving out. The beauty of inflection, in other words, can give rise to the beauty of innuendo. Profusions of style can sharpen sense.

The development of the 'The Skaters' is a looping exploration of this insight. In the second part of the poem Ashbery develops his argument by wondering how it is he has come to be in experimental exile in the first place. How is it, he asks, 'that you are always indoors, peering at too / heavily canceled stamps through a greasy magnifying / glass?' (RM, 42). The answer to this question is not so hard, the poet telling the history of the poem's coming into being by offering a semi-autobiographical account of leaving New York for Paris. The harder question is how, now he finds himself in exile, he can justify the impoverished conditions in which he finds himself, 'How excuse it to oneself? The wetness and coldness?' (RM, 48). The justification for his ascetic lifestyle – and Ashbery, it should be recalled, could not afford to travel home at this point – is the heightened attention it produces. The logic is straight from Thoreau, the relative poverty which follows from experimental writing being the necessary condition for the success of the experiment. Thus the poem finds the poet gazing at a 'rusted tomato can' (RM, 48). Nothing, it seems, is too insignificant for his democratic attention.

Part three deepens the theme by posing the question of communication, the poet reflecting on the irony that his commitment to the language leaves him '"Frei aber Einsam" (Free but Alone)' (RM, 54). Free to fantasise at length that he is marooned on a desert island, but cut off from 'life in the streets'. Free to develop a form of expression equal to the flow of its contemporary environment, but lonely by dint of being peculiar in having done so. It is the experimental poet's dilemma, and one with which Thoreau was happy to live. 'It is', he judged, 'a ridiculous demand which England and America make, that you shall speak so that they can understand you. Neither men nor toad-stols grow so.'[45] It is not a ridiculous demand, and only a writer who was entirely persuaded of the virtues of self-reliance could think it so. Ashbery is not so persuaded, not least because in his late twentieth-century environment he can barely credit the idea of an independent self. Self, as he sees it, is not at odds with its social environment, but as Pasternak thought, reliant for its identity upon it. Hence the acute awkwardness of Ashbery's necessary self-exile, and hence also his eagerness, in the final part of 'The Skaters', to mingle with others once again. His house, he tells us, 'could use a coat of paint / Except that I am too poor to hire a workman' (RM, 61). Thoreau, was also to poor to hire a workman, but took it as a test of his independence not to do so. Ashbery, by contrast, knows he needs help. Having holed himself up in order to develop a language porous enough to articulate its environment and the self it shapes, it was time to integrate once again.

It's hard to imagine a poem Susan Sontag would like more than 'The Skaters'. By calling attention both to the environment of its own writing and to the styles by which it does and does not express that environment, the poem clarifies the readers' sense of their own situation.

> We step out into the street, not realizing that the street is different,
> And so it shall be all our lives; only from this moment on, nothing
>   will ever be the same again.
>
> (RM, 57)

The poet imaging his impact on his ideal reader, a moment such is this is wishful thinking. It is not however, unjustified, the very real effect of the poem's attention to its present being (if one will let it) to insert the reader into his or her own. The poem thus demonstrates all that is best about the Sontag thesis. It also, however, shares Sontag's weakness. Witness,

>   A revolution
>   in Argentina! Think of it! Bullets flying through
>   the air, men on the move;
> Great passions inciting to massive expenditures of energy,
>   changing the lives of many individuals.
> Yet it is all offered as "today's news," as if we somehow
>   had a right to it, as though it were a part of our lives
> That we'd be silly to refuse. Here, have another – crime or
>   revolution? Take your pick.
>
> (RM, 57)[46]

The trouble here is that, as the passage is well aware, having adjusted his language to the intensity of minor acts, the poet can't really think about major ones: their distance from him and the manner in which they are mediated rendering them practically meaningless. All he can think about, in fact, is the difficult of thinking about them. Which would, perhaps, have been acceptable, except that by the time *Rivers and Mountains* was published the pressure to think meaningfully about distant events had become immense, and even the most professional of exiles could not afford to be so sanguine. *The Double Dream of Spring* responds to that pressure.

The Double Dream of Spring opens with a statement of fresh concerns, the first poem, 'The Task', outlining the volume's objectives.

> They are preparing to begin again:
> Problems, new pennant up the flagpole
> In a predicated romance.

(RM, 13)

The present volume, the reader is advised, means to make a new beginning. There are new problems to be addressed; problems that have something to do with flags – and so something, apparently, to do with the state of the nation – and which appear in turn to entail what the poet calls a 'predicated romance'. This is a tense phrase, casting back for its meaning to the nature of the previous volume. *Rivers and Mountains* was an unpredicated romance, its extraordinary inventiveness owing largely to the fact that there was nothing pressing in the poet's environment. It was, as 'The Task' harshly observes, 'only / Cloud-castles'. Mostly written after the poet's return to America, and with the pressure mounting on the American poet to declare his opposition to the nation's foreign policy, *The Double Dream of Spring* could not afford to be so fanciful. It is, then, by contrast, a 'predicated romance': the poet still insisting on the need for free expression, while in the same breath acknowledging that his utterances are now necessarily coloured by prevailing conditions.

The particular condition 'The Task' observes is the need to develop a form of expression which, without sacrificing attention to the minor acts which make up its environment, somehow takes account of distant events. The second paragraph of the poem thus outlines the poet's sense that his writing must now be more worldly. Worldly in the sense of extending its scope: 'About the time the sun begins to cut laterally across / The western hemisphere with its shadows, its carnival echoes, / The fugitive lands crowd under separate names' (DDS, 13). Worldly also in the sense that the poet must now immerse himself again in the realities of American life: 'And the way is clear / Now for linear acting into that time / In whose corrosive mass he first discovered how to breathe'. What this adds up to is the intention the poem outlines in its final paragraph. 'I plan to stay here a little while / For these are moments only, moments of insight, / And there are reaches to be attained.' Without sacrificing his attention to the momentary, Ashbery's plan in *The Double Dream of Spring* is to give his poetry new reach.

In expanding the reach of his utterance to take account of distant events which, one way or another, have a shaping impact on the occasion of the poem

– and in so doing taking account of the process of globalisation that, in a certain sense, first makes itself felt through the televising of the war in Vietnam – Ashbery does not abandon his fundamental poetic procedures. Indeed there is a certain sense in which the extended experiments of *Rivers and Mountains* have their real pay-off in *The Double Dream Spring*, Ashbery's fourth volume proving able to incorporate more styles and more voices (and so, in the process, more kinds of information) than ever before. The volume's title is borrowed from a painting by De Chirico, a section of whose experimental novel *Hebdomeros* Ashbery had recently translated. The title of the opening poem is borrowed from a poem by William Cowper, Cowper's 'The Task' being a poem of epic proportions addressed to a sofa, and so which itself negotiates the demands of the apparently major and the apparently minor. The Clare-like prose poem 'For John Clare' honours the minor British Romantic who would eventually become the subject of one of Ashbery's Charles Eliot Norton Lectures. Arthur Cravan, early twentieth-century experimental French poet and founder of the magazine *Maintenant*, is roughly translated, Ashbery's 'Some Words' being a version of Cravan's 'Des Paroles'. Ella Wheeler Wilcox, writer of popular doggerel, is treated to a parody. Auden makes an appearance in the black doggerel of 'It Was Raining in the Capital'. Popeye, Olive and Swee'pea figure in the cartoon sestina 'Farm Implements and Rutabagas in a Landscape'. 'Happy Hooligan', a cartoon character designed to aid the American Army's recruitment drive during the campaign in Vietnam, crops up in 'Soonest Mended'. Two poems, Decoy' and 'Definition of Blue', are spoken by lecturers, public orators with something to declare. 'French Poems' is a translation into English of poems Ashbery first wrote in French. And, throughout, the volume is a mixture of *vers libre* and regular form: the first poem, 'The Task', with its deliberate intent, being an instance of free verse; the last, the meditative, improvisional long poem 'Fragment', taking the disciplined form of a series of dizains.

The effect of this absorbing of differing voices – high and low, comic and serious, declarative and experimental, free and constrained – is to render more fully than ever the occasion of the poetry's writing. Whether quoted directly or incorporated obliquely, the impression given is of poetry which contains all the voices of its moment: all those voices which, while they are not exactly in conversation here, constitute the cultural background against (and in knowledge of) which successful communication has to take place. Written at a moment of great divergence and dispute in American society, *The Double Dream of Spring* is thus, according to the assumptions of the Ashberyan aesthetic, a poetic utterance appropriate to its occasion. Or at least it would be, were it not that the really pressing question posed by this volume, for both the reader and the poet himself, is whether that aesthetic is itself now appropriate: whether, at a time when, from one point of view at least, the call is for tough talk, poetry as sponge can afford a suitable response. That this question occurs to Ashbery is apparent from the presence in *The Double Dream of Spring* of a voice new to his poetry: the voice of a critic (or, more precisely, a poet-critic) urging him to make a protest. In 'The

Hod Carrier', for instance, the poet is chastised, or chastises himself, for his poetry's refusal to make itself clear.

Are these floorboards, to be stared at
In moments of guilt, as wallpaper can stream away and yet

You cannot declare it?

(DDS, 58)

With the poet's aesthetic insistence on matters of background trivialised as 'wallpaper', the salient voice here is the accusatory one, castigating the poet for his inability to declare. Likewise in 'An Outing', a speaker resembling (but also, again, parodying) the poet observes how '"My activity is as random as the wind. / Why should I insist? The visitor is free to go, / Or to stay, as he chooses"' (DDS, 60). To which a tougher, terser, voice objects: '"I think you shd make yr decision"'. The abbreviations are from Corso, or Ginsberg perhaps; from the voice, anyway, of the protesting poet.

With this voice firmly in mind, there are moments throughout this volume when the poetry can be heard responding to the pressure to declare. 'Variations, Calypso and Fugue on a Theme of Ella Wheeler Wilcox' (which, as the medley of its title suggests, is one of Ashbery's more absorbent poems) concludes by resisting just such a pressure.

Weak as he was, Gustavus Hertz raised himself on his elbow. He stared wildly about him, peering fearfully into the shadowy corners of the room.
'I will tell you nothing! Nothing, do you hear?' he shrieked. 'Go away! Go away!' (DDS, 29)

'For John Clare' arrives at a similarly defensive conclusion:

But the others – and they in some way must know too – it would never occur to them to want to, even if they could take the first step of the terrible journey toward feeling somebody should act, that ends in utter confusion and hopelessness, east of the sun and west of the moon. So their comment is: 'No comment'. (DDS, 36)

The pressure here is for an action not a declaration, but the result, as before, is 'confusion and hopelessness'. The call for comment is met with '"No comment"'.

This protesting voice makes itself felt also in the poet's seemingly defensive need, at various points, and with various degrees of conviction, to articulate the tenets of his poetry. Half-way through 'Evening in the Country', for instance, the poem points beyond its immediate circumstances and into the distance at 'ten thousand helmeted footsoldiers, / A Spanish armada stretching to the horizon, all / Absolutely motionless until the hour to strike ...' (DDS, 33). As it waits to strike, this armada plainly weighs a good deal more heavily on the poet's consciousness than did the revolution in Argentina. Still, though, the poet refuses to allow such events to dominate his thinking. 'But I think there is not too much to be said or be done / And that these things eventually take care of themselves ...'

(DDS, 33). This moves beyond *Rivers and Mountains* in that there was no 'but' in 'The Skaters', no real sense of counterpressures. Even so, the outcome of the deliberation is much the same, the poet resolving to 'pass over this to the real / Subject of our concern, and that is / Have you begun to be in the context you feel …' (DDS, 33–4). He reiterates this resolve in 'The Bungalows', where, if faced with a choice, he is clear that he would 'Rather decaying art, genius, inspiration to hold to / An impossible "calque" of reality, than / "The new school of the trivial, rising up on the field of battle, / Something of sludge and leaf-mold" and life / Goes trickling out through the holes' (DDS 71). A calque is another word for loan (or literal) translation. Given the choice, then, Ashbery would rather be about the business of translating reality than writing the kind of protest poetry which is sieve-like (not sponge-like) in its relation to its environment. Better still, though, he would prefer not to have to choose, the choice itself, as the *The Double Dream of Spring* makes clear, giving a false because polarised impression of what poetry ought to be about. Thus for all that he is not about to join the new school of the trivial to which the war has given rise, and for all that he would never write the kind of abbreviated imperatives protest poetry appears to call for, he appreciates the pressure to do so. Why else would he allow such voices into his writing? *The Double Dream of Spring* is thus not, in any straightforward sense, the result of a choice between experiment and declaration. It is rather, as the twin perspectives of its title suggest, an ongoing negotiation of these competing impulses, its object, throughout, and its achievement, at its best, being a form of utterance that responds to both.[47]

The ongoing negotiation takes various guises. In 'Decoy', for instance, he responds to both impulses by experimenting with a form of poetic declaration, teasing out the strengths and weaknesses of the orator's address. The quality of this teasing is evident from the poem's opening lines:

> We hold these truths to be self-evident:
> That ostracism, both political and moral, has
> Its place in the twentieth-century scheme of things;
> That urban chaos is the problem we have been seeing into and seeing
>   into,
> For the factory, deadpanned by its very existence into a
> Descending code of values, has moved right across the road from
>   total financial upheaval
> And caught regression head-on.

(DDS, 31)

The force of this statement depends on the multiple ironies Ashbery introduces into his poem through his title: a 'Decoy' being a risky means of distracting attention from something more important; the risk being that, if decoded as such, the effect of a decoy is to heighten suspicion. Controlling these possibilities by its carefully managed ironies, Ashbery's poem draws attention both away from and towards the matter in hand.

Thus, once alerted by the title to the poem's ironic possibilities, the opening statement appears to render itself practically redundant. If the content of the statement is self-evident, why state it? Arguably the gesture is not totally redundant in that to express that which is self-evident is to consolidate a audience's collective sense of their situation. However, as Ashbery's poem indicates, the very fact of the situation being felt self-evident tends to lead the speaker into over-complicating rhetoric, the effect of which is to cause the self-evident thing to slip from view: 'Deadpanned by its very existence into a / Descending code of values'. The orator's address is thus, at best, only useful ironically, its failure to bring its subject into view prompting a suspicious audience to reflect for themselves on what it leaves out.

Given these various ironic twists, there is a danger that the reader will not grasp the force of Ashbery's 'Decoy', that he or she will simply lose sight of whatever it was the speaker lost sight of. The poem thus concludes by commenting directly on what the orator left out. 'There was never any excuse for this and perhaps there need be none / For kicking out into the morning, on the wide bed, / Waking far apart on the bed, the two of them: / Husband and wife / Man and wife' (DDS, 32). This closing image of a man and wife apart speaks much more forcefully of 'ostracism' than the orator was able to. The abstract nouns of the act of declaration are replaced by the emblematic images of the act of calling attention. The poet says more than the public speaker.

In so far as 'Decoy' makes knowing use of a style of utterance the poet thinks inappropriate to its situation, it is typical of *The Double Dream of Spring*, the book being characterised throughout by a wilful infelicity. 'Variations, Calypso and Fugue on a theme of Ella Wheeler Wilcox', 'It Was Raining in the Capital', and 'Some Words' each offer knowingly maladroit poetry, as if to observe that the appropriate poetic utterance can hardly now be found. The arguments dividing contemporary poets confirm the difficulty of arriving at such an utterance, a difficulty which, as George Oppen saw it, owed to the fact that poetry itself could hardly be thought the most appropriate activity in time of war. Writing to his niece in 1966, Oppen reported, 'I'm finding it difficult to write poetry – An eerie feeling writing poetry with the war going on. I don't know if I can.'[48] Ashbery's poetry of the period indicates likewise. So while he did not think it useful for him, as a poet (for reasons Oppen shared) to declare his opposition to the war, nor does he settle comfortably to the task of writing poetry. In various ways *The Double Dream of Spring* sets up obstacles for itself, building in resistance to its own most seductive cadences.

The most obvious instance of the poet making life difficult for himself is the group of poems called 'French Poems', which Ashbery wrote in France and translated into English as a means, as he puts it in his notes on the volume, of 'avoiding customary word-patterns and associations' (DDS, 95). 'Variations, Calypso and Fuge' and 'It Was Raining in the Capital' also build in obstacles, both poems questioning the value of Ashbery's poetry by translating its tenets into the terms of noticeably less fluent poets. As 'It Was Raining in the Capital' has it, '"This is what my learning / Teaches," the Aquarian said, / "To absorb life through the pores / For the life around you is dead'" (DDS, 23). This is what Ashbery's poetry teaches, except that to put the point this way is to trivialize it. And the effect of such knowing trivialisation is to raise doubts about the value of the act of writing poetry. 'The Bungalows' and 'Sunrise in Suburbia' build obstacles to themselves if only by locating poetry in environments where it is likely to meet with resistance. By contrast, 'The Double Dream of Spring' would seem to promise a traditional, and so relatively untroubled kind of poetic utterance. In fact the poetic enterprise is thwarted at every turn: 'I had thought of all this years before / But now it was making no sense. And the song had finished: / This was the story' (DDS, 41). The new story being the failure of the poet's old song now to make sense, 'The Double Dream of Spring' is an act of rhythmical resistance, the poet's expression refusing at every stage to swell into the kind of affecting cadences he is so easily capable of. Hence the ending, 'Like so much blond hair awash / Sick starlight on the night / That is readying its defenses again / As day comes up' (DDS, 42). This is poetry forbidding its own sense of morning, the monosyllabic bluntness of 'As day comes up' having little of the dawn about it.

The most important way, however, in which *The Double Dream of Spring* negotiates the conflicting impulses bearing on the contemporary American poet in the late 1960s lies in the scrutiny it brings to the matter of individuality. In *Rivers and Mountains*, Ashbery's reluctance fully to embrace Thoreau-like isolation flowed, in part, from a resistance to the image of the self-reliant individual such isolation implies. The Ashberyan self, by contrast is radically porous, dependent for its sense of identity on the things and people it has around it. And this is the core of the dilemma posed the American poet by his or her nation's actions in Vietnam. What the call for the poet to protest implies is a measure of authority and sovereignty, a sense of self, which Ashbery, among others, found unsustainable in late twentieth-century America. A number of the most challenging poems in *The Double Dream of Spring* – 'Definition of Blue', 'Some Words' and 'Soonest Mended' – argue this problem out, aiming, as they do, to arrive at what one might call a lightly contoured self: an image of a self which appreciates its lack of sovereignty, and knows itself to be the subject of forces beyond its control, but which through that knowledge manages to retain just sufficient integrity to give expression to those forces.[49]

As a dramatic monologue, 'Definition of Blue' is the expression of a single voice, a lecturer. The argument of the lecture, its academic discourse immaculately rendered, is that 'in our own time' the Romantic individual has been submerged by what are termed 'mass practices'. Ashbery invariably has a disagreement with his lecturers, and this poem is no exception. Thus for all that the poem argues for a correspondence between the self and the environment in which it happens to find itself – for self and world as mutually revealing media – it does so in the untroubled continuous voice of the self-confident orator. In this case the poet does not comment on the paradox that results, on the fact that the style and content of the utterance undermine one another. Rather, and because it would reproduce the paradox to do otherwise, he allows the reader to get it for himself or herself.

'Some Words' is more positive than 'Definition of Blue', being less concerned with presenting the problems implicit in contemporary articulations of self, and more concerned to find their solution. In so far as it depends on another poet's words (Arthur Cravan's) and as it is written throughout in knowingly banal rhyming couplets, the poem has a flattening effect on the writing self. Nor is this effective flattening of the self only formal, the poem's narrative being the kind of all-purpose, universal and so de-personalising autobiography Ashbery tries out at various moments in *The Double Spring* – in 'Variations, Calypso and Fugue' for instance. Again, though, 'Some Words' is the more exacting poem, its universal, self-denying story giving rise to the kind of expression of anger that is currently on many people's lips:

> When, beside a window, one feels evening prevail
> Who is there who can receive its slanting veil
> And not regret day that bore it on its stream
> Whether day was joy or under evil's regime
> Drawing us to the one and deploring the other
> Regretting the departure of all our brothers
> And all that made the day, including its stains.

(DDS, 65)

There is, unmistakably, a protest here. In issuing it, however, the poet presumes neither the sense of special status implicit in poetry, nor even a sovereignty of self. This is the protest, rather, of a citizen no less shaped by the present 'regime' than those 'brothers' who have gone away. A protest, that is, in its own, undemonstrative, understated way, in the manner of Whitman: the poet identifying, but taking care not to over-identify, with fellow Americans elsewhere.

It is with 'Soonest Mended', however, that Ashbery comes closest to a sense of self equal to its moment: a sense of self located in because shaped by its situation, but just sufficiently distinct from that situation to give it coherent expression.[50] Moving at the kind of speed he developed in 'Clepsydra', but expanding the scope of its utterance with every step, 'Soonest Mended' is both Ashbery's most fleet-footed and his most thoroughly absorbent poem to date. The opening line is an image of the contemporary poet at work, 'Barely tolerated, living on the margin / In our technological society' (DDS, 17). The image is a response to competing pressures: questioning the suggestion that, because the likes of Ginsberg had become such popular public figures, poetry was therefore central enough for its declarations really to be heard; acknowledging the fact that, by their willingness to experiment with ways of seeing the world, American poets had set themselves apart from society en masse. Ashbery's object in 'Soonest Mended' is to steer a middle course, the poem continuing to practise now familiar experimental strategies, while at the same time meaning to communicate on matters of general concern. Briefly, brilliantly, it manages to do so.

The poem's experimental quality has to do with its sponginess, the first paragraph absorbing among others *Orlando Furioso* (Ariosto's mock epic having been important background reading in the early days of the New York School), Ingres, 'Happy Hooligan' and (in the dead-pan allusion of 'summer's energy wanes quickly') Shakespeare's Sonnet 18. Set against this hazardous combining of registers – the poem's rapid juxtapositions steering it, close, early on, to the brink of unintelligibility – the poem asserts it desire to communicate, turning its attention to domestic concerns (and so to a Marianne-Moore-like neutral ground on which poet and reader can meet); to 'thoughts in a mind / With room enough and to spare for our little problems (so they began / to seem), / Our daily quandary about food and the rent and bills to be paid?' (DDS, 17). Even as he mentions such common concerns, however, another impulse looms into view, the poet reminding himself and his reader that in the present climate such 'problems' inevitably seem 'little'. Which is not to say that he wants to disregard such little concerns. Rather he wants somehow to reconcile intimacy with one's immediate environment with an awareness also of distant events. Hence,

> a robin flies across
> The upper corner of the window, you brush your hair away
> And cannot quite see, or a wound will flash
> Against the sweet faces of the others, something like:
> This is what you wanted to hear, so why
> Did you think of listening to something else?
>
> (DDS, 18)

Intimacy and distance are beautifully handled here: that which is intimate (the poet's hair) brushed away; that which is distant (the wounded faces of the others) brought close by the felt word 'sweet'. The poet himself thinks this is 'something like', and he is surely right. Extending the range of his utterance by widening his sense of what constitutes its occasion, 'Soonest Mended' brings, without forcing, apparently conflicting impulses together.

The poem is generally a bringing together of competing impulses. Voices holding different opinions find a measure of agreement:

> Better, you said, to stay cowering
> Like this in the early lessons, since the promise of learning
> Is a delusion, and I agreed, adding that
> Tomorrow would alter the sense of what had already been learned,
> That the learning process is extended in this way
>
> (DDS, 18–19)

A seemingly passive poetry becomes a form of action:

> learning to accept
> The charity of the hard moments as they are doled out,
> For this is action, this not being sure, this careless
> Preparing, sowing the seeds crooked in the furrow
>
> (DDS, 19)

And, crucially to the success of the poem, it brings together different senses of the poetic occasion. We glimpse the poet at his desk a robin flying across the window, and we see him in his climate, the climate, as he tells us, that fostered his sentences. We see him, also, leaving a stadium after some grand occasion (a protest reading perhaps) at which *'They'* were the players, while 'we who had struggled at the game / Were merely spectators' (DDS, 18).

An experimental poem with a public dimension, indicating its protest without having to declare, communicating intimacy while managing distance – few Ashbery poems, few poems, have been more fit for their occasion than 'Soonest Mended'.

NOTES

1 John Ashbery, 'Frank O'Hara's question', p. 1.
2 Louis Simpson, 'Dead horses and live issues', p. 521.
3 John Ashbery, letter to the editor, *The Nation*, 29 May 1967, p. 692.
4 Ibid.
5 Simpson, 'Dead horses and live issues', p. 521.
6 'An interview in Warsaw', p. 273.
7 For other useful accounts of this exchange see James Longenbach, *Modern Poetry After Modernism*, pp. 85–101; and John Shoptaw, *On The Outside Looking Out*, pp.101–2.
8 Paul Carroll, *The Poem In Its Skin*, p. 230.
9 Cited in Carroll, *The Poem in its Skin*, pp. 258–9.
10 Susan Sontag, *Against Interpretation*, pp. 5, 7, 14.
11 Ibid., pp. 15, 21, 25–6, 277.
12 Ibid., p. 301.
13 Carroll, *The Poem in its Skin*, p. 237.
14 Ibid.
15 Ibid., pp. 255, 248, 251.
16 Robert Bly, for instance, a poet as active as anybody in the protests against Vietnam, tried to address the problem in terms of his deep image poetic, arguing that 'Those poets who try to write political poems, without having developed any inwardness, have embarked on an impossible task. Paradoxically what is needed to write true poems about the outward world is inwardness.' 'On political poetry', p. 522. Bly does not explain, however, how inward-looking poetry results in outward-looking poetry.
17 Cary Nelson, *Our Last First Poets*, p. ix.
18 Ibid., p. xv.
19 Charles Altieri, *Enlarging the Temple*, p. 20.
20 Ibid.
21 John Plotz *et al.*, 'An interview with John Berryman', p. 11.
22 Ibid.
23 L.S. Dembo, 'The "objectivist" poet: four interviews', p. 174.
24 For a compelling account of this exchange, see Marjorie Perloff, *Poetry On and Off the Page*, pp. 208–21.
25 Sontag, *Against Interpretation*, p. 268.
26 Ibid., p. 267.

27 Nelson, *Our Last First Poets*, p. 15.

28 Ibid., p. 16.

29 John Ashbery, 'The decline of the verbs', p. 5.

30 Ibid.

31 Sontag, *Against Interpretation*, p. 303.

32 John Ashbery, 'Tradition and talent', p. 2.

33 Ibid. Ashbery has confirmed that he meant 'flouting', not 'flaunting'.

34 John Ashbery, 'Jerboas, pelicans and Peewee Peese', p. 1.

35 Stein and Stevens also played with the idea of the lecture, Stein most notably in 'Composition as explanation', and Stevens in his ironically academic poems.

36 Charles Molesworth, *The Fierce Embrace*, p. 166.

37 For an extended close reading of this poem see David Rigsbee, 'Against monuments: a reading of Ashbery's "These Lacustrine Cities"'. For other interesting considerations see Alan Williamson, *Introspection and Contemporary Poetry*, p. 138; and Norman Finkelstein, *The Utopian Moment in Contemporary Poetry*, pp. 56–58.

38 Marjorie Perloff discusses the partly Audenesque character of *Rivers and Mountains* in *The Poetics of Indeterminacy: Rimbaud to Cage*, pp. 252–4.

39 It is the explicit point of *Walden* to wake American readers from their culturally induced slumbers. William James repeatedly insists on the need to break through the husk of outmoded language, while famously locating his pragmatism between the 'toughness' of empiricism and the tenderness of 'idealism'.

40 Henry David Thoreau, *Walden*, p. 34.

41 For extended discussions of the idea of verbal performance in Ashbery, see Margueritte S. Murphy's Bakhtinian account of *Three Poems* in *A Tradition of Subversion*, pp. 168–98; and James McCorkle's deconstructive reading of Ashbery in *The Still Performance*, pp. 46–86.

42 Thoreau, *Walden*, p. 169–72.

43 Paris Leary and Robert Kelly (eds), *A Controversy of Poets*, p. 523.

44 Thoreau, *Walden*, pp. 144. The titles of Thoreau's early chapters act as a kind of guide to the main themes of Ashbery's poem: Economy, Where I Lived, And What I Lived For, Reading, Sounds, Solitude, Visitors.

45 Ibid., p. 288.

46 In an eloquent discussion of this passage, Geoff Ward identifies what he takes to be Ashbery's liberal individualism with Emersonian self-reliance. See Ward, *Statutes of Liberty*, pp. 140–5.

47 For other discussions of the way *The Double Dream of Spring* handles the voice of the protest poet see James Longenback, *Modern Poetry after Modernism*, pp. 85–101, and Shoptaw, *On The Outside Looking Out*, pp. 100–11.

48 George Oppen, *Collected Letters*, p. 114.

49 One might add 'Fragment' to this list, in that, as the title suggests, the poem traces the meditations of a mind which knows itself to be the product of a situation larger than itself. But 'Fragment' constitutes a rather disappointing end to the book, its digressive style resulting in a rather uninteresting disorientation. Very arguably this degree of disorientation owes to the fact that Ashbery wrote the poem soon after the death of his father. For an extended consideration of the impact of this event on the writing of the poem see Shoptaw, pp. 111–24.

50 'Soonest Mended' has attracted some very helpful criticism. Particularly insightful are Harold Bloom, *Figures of Capable Imagination*, pp. 185–7; John Hollander, 'Soonest

Mended'; Shoptaw, *On the Outside Looking Out*, pp. 105–07; J.D. McClatchy, *White Paper: On American Poetry*, pp. 51–4.

CHAPTER FIVE

From poetry to prose: the sceptical tradition of *Three Poems*

There was something negative about Ashbery's poetry in *The Double Dream of Spring*. Like O'Hara's, as we have seen:

> It does not advocate sex and dope as a panacea for the ills of modern society; it does not speak out against the war in Viet Nam or in favor of civil rights; it does not paint gothic vignettes of the post-Atomic age: in a word, it does not attack the establishment.

The strength of this argument is that it resists delusions of grandeur, such things, Ashbery observing, falling outside the remit of poetry. The weakness of the position is that even to formulate it is to accommodate a perspective on poetry that makes it look like a most inconsequential activity. Concerned as it is, in other words, not to falsify its situation 'on the margin / In our technological society', Ashbery's poetry in *The Double Dream of Spring* is sometimes preoccupied with what it cannot do. In *Three Poems* he is concerned with what it can. Changing the angle by stepping through the looking glass, Ashbery's realm in his prose poetry is art, that 'neutral space', as Auden puts it in 'The Sea and the Mirror', which 'accommodates the conspirator and his victim'.[1] His subject is ideas of order, such ideas being, according to Stevens, the province of art in a secular society. Its lasting impression is a sense of grace reminiscent of, but much more deeply explored than, the delightful harmonies of 'Some Trees'. *Three Poems* is Ashbery's version of the supreme fiction.

Kenneth Koch's poetry had recently taken a comparable turn. Speaking about the evolution of 'The Pleasures of Peace' (published in 1969, the year Ashbery started *Three Poems*), Koch describes his poem's relation to the protest movement:

> I had never written a political poem before and I wanted to see what I could do. I was involved a little bit in the peace movement ... I would march on marches, and give poetry readings against war – that didn't do much good. You know I signed all sorts of petitions and wrote things, and I thought, well this is crazy, I am very involved in this, I hate this war, and what am I writing love poems for, I want to write about this. It took me three years to write that poem and the parts that were about the war actually kept sort of being rejected by the poem, in the way that an

artificial heart might be. I didn't seem to have a talent to do that, and it ended up being a poem about the peace movement, and the pleasures of peace.[2]

Koch's poem is an exuberant story of the writing of a poem called 'The Pleasures of Peace', a reflexive gesture which combines Pasternak's notion that 'the finest works in the world in fact all tell us of their own birth', Auden's suggestion that the poet's task in time of crisis is to affirm, and Stevens's insistence that poetry is the proper subject of the poem. Showing an affirming flame by affirming poetry, the poem's intention is to make one actively glad of the state of affairs – peace – in which such pleasures are possible.

Three Poems is similarly poised, Ashbery affirming poetry by staging an inquiry into its capacity for harmony and order. So why does he write it in prose? This is not quite the contradictory gesture it might seem, American poetry having always enjoyed a close relationship with prose. Arguably it started with prose, its characteristic style of thought having its origin in Emerson's essays. Certainly Whitman's line was intimate with prose. Williams coupled his prosody to it. Even Eliot, while always preserving a proper distance between the two, took good prose as his model for poetic clarity. But if these precedents afford a context within which to situate Ashbery's seemingly contradictory gesture, they do not resolve it: *Three Poems* having Stevens-like aspirations for poetry, and Stevens being the most self-consciously poetic of major American poets. The more pertinent question to ask of *Three Poems*, therefore, is, how can one reconcile Ashbery's turn to prose with the book's Stevens-like aspirations for poetry?

There are moments in Stevens's poetry when a shift into prose seems all but inevitable, and when the decision not to permit the shift produces an acute tension in the verse. 'Sad Strains of a Gay Waltz' is a case in point. A meditation on the perishability of artistic form, the poem concludes on a prophetic note:

Too many waltzes have ended. Yet the shapes
For which the voices cry, these, too, may be
Modes of desire, modes of revealing desire.

Too many waltzes – The epic of disbelief
Blares oftener and soon, will soon be constant.
Some harmonious skeptic soon in a skeptical music

Will unite these figures of men and their shapes
Will glisten again with motion, the music
Will be motion and full of shadows.[3]

Early as it is, 'Sad Strains of a Gay Waltz' sketches the limit of Stevens's achievement. Acutely aware that certain old ideas of order are inadequate to modern life – the civilities of the Enlightenment as figured by the waltz, Romanticism as embodied by that 'Mountain-minded Hoon' – the poem is also troublingly aware of the form a now adequate idea of order must take. Only an idea of order, Stevens suggests, which is unimposing enough to accommodate the scepticism of a Godless culture and mobile enough to accommodate the realities of the crowd (these 'sudden mobs of men') could begin to warrant belief in the modern age. It would be an idea of order, in other words, that took full account of the disorder that made it desirable; an 'epic', as he puts it, 'of disbelief'. The limitation of Stevens's poem, against which every line strains, is its form. The rhythmically regular three-line stanzas conspicuously owe more to the strict ¾ time of the outmoded waltz than to the 'motion' and 'shadows' of contemporary existence. Stevens, of course, is aware of the disjunction, so making it all the more poignant. It is as if he cannot bring himself to mobilise his poetry to the degree the age demands because to do so would be to risk collapsing the distinction between poetry and prose.

Ashbery, attracted no doubt by the recklessness of the gesture, had been testing the boundaries between poetry and prose long before *Three Poems*: in *Some Trees*, which contains the prose poem 'The Young Son'; in *The Tennis Court Oath* where 'The Ascetic Sensualists', 'Europe' and 'Idaho' all incorporate gobbets of popular fiction; and in *The Double Dream of Spring* with its prose poem 'For John Clare', and 'Variations, Calypso and Fugue on a Theme of Ella Wheeler Wilcox', a poem which turns into prose. In all these cases, however, the distinction between the two modes is kept clear: the prose poems being exceptions; and the poems which incorporate prose – especially in *The Tennis Court Oath* – doing so in order to argue with it. It is with *Three Poems* that Ashbery properly merges the modes for the first time.

He chose to do so, as he has observed in interview, in the interests of greater mobility:

> the poems in *The Double Dream of Spring* ... had gotten to a tightness and strictness that bothered me, and I began to feel that I'd have to start moving in some other direction because I had become too narrow, even though I liked those poems.[4]

Stephen Fredman, who has written the most discriminating account of *Three Poems*, provides a helpful gloss on this new departure. Locating Ashbery in the tradition of American poetry in prose – a tradition that includes Williams, Stein and Creeley – he observes that

> the American poet uses prose not to give evidence of genius and the ability to impose order but instead to create, through attentive receptivity, a space of permission in which the world is allowed to appear as it is. In this context the eschewal of verse can be seen as a conscious abnegation of the tremendous 'disciplinary' force inherent in verse.[5]

What this formulation gets at is the Stevens-like impulse guiding Ashbery's eschewal of the tight, restrictive forms of *The Double Dream of Spring*. Ashbery's ambition in *Three Poems* is nothing less than a form of order commensurate with the world as it is: an ambition which is consonant with the highest ideals of poetry but which requires the mobility of prose for its fulfilment. Far, that is, from contradicting his Stevens-like intention to affirm poetry by affirming its capacity to order, Ashbery's turn to prose is necessary to the expression of the supreme fiction shadowed forth by 'Sad Strains of a Gay Waltz'. Or, to put it another way, the prose of *Three Poems* is the appropriate mode of revealing the desire for order which makes it right to describe the writing as poetry.

In principle, then, there is no fundamental contradiction between Ashbery's desire to affirm poetry and his decision to write prose. Which is not to say that it is not a precarious move to make. To use prose as the means of revealing poetic desire is to undermine the opposition between poetry and prose and so to desta-bilise conventions and hierarchies that historically have tended to work to the poet's advantage, enhancing his or her prestige. It is, moreover, a move that, once made, would seem hard to reverse. This, perhaps, is why 'Sad Strains of a Gay Waltz' stops where it does, and probably also why it is that since *Three Poems* Ashbery's poetry, whatever its form, has been characterised by that prosiness one would now call 'Ashberyan'. Indeed, Ashbery's poetry has stayed prosy because poetry as prose would seem a most appropriate medium through which to respond to the ordinary, uncertain occasions which Stevens did much to make the subject of American poetry.

None of this, however, gets at the real difficulty of *Three Poems*; the difficulty, that is, of actually reading it. The really pertinent question to ask of *Three Poems* is not why, given all the impulses described, Ashbery should have chosen to write prose, but why, with all those impulses in mind, he should have chosen to write prose like this:

> Here it is that our sensuality can save us *in extremis*: the atmosphere of the day that event took place, the way the trees and buildings looked, what we said to the per-son who was both the bearer and fellow recipient of that message and what that person replied, words that were not words but sounds out of time, taken out of any external context in which their content would be recognizable - these facts have entered our consciousness once and for all, have spread through us even into our pores like a marvelous antidote to the cup that the next moment had already pre-pared and which, whether hemlock or nectar, could only have proved fatal because it *was* the next, bringing with it the unspoken message that motion could be accomplished only in time, that is in a preordained succession of moments which must carry us far from here, far from this impassive but real moment of under-standing which may be the only one we shall ever know, even if it is merely the first of an implied infinite series. (TP, 76)

In the coils of its syntax, the mix of its idioms, its shifting perspectives, and its sheer, seemingly unreadable length, this sentence is by no means untypical of *Three Poems*. Indeed if, to the sympathetic reader, the abiding image of this volume is of the grace of those few hours in early spring when 'the air seems suffused with an unearthly tenderness', to the antagonistic reader the lasting impression will be of the kind of disorientation produced by such sentences (TP, 73). So how is one to understand such a sentence?

To answer this question one needs first to be clear what kind of understand-ing one is after. What the most sceptical reader will probably be after is a paraphrasable meaning. What, such a reader will want to know, is the sense of this sentence? This is neither an unreasonable nor an unanswerable question. Occurring shortly after the image of a spring day with its air of 'unearthly tenderness', this long sentence meditates on the meaning of such moments. What, it wonders, are we to make of such epiphanic sensations of harmony? Are we to preserve them in the memory, and draw on them, like 'still points', when faced, as more commonly, by moments of disharmony? Or are we to let them pass, according them no privileged status in our negotiation with the world? These questions catch the broad theme of Ashbery's sentence, and perhaps satisfy the demand for a 'sense'. But they hardly amount to a satisfying account of the sentence, because they do not meet the experience of reading it.

Better to say that this sentence is understandable not in so far as one can paraphrase its sense (which one can, at a cost) but that one can, as it were, track its meaning. Fredman observes a link between *Three Poems* and late Henry James. Using Ashbery's review of Gertrude Stein's *Stanzas in Meditation* as a means of orientating himself in *Three Poems*, he quotes Ashbery's comparison of Stein's *Stanzas* with *The Golden Bowl*. 'If these works are highly complex, and, for some, unreadable,' Ashbery remarks, 'it is not only because of the complicatedness of life, the subject, but also because they actually imitate its rhythm, its way of happening, in an attempt to draw our attention to another aspect of its true nature'.[6] The link with James, who is not now, on the whole, thought unreadable, is helpful. Reading late James one can follow, from clause to clause, how one thought leads to another, even as one is aware that the point of departure, the beginning of the sentence, is receding further and further from view. So it is with Ashbery's long sentence: his syntax calling on the reader to think of understanding as a process not an end-point. This in turn points one to a further dimension of the sentence, which is its performative quality. Searching for the meaning of the harmonious moment, the sentence performs the process whereby – language being what it is – the search for meaning tends to carry one further and further from the experience or fact one was trying to understand in the first place. Which is not to say, as David Lehman does, that for Ashbery '"understanding" is a doomed project'.[7] To say so is to cut the process short by failing to appreciate the uses of error in Ashbery. To recognise that the search for understanding has modulated into misunderstanding is to appreciate what is wrong with one's understanding and so to arrive at a sharper understanding of its object. Ashbery, that is, like Stevens, uses the beauty of inflections to get at the beauty of innuendoes; the act of saying to get at what has gone unsaid.

So, there are various ways one might understand Ashbery's demanding sentence, and one does so the more fully as one allows it to challenge such presuppositions about meaning as one might bring to it. To a certain degree, though, as we have become embroiled in the workings of Ashbery's prose, we have lost sight of the point. Important as it is to indicate that one can in fact read the more difficult passages of *Three Poems*, the fact that one can does not in itself justify their difficulty. Why, one still wants to know, should a text that has as its object the idea of the supreme fiction incorporate such difficult writing? The answer to this question lies in Ashbery's reading.

Reading Ashbery's reading is always illuminating, but it is especially so in the case of *Three Poems* because it is in this volume that he first discusses the 'other tradition':

> There was, however, a residue, a kind of fiction that developed parallel to the classic truths of daily life (as it was in that heroic but commonplace age) as they unfolded with the foreseeable majesty of a holocaust, an unfrightening one, and went unrecognized, drawing force and grandeur from this like the illegitimate offspring of a king. It is this 'other tradition' which we propose to explore. (TP, 55–6)

Of continuing importance to Ashbery – witness his poem 'The Other Tradition' in *Houseboat Days*, and the title of his Charles Eliot Norton Lectures – this other tradition is a story of neglect. As it concerns history it refers to all those 'happenings', those 'obscure phenomena' which history neglects to mention, and which to a very large extent constitute the stuff of people's lives. As it concerns literature it concerns those writers who have tried to address themselves to these happenings and the unspoken sequences they generate. This is Ashbery's other tradition. It consists of many writers who have been neglected, and of the neglected works and aspects of important writers. It is that body of writing which deals with what George Eliot called the 'roar' of being and what Paul H. Fry calls the 'hum of the occasion'.

As Ashbery's readers catch up with his 'other tradition', his own writing comes to seem less and less strange, more and more the necessary development of a most significant line of thought, and the best discussions of *Three Poems* rightly aim to explain the book in this way.[8] What critical writing on Ashbery's prose poetry has not yet done, however, is locate it in the particular discursive tradition from which the text itself advises us it has emerged, the reason being that as yet critics have paid little or no attention to Ashbery's most significant allusion in *Three Poems*, to Pascal. Pascal is, in fact, the only writer Ashbery refers to by name in *Three Poems* (mentioning him in 'The System' just after he introduces the idea of the 'other tradition') and the book's aspirations and difficulties are best understood as the latest in a genealogy of spiritually inclined texts linked by their dialogue with *The Pensées*. To consider Ashbery's prose poetry in these terms is to appreciate that Ashbery's demanding syntax, far from being a needlessly obscurantist gesture, is a necessary move in an ongoing argument: Pascal's challenge to atheism becoming, in twentieth-century poetics, above all a question of style.

There are times when Pascal sounds very like Ashbery. Witness, from the 84th pensée:

> This is our true state; which makes us incapable both of certain knowledge and of absolute ignorance. We sail on a vast expanse, always drifting in uncertainty, and carried hither and thither. If there is any point to which we think we can attach

ourselves, to steady our position, it shifts and leaves us; if we pursue it, it escapes our grasp, slides past us and vanishes on its eternal course. Nothing stays for us. This is our natural condition, and yet most contrary to our wishes; we burn with desire to find firm ground, and a final fixed foundation on which we can build a tower to rise to infinity. But our whole foundation cracks, and the earth opens upon abysses.

Then let us not look for certainty and stability. Our mind is always deceived by changing appearances; nothing can fix the finite between two infinities which enclose it and escape it.

Once this is well understood, I think we shall tend to rest, each in the place where nature has put him.[9]

One could be reading *Three Poems*. Like Ashbery, Pascal conjures an illusion of surface and depth. There is an air of order at the surface of the writing, the passage having the veneer of argument. Look closely, however, and the surface disappears as all the elements of Pascal's prose – the accumulation of verbs, the vertiginous shifts of perspective, the paradoxical logic – conspire to generate a perpetually restless syntax. As in Ashbery the sentence performs its meaning: a seemingly composed argument about the uncertainty of the human condition becoming entangled in a syntax of uncertainty. Running through this restless syntax is an argument about chance. The human mind, as Pascal sees it,

is not so independent that it is not liable to be disturbed by the first clatter that arises near it. It does not need the noise of a cannon to interrupt its thoughts; the creaking of a weathercock or a pulley is enough. Do not be surprised if it is not reasoning well at the moment. A fly is buzzing in its ears, and that is enough to make it incapable of sound judgement.

Sympathetic as he is to the music of John Cage, Ashbery would find little to disagree with in Pascal's estimation of the chance occurrence, and he would surely also agree with Pascal's proto-surreal suggestion that

Chance provides thoughts and chance sweeps them away; there is no art of keeping or getting them.

A thought has escaped me. I wanted to write it down, but instead I write that it has escaped me.[10]

Again the articulation is uncannily Ashberyan, Pascal illustrating the importance of chance on his thinking by writing an utterance which reports on its own occasion. It is not without good reason, then, that Ashbery directs the reader back to Pascal in 'The System', *The Pensées* offering an image of the universe – vast, mobile, uncertain, contingent – that chimes with, and so serves to legitimise, Ashbery's own. *Three Poems*, as 'The System' implies, is 'as Pascal says' (TP, 57).

Except, of course, that, far from sustaining this uncertain world view *The Pensées* argues fiercely against it. Pascal's meditation is dramatically structured. The passages which find an echo in Ashbery are from the first part of the discourse 'Man Without God', in which Pascal presents the world according to the perspective of an atheist. As Pascal sees it this perspective is so wretched that, when

he presents the second part of his thesis, 'Man With God', the intricately con-
structed offer of grace he presents will come as such relief to the reader that
it will prove undeniably compelling. The broad and enduring value of Pascal to
the twentieth-century reader is the force with which he challenges the Godless
condition. His rendering of that condition is unerringly accurate, as evidenced
by its affinities with the immaculately modern mind of Ashbery's poetry. His
challenge lies in his reminder that disbelieving is no less a belief than belief itself,
and in the sheer force of his Christian rhetoric. The atheist can read *The Pensées*
without being converted. But it is hard to imagine he or she could do so with-
out realising the seriousness of their position.

When Ashbery alludes to Pascal in 'The System', therefore, he is directing
the reader not to an authority by whom he is legitimated but to a writer with
whom he has an argument. Indeed, one way of describing the task Ashbery sets
himself in *Three Poems* is as an attempt to discern a supreme fiction in Pascal's
description of 'Man Without God' which answers the questions Pascal poses the
atheistic mind set in 'Man With God'. To do so would be, in an exact sense, to
achieve the harmonious scepticism necessary, as Stevens put it, to the 'epic of
disbelief'. Pascal's value to Ashbery, in other words, lies in the challenges he
poses to his sensibility; the most sublime of these challenges concerning the
question of time.

In the Conclusion to the first part of the discourse (subtitled 'That We Must
Seek God'), Pascal fixes the question of perceptions of time at the heart of his
argument. 'Certainly,' he asserts, in a passage worth hearing at length,

> the duration of this life is but a moment, and the state of death, whatever its nature,
> is eternal. All our thoughts and actions must therefore be directed along very dif-
> ferent paths according to the nature of this eternity, and it is impossible to take a
> single sensible and judicious step unless we are guided by the sight of that point
> which should be our final goal.
>
> Nothing is clearer than this, and so, by the laws of reason, men's conduct is alto-
> gether unreasonable if they do not take a different course.
>
> Let us use this criterion to judge those who live without thought of their life's
> latter end, who let themselves be guided by their whims and pleasures, without
> reflection or disquiet, and who only think of making themselves happy in the
> moment, as if they could abolish eternity by turning away their thoughts.
>
> Yet this eternity exists; and death, which will lead into it and threatens them
> every hour, must infallibly confront them in a short time with the awful inevitabil-
> ity of either eternal annihilation or eternal misery. And they do not know which of
> these eternities is to be theirs for ever.
>
> Here is a dilemma with terrible consequences.[11]

With this passage Pascal offers as forceful a challenge as one is likely to find to
the Ashberyan sensibility. In so far as it offers an account of that sensibility, its
description is pejorative. Ashbery's poetry is shaped by more than personal
whims and pleasures, and is concerned with much more than its own happiness.
Undeniably, however, concerned as it is meet the demands of the occasion, it

lives 'in the moment'. At one point in his career this constituted an argument with a Lowellian poetic of endurance. Reading Pascal raises the stakes of the argument. To live 'in the moment' is to deny eternity, and to deny eternity is to live with the threat, from moment to moment, of 'either eternal annihilation or eternal misery'. It is only, one might argue, at the point at which Ashbery has engaged with Pascal's argument for divine time that his occasional poetic can be treated with all seriousness, because only then can he be thought to have contemplated the full implications of his sensibility.

To get the full measure of Ashbery's prose in *Three Poems* one would want first to get the measure of the genealogy of responses to the Pascalian challenge which are the background to Ashbery's own: Emerson's 'Experience', James's discussion of 'Pragmatism and religion', and Auden's 'The Sea and the Mirror'. Ashbery's prose is shaped by his absorption of such texts, his style being, as much as ever, the product of his reading. But if Ashbery's sentences echo, and so owe some kind of debt to, the prose of a number of writers addressing themselves to Pascal, they are unthinkable without 'The Sea and the Mirror', Auden appreciating, more clearly than Emerson or James that Pascal's question to the modern atheist is a question of style.

The premise of 'The Sea and the Mirror' is a Pascalian predicament, the whole poem 'swaying out on the ultimate wind-whipped cornice that overhangs the unaiding void'.[12] *The Pensées* also hung over a void, Pascal imagining man 'suspended in the material body that nature has given him between the two abysses of infinity and nothingness'.[13] For Pascal this was reason to gamble on God's existence, the vertiginous uncertainty of human existence prompting faith in the divine order. Auden responds differently, preferring to value the 'ever giddier collective gallop' (the 'Grand Gallop' as Ashbery calls it) rather than succumb to the blandishments of the 'everlasting Not Yet'. Like Emerson, that is, Auden understood Pascal's challenge to the atheist as the challenge to establish what Emerson termed 'the strong present tense', a way of talking about the present which appreciated its value; which did not allow it to pale in the face of the 'everlasting Not Yet'. What this meant for Auden, as for Emerson, was not abandoning ideas of order, but discerning order in the present, or, as Sebastian puts it in 'The Sea and the Mirror',

> Just Now is what it might be every day,
> Right Here is absolute and needs no crown,
> Ermine or trumpets, protocol or sword.[14]

Enthusiastic, and mildly exhilarating as it is, Sebastian's remark, as Auden well knows, is blithe: asserting the value of the present – the 'Right here', 'Just Now' – but by its 'trumpets, protocol and sword' signalling a distance from its actuality. Sebastian's present might be ideal, but that is only because it is unlike any present that anybody actually inhabits. His language is quite free of the 'tangled, muddy, painful, perplexed' situations which are the stuff of most people's lives most of the time. What Sebastian opens up, therefore, is what Auden (or at least

Caliban) terms 'the ungarnished offended gap between what you so question-
ably are and what you are commanded without any question to become'.[15] This
gap has been the substance of responses to Pascal since Emerson noticed that
'the world I converse with in the city and in the farms, is not the world I *think*. I
observe that difference, and shall observe it. One day I shall know the value and
law of this discrepance'.[16] Emerson is particularly prone to such a discrepancy,
his language, conditioned by the abstract requirements of Transcendentalism,
being quite incapable of gripping the actuality of life in the city. Auden's
response to such a discrepance is the prose of Caliban's address to the audience.

The young Ashbery was much taken with Caliban's prose. In his Harvard
University senior thesis on Auden, Ashbery praised the older poet for having
'brought innumerable people closer to the world in which they have to live'. He
also thought 'Caliban to the Audience' was 'probably the most brilliant writing
Auden has ever done', observing that, '[o]ddly enough, it is in prose, beginning
as a parody of the late-style of Henry James'.[17] There is a tension between these
two judgements of which Auden and the mature (though perhaps not the
undergraduate) Ashbery are acutely aware, and which takes one to the difficult
truth of 'The Sea and the Mirror'. Caliban's prose does mean to bring readers
closer to the world in which they have to live, and is happier than ever Sebastian
(or for that matter Emerson) could be in a world in which people have 'one bout
of flu per winter, an occasional twinge of toothache', in which shoelaces are bro-
ken, soup is spilled, cigarettes burn holes into tablecloths, and letters are lost. He
also has a way of making such a world seem ideal; of making the 'giddy collec-
tive gallop' seem infinitely preferable to the 'everlasting not yet'. It is exhilarat-
ing – certainly the undergraduate Ashbery appears to have found it so – to be told
that 'you will never feel more secure than you do now in your knowledge that
you *have* your ticket, your passport *is* in order, you have *not* forgotten to pack
your pyjamas and an extra clean shirt', that 'you will never meet a jollier, more
various crowd than you see around you here, sharing with you the throbbing,
suppressed excitement of those to whom the exciting thing is still, perhaps, to
happen'.[18]

This is a world one wants to live in, a strong present worthy of the name – the
choreography of the rush-hour crowd communicating a sense of grace equal to
any desire for order. Sebastian's words ring momentarily true. 'Just Now *is* what
it might be every day, / Right here *is* absolute and needs no crown.'

Except, of course, that, soup and shoelaces notwithstanding, Caliban's scene
is a composition, the station crowd not bumping and swearing but choreo-
graphed by Caliban's effortlessly fluent, multi-clausal Jamesian syntax. Auden
knows this of course, the audience telling Caliban that the effect of his writing
is a 'distorted parody' of an actual situation, 'all grossness turned to glory'. The
argument of Auden's prose poem is that there is no alternative to this parody.
Only by bathing the ordinary in an extraordinarily positive light, so Caliban's
argument goes, can the poet encourage the reader to attend closely enough to
their life to make it worth living. The gamble is that, while the gap between the

two states might induce the wish to meliorate things, it is equally possible, as Caliban observes, that the reader will feel further estranged from the life he or she has to live.

The critical question to ask of 'The Sea and the Mirror', which the under-graduate Ashbery appears not to have asked but which mature Ashbery certainly does, is whose estrangement is really at issue in Caliban's prose. Thus for all that Auden (as Caliban) has a winning way with reality, and close as he gets to the 'drabness and sham', he is also always protecting himself from it. So if, in part, Auden's Jamesian syntax is a comment on the inevitable choreographic effect of language, it is also a double-bluff, the further point of which is to preserve a camp distance between the poet and a life whose 'grossness' he can come to terms with it only by 'glorifying' it. It is not altogether surprising, then, that 'The Sea and the Mirror', for all that, for the most part, it is caught up in the giddy collective gallop, should resort in the end to the cadences of the everlasting not yet – Caliban's concluding sentence reminding us of 'the perfected Work which is not ours', whose 'great coherences stand out through our secular blur in all their overwhelmingly righteous obligation'.[19] Auden's is thus only a partial response to Pascal, the stylishness of his 'drabness and sham' – nicely illustrated by the elegant assonance of the phrase – refusing to acknowledge how drab and sham it really gets.

The crux of *Three Poems* is an Audenesque moment, one of those moments when, as Ashbery puts it, a 'sudden balm suffuses the soul without warning, as a kind of bloom or grace':

> those periods of balmy weather in early spring, sometimes even before spring has officially begun: days or even a few hours when the air seems suffused with an unearthly tenderness, as though love were about to start, now, at this moment, on an endless journey put off since the beginning of time. Just to walk a few steps in this romantic atmosphere is to experience a magical but quiescent bliss, as though the torch of life were about to be placed in one's hands: after having anticipated it for so long, what is one now to do? (TP, 73)

This luminous moment occurs midway through 'The System' – the middle, and by some measure the most important, of the *Three Poems* – and at the end of a remarkably controlled and extended argument, the premise of which is that, as the opening line of the poem has it, 'The system was breaking down' (TP, 53). The argument itself has two phases. The first phase is a history of the process whereby the system – by which is meant nothing more precise than the sense of a controlling order – has come to break down. A kind of mythology of con-sciousness, the narrative ascribes the breakdown to the tendency in human thought to render things coherent, a tendency which has required all manner of things to fall outside human reckoning, with the consequence that now so much goes unaccounted for that the system of thought that excluded them is breaking down. Vaguely but not completely plausible – being itself an instance of the kind of organising thought it means to argue against – the narrative is difficult, but by no means impossible to follow, and so one is prepared, as one enters it, for the second phase of the argument. The subject of the second phase of the argument, which is more like a lecture than the first, is how to cope with the reality of a living in a world in which the system has broken down. Working through alternative theories, in the maner of a good lecture, the poem advances the pros and cons of a series of ways of (or through) life: of just sailing along (so acquiring a 'visceral knowledge' of life but losing any sense of order); of persisting in the search for order (and so, in the present disorganised state of affairs, suffering terribly); of the great career model (which shapes a life by inscribing it with an objective, but which requires single-mindedness and so tends to produce separation); or of the '"life-as-ritual" concept' (an Emersonian image of a mobile self, which exhilarates as it allows for rapid change, but disorientates as it tends to loss of identity). This phase of the argument is also ironically poised, the poem engaging in intelligently abstract discussions of these alternative ways of life, but all the time signalling that abstraction is part of the problem, that the system is breaking down because thought has become so abstracted. It is at this point that Ashbery's poetic lecture turns its attention to the value of the moment of grace. 'In addition', we are told (in best lecturese), 'to these twin notions of growth, two kinds of happiness are possible: the frontal and the latent' (TP, 71). This opaque, almost entirely meaningless, terminology indicates that we have reached the end of the line, that the lecturer's abstractions have finally lost touch with anything resembling reality. It is in these circumstances, and under the name of frontal happiness, that the balmy Audenesque moment is introduced.

For Auden, in 'The Sea and the Mirror', this was the end of the argument: his glimpse of order in the daily round carrying his dialogue with Pascal as far it could go. In this Auden was with Frank Kermode, who in *The Sense of an Ending* (a critical text situated on precisely the same quasi-spiritual, post-Stevens territory as *Three Poems*) argued that it is only by such moments that any shape can be given to existence. They are, as Kermode sees it, the 'hiding places of power', 'the agents of time's defeat': 'sempiternal moments that transcend the giddy successiveness of world-time'.[20] But there's the problem, because, while for Auden such moments were a means of establishing the value of the 'ever giddier collective gallop' against the allure of the 'everlasting Not Yet', now for Kermode they transcend that 'giddiness'. And Kermode (as Auden comes to concede in 'The Sea and the Mirror') is surely right, the moment of grace (the epiphany) serving no more to reveal the possibility of order in the daily round than to disclose the fact that being in the middle of the daily round does not usually feel like this, the present situation being typically 'tangled, muddy, painful, perplexed'. Auden's choreographed sense of the here and now is not an adequate answer either to Pascal's challenge to the Godless mind-set (living in the present not being shown preferable to gambling on an eternal future) or (because it does not arrive at an idea of poetic order which takes full account of the disorder of daily life) to Stevens's call for a harmonious scepticism. Whether one likes it or not, it is a great strength of Ashbery's poetry that he squares up to this short-fall in Auden, that rather than, as Kermode implies he should, revive a Romantic (bad) faith in the power of the sempiternal moment, he writes a poetry, as Bloom describes it, without privileged moments. That poetry comes fully into being in *Three Poems*, with the moment of grace proving not the end of the argument but a point of departure – the moment at which Ashbery's contribution to the Pascalian discourse can properly be thought to begin.

Put stylistically, the question for the poet writing after Auden (or at least for the poet for whom religion is no longer a viable option) is how to make poetry, even prose poetry, more prosaic. One way to do this, as Ashbery sometimes shows in *Three Poems*, is simply to incorporate things prosaic – 'a battery jar, a rusted pulley' – into one's poetry. In itself, however, absorbing the things of the world into poetry is not sufficient to make poetry more prosaic, Auden showing – with his soup and shoelaces – that poetry can accommodate things of the everyday world while also keeping its distance. The effect is not so much to make poetry more prosaic as to poeticise the prosaic things that get included. What Ashbery sets out to include in his prose poetry, therefore, is the sensation not the objects of everyday life.

One way he does this is by allowing his writing to knot. The passage inquiring into latent happiness becomes just such a tangle:

> So that this second kind of happiness is merely a fleshed-out, realized version of that ideal first kind, and more to be prized because its now ripe contours enfold both the promise and the shame of our human state, which they therefore proceed to transmute into something that is an amalgam of both, the faithful reflection of the idealistic concept that got us started along this path, but a reflection which is truer than the original because more suited to us, and whose shining perspectives we can feel and hold, clenching the journey to us like the bread and meat left by the wayside for the fatigued traveler by an anonymous Good Samaritan – ourselves, perhaps, just as Hop-o'-My-Thumb distributed crumbs along the way to guide him back in the dark, only these the birds have miraculously spared: they are ours. (TP, 81)

This is a difficult sentence, an initially clear argument becoming a complex tangle. The sentence's argument is for a fleshed out, realised version of the kind of idealised happiness offered by Auden – for an image of happiness that somehow narrows and straddles the 'ungarnished offended gap'. This is not so easy to achieve and the tangle that the sentence becomes results from the intertwining of the discursive strands – abstract and detailed (concepts and crumbs) – that would enable such a fleshy ideal to be articulated. Such tangles are easy to dismiss: as the work of a poet, incapable of, or simply resistant to, coherent thought. And probably there is no way of convincing the most sceptical reader of Ashbery that this is not all it amounts to. But there is another way to look at the knottedness of *Three Poems* and that is as evidence that more than Auden (or Emerson, or James) Ashbery rises to the challenge of Pascal's writing.

In the section of *The Pensées* entitled 'The knot' Pascal argues for the inadequacy of rational argument. 'There is nothing', he suggests, 'that so conforms with reason as [the] renunciation of reason.' 'The last step that reason takes', he argues, 'is to recognize that there is an infinity of things beyond it; it is but weak if it does not succeed in recognizing that.'[21] 'The knot' is the paradoxical heart of *The Pensées*, Pascal's argument for belief in God insisting on the inadequacy of rational argument. To dispute the power of argument, for Pascal, is to foster the degree of humility necessary if the individual is to submit to Christ. However, to argue against argument is also, as Pascal is very well aware, to affirm the power of rational thought. The problem is solved by allowing the argument to argue against itself. In other words, Pascal demonstrates the inadequacy of argument by allowing his seemingly composed disquisition to become so tangled that the reader loses faith in the discursive structures that had promised order. This is most clearly the case in his account of 'Man without God', the individual pen-sées being reasonable in themselves but combining to produce a feeling of extreme disarray. For Pascal this feeling of extreme disarray is what it means to be without God, his prose thereby embodying the belief that only in God (and not in rational argument) does one find the answer to the call to order.

Pascal's knotted prose is thus the measure of his challenge to the would-be harmonious sceptic. Only writing that is fully cognisant of the 'tangled' state which is part of the actual condition of living in the moment can seriously be thought to argue that living in the moment is ideal. Emerson, James and Auden all have ways of signalling the confusions that are part and parcel of present experience: Emerson spoke of his disorientation; James talked of the hurly-burly of real life; Auden observed the paradoxes of representation. But eager as each writer is to establish that happiness can and should be found 'in the moment', each also understates just how perplexing the present can be. By contrast, *Three Poems* in general, and 'The System' in particular, are an attempt to write it how it feels.

Not, of course, that getting one's writing in a tangle is itself a sufficient response to Pascal, because in and of itself knottedness only confirms Pascal's opinion of 'Man without God': as a wretch caught up in the tangles of his own inadequate thought processes. What redeems the tangles of Ashbery's prose poetry – and what makes it the work not of a sceptic but of a harmonious scep-tic – is that such tangles do not here preclude poetic order but are, in fact, its precondition. There are two ways to understand this. The first, and most straightforward, is that the difficulties of Ashbery's writing serve to enhance the pleasures of its clarities and so serve to enhance one's sense of the situation present. This was one of the reasons why, in his review of *Stanzas in Meditation*, Ashbery suggested the reader should bear with Stein. We should bear with those 'highly complex, and, for some, unreadable' poems not only because they 'imi-tate [life's] rhythm, its way of happening', but also, he told us, because

> the almost physical pain with which we strive to accompany the evolving thought of one of James's or Gertrude Stein's characters is perhaps a counterpart of the painful continual projection of the individual into life. As in life, perseverance has its rewards – moments when we emerge suddenly on a high plateau with a view of the whole distance we have come.[22]

Ashbery's response to Stein and Henry James finds an echo, as one might expect, in William James, it being part of James's response to Pascal to ask:

> Is all 'yes, yes' in the universe? Doesn't the fact of 'no' stand at the very core of life? Doesn't the very 'seriousness' that we attribute to life mean that ineluctable noes and losses form a part of it, that there are genuine sacrifices somewhere, and that something permanently drastic and bitter always remains at the bottom of its cup?[23]

If there are moments in life that make Pascal's odds worth resisting, James suggests, they are the more valuable for not being the norm. Forceful (invigorating even) as this is, it raises familiar problems. If, as Ashbery suggests, such moments offer 'a view of the whole distance we have come', that 'whole distance' is also another version of the Emersonian discrepance, the Audenesque 'gap'; and so, while the difficult quality of Ashbery's writing in *Three Poems* does make the rewards it comes ultimately to offer that much the sweeter, there is a more precise sense in which the knots of his prose are a precondition for its idea of poetic order.

The flipside of the knottedness by which Ashbery represents the sensation of living in the absence of an ordering presence is what, in 'The New Spirit', he calls 'the new merging' (TP, 5).

> This is shaped in the new merging, like ancestral smiles, common memories, remembering just how the light stood on the water that time. But it is also something new. Outside, can't you hear it, the traffic, the trees, everything getting nearer. To end up with, inside each other, moving upward like penance. For the continual pilgrimage has not stopped. It is only that you are both moving at the same rate of speed and cannot apprehend the motion. Which carries you beyond, alarmingly fast out into the confusion where the river pours into the sea. That place that seems even farther from the shore. (TP, 5)

The 'new merging' is an important phrase. What it points to is Ashbery's poetic prose: its strong present aiming to keep pace with the way people and things actually come together, so discerning the shape (if not exactly the order) in everyday life. And crucially, the qualities of Ashbery's prose which make it right to speak of it as a 'new merging' are also the qualities which constitute its knottedness: speed, a blurred sense of self, the intertwining of discourses, and what one might call its deictic relation to the world. A passage from page 7 of 'The New Spirit', in which the poet is endeavouring both to define and to exemplify this condition he calls the 'new merging', helps bring these now harmonious elements of Ashbery's writing into view.

> It's just beginning. Now it's started to work again. The visitation, was it more or less over. No, it had not yet begun, except as a preparatory dream which seemed to have the rough texture of life, but which dwindled into starshine like all the unwanted memories. There was no holding on to it. But for that we ought to be glad, no one really needed it, yet it was not utterly worthless, it taught us the forms of this our present waking life, the manners of the unreachable. And its judge-

ments, though harmless and playful, were yet the form of utterance by which judgement shall come to be known. For we judge not, lest we be judged, yet we are judged all the same, without noticing, until one day we wake up a different color, the color of the filter of the opinions and ideas everyone has ever entertained about us. And in this form we must prepare, now, to try to live. (TP 7–8)

The speed, which, as Ashbery puts it elsewhere, 'has become the element in which you live and which is you', is felt here in the phrase 'There was no holding on to it'. The suggestion is that things are moving too quickly to be retained, and as we have seen this can be a source of difficulty in Ashbery's prose, his sentences accelerating away from their point of departure at escape velocity. Here, however, as elsewhere, speed is also a cause for gratitude. 'For that', as the poet puts it, echoing the act of grace given before a meal, 'we ought to be glad.' Speed, as Ashbery regards it, is not just a defining quality of contemporary existence, it is also, potentially, a source of grace: the pace of events blurring distinctions, collapsing divisions and so becoming a medium of unity. Keeping pace with the 'secular blur' in order to show how people and things now run together, Ashbery's accelerated prose means, as Kermode put it, to acknowledge mere successiveness without being merely successive.

The new merging that comes of a blurred sense of self is linked, in the passage in question, to the merging that comes of an intertwining of registers. Ashbery's sense of the relation of self to others is defined not so much by Rimbaud's suggestion that 'Je est un autre' as by Pasternak's idea, articulated by Zhivago, that 'You in others are yourself'. This is a hard thought to accept – other people's ideas of oneself constituting one's identity – but Ashbery clearly articulates it here, hence the fact that 'one day we wake up a different color, the color of the filter of the opinions and ideas everyone has ever entertained about us'. Hence also the allusion to Matthew 7:1. As Matthew has it, one should judge not in case one should be judged. It is an argument for a unity, judgements, as Matthew puts it, suggesting divisions. But if there is an ideal of unity implicit in not judging, it is not the fleshed-out kind of ideal Ashbery is aiming at. People do judge, Ashbery suggests, but do not necessarily divide against one another as they do so. Indeed to judge is to take an interest, and so to realise one's connection to others. So, if our judgements of others sometimes get us into tangles, and if Ashbery's attempt to articulate a self which finds itself in others can sometimes produce rather knotted writing, each gesture, also results in a merging of sorts. Indeed, the merging of individuals through the act of judgement is an almost religious state, which the passage communicates by its almost religious tone. It achieves this tone by its way of absorbing the cadences from Matthew's gospel, sacred language and secular talk running together with barely a seam. Ashbery, that is, unlike Auden, does not preserve a dramatic distance between spiritual and demotic idioms, but here, as throughout *Three Poems*, allows them to bleed together.

Finally, and much more than Auden, Ashbery's prose permits an interfusing of language and events. This passage is typical of *Three Poems* in opening itself up to events, that openness being achieved, here as elsewhere, through the impersonal pronoun 'it'. At times, in Ashbery, 'it' is an index of the difficulty of the writing, referring the reader back to an antecedent that has already slipped too far into the past to be recoverable. Here, however, 'it' functions deictically, taking its meaning from the events that surround it, events which, as they are not specified, can be those of either the poet's situation or the readers, or, ideally, of both. Events are thus allowed to spill on to the stage of Ashbery's writing. Always deictically poised – his 'this' and 'that' always sucking in 'the other' – Ashbery's writing means to narrow the gap between word and world.

Ashbery is not the only poet writing after (and under the influence of) Auden to realise that the problem Auden leaves the contemporary poet – or at least, the contemporary poet for whom the religious drama is not an alternative to the secular blur – is how to make poetry more prosaic. Another such poet, offering a very different solution, is Larkin: the difference between Ashbery and Larkin being never so marked as between 'High Windows' and *Three Poems*. I am aware, of course, that to a certain reader of Larkin – the kind of reader drawn especially, perhaps, to the structures of his poetry – no amount of extended explanations of Ashbery's demanding prose poetry will be sufficient to convince of its value (the need for explanation only proving, from a certain viewpoint, that the poetry is too complicated). Nor do I want to imply that one has to choose between Ashbery and Larkin. This would be to reinforce a division which, for instance, the writing of the British poet John Ash – who manages not only to like but to write like both of them – has shown to be false. However, it does help to understand Ashbery if one appreciates the cost of Larkin's more structured approach to the prosaic.

'High Windows' begins with the poet observing how,

> When I see a couple of kids
> And guess he's fucking her and she's
> Taking pills or wearing a diaphragm,
> I know this is paradise[24]

Larkin's rhythms being strictly those of poetry, this is not as prosaic as it looks. Metrically, it is a virtuoso performance, spondees, trochees and dactyls playing across the less than elegant diction, and signalling, as they do, the poet's mastery of his craft. This is not, then, a happy merging of poetry and prose, but a triumph of poetry over prose, the high points of which are the trochaic 'fucking' and the dactylic 'diaphragm'. Larkin's poetry does not come to terms with grossness by glorifying it, as Auden did. Rather he produces a disjunction of self-consciously poetic form and manifestly prosaic subject matter that serves to accentuate the grossness of the latter. He develops Auden in that he incorporates a level of drabness Auden could not tolerate, but he departs from Auden in that he incorporates such drabness only to dismiss it. The whole point of the poem, in fact, is to show that the poet's vision of the kids' behaviour is not 'paradise', hence the recourse to the very different register of the final stanza, with its 'thought of high windows', its 'sun-comprehending glass' and 'beyond it, the deep blue air, that shows / Nothing, and is nowhere, and is endless'.[25]

'High Windows' is thus a significant failure. It does not believe in God, but in its disregard for the prosaic it fails to show that one would have anything to lose by doing so. In Pascalian terms this is a wretched position to assume, and one that, in the process, betrays a limited reading of Auden. Witness the poem's weak use of the word 'beyond'. 'Beyond', for Larkin, points to an escape from the present. It denotes the realm of the imagination, but, in so far as imagination in this poem is nothing more than the ethereal other of a contemptible reality, then 'beyond', as Larkin uses it, also signals a failure of imagination. At his strenuous best, Auden's use of 'beyond' is altogether more imaginative. 'Is there,' the audience, speaking through Caliban, asks,

> could there be, *any* miraculous suspension of the wearily historic, the dingily geographic, the dully drearily sensible beyond her faith, her charm, her love to command? Yes, there could be, yes, alas, indeed yes, O there is, right here, right now before us, the situation present.[26]

The way to get 'beyond' the dully drearily sensible – the prophylactic world of Larkin's couple – is not, Auden suggests, to escape it but to think of it in terms of 'the situation present': the present situation being that which people have in common, which binds them, which 'right here, right now' affords an image of unity in action.

What Auden calls the 'situation present' is what Ashbery calls the occasion, the point of occasional poetry being, as Paul Goodman suggested, precisely to get beyond the 'wearily historic, the dingily geographic' by bathing 'the world in such a light of imagination and criticism that the persons who are living in it without meaning or feeling suddenly find that it is meaningful and exciting to live in it'.[27] The effect of such writing, Goodman observed, was to integrate those it concerned itself with, to reacquaint people with their circumstances and so with one another. Such an act of integration is what Ashbery calls 'the new merging', this being a poetry of the occasion by any other name. As he puts it in 'The New Spirit': 'The various segments of knowledge are by definition divided up and distributed in an equilibrium guaranteed by the nature of their existence, yet it can all be grasped and used quite handily when an occasion presents itself' (TP, 31). Or as he exhorts in 'The System':

> The day is not far advanced: it still half-seriously offers with one hand the promise that it pockets with the other, and it is still up to you to seize the occasion, jump into the fray, not be ruled by its cruel if only human whims. The person sitting opposite you who asked you a question is still waiting for the answer; he has not yet found your hesitation unusual, but it is up to you to grasp it with both hands, wrenching it from the web of connectives to rub off the grime that has obscured its brilliance so as to restore it to him, that pause which is the answer you have both been expecting. (TP, 97)

With its language of merging growing out of its knots and tangles, *Three Poems*, and 'The System' in particular, offers the reader, more than ever, a way of writing and viewing the world which might enable him or her to seize the occasion, to apprehend from moment to moment (not just at privileged moments) one's connectedness to the things going on around one.

Writing that aims to do this sets itself, as he observed of Stein, an impossible task, but one to which Ashbery was never more equal than in *Three Poems*. Hence the conclusion to 'The System', the exhilaration of which speaks clearly of a writer at the height of his powers:

> I have been watching this film, therefore, and now I have seen enough; as I leave the theater I am surprised to find that it is still daylight outside (the darkness of the film as well as its specks of light were so intense); I am forced to squint; in this way I gradually get an idea of where I am. Only this world is not as light as the other one; it is made grey with shadows like cobwebs that deepen as the memory of the film begins to fade. This is the way all movies are meant to end, but how is it possible to go on living just now except by plunging into the middle of some other one that you have doubtless seen before? It seems truly impossible, but invariably at this point we are walking together along a street in some well-known city. The allegory is ended, its coils absorbed into the past, and this afternoon is as wide as an ocean. It is the time we have now, and all our wasted time sinks into the sea and is swallowed up without a trace. The past is dust and ashes, and this incommensurably wide way leads to the pragmatic and kinetic future. (TP, 105-6)

Ashbery's deep immersion in Pascal notwithstanding, 'it is the time we have now' that matters here. And as the reader is propelled from the poem, urged out by the poetry's inspirational pragmatism, so the poem has equipped him or her to understand the shape of events, to discern, ideally, the order in disorder. What the poet apprehends is thus no longer the question. What the reader can come to apprehend is. Ashbery's prose poetry is thus the act of *some* harmonious sceptic.

NOTES

1 W.H. Auden, *Collected Poems*, p. 328.
2 David Herd, 'Kenneth Koch in conversation', p. 30.
3 Wallace Stevens, *Collected Poems*, p. 122.
4 A. Poulin Jnr, 'The experience of experience', p. 254.
5 Stephen Fredman, *Poet's Prose*, p. 6.
6 Ibid., p. 100.
7 David Lehman, *The Last Avant-Garde*, p. 100.
8 Shoptaw considers Clare, Auden and de Chirico as models. Fredman, whose selections show a very fine ear for cadence, goes much further in his respect, offering, among others, Stein, James, Roussel, Rilke and again de Chirico as precursors to Ashbery. He defines the tone and ambition of Ashbery's prose by distinguishing it clearly from the French prose poem (which Ashbery finds too 'self-consciously poetic' for his tastes). He hints at, but does not develop, Ashbery's affinities with

Emerson's meditative essay style. And most helpfully he links it with other mid–life spiritual meditations, for instance Dante's *La Vita Nuova* and the *Commedia*, Stevens's disquisitions on the nature of supreme fictions and Rilke's *Letters to a Young Poet*.

9 Blaise Pascal, *The Pensées*, p. 54.
10 Ibid., p. 59.
11 Ibid., p. 116.
12 W.H. Auden, *Collected Poems*, p. 340.
13 Pascal, *The Pensées*, p. 52.
14 W.H. Auden, *Collected Poems*, pp. 324, 338.
15 Ibid., p. 339.
16 Ralph Waldo Emerson, *Essays*, p. 85.
17 Cited in John Shoptaw, *On The Outside Looking Out*, p. 133.
18 W.H. Auden, *Collected Poems*, pp. 334, 335.
19 Ibid., p. 340.
20 Frank Kermode, *The Sense of an Ending*, p. 169.
21 Pascal, *The Pensées*, p. 161–2.
22 John Ashbery, 'The impossible', p. 252.
23 William James, *Pragmatism*, p114.
24 Philip Larkin, *Collected Poems*, p. 165.
25 Ibid.
26 W.H. Auden, *Collected Poems*, pp. 326, 327.
27 Paul Goodman, 'Advance-Guard Writing', p. 376.

CHAPTER SIX

John Ashbery in conversation: the communicative value of *Self-Portrait in a Convex Mirror* and *Houseboat Days*

Ashbery: Isn't that true of all of us? We want to communicate and we hate the idea
of being forced to. I think it's something that should be noticed ...
Poulin: Can we get back, then, to the central question of what it is you're
communicating. My feeling is that in the middle of the difficulty of your
poetry there is a very personal element, disguised by this difficulty.
Ashbery: Is that all? I don't see quite what you mean by a very personal element.[1]

> Something
> Ought to be written about how this affects
> You when you write poetry:
> The extreme austerity of an almost empty mind
> Colliding with the lush, Rousseau-like foliage of its desire to
>   communicate
> Something between breaths, if only for the sake
> Of others and their desire to understand you and desert you
> For other centers of communication, so that understanding
> May begin, and in doing so be undone.

(HD, 45–6)

During the eight years following the completion of *Three Poems*, Ashbery wrote two of his finest volumes of poetry, *Self-Portrait in a Convex Mirror* (1975) and *Houseboat Days* (1977), one of his most formally inventive, *As We Know* (1979), and a scurrilously funny work of prose poetry, *The Vermont Notebook* (1975). Each of the first three of these included a remarkable long poem – 'Self-Portrait in a Convex Mirror', 'Fantasia on "The Nut-Brown Maid"' and 'Litany' – and between them they contain upwards of a dozen of the best lyric poems he (or any American poet) has ever written. All this amongst and between the art criticism (for *ArtNews*, *Art in America* and *New York*, among others) and the creative writing classes (at Brooklyn College) by which he was making his living. It was a brilliantly inventive period in Ashbery's career, and entirely appropriate, therefore, that it was at this moment he should emerge as America's most celebrated contemporary poet: *Self-Portrait in a Convex Mirror* winning the triple crown of Pulitzer Prize, National Book Award and National Book Critics' Circle Award in 1976; Harold Bloom speaking for a large part of the critical community when

he proclaimed Ashbery, simply, 'the poet of our moment'; and the media show-
ing him a degree of attention that would once have seemed unthinkable for an
experimental poet.

But Ashbery's new-found celebrity was also a most perplexing development,
as the poet himself observed to John Ash.

> I think there are now people who know my name but don't know what I do. I'm
> famous for being famous – I'm a superstar, almost like Edna Everage! I find this
> very strange. I'm certainly still terribly controversial as a poet. The jury is still out
> on the question of whether I'm a poet at all, yet I get my picture taken for *Women's*
> *Wear Daily*.[2]

Or as he put it, rather less flamboyantly, to *The Paris Review*:

> Let me read you a comment which appeared in a review of my most recent book,
> from some newspaper in Virginia. It says: 'John Ashbery is emerging as a very
> important poet, if not by unanimous critical consent then certainly by the admira-
> tion and awe he inspires in younger poets. Oddly, no one understands Ashbery.' ...
> So I live with this paradox: on the one hand, I am an important poet, read by
> younger writers, and on the other hand, nobody understands me. I am often asked
> to account for this state of affairs, but I can't.[3]

To voice this state of affairs in interview is to perpetuate it, the interview itself
being one of these means whereby the contemporary poet becomes known
without being understood. So if, to understand Ashbery's poetry of this period,
one needs to consider his paradox – how it arose, what it meant to the poet and
what it tells us about postmodern American culture and the place of poetry in
that culture – one way to start is with his experience of the interview.

Ashbery hates interviews. He hates them because, as he told Kenneth Koch
in the mutual interview they conducted in 1965, he believes that 'It's rather hard
to be a good artist and also be able to explain intelligently what your art is about.
In fact, the worse your art is the easier it is to talk about it. At least, I'd like to
think so.'[4] Ashbery's comment to Koch recalls the much observed moment in
'The Skaters' (first published a year before the interview) when Ashbery intro-
duces the vexed question of what to leave out:

> But this is an important aspect of the question
> Which I am not ready to discuss, am not at all ready to,
> This leaving-out business. On it hinges the very importance
>   of what's novel
> Or autocratic, or dense or silly. It is as well to call attention
> To it by exaggeration, perhaps. But calling attention
> Isn't the same thing as explaning, and as I said I am not ready
> To line phrases with the costly stuff of explanation, and shall not,
> Will not do so for the moment.

(RM, 39)

Always preferring to call attention rather than explain, Ashbery dislikes the
interview because it cuts against the grain of his poetic; the act of explanation the

interview involves presupposing a relation between poet and reader to which he is antipathetic, and which he catches here in the term 'autocratic'. Or as he put it when asked by Sue Gangel in 1977 how he felt about discussing his poetry in interview: 'I find it distasteful.'[5] In a general sense the interview is 'distasteful' to Ashbery because he has a horror of the kind of confessional conversation it is always likely to become. But it is more precisely distasteful in that to explain one's poetry to the reader through the interview is to impede the exercise of readerly judgement, and so taste, that his poetry means to encourage. This explains Peter Stitt's slightly baffled (and not untypical) observation in the preface to Ashbery's *Paris Review* interview that 'Ashbery's answers to my questions required little editing. He did, however, throughout the conversation give the impression of distraction, as though he wasn't quite sure just what his role in the proceedings might be.'[6] Ashbery, it will be recalled, has said that 'the ideal situation for the poet is to have the reader speak the poem'. The ideal reader of an Ashbery poem will therefore be active like Emerson's, the activity of reading bringing the reader to the point at which he or she might (ideally) write the poem for themselves. To explain the poem to the reader (in so far as that is possible) is thus to allow for less than active reading, and so to militate against the poet's ideal. It is not altogether surprising, then, that Ashbery should be unsure what his role in the proceedings of the interview should be.

This said, Ashbery has given scores of interviews – to little magazines, academic journals, newspapers and radio programmes – being, like most contemporary poets, scarcely in a position to decline them.[7] Partly this is because the interview promises the poet the much-needed oxygen of publicity. But more importantly, as Donald Hall has observed, in the best interviews, 'the questioner is a version of ourselves; dressed in the costume of the common reader'.[8] To refuse an interview, in other words, would be to refuse to meet the reader. So while Ashbery hates interviews because they presuppose an image of poet-reader communication with which he is at odds, he continues to give them because, in theory at least, they promise the kind of close contact with the reader for which his poetry (after Whitman) is constantly striving. It follows that for Ashbery the interview is a deeply ambivalent occasion.

Ashbery's first published interview was his 1965 'Conversation' with Koch. Conventionally speaking, the exchange is a failure, the pair being far too intimate with one another's work to want explanations of it. The result was an anti-interview, or, more accurately perhaps, a collaboration of which the only rule was that one shouldn't give anything away. The interviewer proper began to arrive a few years later, Bill Berkson showing up at the *ArtNews* offices in 1970 to interview Ashbery for the *Paris Review*. Berkson's commission never materialised, the conversation never making it into print – a sign, no doubt, of Ashbery's ambivalence to the form. After Berkson the interviewer proceeded to arrive so frequently – often as not at the poet's Chelsea apartment – that, when asked by Gerrit Henry in 1979 (in an interview published in *The Spectator*) whether he was working on a new book of poems, a besieged Ashbery complained, 'I don't have any time. People are always coming to interview me these days.'[9]

Over and above the time they consumed, there are good reasons for supposing that the stream of interviewers affected (or disaffected) Ashbery's poetry. The first has to do with his poetic practice. Describing the origin of his centrifugal procedure to Gangel, he observed that

> The room, wherever I happen to be when I am writing is, of course, very important to me. They are frames for the poet, which lead him into a kind of reflection … Somehow I make connections and want to find out why I'm doing that, at this particular time.[10]

For Ashbery, it follows from this that anything that passes through the room in which he writes can have an impact on the poetry – a telephone call, as he puts it, can divert the progress of a poem. How much more affecting is it going to be, then, when the reader (in the guise of interviewer), who only a decade or so before had seemed to turn his back on Ashbery, starts passing through his sitting room?

The second reason for thinking the coming of the interviewers might have affected Ashbery has to do with the kind of questions they asked. In March 1971, as he finished 'The System', Ashbery's poetry acquired new strength. Sublimely inspirational, the poem left Ashbery understandably confident of his capacity to negotiate the reality of experience. So much so that 'the problem', if anything – as he put it in the third of his *Three Poems*, 'The Recital' – was that 'there is no new problem' (TP, 107). So adapted had his poetry become to the fact of change that little or nothing, so it must temporarily have seemed, could exceed its grasp. By the beginning of his next book, *Self-Portrait in a Convex Mirror*, that confidence had dramatically ebbed away. In 'As One Put Drunk into the Packet-Boat', the first poem in *Self-Portrait*, 'Harsh words are spoken'. In 'Worsening Situation', the second, the poet receives a visitor:

> One day a man called while I was out
> And left this message: 'You got the whole thing wrong
> From start to finish. Luckily, there's still time
> To correct the situation, but you must act fast.
> See me at your earliest convenience. And please
> Tell no one of this. Much besides your life depends on it.'
> I thought nothing of it at the time. Lately
> I've been looking at old-fashioned plaids, fingering
> Starched white collars, wondering whether there's a way
> To get them really white again. My wife
> Thinks I'm in Oslo – Oslo, France, that is.

(SP, 3-4)

The bathos of this transition – from the sublime chords of the end of the 'The System' to the bum notes of advertising diction – recalls the shift in Whitman from 'Song of Myself' to 'As I Ebb'd With the Ocean of Life'. Dismayed by the reception of his great long poem, Whitman dismantled the rhetoric that held it together. The first poems of *Self-Portrait in a Convex Mirror* are similarly dismayed, the final sentence of 'Worsening Situation', with its lack of understanding born of inadquate knowledge, being tonally typical.

There might be many reasons for the dispirited self-examination Ashbery undertakes in the first poems of *Self-Portrait*, but one prompt, as the 'harsh words' and the critical visitor suggest, was the early interview, of which A. Poulin Jnr's conversation with Ashbery, conducted at the 1972 Brockport Writer's Convention, was a typical example. Poulin's questioning, hostile and flustered by turn, had almost exclusively to do with Ashbery's 'difficulty'. Noting a certain bafflement in Ashbery's critics, Poulin asked, 'What is it about your poetry that produces these reactions in readers?', a dismayingly blunt question issuing in some very unsatisfactory exchanges.

> Poulin: Everyone speaks about the difficulty of your poetry and it seems to me that any discussion of your work must center around what is, or what seems to be, the core of your poem, of your poetry, of your work.
> Ashbery: I don't know what that core is. Maybe it would help if you explained exactly what you mean by 'difficulty'.
> Poulin: The difficulty of language, for one, of syntax. Reading one of your poems, one is not prepared for the kinds of juxtapositions that occur in many of the poems.
> Ashbery: I don't think one is prepared for juxtapositions in general, is one?[11]

Poulin, it will be observed, for all that he is a professional reader, is hardly an Emersonian one, his ill-considered questions collapsing into decidedly inactive tautologies. Even so, it is hard to see that Ashbery could ignore exchanges of this sort. Certainly it had always concerned Ashbery that his poetry had few takers. The very fact of the reader's absence, however, had meant that his or her reactions could not press heavily on the poet's consciousness. This state of affairs alters radically when the reader, in the form of the interviewer, tells the poet to his face that 'Everyone speaks of the difficulty of your poetry'. One way or another, whether he likes it or not, the poet has to take account of this voice.

Introducing his anthology of interviews with American poets, Joe David Bellamy recalls first noticing what he calls 'the interview swell' in 1970.[12] Explaining this development, which he regards as an unambiguously good thing, Bellamy observes that with the death of Randall Jarrell 'a critical vacuum ensued' just as a new generation of poets emerged, with the result that 'the poets themselves felt called upon to explicate the mysteries of their art with some new urgency in ritualistic collaboration with a tape recorder and a determinedly curious, and usually appreciative, interrogator'.[13] Bellamy's over-emphasis on Jarrell simplifies things, but there is some truth in the implication that, two decades after having counterposed themselves to the conventions of the prevailing critical practice, the avant-gardes of the 1950s lacked critical interlocutors. At their strongest, the modernist avant-gardes had a mutually nurturing relationship with the critical languages to which they gave rise, Russian formalism being the prime example. As these languages atrophied into the stifling prescriptions of the New Criticism, the postmodern avant-gardes developed in part out of an anti-critical impulse, one consequence of which was that by 1970 this generation of poets found itself speaking into a critical vacuum. By the mid-1970s this situation had begun to change. The publication of such works as Bloom's *The Anxiety of Influence* and *A Map of Misreading* (1973 and 1975) and Perloff's *Frank O'Hara: Poet Among Painters* (1977) and the bubbling through of post-structuralist theory into the practice of LANGUAGE poetry, indicated that, for good and ill, the languages of criticism and poetry were beginning to get back in step with one another. But all this, as Bellamy reports, was only after the poets had for some time been called on to explain themselves in interview. One effect of this is a tension in postmodern critical practice: the insistence on the death of the author coinciding with the equally insistent requirement that the writer give the authorized version of their work.

Bellamy is unusual in the unsuspicious way he treats the interview. Writing in 1967, in his introduction to the third series of *Writers at Work* (selections from *The Paris Review* interviews), Alfred Kazin noted that 'the "personal" is more and more the theme, the occasion, the dilemma of contemporary literature', and warned the reader that the interviews that follow reveal both 'the eloquence and the danger of the personal mode'.[14] The danger was that, in attending to the personal character of literature, they fostered the cult of the authorial personality, and so, rather than providing access to the writing, diverted attention from it. The interview 'is due someone currently important … is our way of understanding his fame. It is not wisdom that we are trying to understand; it is exceptionality.'[15] The proliferation of literary interviews thus marks an increased interest not so much in writing but in the fact of being a writer, which is just another version of being a celebrity, and, so far from constituting a point of contact between writer and public, the interview marks a breakdown of communication. Writing in 1983 (in the introduction to the fifth series of *Writers at Work*), Francine du Plessix Gray gave Kazin's discussion of 'celebrity' a sophisticated twist, observing that, while it would seem to make writers more special, the interview actually diminishes them. 'In the past half century,' she argues, 'we [the American public] have swung from the traditional custom of letting artists famish in their garrets to the current fashion of force-feeding them into stardom for consumption in media and salon'.[16] She too warns artists to guard against 'the seductive immediacy' of the interview, which, she argues, tends to contaminate, rather than to alleviate 'their traditional solitude'.[17]

The overlap between Du Plessix Gray's argument against the interview and Fredric Jameson's pessimistic account of the avant-garde in postmodern culture tells us something about the centrality of the interview to that culture. It is central because it brings into collision two opposed but inextricably linked themes in contemporary existence: democracy and celebrity. The interview democratises poetry in that the poet has never been so accountable, readers of various stripes and qualifications telling him or her what they do and don't like, do and don't understand about the poetry, almost as soon as it has been written – diminishing, in the process, the distance between poet and reader which for good and ill has contributed to the poet's cultural prestige. On the other hand, the interview makes a celebrity of the poet, it being the poet's aura of importance which attracts a certain kind of interviewer in the first place, the poetry, as a result, becoming secondary to the fact that the poet is a poet. What results is a strictly double-edged form of communication – apparently promising the poet contact with a wider audience but actually affirming that communications have broken down. The effect of this is a peculiar kind of marginality, the figure of the poet being invested with great significance, while the poetry itself slips further from consideration. It is in a cultural climate characterised by such a paradoxical form of communication that a highly controversial poet can have his photograph taken for a women's fashion magazine.

A further recognisably postmodern effect of the interview is self-consciousness. Interviewing Ashbery at his Chelsea apartment in 1976, Richard Kostelanetz echoed Poulin in asking how Ashbery felt when 'readers tell him … that they were unable to "understand" his poetry', while the *New York Times Magazine* profile that resulted from the interview ran under the somewhat uninviting title 'How to be a difficult poet'.[18] There is no denying, of course, that Ashbery's poetry makes demands on the reader. But the charge of literary difficulty is self-fulfilling: the reader finding the poetry difficult because that is how the interviewer encourages him (or otherwise) to approach it. Certainly by the early 1980s the question of difficulty had been asked so often that even the interviewers were beginning to tire of it. Speaking to Ashbery for the *American Poetry Review*, Ross Labrie observed

> the number of times the matter of obscurity has been brought up in connection with your poems. Of course you have rejoined consistently that you didn't mean to be obscure, that you were obviously trying to communicate to others. When you look back over your poems, are you ever surprised by what appears there?[19]

Ashbery's reactions to the reiterated charge of difficulty have been various, one response, as Labrie indicates, being simply to repeat his insistence that he means to communicate. 'My poetry is often criticized for a failure to communicate,' he told the *New York Quarterly*,

> but I take issue with this; my intention is to communicate and my feeling is that a poem that communicates something that's already known by the reader is not really communicating anything to him and in fact shows a lack of respect for him.[20]

This often repeated, bite-size retort tells part of the truth of his poetry; the telling communication, as he sees it, being that which conveys something new and so unfamiliar. But this is only a partial understanding of 'communication', which, although it does mean imparting or transmitting information, also means connection and mutual understanding. Ashbery's poetry appreciates the relation between these apparently contradictory elements, and wherever possible in interview he deepens his meditation on communication to explore that relation. Indeed, in a certain sense the interview is the ideal form for Ashbery to explain this aspect of his poetic, the interview, like the collaboration, succeeding only if both parties have a shared sense of the occasion. Putting this philosophically, John Searle has observed that, because conversations, unlike Austinian speech-acts, are made up as the speakers go along, it is difficult to generalise about their rules beyond observing the 'role background plays in determining conversational relevance'.[21] From which it follows that a successful conversation with a stranger will largely be an act of preparation, both parties filling in the background in a prelude to, a preamble towards the possibility of, a conversation. One way for Ashbery to make the communicative character of his poetry clear, therefore, is to draw attention to this necessary preparation in relation to the interview itself, foregrounding the background in order to stage the conversation. Thus as he tells Poulin,

> We're sitting here, presumably having a nice discussion about somebody's poetry, and yet the occasion is something else also. First of all, I'm in a strange place with lots of lights whose meaning I don't quite understand, and I'm talking about a poem I wrote years ago and which no longer means very much to me. I have a feeling that everything is slipping away from me as I'm trying to talk about it – a feeling I have most of the time, in fact – and I think I was probably trying to call attention to this same feeling in 'Leaving the Atocha Station' and in other poems as well. Not because of any intrinsic importance the feeling might have, but because I feel that somebody should call attention to this. Maybe once it's called attention to we can think about something else, which is what I'd like to do.[22]

This is subtly done, Ashbery explaining the deictic character of his poetry, its intention always to 'call attention to this', by calling attention to the occasion of the interview, the background becoming the foreground in the way that in Bonnard the wallpaper, or in Rousseau the foliage, becomes the subject.

A reply to a question by Richard Jackson makes a similar point in a more scholarly fashion, Ashbery noting that at the end of his essay 'The Wall and the Books',

> Borges gives an almost Paterian definition of creativity: 'Music, states of happiness, mythology, faces molded by time, certain twilights in certain places - all these are trying to tell us something, or have told us something we should not have missed or are about to tell us something. The imminence of the revelation that is not yet produced is, perhaps, the aesthetic reality.' The imminence of a revelation not yet produced is very important and hard to define in poetry and probably is the source of some of the difficulty with my own poems. But I don't think it would serve any useful purpose to spare myself or the reader the difficulty of that imminence, of always being on the edge of things.[23]

This is a highly considered answer – Ashbery acknowledging that his poetry causes difficulty, but legitimising it by articulating his own concern to bring the reader to 'the edge of things' in terms of Borges and Pater. The result of such consideration is, as Ashbery has observed, a heightening of a certain kind of self-consciousness. Speaking to David Remnick in 1979, he remarked that the poem 'Wet Casements' was occasioned by the visit of a poet:

> He began asking questions that I found very deep and almost painful to contemplate. This strange transformation interested me very much. At one point it was almost as if we were seeing ourselves in each other. I was looking at him but it seemed as though I was looking at myself. He pointed out this phenomenon.[24]

If a certain kind of heightened self-consciousness is one means of distinguishing postmodern from modernist writing, the discomforting reflection the literary interview provides the writer would appear to be one prompt towards the new condition.

The fact that the interview sometimes allows for such careful statements of purpose as Ashbery presents to Jackson would seem to redeem it as a form, the poetry not the personality being clearly to the fore here. But, as Ashbery complained to John Tranter, such statements carry a cost. 'It seems', he observed,

> that people will do almost anything rather than read a poem and try and come to terms with it, you know. A statement from the poet about what he meant in the poem is considered to be very helpful, but my point is that it really isn't going to help anybody since it's just a paraphrase operating at some distance.[25]

Ashbery's response to this tension is whenever possible to return the interview to the poetry itself, the best example of this (and his most successful interview to date) being his conversation with the British poet John Ash. A friend and Chelsea neighbour, Ash knew Ashbery's aesthetic background well enough to ask informed questions about it, but well enough also to understand the importance of background to that aesthetic. He shows this understanding both in the body of the interview, by drawing Ashbery on composers and writers who have been important in his formation, but also in his prose preamble to it.

'The interview', Ash tells us,

> took place in John Ashbery's apartment in Chelsea. It was repeatedly interrupted by the sound of sirens rising from 9th Avenue and a ringing telephone. Chelsea is located north of Greenwich Village on the west side of Manhattan. Ashbery's apartment looks out towards the Hudson River and the heights of New Jersey. To one side of the view is a seminary with a very English-looking Gothic belfry, on the other is the massive red brick bulk of London Terrace, a complex of apartments constructed in vaguely Byzantine Romanesque style, surmounted by strange pavilions concealing water tanks. Shortly before the interview began this entire panorama had been set alight by one of the gaudiest sunsets I have ever seen.[26]

The interview, Ash wants us to notice, was like an Ashbery poem, 'interrupted by the sound of sirens rising from 9th Avenue and a ringing telephone', and affected, in some unspecified way, by 'one of the gaudiest sunsets' he had ever seen. As in an Ashbery poem, in other words, we are given to understand that the occasion of the interview mattered seriously. The most pleasing feature of the interview, however, is the manner in which it returns the reader to the poetry, with fragments of poems ('Houseboat Days' and 'The One Thing That Can Save America') twice being spliced into the body of the conversation. Both times the quotation is positioned such as to cause the reader to contemplate the relation between it and the answer that went before. In each case the relation is hard to specify – the poet's remarks not explaining the poetry as such, only leading to it.

Of the new elements in Ashbery's poetry in *Self-Portrait in a Convex Mirror*, among the more obtrusive is a steady flow of visitors. 'As One Put Drunk into the Packet-Boat' opens with the narrative voice 'waiting for someone to come' (SP, 1). 'Harsh words are spoken' and the poem reflects anxiously on the encounter:

> A look of glass stops you
> And you walk on shaken: was I the perceived?
> Did they notice me, this time, as I am,
> Or is it postponed again?

(SP, 1)

The speaker, it would appear, is only too used to visitors who fail to notice him, and in so doing induce a crisis of identity. 'De Imagine Mundi' opens with another perplexing reflection:

> The many as noticed by the one:
> The noticed one, confusing itself with the many
> Yet perceives itself as an individual
> Traveling between two fixed points.

(SP, 34)

This deepens the problem of being noticed. In the image of the one both noticing and confusing itself with the many, one catches a glimpse of a Whitmanesque self: at one with the populace (en masse), but in being in a position to speak of it clearly also somehow distinct. The formulation describes the characteristic Ashberyan 'I' quite accurately, the faint contours of a discernible self always being shaped (as in 'When a Child Went Forth') by the situation it is entering. Here, though, the distance between the one and the many is accentuated as the noticing one has himself been noticed, and as a consequence assumes a more separate identity. The problem here, then, is not that the individual has not been noticed, but that he has, or rather, that in being noticed he is missed: the individual's relation to the mass slipping from view with the fact of recognition.

This problematic development is somehow linked to the unsatisfactory meeting in the third stanza:

Skeeter collecting info: 'Did you know
About the Mugwump of the Final Hour?'
Their even flesh tone
A sign of 'Day off,'
The buses moving along quite quickly on the nearby island
Also registered, as per his plan.

(SP, 34–5)

It is not the content of Skeeter's question but his or her tone that matters: the functional diction, the disengaged expression, the determination to make everything fit. In all this Skeeter is like an interviewer and as such is just the sort of visitor who gives the poet the wrong kind of notice.[27] For this reason, perhaps, the visitors in *Self-Portrait in a Convex Mirror*, who invariably butt into the poem unannounced (in 'Märchenbilder' 'Everybody wondered who the new arrival was'), frequently have an air of forboding about them, as in 'No Way of Knowing' where the speaker is

Waiting
In vanilla corridors for an austere
Young nurse to appear, an opaque glass vase of snapdragons
On one arm, the dangerously slender heroine
Backbending over the other, won't save the denouement
Already drenched in the perfume of fatality.

(SP, 56)

To paraphrase Ashbery's favourite remark from Nijinsky's diary, for all their seductive appeal and apparent concern, these critical visitors would seem to spell death. Or as he puts it, more explicitly, and combatively, in 'Litany':

They are anxious to be done with us,
For the interview to be over, and we,
We have just begun.

(AWK, 9)

With this increase in visitors, Ashbery's poetry is obliged to become more conversational, poem after poem in the 1970s breaking into dialogue, and many of the dialogues asking or answering the kind of question an interviewer might put. 'Ode to Bill' replies to the most rudimentary of these:

What is writing?
Well, in my case, it's getting down on paper
Not thoughts, exactly, but ideas, maybe:
Ideas about thoughts.

(SP, 50)

'Grand Galop' is more informed:

What precisely is it
About the time of day it is, the weather, that causes people to
note it painstakingly in their diaries

[154]

For them to read who shall come after?

(SP, 17)

'Foreboding' is troubled:

> I feel as though
> Somebody had just brought me an equation.
> I say, 'I can't answer this – I know
> That it's true, please believe me,
> I can see the proof, lofty, invisible
> In the sky far above the striped awnings ...'

(SP, 36)

'Absolute Clearance' gives an all-purpose answer to one of those all-purpose questions about the poet's early career:

> 'I put away childish things.
> It was for this I came to Riverside
> And lived here for three years
> Now coming to a not uncertain
> Ending or flowering as some would call it.'

(SP, 13)

'The Tomb of Stuart Merrill' absorbs one of those enthusiasitic, if unctuous, platitudes by which the interviewer curries favour with the poet:

> 'I really would like to know what it is you do to "magnetize" your poetry, where the curious reader, always a bit puzzled, comes back for a clearer insight.' (SP, 38)

The questions, like the visitors, continue into *Houseboat Days*, 'Variant' opening with the poet's response to that most common of interview questions, what gets you started in writing a poem? Answering *The Paris Review*'s version of this question, Ashbery observed that 'I often put in things that I have overheard people say, on the street for instance. Suddenly something fixes itself in the flow that is going on around one and seems to have significance'.[28] 'Variant' offers a comparable response:

> Sometimes a word will start it, like
> Hands and feet, sun and gloves. The way
> Is fraught with danger, you say, and I
> Notice the word 'fraught'

(HD, 4)

In 'And Others, Vaguer Presences' (a title heavy with unwelcome visitors), he tackles the trickier question of form.

> It is argued that these structures address themselves
> To exclusively aesthetic concerns, like windmills
> On a vast plain. To which it is answered
> That there are no other questions than these,
> Half squashed in mud, emerging out of the moment

[155]

We all live, learning to like it. No sonnet
On this furthest strip of land

(HD, 48)

Answering the vague charge that form is an 'exclusively aesthetic concern' (whatever that might mean), the speaker replies that a poem's form must emerge 'out of the moment' itself because its purpose is to make that moment more inhabitable, hence the fact that the sonnet is now obsolete. Which is more or less how Ashbery put it when answering the *New York Quarterly*'s question on this subject: 'I don't think I have any criteria. It's what seems suitable at the moment and I can't say any more than that.'[29]

What these exchanges indicate is that one way or another Ashbery incorporates the interview into this poetry; that because 'a word will start it, like / Hands and feet' then sometimes, by the kind of reflexive logic the poet enjoys, that word is the word of an interviewer. The point of mentioning these exchanges, however, is not just to register that they occur but to notice what they point towards: the deeper structures of Ashbery's writing of this period indicating an involved relation between poetry and interview, with that involved relation having, in turn, to do with the act of self-explanation.[30]

At the outset, self-explanation was anathema to the New York School, the poets declining to publish manifestos (O'Hara's 'Personism' the ironic exception), being more interested in the act of writing than in the act of explaining writing. In this respect they were most unlike Charles Olson, for instance, who arrived at and published his poetic before he had written the majority of his poetry. Not that Ashbery *et al.* did not know what they were doing, but that central to what they were doing was allowing the act of writing poetry to lead them to new insights. 'If you understand how you're doing it you're not doing it right', as Koch put it.[31] By the early 1970s this had changed, Koch publishing his skilfully lucid explanatory poem 'The Art of Poetry', and Ashbery, in part because he was forever being obliged to explain his poetic, arriving at a sharpened sense of his self-reflexive poetic procedures. In Ashbery's case it is a consequence of this understanding that the poetry itself has a consistently surer idea of its own sense of occasion, and in turn that, because this sense of the poetic occasion is informed by the Pasternakian idea that art tells the history of its own coming into being, the implications of the interview cut deep into the poetry. Viewed from the reader's perspective, what this means is that to understand the relation between casual interview-like exchanges at the surface of Ashbery's writing and poems of such reach and moment as 'Self-Portrait in a Convex Mirror' and 'Fantasia on "The Nut-Brown Maid"', is to gain a strong hold on his poetic process.

Central to this process is the fact that Ashbery is 'one of those on whom nothing is lost'. As he describes it, events in his immediate environment are as signals from the culture, his poetry working by the kind of synecdochic logic he voices in relation to 'Fragment', the title of which 'was a kind of a joke because it's very long and yet like any poem it's a fragment of something bigger than itself'.[32]

Thus '[a]ll I need is the time and a not too depressed state of mind to be able to pick up whatever is in the air'.[33] As signals from the culture to the poet go, the interview, with its harsh words and cross-purposes, does not require the most sensitive of antennae. What it clearly communicates is a culture ill equipped for the kind of demanding poetic communications Ashbery has to offer, and so, by the pragmatic logic articulated in the introduction to this book at least, ill-equipped for communication, period. It is this cultural condition, not the experience of the interview that signals it, which is the characteristic occasion of Ashbery's poetry in the 1970s – the interview-like exchanges acting as indices of a shared background.

Ashbery's responses to this shared background of fraught communication push in conflicting directions, the poetry experimenting with forms, modes, tones and registers in an effort to arrive at an appropriate utterance. Thus it is a distinctive, if dissonant (and little-noticed), aspect of *Self-Portrait in a Convex Mirror* that a number of the poems amount to uncharacteristically harsh complaints against the American reading public. 'The Tomb of Stuart Merrill' is a case in point. The 'Tomb' of the title is ambiguous, referring in part to the poem itself, which in mentioning Merrill – a little-read Symbolist poet – mounts a monument to his neglected achievement, but also to the 'basement' in which the action of the opening lines of the poem take place.[34]

> It is the first soir of March
> They have taken the plants away.
>
> Martha Hoople wanted a big 'gnossienne' hydrangea
> Smelling all over of Jicky for her
> Card party: the basement couldn't
> Hold up all that wildness.
>
> The petits fours have left.
>
> Then up and spake the Major:
> The new conservatism is
> Sitting down beside you.

(SP, 37)

Martha Hoople is sensitive in just the wrong way, her precisely specified '"gnossienne" hydrangea' proving just too wild for a basement card party so refined that even those most delicate of delicacies the 'petits fours have left'. The poem is a satire, in other words, on middle-class taste, Martha's behaviour and the presence at her party of the Major leading the poet to diagnose a 'new conservatism'. Like one of Stevens's anecdotes the poem thus reaches beyond itself, giving out on to a cultural climate which was, politically at least, newly conservative (the radical utopianism of the 1960s having given way to the Nixon-led Republicanism of the early 1970s). But in staging a satire on bourgeois taste (such taste spelling death for the likes of Stuart Merrill) the poem also indicates how and why it came to do so, recording the history of its own coming into being by incorporating a remark from a reader:

[157]

'I have become attracted to your style. You seem to possess within your work an air
of total freedom of expression and imagery, somewhat interesting and puzzling.
After I read one of your poems, I'm always tempted to read and reread it. It seems
that my inexperience holds me back from understanding your meanings ...'

(SP, 38)

Whether quotation or parody, this reader's report is problematically poised. On
the one hand, it is mildly (if banally) flattering, the speaker finding the poetry
attractive and 'interesting'. On the other, it misses the point almost entirely. Like
Martha, the reader is delicate in just the wrong kind of way, the qualifying
'somewhat', and the carefully non-committal 'always tempted' indicating a
polite reluctance really to engage with, and so actually to be affected by, the
poetry. The result is a profound misunderstanding, the reader failing to appreci-
ate that Ashbery's poetry, far from requiring a particular kind of experience,
means the reader to better understand their own.

'The Tomb of Stuart Merrill' is a paradigmatic Ashbery poem, telling the his-
tory of its own coming into being by incorporating the experience which
prompted it, but in the process moving from that experience to a consideration
of the wider cultural condition of which it is a symptom. Simultaneously self-
reflexive and synecdochic, it demonstrates not just a sure sense of its own occa-
sion but a clarified sense of its relation to that occasion. It is also, however, a
deeply problematic poem. What, one might wonder, is the poet to make of the
reader's enthusiastic misunderstanding? Where does the fault lie, and what is the
appropriate response?

One response in *Self-Portrait in a Convex Mirror* is a form of poetic disaffection
typified by the resolutely flat conclusion of 'Grand Galop'.

It seems only yesterday that we saw
The movie with the cows in it
And turned to one at your side, who burped
As morning saw a new garnet-and-pea-green order propose
Itself out of the endless bathos, like science-fiction lumps.
Impossible not to be moved by the tiny number
Those people wore, indicating they should be raised to this or
    that power.
But now we are at Cape Fear and the overland trail
Is impassable, and a dense curtain of mist hangs over the sea.

(SP, 21)

There is an ironic echo here of the ending to 'The System', the 'movie with the
cows in it' recalling the inverted Platonic transition at the end of Ashbery's prose
poem from the darkness of the movie house into the brightness of real experi-
ence. In every other respect, though, this conclusion is different, ending not
with the openness of a kinetic future but at an impasse, and emerging not into
the light but into the obscurity of 'a dense curtain of mist'. Mostly it differs,
however, in its steadfast refusal to swell into anything approaching the sublime.
It is the sublime cadences of the end of 'The System' that finally enact the

poem's meaning, their inspirational force propelling the reader out from the poem into an encounter with his or her experience, and signifying, as they do, a poet confident in his capacity to affect. In the face of such reserved reader responses as the one in 'The Tomb of Stuart Merrill', such confidence would seem misplaced, hence the disaffected poetry at the end of 'Grand Galop'. The disaffection is precise: the alienated poet feeling unable to move his reader, and so stripping his lines of emotional content. At every point, then, when the poetry seems likely to elevate the reader, it opts instead to bring him back to earth. So whereas in Eliot 'the one at your side' signifies the presence of Christ, here he burps. And whereas 'science fiction' and the 'overland trail' would usually intimate the exhilarations of the frontier, here they lead only to 'lumps' and impasses. Rightly uncertain of his capacity to inspire the reader, Ashbery dismantles the sublime in favour of an endless bathos.

How and whether to risk the sublime in a cultural climate in which poetry is failing to communicate are problems which persist throughout Ashbery's poetry of the 1970s. A poet at the height of his powers, his power to affect is seriously in doubt and the result is writing often at odds with itself. This is apparent in the three poems of 'Poem in Three Parts', 'Love', 'Courage' and 'I Love the Sea', and the poem that follows them, 'Voyage in the Blue', in each case the noble titles being undercut by lumpy syntax and dumpy diction. The anti-sublime strategy is pushed furthest, however, in 'The One Thing That Can Save America', an exceptional poem in *Self-Portrait* in that it does dare a surging ending.

> The message was wise, and seemingly
> Dictated a long time ago.
> Its truth is timeless, but its time has still
> Not arrived, telling of danger, and the mostly limited
> Steps that can be taken against danger
> Now and in the future, in cool yards,
> In quiet small houses in the country,
> Our country, in fenced areas, in cool shady streets.
>
> (SP, 45)

One wants very much to be moved by this, the various refrains and the gentle allusion to Whitman's 'Dooryard' conspiring to provoke a feeling of unity. But the lines are shot through with limitations also, the 'limited / Steps', the 'fenced areas' and the recollection that 'When Lilacs Last in the Dooryard Bloom'd' is an elegy (and so an expression of weakness) combining to thwart the poem's grander impulse. Hence, also, the title, the comic-strip language of which lampoons a Shelleyan aspiration to which the poem confesses but proceeds to suppress.

'The Tomb of Stuart Merrill' explores a more hostile expression of disaffection.

> Once when the bus slid out past Place Pereire
> I caught the lens-cover reflection: lilacs
> Won't make much difference it said.

Otherwise in Paris why
You never approved much of my pet remedies.
I spoke once of a palliative for piles
You wouldn't try or admit to trying any other.
Now we live without or rather we get along without
Each other. Each of us does
Live within that conundrum
We don't call living
Both shut up and open.
Can knowledge ever be harmful?
How about a mandate? I think
Of throwing myself on the mercy of the court.

(SP, 37)

Paris is where Ashbery wrote *The Tennis Court Oath*, with the 'palliative for piles' he once spoke of referring to 'America', one of the more unaccommodating poems in that reader-unfriendly volume.

Piling upward
the fact the stars
In America the office hid
archives in his
stall ...
Enormous stars on them
The cold anarchist standing
in his hat

(TCO, 15)

What Ashbery's allusion to his Paris poems indicates is that in *Self-Portrait in a Convex Mirror* he finds himself at a crux in his career. Confronted by middle-class readers who don't understand him, and disaffected by their seeming unwillingness to do so, one course of action might be to take refuge in the anti-bourgeois shock tactics of the historic avant-garde. If the reader resists the poems, why should the poems not resist the reader? That this possible strategy figured significantly in Ashbery's thinking at this time is apparent from the poetry's antagonism to such American types as the 'Ruths, Lindas, Pats and Sheilas' in 'Mixed Feelings', and 'the riffraff at the boat show' in 'Tenth Symphony'. It is evident, also, in *The Vermont Notebook*, the scandalous catalogues of which represent a Steinian assault on the sensibilities of a reading public desensitised by commodity culture, and from whom, as the last page of the book indicates, the poet feels himself seriously distanced:

If I don't hear from you again, I shall wonder whether or not you got so wrapped up in your 'canning and freezing' that you are either somewhere on a shelf full of preserves with a metal lid on you head or holing up with the frozen peas in your freezer compartment, from life to something else swiftly translated. Be of good cheer.
    Beverly

(VN, 101)

But if *Self-Portrait in a Convex Mirror* is more disaffected than has tended to be observed, and if therefore it is closer in spirit to *The Vermont Notebook* than is usually supposed, Ashbery's prevailing response to misunderstanding readers was not to wave them farewell. His tendency, rather, was to explain himself, witness the coyly self-revealing title poem.

'Self-Portrait in a Convex Mirror' is a brilliantly conceived and superbly executed, if ultimately costly, act of poetic self-explanation. The poem's title is taken from the painting by the sixteenth-century Italian painter Parmigianino on which it hangs, and whose own conception and execution Vasari describes in detail:

> Francesco one day set himself to take his own portrait, looking at himself in a convex mirror, such as is used by barbers. While doing this he remarked the curious effect produced by the rotundity of the glass, which causes the beams of the ceiling to look bent, while the doors and all other parts of the buildings are in like fashion distorted, and recede in a very peculiar manner. All this, Francesco took it into his head to imitate for his diversion. He accordingly caused a globe or ball of wood to be made by a turner, and having divided it in half and brought it to the size of the mirror, he set himself with great art to copy all that he saw in the glass, more particularly his own likeness ... But as all the nearer objects thus depicted in the glass were dimished, he painted a hand, which he represented as employed in drawing, making it look a little larger than true size, as it does in the glass, and so beautifully done that it appears to be the living member itself.[35]

The history of the poem, as Ashbery reports, is more protracted.

> I began writing 'Self-Portrait in a Convex Mirror' during a month's residence at the Fine Arts Work Center in Provincetown in February 1973. I always wanted to 'do something' with Parmigianino's self-portrait ever since I saw it reproduced in the New York Times Book Review in 1950, accompanying a review of Sidney Freedberg's monograph on the painter. This half-conscious wish was reinforced when I saw the original in Vienna in 1959. Then one day when I was walking around Provincetown during my stay there I passed a bookshop with an inexpensive portfolio of Parmigianino's work displayed in the window – the self-portrait was illustrated on the cover. I bought the book, took it back to my studio and slowly began to write a poem about it, or off it.[36]

Both Ashbery's initial fascination with Parmigianino's painting in 1950 and his decision, in 1973, finally to realise a long-nurtured poetic desire to 'do something' with it are understandable. The year 1950 was when Ashbery wrote 'Picture of Little J.A. in a Prospect of Flowers', the poem in which he first directed the reader to Pasternak's *Safe Conduct*, and to which 'Self-Portrait' (as one might expect given the poems' shared reflective quality) alludes – the painter, like the young J.A., being described as 'accepting everything' (SP, 71). For the young poet with Pasternak's aesthetic on his mind, Parmigianino's 'Self-Portrait' would have seemed intriguing. As a painting of the painter painting himself, it is an immaculate instance of a work of art telling the history of its own making, and so in an important sense it speaks directly to Ashbery's sense of occasion. In another respect, however, it is a most unAshberyan artefact in that its apparent sense of its own occasion is radically truncated, the problem having to do with the relation of background to foreground the painting construes.

In so far as Ashbery tends to prefer self-explanation to self-alienation in *Self-Portrait in a Convex Mirror*, it is central to his strategy that he should find ways of shifting the reader's focus of attention, foregrounding background in an effort to signal his concern with their shared situation. Key to this realignment of background and foreground, and in some ways the term on which the volume hinges, is the word 'as': the book opening with it, the first poem being 'As One Put Drunk into the Packet-Boat', as does the title poem – 'As Parmigianino did it, the right hand / Bigger than the head' – the trochaic rhythm of the first line swinging down heavily on the opening word.[37] It is most to the fore, however, in 'As You Came from the Holy Land' a poem which explicitly calls for a shift of attention:

> as you came from that holy land
> what other signs of earth's dependency were upon you
> what fixed sign at the crossroads
> what lethargy in the avenues
> where all is said in a whisper
> what tone of voice among the hedges
> what tone under the apple trees

> (SP, 6)

The 'as' of Auden's 'Musée des Beaux Arts' rather than the 'as' of 'as if' in Stevens's 'Notes Towards a Supreme Fiction', the term functions here as a subordinating conjunction, Ashbery indicating what is going on while an apparently more important event is taking place. 'As You Came from the Holy Land' it was not your coming but what was going on as you were coming that counts.

The problem with Parmigianino's painting from Ashbery's perspective is that because of the manner in which it is painted it is all foreground: the hand, larger than life, swimming out towards the viewer, the head it seems to protect occupying the middle distance, and the studio window, through which one might catch sight of the world beyond, and the background to, the action of the painting being reduced by the optical illusion to a most insignificant opening. Or as Freedberg, in the monograph of 1950 from which Ashbery quotes in the poem, puts it

> The hand, distortedly large as it would in fact appear in such a mirror, looms in the very foremost plane and instantly catches the spectator's eye, but does not hold it: the hand serves as a bridge into the depth of the picture where the head is placed. Details of clothing, background, etc. are reduced to quite summary terms.[38]

At its grandest, art historical, level, Ashbery's argument with Parmigianino is an argument about perspective. Using a term Ashbery cites in his poem, Freedberg describes the painting as a 'bizarria' on 'High Rennaissance style', which comments on that style by carrying it to its logical conclusion. By his use of the convex mirror, Parmigianino accentuates the laws of perspective to an incredible degree, the background disappearing behind a shockingly over-emphasised individual. From Ashbery's point of view, then, Parmigianino's 'Self-Portrait in a Convex Mirror' is both an immaculate instance of art telling the history of its own coming into being and a radical manifestation of the self-absorbed artist. Ashbery's rediscovery of the painting in Provincetown in 1973 might thus be thought serendipitous. At a time when interviewers where trying to pin his poetry down to a 'personal element', and when he was trying to correct this view of his work by indicating what was going on as they presented it, Parmigianino's painting provided an opportunity for self-explanation.

That Ashbery meant to explain himself in terms the reader would understand is evident from the poem's generally more conventional manner and structure. For a start it appears to have a continuous subject. This is not precisely true in that the painting is less the subject of the poem than the hook on which its meditations hang, but the fact that the poet allows the appearance of the subject indicates his willingness to accommodate readerly expectations. It also differs from most Ashbery poems in having a clearly identifiable and sustained narrative voice, the speaker, who seems indistinguishable from the poet, engaging in a dialogue with Parmigianino and the presuppositions of his painting, often addressing the painter directly ('Francesco, your hand is big enough / To wreck the sphere'). Ashbery addresses the painter in this way as a means of addressing the needs of the reader, the effect of this new style of address being, as critics have variously remarked, that the poem is 'more realized in terms of the reader'; that 'here Ashbery himself has been reader'; and that in this poem the poet is a 'one-way interviewer of Parmigianino'.[39] Aiming to draw the reader, and his surrogate the interviewer, into his poetic, Ashbery accommodates them by incorporating their voice into his poem.

Having thus drawn the reader to his poem, Ashbery proceeds to emphasise its explanatory purpose by what he calls its 'essayistic thrust': the poem making scholarly references (it quotes Vasari and Freedberg); offering etymological digressions (the word 'speculation', we are advised, derives from 'the Latin *speculum*, mirror'); and unpacking allusions that ordinarily readers might be expected to get for themselves ('As Berg said of a phrase in Mahler's Ninth; / Or, to quote Imogen in *Cymbeline*') (SP, 69, 76). Chiefly, though, the poem accommodates itself to the need to explain by conducting the reader through a carefully staged argument.

The logic of the poem's argument is contained in the ambiguity of its opening clause.

> As Parmigianino did it, the right hand
> Bigger than the head, thrust at the viewer
> And swerving easily away, as though to protect
> What it advertises.

(SP, 68)

On the one hand, as John Shoptaw has observed, what this indicates is that the poet will write in the manner of the painting.[40] It will be coherent, autonomous (in that it is self-explanatory) and its contents will appear organised because presented from a single point of view. On the other hand, however, the purpose of the poem is to draw readers way from the self-regarding view of art articulated by the painting, and to encourage them to consider what it appears to exclude. Its object, in other words, is to indicate what was and is happening 'As Parmigianino did it', as the poet contemplates him doing it, and as the reader contemplates both.

The beauty of the argument is the incremental pace at which it draws the reader towards this new way of seeing. Thus, in the first of the poem's six sections the painting is presented in its own terms. Ashbery quotes Vasari on the making of the painting, and offers a more or less faithful verbal reproduction of the image of self the painting contrives:

> The surface
> Of the mirror being convex, the distance increases
> Significantly; that is, enough to make the point
> That the soul is a captive, treated humanely, kept
> In suspension, unable to advance much farther
> Than your look as it intercepts the picture.

(SP, 68–9)

'What the portrait says', as the poet makes clear, is that one's soul, or self is private, sealed off from factors outside it and so, by definition, incommunicable. Viewing the painting from his Emersonian point of view, what the poet would like to believe is that therefore the self in Parmigianino's 'Self-Portrait' is 'restless', 'longing to be free'. In itself, however, the painting does not say this but insists, rather, that one's life is 'englobed'.

> One would like to stick one's hand
> Out of the globe, but its dimension,
> What carries it, will not allow it.

(SP, 69)

So convincing is Parmigianino's Self-Portrait (so persuasive is the illusion he creates) that nothing in the painting itself would seem to allow one to argue, on the contrary, that one's life is not englobed. To make that argument requires one, first, to step beyond the confines of the painting, and so to show what Parmigianino excludes in the achievement of his trompe l'oeil.

Each of the five sections that follow is a digression from the painting. In section two the poet's attention begins to drift – as it does when one is looking at a painting – and he finds himself thinking first of his own circumstances

> I think of the friends
> Who came to see me, of what yesterday
> Was like.

(SP, 71)

and then, by association, of the circumstances that might have been passing through the painter's mind

> In the silence of the studio as he considers
> Lifting the pencil to the self-portrait.
> How many people came and stayed a certain time,
> Uttered light or dark speech that became part of you
> Like light behind windblown fog and sand,
> Filtered and influenced by it, until no part
> Remains that is surely you.

(SP, 71)

The self, this passage suggests, like Ashbery's poetry, is a collaboration, so much the product of factors beyond oneself that the individual self, as such, barely exists. Section three follows this consideration of what takes place as one views or produces a painting by considering how much more difficult it is to represent such experiences.

> Tomorrow is easy, but today is uncharted,
> Desolate, reluctant as any landscape
> To yield what are laws of perspective
> After all only to the painter's deep
> Mistrust, a weak instrument though
> Necessary.

(SP, 72)

Nothing is more difficult to get into perspective than the present, and so art which works according to the laws of perspective necessarily falsifies the circumstances in which it finds itself. Section four develops the point historically, drawing on Freedberg to present the High Renaissance background out of which Parmigianino's painting emerges. 'Later portraits,' Ashbery observes,

>   such as the Uffizi
> 'Gentlemen,' the Borghese 'Young Prelate' and
> The Naples 'Antea' issue from Mannerist
> Tensions, but here, as Freedberg points out,
> The surprise, the tension are in the concept
> Rather than its realization.
> The consonance of the High Renaissance
> Is present, though distorted by the mirror.

(SP, 74)

Moving from Parmigianino's situation to a contemplation of the poet's own, section five remarks how

> The shadow of the city injects its own
> Urgency: Rome where Francesco
> Was at work during the Sack: his inventions
> Amazed the soldiers who burst in on him;
> They decided to spare his life, but he left soon after;

[165]

Vienna where the painting is today, where
I saw it with Pierre in the summer of 1959; New York
Where I am now, which is a logarithm
Of other cities. Our landscape
Is alive with filiations, shuttlings;
Business is carried on by look, gesture,
Hearsay.

(SP, 75)

This is a beautiful transition, the history of Parmigianino's painting leading Ashbery to recount the history of his relationship with the painting, and so the history of the writing of his poem; a history which does not, as Parmigianino pretends, begin and end in the studio but extends outwards to incorporate the city (and all it contains and stands for) in which the poem was written. Step by step, then, the poem indicates what Parmigianino's painting excludes, and what it encourages its viewer to exclude, drawing the reader in the process away from the painter's aesthetic and towards the poet's own. The result is that by the sixth section – the painting by now having all but disappeared from view – both poet and reader experience a release. The poet is released in that, having illustrated the limitations of another's aesthetic, he is now in a position to propose his own:

Is there anything
To be serious about beyond this otherness
That gets included in the most ordinary
Forms of daily activity, changing everything
Slightly and profoundly, and tearing the matter
Of creation, any creation, not just artistic creation
Out of our hands, to install it on some monstrous, near
Peak, too close to ignore, too far
For one to intervene?

(SP, 80–1)

And because Ashbery's poem, unlike Parmigianino's painting, is serious about this 'otherness', about the circumstances that surround us as we produce or consume art, and because his poem, as he hopes, has re-directed our attention to that 'otherness', so the reader also should, at this point, feel a release:

And we must get out of it even as the public
Is pushing through the museum now so as to
Be out by closing time. You can't live there.

(SP, 79)

Ashbery's poetic, like Emerson's 'American Scholar', but unlike Parmigianino's painting, leads the reader beyond the confines and conventions of artistic practice and into an encounter with their own experience.

Ashbery's 'Self-Portrait' could hardly have been more subtly done. Deeply resistant to the idea of self-explanation, Ashbery reveals himself in the negative, presenting himself to the reader by showing what another artist, apparently unlike him, is not. As such the poem works like Stein's *Autobiography of Alice B. Toklas*, or, more so, like Pasternak's account of Mayakovsky in *Safe Conduct*, the writer revealing himself as the other of his subject. More subtly still, and at the risk of contradiction, Ashbery not only shows himself by indicating what Parmigianino's 'Self-Portrait' isn't, but in its most far-reaching gesture shows that the painting itself is not itself. Actually he has to do this because in so far as he believes that all great art tells the history of its own making, and that that history incorporates more than the artist's immediate circumstances, then somehow or other it should be possible to show how Parmigianino's painting itself communicates that 'otherness / That gets included in the most ordinary / Forms of daily activity'. And of course the poem shows that it does, not only because, as Vasari and Freedberg both indicate, the painting carries with it the whole history of Renaissance art and politics but also because the effect on first viewing the painting is that

> you could be fooled for a moment
> Before you realize the reflection
> Isn't yours. You feel then like one of those
> Hoffmann characters who have been deprived
> Of a reflection, except that the whole of me
> Is seen to be supplanted by the strict
> Otherness of the painter in his
> Other room.

(SP, 74)

Its extreme self-absorption notwithstanding, the effect of the painting on the viewer can be to locate his or her self in what Emerson calls 'not-me'.

And yet for all the brilliant ironies of his explanatory poem, Ashbery has consistently sought to distance both the reader and himself from 'Self-Portrait in a Convex Mirror'. 'What makes it seem more accessible', he observed soon after its publication, 'is an essayistic thrust, but if one sat down and analyzed it closely, it would seem as disjunct and fragmented as "Europe"'.[41] More recently he has described it as the product of 'three months of not very inspired writing'.[42] Such distancing tactics are a response to the poem's reception. David Trotter has argued that Ashbery's poetry has become lost behind its critical mediations because, having neglected, or declined to make a readership for itself in the way that, say, O'Hara did, he was thus prey to institutional readers whose first loyalty was not to the poetry but to one of the critical discourses vying for power within the academy. This point can be developed with respect to 'Self-Portrait in a Convex Mirror'. Ashbery wrote the poem by way of a bargain, going over to the reader's way of speaking in the hope that the reader would in turn be drawn to his. While many readers have, undoubtedly, fulfilled the terms of Ashbery's bargain, very many, also, have not, academic readers in particular having been attracted more to the manner of the poem's argument than to its implications. The concrete result of this has been that a poem which was intended to draw readers into the rest of Ashbery's work has instead, all too often, been singled out from it, article after article on Ashbery focusing

[167]

exclusively on 'Self-Portrait'.[43] Deft as it is, then, Ashbery's explanatory poem has had its cost, the poet becoming widely known for a poem which is untypical of him. Which perhaps, in turn, helps explain the paradox that while he is widely celebrated he is little understood.

The most pressing question Ashbery was posed by the interviewer was the question of communication, Ashbery being obliged repeatedly to insist that 'I'm interested in communicating but I feel that saying something the reader has already known is not communicating anything. It's a veiled insult to the reader.'[44] Raised by the interviewer as a simple matter of poetic difficulty, the question of communication resonated deeply through the culture, key developments in contemporary theory implying that the poet's failure to communicate to his readers signalled the readers' failure to communicate with one another. Writing in 1976 Peter Bürger announced the death of the avant-garde. Always, as he saw it, doomed to isolation by its self-appointed task of reacquainting society with a reality from which society did not feel itself alienated, the avant-garde had of late – and for the kind of media-related reasons Ashbery had touched on in 'The invisible avant-garde' some eight years previously – finally ceased to function. The alternatives, Bürger gloomily proposed, for post-avant-garde art were either the institutionalization of avant-garde art (Damian Hirst hanging in the Royal Academy) or an absolute, but non-communicating autonomy. Writing around the same time, and with Bürger among many others in mind, Habermas diagnosed what he called the crisis of legitimation in liberal democratic societies. The rapid modernising and relentless rationalising characteristic of those cultures were resulting in the steady erosion of meanings and norms fixed by tradition and as this occurred so the culture's capacity for communication – the capacity of democratic citizens to communicate with one another – gradually broke down. The poems Ashbery wrote after *Self-Portrait in a Convex Mirror* address these developments. Envisaging a future for post-avant-garde writing which entails neither institutionalisation nor autonomy but a traditional poetic function in a culture marked by ceaseless change, the temporary structures of Ashbery's *Houseboat Days* are as much as ever fit for their occasion.

Communication is more than ever the issue in *Houseboat Days*. In an important sense, of course, it had always been germane to Ashbery's poetry, the point of his occasional poetic having always been to make communication possible. It had always been the case that, as he told the readership of the *New York Times Magazine* in 1976, 'The inaccuracies and anomalies of common speech are particularly poignant to me. This essence of communication is what interests me in poetry.'[45] It had never, however, been so explicitly his theme, poem after poem in *Houseboat Days* naming, or clearly signalling, an interest in communication. Sometimes, as in 'And *Ut Pictura Poesis* Is Her Name', it is the poet's capacity to communicate that is the issue:

Something
Ought to be written about how this affects
You when you write poetry:
The extreme austerity of an almost empty mind
Colliding with the lush, Rousseau-like foliage of its desire to
    communicate
Something between breaths, if only for the sake
Of others and their desire to understand you and desert you
For other centers of communication, so that understanding
May begin, and in doing so be undone.

(HD, 45–6)

Another poem in answer to a question, 'And *Ut Pictura Poesis* Is Her Name'
says better than Ashbery has been able to in interview what he means by poetic
communication. Expressing its desire to communicate by presenting an image
of the environment, the 'Rousseau-like foliage', which is the precondition
of understanding, Ashbery's poetry presents what's new in order for obsolete
ways of understanding to be 'undone', so that, in turn, understanding can begin
again. Elsewhere the issue is not so much the poet's capacity to communicate
as the culture's. 'Pyrography' – a poem commissioned by the United
States Department for the Interior for a touring exhibition ('America 1976') to
celebrate the nation's Bicentenary – considers the state of the nation in terms of
its communications:

This is America calling:
The mirroring of state to state,
Of voice to voice on the wires,
The force of colloquial greetings like golden
Pollen sinking on the afternoon breeze.
In service stairs the sweet corruption thrives;
The page of dusk turns like a creaking revolving stage in
    Warren, Ohio.

(HD, 8)

The voice of the media sounding loud, what, 'Pyrography' wonders, is to be done
for a culture in which the intimacy of the colloquial greeting has been displaced
by the big, homogenising voices of the national networks? The answer, the poem
tentatively suggests, is to write a 'history of our time' which incorporates all those
'unimportant details', so giving texture to those banally general utterances which
the poem describes as having 'that flat, sandpapered look the sky gets / Out in the
middle west toward the end of the summer' (HD, 10). Ironically poised, the
image is an instance of precisely the kind of apparently unimportant detail the
poet requires, the poem being a gesture towards a textured 'history of our time'.
In the most telling poems in the book, however – 'Daffy Duck in Hollywood',
for instance, or 'Fantasia on "The Nut-Brown Maid"' – the question of the poet's
capacity to communicate and the question of the culture's are one and the same,
the term that yokes them together being 'tradition'.

The issue of tradition is introduced early in *Houseboat Days*, the volume's second poem, 'The Other Tradition', meditating on the canonical sense of the term.

> They all came, some wore sentiments
> Emblazoned on T-shirts, proclaiming the lateness
> Of the hour, and indeed the sun slanted its rays
> Through branches of Norfolk Island pine, as though
> Politely clearing its throat, and all ideas settled
> In a fuzz of dust under trees when it's drizzling:
> The endless games of Scrabble, the boosters,
> The celebrated omelette au Cantal, and through it
> The roar of time plunging unchecked through the sluices
> Of the days, dragging every sexual moment of it
> Past the lenses: the end of something.
> Only then did you glance up from your book,
> Unable to comprehend what had been taking place, or
> Say what you had been reading. More chairs
> Were brought, and lamps were lit, but it tells
> Nothing of how all this proceeded to materialize
> Before you and the people waiting outside and in the next
> Street, repeating its name over and over, until silence
> Moved halfway up the darkened trunks,
> And the meeting was called to order.

> (HD, 2)

When Ashbery raised the question of tradition in 'The Invisible Avant-Garde' a decade or so earlier, his anxiety was that, as Bernard Shaw and Gertrude Stein had both warned, 'it is the fate of some artists, and perhaps the best ones, to pass from unacceptability to acceptance without an intervening period of appreciation' (RS, 390). The success of *Self-Portrait* having secured him this unenviable passage, 'The Other Tradition' contemplates the reality of life in the canon.[46] Taking an institutional setting – the occasion is a meeting – the poem contemplates its contemplators: their critical loyalties worn like legends on T-shirts, their fuzzy ideas, their enthusiastic boosting and the almost pornographic detail of their endless word games. The result of their discusssions, as the poem tells it, is an inability 'to comprehend what has been taking place': either outside the meeting, where the setting sun and the people in the street go unnoticed, or inside the poetry, it being such things that the poetry means to indicate. Attracting attention to itself rather than drawing attention to the things going on around it, poetry which enters the tradition, as Ashbery's chief booster Harold Bloom has sought to ensure, comes to speak of the tradition and little else.

Ashbery's argument in *Houseboat Days* is not with the idea of tradition as such, but with the idea of tradition as canon. As Ashbery's poetry understands it, this sense of tradition is tantamount to a self-contradiction, the alternative formulation being Daffy Duck's suggestion that 'to be ambling on's / The tradition more than the safe-keeping of it' (HD, 34). This makes good sense. In so far as tradition stands for a set of customs and conventions evolved to enable effective communication within a society or culture, and in so far as effective communication requires, as Habermas points out, a shared 'background knowledge' among a 'community of speaking and acting subjects' about 'what takes place in the world or is to be effected in it', then the idea of a tradition preoccupied with its own 'safe-keeping' (in the guise of a canon) is indeed a contradiction in terms. It must change (it must be ambling on) if people are not to lose contact with one another by losing contact with that which binds them together. 'Daffy Duck in Hollywood' is Ashbery's most vivid meditation on this issue.

The poem opens with a slew of details:

> Something strange is creeping across me.
> La Celestina has only to warble the first few bars
> Of "I Thought about You" or something mellow from
> *Amadigi di Gaula* for everything – a mint-conditioned can
> Of Romford's Baking powder, a celluloid earring, Speedy
> Gonzales, the latest from Helen Topping Miller's fertile
> Escritoire, a sheaf of suggestive pix on greige, deckle-edged
> Stock – to come clattering through the rainbow trellis
> Where Pistachio Avenue rams the 2300 block of Highland
> Fling Terrace.

(HD, 31)

The picture is of a culture so diversely productive that it has exceeded, and is always exceeding, the customs and conventions by which it understands itself. Alarmed at the prospects for such a culture – and barely able to make himself heard over the cacophony produced as Billie Holiday ('I thought about you') rams into Handel ('*Amadigi di Gaula*') – the poet, as 'Daffy', makes an announcement:

> This wide, tepidly meandering,
> Civilized Lethe (one can barely make out the maypoles
> And *châlets de nécessité* on its sedgy shore) leads to Tophet,
> that
> Landfill-haunted, not-so-residential resort from which
> Some travellers return!

(HD, 32)

The problem is that the culture continues to cling to customs and conventions – witness the barely visible 'maypoles' – designed for occasions now past. What such outmoded conventions are not equipped to deal with is what the poem calls the 'Civilized Lethe': that flow of details with which the poem opened, and which by its sheer volume threatens to obliterate all memory of culture. What are needed, accordingly, and what it is the poet's task to provide, are structures of understanding flexible enough to absorb and make sense of the deluge. Hence,

> While I
> Abroad through all the coasts of dark destruction seek

> Deliverance for us all, think in that language: its
> Grammar, though tortured, offers pavilions
> At each new parting of the ways.

(HD, 33)

A pavilion is a temporary structure assembled and disassembled quickly enough to serve the needs of a particular, fleeting occasion. This, Daffy argues, is what is required if the culture is to be delivered from Tophet, and of course the poem is just such a structure: its heavily allusive diction (to Milton, here, for instance) combining with the cartoonic speed of its transitional syntax to generate a language alive both to the requirement of tradition and to the need for that tradition always to be adapting itself anew.

Ashbery's over-arching term for this way of writing is 'the other tradition', and one way of reading *Houseboat Days* is an extended exploration and exposition of that crucial phrase. First mentioned in 'The System', what the phrase implies (as discussed above) is writing which addresses itself to the apparently unimportant details of day-to-day existence (the background to people's lives) and which has tended either to be neglected or misconstrued by virtue of taking such a subject matter. *Houseboat Days* signals its involvement in the other tradition in two distinct ways. On the one hand, the poetry is forever opening on to that 'otherness / That gets included in the most ordinary / Forms of daily activity' which 'Self-Portrait in a Convex Mirror' advised us we should be serious about but to which it could not attend because too busy explaining itself. Like *The Vermont Notebook*, *Houseboat Days* is ready, often, just to draw attention to what in 'Business Personals' the poet calls '"leftovers"'; to the 'trash, sperm and excrement' which litter the picnic sites in 'Street Musicians' (HD, 18, 1). On the other hand *Houseboat Days* signals its interest in the other tradition by continually reminding the reader of more intimate forms of literary communication: traditions of writing and speaking in which a background of shared knowledge made it possible for the poet to assume a more central role in people's lives; one aspect of his or her role being the maintenance of that knowledge. 'The Other Tradition' recalls 'the troubadours' the New York School had first associated themselves with in the collaborations special issue of *Locus Solus* (HD, 2). 'On The Towpath' names the fairy tales ('Red Riding Hood, Cinderella, the Sleeping Beauty') by which children are introduced to the norms of their community. (HD, 22) 'Syringa' tells the tale of 'Orpheus', who liked 'the glad personal quality / Of the things beneath the sky', but who in this re-telling is now followed only by 'birds of dusty feather', in their 'libraries, onto microfilm' (HD, 69, 71). The point of such references is not to express nostalgia for any given model of poetic community, but to register the need for a form of modern poetry which might perform a comparable function – 'Fantasia on "The Nut-Brown Maid"' being Ashbery's most exacting variation on this theme.

By conspicuously referring, in the title of his long poem, to an anonymous fifteenth-century ballad Ashbery alludes to a kind of poem which could and did

[172]

presuppose a shared body of allusions, the ballad form being deeply embedded in the activities of daily life. As Tessa Watt observes, anonymous ballads such as 'The Nut-Brown Maid' met the audience's 'need for role models, for inspirational stories, for behavioural rules to give to their children, for guidance on the approach to death'.[47] The ballad was part of life, or, to be precise, a ballad was a ballad only in so far as it succeeded in becoming part of life. Made, as Puttenham observed, 'purposely for recreation of the common people at Christmasse drives and brideales, and in taverns and alehouses, and other such places of base report', the ballad had, as Gordon Gerould puts it, 'no real existence save when held in memory and sung by those who have learned it from the lips of others'.[48] Generically, then, the ballad was a model of integrated poetic communication, influencing people and holding communities together by fitting itself for their occasions.

However, as Ashbery trawled *The Oxford Book of English Verse* for formal models – 'The Nut-Brown Maid' falls opposite 'As You Came from the Holy Land' in Quiller-Couch's edition – it would have been for specific as well as generic reasons that this particular ballad caught his imagination. 'The Nut-Brown Maid' is a dialogue between 'He' and 'She', its traditional topic being the question of woman's fidelity. To dramatise the topic the speakers perform the story of 'The Nut-Brown Maid' – the poem thus alluding to a story of which it is confident its audience has knowledge – 'She' playing the Maid, 'He' her suitor. Claiming to have committed a crime, and to be, as a result, 'a banished man' who 'must withdraw as an outlaw' to 'the green-wood', he tests her loyalty by asking whether she will follow him into an environment where one must be always 'ready' to draw one's bow, where 'fortune' is the only guide, and which is proscribed by taboo and so requires one to sever relations with polite society.[49]

One can see why Ashbery might have been drawn to such a poem. For Harold Rosenberg the forest was the site of the new; the place where, precisely because it required readiness in the face of chance and the absence of convention, the mobile American sensibility was founded. 'The Nut-Brown Maid' thus speaks quite directly to Ashbery's situation. And all the more so because, whereas Rosenberg was content to accept the incommunicability of the specific encounter which for him found paradigmatic form on the Abstract Expressionist canvas, 'The Nut-Brown Maid' imagines such experiences to be communicable. Because the argument of the poem consists in the suitor presenting the hardships of the forest to the maid who has not experienced them, it challenges its own suggestion that to enter such an environment is to excommunicate oneself from society. Indeed, the poem is predicated on the communicability of life in the forest, its interlocutors occupying a position between the forest and society, and so integrating the way of chance and risk with the ways of conventional society. In its simplified form, in other words, 'The Nut-Brown Maid' imagines just the kind of poet-audience communication Ashbery's own occasion required

Ashbery's 'Fantasia' is also a dialogue between 'He' and 'She'. It is not, however, an easy one, the reason being, as a typically densely oxymoronic passage puts it,

> The period of civilities is long past.
> Strange we should be continually waking up
> To a barbaric calm that has probably
> Always supported us, while still
> Apologizing to the off-white walls we saw through
> Years ago. But it stays this way.

(HD, 76)

'The period of civilities', of clearly codified ways of behaving, has passed. In its stead is a constant waking up to an uncodified present which is strange in that it brings new tasks and challenges, but familiar in the minimal sense that the present is always like this, hence the 'barbaric calm'. The question the poem asks itself is implicit in the punning suggestion that 'it stays this way'. How, the poem, wonders, can anything stay this way? And in particular, how can poetry which is permanently engaging with the present situation offer the kind of cultural support that in a period of civilities would have constituted its role?

At its bleakest, and Ashbery is very bleak at times in 'Fantasia', the poem squares up to the possibility that actually it can't perform anything like the communal role which was the raison d'être of its ur-text, that it is a big mistake to suppose

> That the glint of light from a silver ball on that far-off flagpole is the equivalent of a career devoted to life, to improving the minds and the welfare of others, when in reality it is a common thing like these, and less profitable than any hobby or sideline that is a source of retirement income, such as an antique stall, pecan harvest or root-beer stand. In short, although the broad outlines of your intentions are a credit to you, what fills them up isn't. (HD, 84)

Reading like the culmination of all those harsh words interviewers have been impressing him with of late, this is a desperate reflection. Looking again into the silver ball of his 'Self-Portrait in a Convex Mirror' the poet discerns not an important career but a hugely costly, largely unprofitable hobby, equivalent, perhaps, to dabbling in antiques or root beer. This is a chilling possibility, which the poem takes account of in the form of its strained dialogue, 'He' and 'She' – like poet and reader – constantly struggling to find the common ground necessary for a satisfactory conversation.

Yet for all their problems in coming to terms with one another, the dialogue between 'He' and 'She' continues throughout, the conversation proving most harmonious when the difficulty of having it comes to the fore.

> He
>
> > You get around this as though
> > The eternally revised geography of spring meant
> > Something beyond its own sense of exaltation,
> > And love were cause for self-congratulation.

She

I might hide somewhere. I want to fly but keep
My morality, motley as it is, just by
Encouraging these branching diversions around an axis.

(HD, 74)

'He' wants to believe that his perpetual encounter with the uncodified present, 'the eternally revised geography of spring', means more than the 'sense of exaltation' it gives rise to. She explains how this is possible, reconciling the independence of experimental expression with the social cohesion denoted by the word 'morality' with her image of 'branching diversions around an axis'.

This formulation describes the progress of the poem. Much more exacting reading than 'Self-Portrait in a Convex Mirror', 'Fantasia on "The Nut-Brown Maid"' is constantly experimenting towards a form of expression suitable for a period marked by change not continuity. As befits such a period, the dialogue is strained, both speakers, more often than not, appearing to move off at a tangent from the previous utterance. But as the poem and the conversation proceed despite themselves so it becomes clear that this is the point: the language evolving from the difficult exchanges being precisely capable of registering each new tangential development.

That's an unusual ... As though a new crescent
Reached out and lapped at a succession of multitudes,
Diminished now, but still lively and true.
It seems to say: there are lots of differences inside.
There were differences when only you knew them.
Now they are an element, not themselves,
And things are idle, or weigh the head
Like an outsize grapefruit, or an ocarina
Closes today with a comical wail.

(HD, 81)

Hard but not impossible to follow, this is a language which has little time for antecedents. Clause by clause, sentence by sentence, Ashbery's phrases do not pause to reflect on what has gone before, but 'as branching diversions around an axis' amble relentlessly on. It is not comfortable writing, but arguably it is necessary, and arguably it warrants the confident peroration with which Ashbery ends 'Fantasia on "The Nut-Brown Maid"'.

Always there was something to see, something going on, *for the historical past owed it to itself, our historical present.* There were visiting firemen, rumors of chattels on a spree, old men made up to look like young women in the polygon of night from which light sometimes breaks, to be sucked back, armies of foreigners who could not understand each other, the sickening hush just before the bleachers collapse, the inevitable uninvited and only guest who writes on the wall: I choose not to believe. It became a part of oral history. Things overheard in cafes assumed an importance previously reserved for letters from the front. The past was a dream of doctors and drugs. This wasn't misspent time. Oh, sometimes it'd seem like doing the same thing over and over, until I had passed beyond whatever the sense of it had been. Besides, hadn't it all ended a long time back, on some clear, washed-out afternoon, with a stiff breeze that seemed to shout; go back! For the moated past lives by these dreams of decorum that take into account any wisecracks made at their expense. It is not called living in a past. If history were only minding one's business, but, once under the gray shade of mist drawn across us ... And who am I to speak this way, into a shoe? I know that evening is busy with lights, cars ... That the curve will include me if I must stand here. My warm regards are cold, falling back to the vase again like a fountain. Responsible to whom? I have chosen this environment and it is handsome: a festive ruching of bare twigs against the sky, masks under the balconies

that

I sing alway

(HD, 88)

The passage claims to marry the poet's concern for contingency with his commitment to solidarity. It casts back in that it dreams of decorum, of the shared understanding of correct forms of behaviour characterised as 'the age of civilities'. But it looks forward in the conviction that only a poetry up to speed with the times, branching off quickly enough from itself to take account of the shifting constituents of our historical present, might perform the communicative role analogous to that of the ballad.

With 'Litany', the third of the period's long poems, Ashbery's dialogical decade ended on a note of failure. The twin columns of Ashbery's most experimental poem to date include some of his most remarkable passages of poetry, and at times it is the work of a poet at the height of his powers. But it is also the work of a poet no longer confident in the power of his poetry to affect. The two columns, which are meant, so the author's note tells us, to be read as independent but simultaneous monologues, almost never interlock. It is a poem one can dip into, as he subsequently observed, like a day book, and as such, as the poem itself observes, it is 'an occasion for all occasions' (AWK, 53). But as an exchange it is underscored by failure, each voice, as in a 'Litany' proper, reading like a prayer in the face of an unvaried response.

But if 'Litany' is only appropriate to its moment in its protracted enactment of communicative breakdown, *Self-Portrait in a Convex Mirror* and *Houseboat Days*, judged by developments in contemporary theory at least, were profoundly timely. Prompted to self-examination by the harsh words of the interviewers, Ashbery reflected first on the need to explain, and then, as his attempts at self-explanation missed their mark, on the cultural condition implied by the difficulties he faced as he endeavoured to communicate his meaning. What emerges in *Houseboat Days* in particular is a radical understanding of his cultural moment, Ashbery's poetry drawing attention to the fact that in a society marked by the communicative difficulties born of the erosion of tradition, it is (*pace* Bürger) towards poetry in the tradition of the new – restless, mobile, adapted to change – that the reader should look for the preconditions of contemporary understanding.

NOTES

1 A. Poulin Jnr, 'The experience of experience', pp. 250–1. The interview took place in 1972, when Ashbery appeared at the Brockport Writers Forum.
2 John Ash, 'John Ashbery in conversation with John Ash', p. 33.
3 Peter Stitt, 'The art of poetry XXXIII: John Ashbery', p. 399.
4 *John Ashbery and Kenneth Koch (A Conversation)*, p. 7.
5 Sue Gangel, 'An interview with John Ashbery' p. 14.
6 Stitt, 'The art of poetry', p. 389.
7 My guess would be that Ashbery rarely says no. The first time I interviewed him, he agreed to see me on his one day in New York between flights from Europe and to the West Coast. On that occasion, he seemed, at times, understandably, a little distracted. But he was also extremely generous, giving me four hours of his time, and being fulsome in his responses to my many questions. The conversation was livelier when the tape-recorder was turned off. He confirmed that he hated giving interviews.
8 Donald Hall, *Poets at Work*, p. xiv.
9 Gerrit Henry, 'In progress', p. 1.
10 Gangel, 'An Interview', p. 19.
11 Poulin, 'The experience of experience', pp. 245–6.
12 Joe David Bellamy, *American Poetry Observed,* p. x.
13 Ibid., p. ix.
14 Alfred Kazin, *Writers at Work*, third series, p. xv.
15 Ibid., p. viii.
16 Francine du Plessix Gray, 'Introduction', *Writers at Work*, fifth series, p. xi.
17 Ibid., pp. xi, xii.
18 Richard Kostelanetz, 'How to be a difficult poet', p. 108.
19 Ross Labrie, 'John Ashbery: an interview with Ross Labrie', p. 30.
20 Janet Bloom and Robert Losada, 'Craft interview with John Ashbery', p. 12.
21 John R. Searle, *(On) Searle On Conversation*, pp. 7, 27.
22 Poulin, 'The experience of experience', p. 245.
23 Richard Jackson, 'The imminence of a revelation (John Ashbery)', p. 70.
24 Cited in John Shaptow, *On The Outside Looking Out*, p. 199.
25 John Tranter, 'An Interview with John Ashbery', p. 94.
26 John Ash, 'John Ashbery in conversation with John Ash', p. 31.
27 A skeet is a form of clay-pigeon shooting.
28 Stitt, 'The art of poetry', p. 408.
29 Bloom and Losada, 'Craft interview with John Ashbery', p. 27.
30 For an illuminating discussion of the dialogical character of Ashbery's poetry of this period see, Charles Altieri's *Self and Sensibility in Contemporary American Poetry*, p. 139.
31 Kenneth Koch, *The Art of Poetry*, p. 208.
32 Bloom and Losada, 'Craft interview with John Ashbery', p. 28.

33 Ibid., p. 13.

34 Ashbery refers to him in his interview with Ash. 'John Ashbery in conversation', p. 32.

35 Giorgio Vasari, *Lives of the Most Eminent Painters, Sculptors and Architects*, pp. 359-60.

36 John Ashbery, Foreword to *Self-Portrait in a Convex Mirror*, Arion Press edition.

37 For a different reading of the word 'as' in *Self-Portrait*, see Shoptaw, *On the Outside Looking Out*, p. 182.

38 Sidney J. Freedberg, *Parmigianino: His Works in Painting*, p. 105.

39 Robert Miklitsch, 'John Ashbery', p. 118; Bonnie Costello, 'John Ashbery and the idea of the reader', p. 507; James A.W. Heffernan, *Museum of Words*, p. 184.

40 Shoptaw, *On the Outside Looking Out*, p. 182.

41 Kostelanetz, 'How to be a difficult poet', p. 108.

42 Shoptaw, '*On the Outside Looking Out*, p. 174.

43 Consider, for instance, Mary E. Eichbauer, *Poetry's Self-Portrait*; John W. Erwin, 'The reader is the medium: Ashbery and Ammons ensphered'; Lee Edelman, 'The Pose of Imposture: Ashbery's "Self-Portrait in a Convex Mirror"; Richard Stamelman, 'Critical Reflections: Poetry and Art Criticism in Ashbery's "Self-Portrait in a Convex Mirror"; Anita Sokolsky, '"A commission that never materialized": narcissism and lucidity in Ashbery's "Self-Portrait in a Convex Mirror"'.

44 Kostelanetz, 'How to be a difficult poet', p. 103.

45 Ibid., p. 106.

46 For a discussion of Ashbery's life in the canon see, Harold Bloom, *Agon: Towards a Theory of Revisionism*, pp. 197–9.

47 Tessa Watt, *Cheap Print and Popular Piety*, p. 7.

48 Puttenham cited in Watt, *Cheap Print and Popular Piety*, p. 13; Gordon Gerould, *The Ballad of Tradition*, p. 19.

49 Sir Arthur Quiller-Couch, *The Oxford Book of English Verse*, pp. 44, 47, 50.

CHAPTER SEVEN

John Ashbery and friends: the poet and his communities in *Shadow Train* and *A Wave*

In Ashbery's *Paris Review* interview, Peter Stitt quizzed the poet on his early influences. When he began writing, Stitt wondered, were there older poets he visited or studied with? Responding at length, and with feeling, Ashbery recalls that he was

> rather shy about putting myself forward, so there weren't very many known poets then that I did have any contact with. I wish I could have visited older poets. But things were different then – young poets simply didn't send their poems to older ones with requests for advice and criticism and 'suggestions for publication' ... Everyone is bolder now. This leads to a sad situation (and I've often discussed this with poets of my generation like Kinnell and Merwin) of having a tremendous pile of unanswered correspondence about poetry – Kinnell calls it his 'guilt pile' – from poets who want help and should receive it; only in this busy world of doing things to make a living and trying to find some time for oneself to write poetry, it isn't usually possible to summon the time and energy it would require to deal seriously with so many requests; at least for me it isn't. But I feel sad because I would like to help; you remember how valuable it would have been for you; and it's an honor to get these requests. People think they have gotten to know you through your poetry and can address you familiarly (I get lots of 'Dear John' letters from strangers) and that in itself is a tremendous reward, a satisfaction – if only we could attend to everybody![1]

Ashbery's feelings on this subject are mixed. He feels honoured and rewarded to receive letters from younger poets, and wishes he had the time to give everybody the attention they deserve. But his inability to deal with the volume of correspondence induces guilt, and, if he regrets his own reticence about approaching older poets, there is a suggestion also that younger poets, with their 'requests for ... "suggestions for publication"' (a phrase which has lodged itself in his memory, if not under his skin) have become bold to the point of intrusiveness. Either way, and for better and for worse, by 1980 Ashbery was becoming consciously absorbed by the writing of younger poets.

Such involvement in the work of younger poets became official eight years later, when David Lehman invited Ashbery to guest-edit the first anthology in the now annual series *The Best American Poetry* (Lehman being the series editor).

The anthology has had mixed reviews. For Susan Schultz it is a sign of Ashbery's 'pervasive presence' that 'so many of the poets he included in *The Best Anthology, 1988* ... sound like him, or – that is – like one of him'.[2] A sign, in other words, that as John Koethe sees it, Ashbery's poetry has been largely responsible for 'remodeling ... the "generic" poem of the age', the poem, that is, which 'the literary culture regards as stereotypical and that younger poets ... try ... to emulate'.[3] For Ian Gregson, on the other hand, the anthology is a closed shop full of Ashbery's 'associates'. Even the poems Ashbery selects by those not associated with him seem to Gregson to have been chosen because they 'occupy his poetic territory', with the effect that, in Gregson's suspicious phrase, established poets like 'Gary Snyder and Charles Simic read like new recruits for Ashbery's post-modernist Village People'.[4] But whether one reads it naively with Schultz, or suspiciously with Gregson, *The Best American Poetry, 1988* confirmed what the letters to the poet had already suggested: that Ashbery had become a highly influential figure in American poetry.

To remodel the '"generic" poem of the age' is an undeniably significant achievement: a sure sign that, one way or another, one's aesthetic has come to meet the requirements of the moment, and a source of satisfaction in particular for a poet who has made meeting the moment the principle of his writing. But it is also a problem, a consequence of remodelling the generic poem of the age being that, as Gregson puts it, younger poets come to occupy one's poetic territory. This is a difficult state of affairs for any poet, the presence of followers and imitators taking the shine off the original, but it is all the more so for a poet of Ashbery's cast of mind, as an early poem by David Lehman helps to make clear.

David Lehman knows the New York School well. He was educated at Columbia where he took Kenneth Koch's writing course. He was the editor of *Beyond Amazement: Essays on the Poetry of John Ashbery* (the first volume of essays on Ashbery's poetry) and of the Ashbery-inclined anthology of writings by poets on poetry, *Ecstatic Occasions*. More recently he has become the New York School's group biographer, and in *The Last Avant-Garde* does a good job of communicating the spirit of a poetry scene with which he is clearly familiar. His first volume of poetry was, however, awkwardly poised, Lehman knowing Ashbery's poetry so well that he found it difficult to write anything else. Witness the beginning of 'How To Think':

> As the hum of a fly surrounds a thinker,
> Lifts his face from the book on his lap –
> And the book is slipping and will surely fall,
> Too fast to be noticed, like a fall asleep –
> It only lasts for the length of a laugh.[5]

We have met this scene before. The image of the writer at his desk tells us that this is a poem concerned with the history of its own making. The writer's pose, head in and out of the book, distracted by a fly, informs us that the poem means to thematise its negotiation of the competing claims of language and reality. The moment is slipping away. Indeed but for the fact that it is so explicitly Ashberyan, one might almost think this was Ashbery writing. And so it continues, with the long sentence which is the heart of the poem:

> And then it occurred to me that in time
> I would know why but never how
> (When people ask why they invariably mean how)
> The forgetting goes on, that even now,
> In the time it takes to formulate a phrase,
> Whole years are reduced to no more than a phrase
> Softly whispered, once and once only,
> Or repeating itself with some slight revision
> Each time, insistent as the tiny hammers
> Of a headache commercial on the television –
> Too slow to seem out of the ordinary
> Or too fast to be noticed, like a fall asleep.[6]

Again the constituent elements are conspicuously Ashberyan: the anxiety that something important has been forgotten, the influx of facts, the distortions of language, the passing glance at the television, the repeated cadences of the insistent ending. Only a poet who had made a close study of Ashbery could reproduce the form of a certain kind of Ashbery poem so faithfully.[7] Precisely because it is the result of study, however, the moves that hold the elements of Lehman's poem together are less fluent than anything Ashbery might offer. Whereas things occur and divert the poetry in Ashbery, here we are told they occur; and whereas Ashbery is always writing against that dismissiveness of language whereby 'In the time it takes to formulate a phrase / Whole years are reduced to no more than a phrase', his poetry is built on the insight that to state the problem so explicitly is only to reproduce the problem. You can't say it that way any more because poetry which does so is dead on the line.

All of which results in a damaging irony. Promising to show the reader 'How To Think', the image of thinking Lehman offers is clearly Ashbery's, and so what the poem actually teaches us is how to think like Ashbery. Against all the odds, in other words, Ashbery's poetic has become an orthodoxy. His gestures have become reducible to a shorthand. His style has become a manner. His way of writing has hardened into the kind of reality denying formulation it evolved to resist in the first place. What Lehman's poem actually shows us, therefore, from a pragmatic point of view at least, is not 'How To Think', but 'How Not To Think', or rather, to put the problem it poses at its most acute, 'How To Not Think In The Manner of Ashbery'.[8]

As inspiring as he was to others during this period, the poems Ashbery himself published between 1980 and 1988 – in *Shadow Train* (1980), *A Wave* (1984) and *April Galleons* (1988) – often felt uninspired. *A Wave* is the exception, being, at times, and for reasons clearly linked to the question of what Gregson terms Ashbery's 'associates', as urgent as anything he has written. In *Shadow Train* and *April Galleons*, however, the prevailing note is one of failure. There are good poems in each, and, as always, the writing is marked with intelligence and grace, but the dominant imagery is of staleness: the breeze on the face being not, now, the gusting of a new wind, but the recycled atmospherics of the air-conditioning system. The titles – 'Another Chain Letter', 'Written in the Dark', 'Ditto, Kiddo', and 'Someone You Have Seen Before' – variously suggest repetition and over-familiarity. Formally also, in Ashberyan terms, the poetry of this period shows signs of failure. The uniformity of *Shadow Train*, the fifty poems of which are all four quatrains long, is a formal declaration that the poetry is less than fully receptive to the state of change which has hitherto provided its element. And of the three books only *A Wave* musters the energy for a long poem – a constituent part of the Ashbery collection since *The Tennis Court Oath*.

As Paul Muldoon sees it such a falling off is to be expected.

> 'This middle stretch of life is bad for poets'. I think often it coincides with a general mid-life stocktaking and getting a few things into perspective. It's very hard to keep on doing it as well. Historically great poets tend to have bad stretches during their middle years.[9]

Because historically, they have tended to start, or at least make their debut, later than British poets, the bad middle stretch tends to happen later for Americans. Emerson, Whitman, Frost and Stevens all published their first volumes in their mid- to late-thirties, and much of their best work at around the age of fifty. Similarly Ashbery, as Harold Bloom has observed, is very much a poet of the middle stretch of life, beginning 'The Skaters' at thirty-seven and finishing *Houseboat Days* at forty-nine. But there are clear signs of staleness in the poetry Ashbery wrote between the ages of fifty and sixty, and no doubt this is partly to be explained by the generally depressing trajectory of a poet's career development. But it has much to do also, so the poetry itself clearly suggests, with the manner in which Ashbery was becoming absorbed by younger poets.

When, later in the *Paris Review* interview, the subject of younger writers came up again, Stitt reminded Ashbery that he once said that one of the primary benefits of reading poets influenced by him was that it warns him to 'watch out for "Ashberyisms" in [his] own work'. Asked to explain what 'Ashberyisms' are, the poet observes:

> there are certain stock words that I have found myself using a great deal. When I become aware of them, it is an alarm signal meaning I was falling back on something that had served in the past – it is a sign of not thinking at the present moment[10]

Ashbery is sanguine here about his relation to his followers. But what might once have seemed a benefit soon becomes a problem the more Ashbery finds himself absorbed by the work of younger writers. What happens when it is not 'Ashberyisms' which are a sign of not really thinking in the present, but Ashberyism? How is the poet to deal with his seeming orthodoxy? How can he write without reading like one of his followers?[11]

Shadow Train is shot through with follower figures. In 'Joe Leviathan', with its titular suggestion of one thing absorbing another, we learn that

> Just because I wear a voluminous cap
> With a wool-covered button at its peak, the cries of children
> Are upon me, passing through me.
>
> (Sh, 19)

In 'Untilted' the 'children' passing through become 'tourists' to whose intrusive presence the poet must accustom himself:

> Why not just

> Breathe in with the courage of each day, recognizing yourself as one
> Who must with difficulty get down from high places? Forget
> The tourists – other people must travel too.
>
> (Sh, 26)

In fact he cannot forget them, because their readiness to encroach on to other people's territory knows no bounds. In 'Tide Music', for instance, the poet observes how

> the welcoming host in you had

> For some reason left the door to the street open and all
> Kinds of amiable boors had taken advantage of it, though the mat
> Isn't out. All the sky, each ragged leaf, have been thoroughly
>   gone over
> And every inch is accounted for in the tune, the wallpaper of dreams.
>
> (Sh, 34)

There is a tension in the air, the poet's generous cast of mind opening people and their poetry to the reality of the street only to find the street now occupied by amiable boors 'taking advantage' of his poetic, 'every inch' of which has been 'thoroughly gone over'.

'Here Everything Is Still Floating' takes the problem further:

> But, it's because the liquor of summer nights
> Accumulates in the bottom of the bottle.
> Suspenders brought it to its, this, level, not
> The tempest in a teapot of a private asylum, laughter on the
>   back steps,
>
> Not mine, in fine; I must concentrate on how disappointing
> It all has to be while rejoicing in my singular
> Un-wholeness that keeps it an event to me.
>
> (Sh, 18)

This is unhappy poetry, images of dissatisfaction multiplying by a process of association to generate a dense weariness of tone. As ever the essence of the poetry is the passage of time, but here it is relentless rather than marvellous. And whereas once the poet's cup ran over, now the bottle he reaches for to assuage his depression contains only the dregs. The poet, in other words, is in a slough, to lift himself out of which he 'must concentrate' on that 'singular / Un-wholeness' of his, that unique openness, which has hitherto ensured his susceptibility to the eventfulness of time. But he can't, he is distracted, and what are distracting him, as the poem makes clear, are

> These, these young guys
> Taking a shower with the truth, living off the interest of their
>
> Sublime receptivity to anything, can disentangle the whole
> Lining of fabricating living from the instantaneous
> Pocket it explodes in, enters the limelight of history from,
> To be gilded and regilded, waning as its legend waxes,
>
> Disproportionate and triumphant.

The presence of these young guys creates tension. The poet admires them, and, like Whitman's young wife gazing at soldiers bathing, he is energised by the thought of them '[t]aking a shower with the truth'. The energy is erotic, and also aesthetic, the poet taking pleasure from the fact that somebody, at least, is still capable of a refreshing Pasternakian encounter with things. But there is something indolent about these young guys, 'living', as they are, 'off the interest'. As quickly as one can say 'sublime receptivity' what had seemed like a solution to the poet's enervated state – the sight of these guys refreshed by the truth – becomes the problem. They have inherited without substantially adding to his sponge-like aesthetic and so Ashbery can no longer rejoice in his 'singular / Un-wholeness', because, in fine, it is 'not mine'.

In one respect the poem makes a concerted effort to free itself of its imitations, the multiple clauses of the long sentence in which the 'young guys' appear shooting off so quickly as to defy the analysis necessary for imitation (or criticism). In the event, though, the poem does not achieve escape velocity and with the final sentence the poet becomes caught once again within the orbit of his followers:

> Still I enjoy
> The long sweetness of the simultaneity, yours and mine,
>   ours and mine,
> The mosquitoey summer night light. Now about your poem
> Called this poem: it stays and must outshine its welcome.

Poets have written to and about their followers before. Whitman wrote to 'he that would become my follower' in 'Whoever You Are Holding Me Now in Hand'.[12] Yeats called for 'upstanding men' to ensure his poetic legacy in 'The Tower'. Stevens addressed 'Notes Towards a Supreme Fiction' to the 'ephebe', and in 'Sad Strains of a Gay Waltz' tried to anticipate how he might be exceeded. Rarely, though, has the follower-figure been such an awkward presence as in *Shadow Train*, young poets being, as Ashbery observed, much 'bolder now'. One reason for this increased boldness is probably the growth of creative writing programmes. Great poets are no longer distant, inaccessible figures because invariably they are also now teachers, and as a medium for the transmission of influence the classroom collapses distance. For the ephebe the consequence of this is that, for the price of a tuition fee, the great poet is on hand to dispense advice and to offer '"suggestions for publication"'. At the time of the publication of *Shadow Train* Ashbery himself had been teaching at Brooklyn College for several years, while Koch had been teaching writing classes at Columbia since the 1950s. And as his former students David Lehman and David Shapiro have shown, it is a only a short hop from Koch's writing class to Ashbery's circle of influence.

For the older poet, one consequence of teaching is that the process of influence no longer takes place at a safe, because largely unnoticed, distance, but right there, in front of him, in the poems he assigns and grades. The feedback that results from this collapsed distance needs to be taken into account, by criticism, but more importantly by the poet himself or herself. Hence the last lines of 'Here Everything Is Still Floating', the poet as teacher – 'Now about your poem' – addressing himself (as he does in his letters) to the young poet's work. Except that the follower's poem isn't strictly their own, but is, rather, 'yours and mine, ours and mine'. It's not only the younger poet, in other words, who needs advice. So does the older, the problem being that it is increasingly difficult to disinter his poetry from its imitations.

So thoroughly does the poet feel his poetic territory has been occupied by his followers that in 'Unusual Precautions' he gives the whole poem over to their collective voice:

'We, we children, why our lives are circumscribed, circumreferential;
Close, too close to the center, we are haunted by perimeters
And our lives seem to go in and out, in and out all the time,
As though yours were diagonal, vertical, shallow, chopped off

At the root like the voice of the famous gadfly: "Oh! Aho!" it
Sits in the middle of the roadway. That's it. Worry and brown desk
Stain it by infusion. There aren't enough tags at the end,
And the grove is blind, blossoming, but we are too porous to hear it ...'

(Sh, 35)

'Unusual Precautions' takes the unusual precaution of alerting his followers (ostensibly in their own voice) to the problems generic to their situation. 'Too close to the center', to the source of their inspiration, they are barely able to inhabit their own lives, and so keen are they to appear porous that they don't even notice that the grove is blossoming. 'Written in the Dark' puts the problem more starkly still.

Telling it five, six times a day,
Telling it like a bedtime story no one knows,
Telling it like a fortune, that happened a short time ago,
Like yesterday afternoon, so recently that it seems not to have

> Quite happened yet ... All these and more were ways
> Our love assumed to look like a state religion,
> Like political wisdom. It's too bad that the two hands
> Clenched between us fail in their concreteness,
>
> That we need some slogan to transform it all into autumn ...
>
> (Sh, 30)

What Ashbery is telling time and time again (in the classroom and in letters to younger poets) is how to write poetry. The new orthodoxy the poem has in mind is thus 'Ashberyism', and the cost of orthodoxy of any stripe is, as the poem suggests, 'concreteness'.[13]

At its most artful *Shadow Train* is not just an extended poetic tussle between the writer and his followers but an inquiry into what one might call the generic condition, the volume endeavouring to make something of the new element shaping his poetic occasions. The volume's uniform form clearly signals some interest in things generic, as does the title: 'Shadow' implying both a looming presence and a pale imitation of a former self; 'Train' connoting both mechanical motion and a uniform succession. Thematically, on the other hand, the poet's awareness of the generic poems he is giving rise to prompts him to a series of telling meditations on the nature of fame, and also to a quite despondent, and quite uncharacteristic, contemplation of the uniform quality of American existence.

The question of fame is an implicit element in the poems addressing the poet's followers, the relationship being predicated on the fact of Ashbery's celebrity. It is the explicit concern of a number of poems which make the degraded condition of celebrity their subject. 'Punishing the Myth', a poem which seems to have the perils of apotheosis firmly in mind, circles towards the realisation that 'After something has passed // You begin to see yourself as you would look to yourself on a stage, / Appearing to someone' (Sh, 2). While in '"*Moi, je suis la tulipe* ..."', the poet is reminded that

> Seriously, the magazines speak of you,
>
> Mention you, a lot. I have seen the articles and the ads recently.
> Your name is on everyone's lips.
>
> (Sh, 38)

The virtue of both poems is the ease with which, Warhol-like, they loosen the paradoxes of contemporary fame. With distinction comes imitators, and so that which initially attracted attention for its uniqueness becomes, through the rapid dissemination processes of the modern media, familiar to the point of banality. Thus in '"*Moi, je suis la tulipe* ..."', someone – the poet perhaps, although the particular identity is by definition not the issue – has achieved fame, in that the magazines (*Women's Wear Daily* perhaps) now speak of him. But rather than confirming his distinctiveness the imitations consequent upon such media recognition make fresh distinctiveness, all the more necessary. Hence the wilfully idiosyncratic title, with its desperate desire to distinguish itself in an environment where, as the poem puts it, 'you get two of everything'.

'Qualm' explores the issue at length. It is one of Ashbery's most straightforward poems, almost none of the sentences stretching the rules of conventional syntax, with the two equal parts of the poem – the first devoted to Warren G. Harding, the second to the summer's latest 'golf star' – making regular use of his four-quatrain form. Both parts of the poem speak to Ashbery's situation: the first observing that Harding died hearing talk of himself; the second that the golf star's fame coincides almost inevitably with the decline in his fortunes. More importantly, both parts also speak to one another, and in so doing to the phenomenon of fame. What connects the two parts is the relation of the one to the many; 'the most central of all philosophical problems … because so pregnant', according to William James, and clearly germane to the structure of fame.[14] Thus the point of the first part of the poem is that while Warren G. Harding is now famous for only one thing – being president of the United States – there is much more in fact that one might know about him: that, ironically, he invented the word 'normalcy', that he died in the Palace Hotel, etc. In part, then, Ashbery's interest in fame is the same as his interest in history, both being forms of remembering which are actually acts of forgetting. Like Harding, the golf star also suffers from the asymmetrical relation of the one to the many, the crowd first sharing in his success and then abandoning him as he becomes a victim of it. He is sacrificed to the hysterical needs of the many, and so, as in Harding's case, his fame is intimately bound up with the act of forgetting. This recalls Warhol, of course, as does the further twist in the poem's handling of the one and the many. Different as they are, Harding, the poem insists, would have noticed the fate of the golf star. Even as it distinguishes them from the crowd, that is, the overwhelming fact of fame effaces difference, ensuring that such diverse individuals as president and golf star are linked by the narrow familiarity the public has with them.

Ashbery's 'fame' poems examine the paradoxically generic quality of the seemingly extraordinary condition of celebrity. They thus complement rather than contrast with a number of poems inspecting the homogeneous quality of contemporary American life. These poems – 'A Prison All the Same', 'Drunken Americans', 'Something Similar', 'Penny Parker's Mistake' and 'Or In My Throat' – appear consecutively in *Shadow Train* and as a group they read like the hollow underside of his own recent writings. As in *The Vermont Notebook* the poet has taken a 'bus trip'. But whereas in his prose work he gleefully documented the variety of American life, the key note now is a deadly similarity. As 'Penny Parker's Mistake' has it, 'Any way she looked, up down, around, around again, always the same'. Travelling from 'a long ways away' in 'Something Similar', the poetry has arrived, as the hick expression suggests, in the dystopically uniform environment of small-town America. Bathed in 'the average light of a college town' the poems are like a series of exceedingly barren Hoppers, their mean exchanges, narrow perspectives, and a seemingly endless series of 'thin, unsatisfactory' moments ensuring that, as 'Something Similar' puts it, 'Elegance has been halted for the duration'.

'A Prison All the Same' is the nadir:

> Many of them drink beer.
> A crisis or catastrophe goes off in their lives
>
> Every few hours. They don't get used to it, having no memory.
> Nor do they think it's better that way. What happens for them
> Is part of them, an appendage. There's no room to step back
> To get a perspective. The old one stops and thinks. The fragrant bulbs
>
> In the cellar are no use either. Last week a man was here.
> But just try sorting it out when you're on top
> Of your destiny, like angels elbowing each other on the head of a pin.
>
> (Sh, 21)

This is the poetry of Main Street not Bleecker, and as such is most unlike Ashbery. His subject is the dreadful consistency of many American lives, mired in drink and lacking memory enough to know whether things have changed or not. What he presents, in other words, is a sensibility quite opposite to that typically embodied by his own poetry, and to do so he has temporarily to remake his language. The sentences are stunted not flowing. The pronouns are not mobile but fixed. The descriptive phrases ('Many are drunk') are dismissively general not nuanced, the general effect of these stylistic reversals being a most unAsbheryan attitude to ordinariness.

Typically, Ashbery's attitude to ordinariness is, as Goodman suggested, to heighten it, to make it meaningful by bathing it in the light of imagination and criticism. The question that haunts Ashbery's dystopic poems is whether that practice is still viable. With so many people now writing like him, the act of heightening has become conventional, and so, by a pragmatic logic, doesn't work any more. Writing about the impact of followers on Ashbery's poetry, Anthony Howell has observed that 'A philosophical perception, like some mathematical formula, may *prove* true forever; but in poetry it only *sounds* true when first stated – repetition falsifies it by turning its expression into cliché.'[15] Or as Ashbery puts it, seeming to identify his own failure now to put things right with his own success and with the overcrowding that has followed:

> just try sorting it out when you're on top
> Of your destiny, like angels elbowing each other on the head of a pin.

All of which leaves Ashbery where in *Shadow Train*? Too many of the poems are private affairs, the poet either irritated with his followers for making his writing seem formulaic, or irritated with himself for his inability to break beyond the formula. 'A Pact With Sullen Death' is typical of this second kind, its keenness to be an Ashbery poem making it sound in fact more like a poem by Lehman:

'Is this life?' Yes, the last minute was too –
And the joy of informing takes over
Like the crackle of artillery fire in the outer suburbs
And I was going to wish that you too were the 'I'

(Sh, 8)

The poems towards the end of the book tend to be less mechanical. 'Catalpas'
informs us that 'All around us an extraordinary effort is being made. / Something
is in the air', and for a brief moment it seems as if Ashbery's quatrains might
cease to be an expression of uniformity, and might instead become, as in Paster-
nak (whose chosen form it was), the familiar background against which change
is registered. But this never quite happens, and in the end the most distinctive
contribution *Shadow Train* makes to Ashbery's writing is to be found in that
clutch of poems which make uniformity their theme. In one respect they con-
stitute an ingenious manoeuvre, the formulaic poetry of imitators giving way to
the poetry of imitation and formula. In another, however, they are an unsus-
tainably desperate measure, Ashbery managing to distinguish himself from
those who write like him only by not writing like himself; by offering an unchar-
acteristically mean response to the business of ordinary life.

A Wave is a much more successful, and altogether more important volume. Here
again the poetry is partly shaped by voices eager to sound like the poet's own, but
now Ashbery's reaction to them is more complex. The poetic forms are looser,
airier than those of *Shadow Train*, and the keen young voices they contain are
permitted, now, to sound rather less like competitors and rather more like col-
laborators. 'Staffage' is a case in point, the poem taking the form of a letter:

Sir, I am one of a new breed
Of inquisitive pest in love with the idea
Of our integrity, programming us over dark seas
Into small offices, where we sit and compete
With you, on your own time.
We want only to be recognized for what we are:
Everything else is secondary.
Consequently, I shall sit on your doorstep
Till you notice me.

(W, 47)

We have come across such letters before – 'Kinnell calls them his guilt pile' –
'Staffage' working through many of the same ambivalent feelings about his
solicitous correspondents that Ashbery articulated in interview. Though not pre-
cisely asking for '"suggestions for publication"', the speaker in 'Staffage' is clearly
bold, pestering the addressee to the point of sitting on his doorstep. As such, and
as in 'Unusual Precautions', the correspondent is presented antagonistically:
encroaching on the older poet's territory in so far as he seeks to 'compete / With
you on your own time'. What 'Staffage' appreciates, however, and what makes it

the better poem, is that relations between generations of poet are complex affairs. So while 'Staffage' opens with the image of ephebe as pre-programmed interloper, it ends more sympathetically:

> Half of me I give
> To do with as you wish – scold, ignore, forget for awhile.
> The other half I keep, and shall feel
> Fully rewarded if you pass by this offer
> Without recognizing it, receding deliberately
> Into the near distance, which speaks no longer
> Of loss, but of brevity rather: short naps, keeping fit.

On the one hand, this suggests, the young poet is beholden to the older poet he so admires; abases himself by offering his own poetry as a tribute; and hopes he will be recognised as participating in the same tradition. On the other, he wants desperately to match the achievement of his elder, which means, as Ashbery has observed in interview, not imitating his style but emulating his uniqueness. 'The more you like a poet', Ashbery observed to Piotr Sommer, 'the less you ought to write like him, because what you were liking in him is a uniqueness, and if you're not being unique you're not being truly influenced.'[16] From which it follows that the highest compliment the older poet can pay the younger is to not recognise his poetry as a continuation of his own; Auden, it will be recalled, paying Ashbery just such a double-edged compliment in his introduction to *Some Trees*.

'Staffage' thus reads like a parody of Bloom's oedipal theorising of the question of influence, both poets struggling to preserve their identity in the face of the other's likeness. But it also goes beyond Bloom, Ashbery opening up the possibility – a possibility Bloom can never allow – that the two poets might collaborate with one another. 'Staffage', that is, allows for the possibility that, just as the shortening of the influential circuit implicit in such letters can produce the kind of negative feedback from which *Shadow Train* suffers, so also it can open the older poet to new possibilities in and for his writing. Half-way through the poem the young poet offers to repay the older poet's generosity:

> I'll flesh out
> The thin warp of your dreams, make them meatier,
> Nuttier. And when a thin pall gathers,
> Leading finally to outraged investigation
> Into what matters next, I'll be there
> On the other side.

Still the lines are threaded with suspicion, and in part we are invited to take the promise of a meatier, nuttier poetry with a pinch of salt. But, when it comes to the question of 'what matters next', the possibility is entertained that the younger poet will be first to the other side; that he or she will be first to the new.

'Thank You For Not Cooperating' is more co-operative still, the poem presenting the two voices in something like harmony. The poem's demotic setting is typically Ashberyan:

Down in the street there are ice-cream parlors to go to
And the pavement is a nice, bluish slate-gray. People laugh a lot.
Here you can see the stars.

(W, 12)

On this occasion, however, the setting is shared:

Two lovers are singing
Separately from the same rooftop: '*Leave your change behind.*
Leave your clothes, and go. It is time now.
It was time before too, but now it is really time.
You will never have enjoyed storms so much
As on these hot sticky evenings that are more like August
Than September. Stay. A fake wind wills you to go
And out there on the stormy river witness buses bound for Connecticut,
And tree-business, and all that we think about when we stop thinking.
The weather is perfect, the season unclear. Weep for your going
But also expect to meet me in the near future, when I shall disclose
New further adventures, and that you shall continue to think of me.'

The difficulty here lies in distinguishing between the two voices the poem refers us to. Possibly they are singing the same song separately. Possibly equally they are singing separate parts of a duet. Either way we cannot tell one from the other. Each, we are invited to suppose, wants the other both to go and to stay. Each feels the other is both more ready now to appreciate the climate, and susceptible to 'fake' winds. Each will be sorry to see the other go, and is confident that the other will continue to think of them. The poem, in other words, is a precarious balancing of dissonance and harmony, of that play of similarity and difference which for Bloom marks the influential relationship. Except that here, as in 'Staffage', the merging of the voices suggests that the respect and anxiety the ephebe feels for the older poet is mutual, both poems contributing to the development of a poetic form which might accommodate the troublesome voices of follower figures.

There are several such poems in *A Wave*: 'At North Farm', 'The Songs We Know Best', 'When The Sun Went Down', 'Just Walking Around', 'A Fly', 'Introduction', and 'Try Me! I'm Different!', all, in their way, finding much more supple ways of absorbing voices like the poet's own than ever he managed in *Shadow Train*. It is not, however, because it arrives at more complex expressions of the influential relationship (important as that is to the state of his art) that *A Wave* is one of Ashbery's most urgent volumes. What makes it urgent, rather, is the way in which, in Ashbery's writing of the early 1980s, his thinking about those around him comes to be shaped by more pressing concerns than that of influence. The occasion of the shift would seem to have been the development of AIDS, one effect of which on Ashbery's poetry was that thinking about the question of coterie became thinking about the question of community, the work of such younger poets as Gerrit Henry helping to make the link. Like Lehman Henry majored in English at Columbia, and, like Lehman also, he knows Ashbery well. Ashbery dedicated 'The Double Dream of Spring' to Henry, Henry interviewed Ashbery in 1979 for *The Spectator*, and Ashbery wrote the introduction to Henry's selected poems, *The Mirrored Clubs of Hell*. Describing him as 'a Dante adrift without a Virgil in the mirrored clubs of hell and their surrounding cityscape', Ashbery's introduction lists Henry's subjects as

> pain and alienation, TV and the movies, relationships with friends, lovers, and parents; life in New York City and the price its transitory pleasures exact; cruising in village bars and celebrating one's birthday in a psychiatric ward; God and death and AIDS.[17]

Henry's poem 'Omnivert' catches much of this. Sad and sassy in equal measure, the poem opens in Henry's apartment. Joan Rivers has just gone off the air. Fauré's 'Requiem' is playing in the background. Henry, who has spent the evening with Jimmy Schuyler and Darragh Park, has learned that J.J. Mitchell has died of AIDS. Unable to absorb the information, the poem speaks of whatever else comes to mind: an accident at a nuclear plant near Kiev, Joan Rivers on the 'Tonight' show, Jimmy, Darragh, 'Dark Victory' ('a great movie the first time you see it'). Only towards the end does the poem approach acceptance. 'What's gone so radically wrong?', the poet asks himself starkly, the question leading, after a further digression (this time into Schuyler's new book) to the sustainable poise of the closing lines:

> 'Isn't that a star?' Jimmy insisted, as we stood outside
> On the sidewalk, looking up to the sky,
> Waiting for Darragh inside to finish parleying
> With John Ashbery and Pierre Martory,
> Later arrivals, at another table.
> 'Why is there only one?'[18]

Galvanised by Schuyler's expression of controlled sentimentality, the poem ends with an image of community: Henry conversing with Schuyler, Park parleying with Ashbery and Martory, and the unattributed last line suggesting a commonality of feeling.

Poetry like Henry's poses a challenge to Ashbery. It is clearly the work of a follower – casually composed, absorbing all elements of the culture, telling the history of its making – and as such threatens to obscure Ashbery by muscling in on his poetic territory. But it also does things that Ashbery's poetry doesn't do, Henry's writing being, in particular, much readier to address himself to a gay readership than Ashbery's own. So while, on the one hand, Henry is one of that coterie of writers who have come to surround and sometimes to impede Ashbery, and from whom Ashbery is understandably keen to distance himself, on the other, his poetry questions that impulse to distance by raising issues of identity and community which Henry clearly thinks urgent – and clearly are urgent – in the face of the emergence of AIDS. The best poems in *A Wave* rise to these challenges, with 'Description of a Masque', Ashbery's lush prose fantasia on the communitarian implications of his own poetic, doing so as clearly as any.

At the centre of 'Description of a Masque' is a character called 'Mania', magnificently dressed 'in a gown of sapphire-blue tulle studded with blue sequins', and who, as 'goddess of confusion', and as inhabitant of 'these ambiguous surroundings, neither true fantasy nor clean-cut reality', bears more than a passing resemblance to the poet himself. The second time we see 'Mania' – the first is in her Miltonic grotto – she is raging against a bunch of hobos who lurk around her door, and whom she finds so oppressive that she can 'no longer see the woman [she] once was'. Accordingly she resolves not to rest 'until I have erased all of this from my thoughts, or (which is more likely) incorporated it into the confusing scheme I have erected around me for my support and glorification'. (W, 22–3) The only person she can trust to help her in this is a character named 'STRANGER', who, hearing of her plight, promises to take her away her to a place where

> beauty and irrationality reign alternately, and never tread on each other's toes as do your unsightly followers ... where your own pronounced contours may flourish and be judged for what they are worth, while the anomalies of the room you happen to be in or the disturbing letters and phone calls that hamper your free unorthodox development will melt away like crystal rivulets leaving a glacier, and you may dwell in the accident of your character forever. (W, 23–4)

This could hardly be more explicit. Obscured by his followers, and hampered by their 'letters and phone calls', the poet wants nothing more than to distance himself from them.

Hospitable as Ashbery's poetry typically is, this unaccommodating impulse is not inconsistent with his poetic. Poetry which aims to accommodate its followers is coterie poetry. Nobody wrote coterie poetry better than O'Hara, and Ashbery, it will be recalled, was wary of the clubbier aspects of O'Hara's writing. ('What is someone who doesn't know who Norman and Jean-Paul and Joan are going to think of this?') Alive to the exclusive implications of such naming, Ashbery has typically sought, by contrast, to cut through the networks that surround him, and to address the reader with something like Whitmanesque directness. Witness, from *Shadow Train*, 'Paradoxes and Oxymorons', which, contrary to the obfuscating jargon of its title, makes itself entirely plain:

> This poem is concerned with language on a very plain level.
> Look at it talking to you. You look out a window
> Or pretend to fidget. You have it but you don't have it.
> You miss it, it misses you. You miss each other.
>
> (Sh, 3)

As in Whitman's 'To You', the unknown reader is everything here, the poet concluding, like a gentle Uncle Sam, by observing that 'the poem / Has set me softly down beside you. The poem is you'.

Ashbery is still not a coterie poet, and so his poetry still does not name names. He is aware, of course, of the limitations of the impersonal address, adverting to them in 'Another Chain Letter' where the Whitmanesque 'you' is compared to the very unintimate 'you' of the mailshot. Still, though, he prefers the inclusive implications of the pronoun to the exclusive implications of the name, the ironic result of which is that his poetry has recruited followers. It is by his anti-coterie strategy, in other words, that Ashbery has acquired a coterie, people who think they have got to know him personally through his poetry addressing him by name in 'their disturbing letters and phone calls'.[19] Thus while Ashbery writes, as he has observed, like Gertrude Stein, 'for himself and for strangers', in the ever shorter circuits of contemporary poetry, strangers become friends and followers before you can say 'Dear John'. Which, if it is a cause of satisfaction on the one hand, is also a cause of anxiety, the followers and the imitations surrounding the poet and hampering his 'free unorthodox development'. Hence Mania's willingness, with the help of 'Stranger', to remove herself from her unsightly followers.

Yet if one tendency, in 'Description of a Masque', is explicitly towards distancing and isolation, the equal and opposite tendency is towards incorporation and identification. In particular, the poem is more explicit than ever in its identification of and with a gay scene. Meticulous in its attention to surface detail (Daffy Down Dilly's 'yellow lace-edged petticoat hung down about an inch and a half below the hem of her gown'), cutting effortlessly between *Mildred Pierce* and *La Bohème*, and offering us, as it does, in 'Mania goddess of confusion' a vision of the poet in drag, one does not, one might think, have to be Susan Sontag to notice that 'Description of a Masque' is camp. But just in case we don't get these signs, and hadn't noticed also that the bar in the second scene (which, with its motionless, gazing barman Georgie Porgie, bears a passing resemblance to the 'Bar at the Folies-Bergère') is a actually a gay bar, Ashbery shows us Little Boy Blue ('entirely clothed in blue denim') 'apparently performing an act of fellatio' on Little Jack Horner ('a tall and roguish-looking young man wearing a trench coat and expensive blue jeans'). Ashbery's poetry has tended not to address the matter of his sexuality. As he put it in *Self-Portrait in a Convex Mirror*, in 'Love' (the first part of 'Poem in Three Parts'):

> 'Once I let a guy blow me.
> I kind of backed away from the experience.
> Now years later, I think of it
> Without emotion. There has been no desire to repeat,
> No hangups either. Probably if the circumstances were right
> It could happen again, but I don't know,
> I just have other things to think about,
> More important feelings. Who goes to bed with what
> Is unimportant ...'

(SP, 22)

'Love' has it both ways, Ashbery speaking frankly about sex, but observing that on the whole he is reluctant to do so. Arguably the poem is a double bluff, and possibly, as Catherine Imbroglio and John Shoptaw have suggested, one should read Ashbery's reluctance explicitly to address the question of his sexuality not as evidence that, as the poet claims, he thinks there are more important things to think about, but as proof, rather, of his closeted sensibility. Following this line both Imbroglio and Shoptaw read the poetry for signs of the repressed subject: for forms of evasion which actually show that homosexuality is the poetry's pressing concern. To do so is to read against the grain of a poetry which is char- acterised, among other things, by its inclusive address. Arguably, of course that inclusive address, as in Whitman, has its origin in a sense of social marginality borne of prevailing attitudes to homosexuality. But if so then, as 'Love' has it, what the poetry is really trying to insist is that 'who goes to bed with what / is unimportant'. But whether you take the poet at his word in 'Love', or read him against the grain, the point about 'Description of a Masque' is that for the gay poet in New York in the early 1980s, and especially for the gay poet who has always sought to absorb what is going on around him, the question of sexual identity could hardly any longer be thought unimportant.

In Edmund White's story 'Palace Days', the central characters, Mark and Ned meet in 'late '81' when the official line had been, '"Limit the number of you part- ners. Know their names."'[20] In White's story, as in Henry's poem, the central issue for the gay writer writing in the face of AIDS is taken to be the question of community and communities. It is a common response, and as such finds its echo in criticism, Suzanne Poirier suggesting in the introduction to the volume of critical essays *Writing AIDS* that the book 'challenges us to resist easy charac- terizations or understandings of the epidemic and to work together to build whatever new communities of care, expression, and action are required'.[21] What form such communities should take is much debated by the contributors. Tak- ing his political lead from Larry Kramer, Joseph Cady draws a distinction between what he calls, not altogether elegantly, 'Immersive and Counter Immersive Writing about Aids'. Immersive writing is characterised by 'pro- longed moments when the reader is thrust into direct imaginative confrontation with the special horrors of AIDS and is required to deal with them with no relief or buffer provided by the writer'. Counterimmersive writing 'typically focuses on characters or speakers who are in various degrees of denial about AIDS them- selves' and treats the reader the same way, 'protecting them from too jarring a confrontation with the subject through a variety of distancing devices'. From which it follows, for Cady, that 'individual counterimmersive texts characteris- tically do nothing to dislodge whatever impulse their audience may have to deny the disease'. His line is clear. 'Silence', as the slogan had it, 'equals death' and so gay writing should be uncompromising in its identification of the disease.[22]

James W. Jones reads such so-called 'counterimmersive writing' altogether differently. Focusing his argument on *The Darker Proof: Stories from a Crisis* – a collection of short stories by Adam Mars-Jones and Edmund White – Jones's starting point is the fact that neither writer uses the name AIDS; a gesture of omission he takes to be a powerful response to the various questions of community to which the crisis gives rise. To refuse the name, he argues, is to resist efforts to cordon off the gay community by labelling. It is also to make the focus of the writing not the condition itself (inseparable as that is from the public mythology) but the lives of individuals and the life of the community affected by it. Which is by no means, as Jones sees it, an act of denial, but a reaction to the 'culturally determined equation of homosexuality=AIDS', a refusal to marginalise an already marginal community. Not that the force of their writing lies only in its negative strategies. In White in particular, while the illness undeniably destroys life, it also gives rise to 'a community of love and strength', with the 'further universalizing discourse' of 'love' allowing White's gay characters not only to consolidate but also to expand their community. Witness the end of 'Palace Days'.[23] All but exclusively concerned with the life of the gay community, and particularly with the possibilities the crisis offers for strengthening that community, the story concludes by momentarily widening its constituency. It ends in Paris – where Mark and Ned have gone because the disease is less prevalent there than in New York – the final scene taking place at the ballet:

> The Robbins ballet was new, but the two Balanchines were old friends, *Apollo* and the Stravinsky *Violin Concerto*. They were both nicely danced, but the somnolent audience scarcely applauded and Mark felt offended. He'd never been able to make Parisians understand that the lobby of the New York State Theater had been the drawing room of America and that we, yes, *we* Americans saw in the elaborate *enchainements* on stage a radiant vision of society.[24]

It is a delicate touch, White lifting his story into a wider society without losing his hold on the gay community: the 'elaborate *enchainements*' of the ballet constituting the necessarily complex link.

Lee Edelman concurs with Jones, arguing that AIDS rhetoric detaches '"high risk groups"' from the '"general population"'. He differs, however, in arguing that therefore 'the politics of "AIDS" as a subject of discourse is inseparable from the politics of "the subject" itself'. Not only then, contra Cody, must writing about AIDS desist from identifying the disease, it must also make the question of identity its subject; the conventional discourse of AIDS effecting the kind of cordon Jones addresses by the restrictive definitions of gay identity it offers. For Edelman, that is, the gay community must develop 'alternative … notions of subjectivity'. By which he means nothing so simplistic as positive images, but rather forms of self-definition which allow identification with the gay community but don't disallow identification with the wider community beyond it.[25]

The complex of problems Jones and Edelman identify – addressing by not naming a crisis, identifying and not identifying with a given community, defining oneself while resisting definition – occasion some of Ashbery's most important writing in *A Wave*, 'Description of a Mask' being a case in point.[26] From the initial isolation of Mania's grotto, the poem enters the bar. This is the setting for a community of sorts – loose-knit certainly, but held together by the spirit of the place. The scene becomes momentarily more ordered when the statue of Mercury steps down from his pedestal to address the people gathered at the bar:

'My fellow prisoners, we have no idea how long each of us has been in this town and how long each of us intends to stay, although I have reason to believe that the lady in green over there is a fairly recent arrival. My point, however, is this. Instead of loitering this way, we should all become part of a collective movement, get involved with each other and with our contemporaries on as many levels as possible. No one will disagree that there is much to be gained from contact with one another, and I, as a god, feel it even more keenly than you do. My understanding, though universal, lacks the personal touch and the local color which would make it meaningful to me.' (W, 20)

A well-meaning attempt both to corral his audience into a 'collective movement' and to encourage involvement with 'our contemporaries', Mercury's earnest lecture judges the situation badly. His words 'produce an uneasiness among the other patrons of the bar' and his attempt to impose a unity on the gathering is decisively resisted when, in an immaculately camp gesture, 'Daffy Down Dilly' pulls a small revolver from her green brocade notebook and shoots the messenger. From here, after Mania's dialogue with the Stranger, the action cuts to 'a busy main street in a large American city', whereupon Mercury (who appears to have chilled out somewhat since he was shot) is delighted to notice

That powder-blue sky of the eternal postcard, with the haze of mountain peaks barely visible; the salmon-coloured pavement with its little green and blue cars that look so still though they are supposed to be in motion? The window shoppers, people like you and me …? (W, 26–7)

Which recognition of the virtues of the setting gives rise to a more general understanding of the virtues of setting:

Then we all realized what should have been obvious from the start: that the setting would go on evolving eternally, rolling its waves across our vision like an ocean, each one new yet recognizably a part of the same series, which was creation itself. (W, 27)

All of which makes 'Description of a Masque' (the campest thing Ashbery has written since he finished *A Nest of Ninnies*) a serious but never earnest response to contemporary questions of community. The poem presents a clearly identified gay scene; gives voice to an all too well intentioned call for that scene's community to develop both a stronger 'collective identity' and a more universal sense of its relations; and concludes with a street scene, and with window shoppers who may or may not have a camp eye for detail, and so which manages, unlike Mercury's speech, to be universal with a personal touch. For all that it is rejected, then, Mercury's speech is pertinent in almost every detail, and fails only in so far as it misjudges the setting. But this is a critical failure, Ashbery's masque, like the genre as a whole, being largely defined by attention to setting. Introducing Milton's 'Comus', of which Ashbery's poem is an uproarious parody ('Mania', in particular, bearing more than a passing resemblance to the unruly 'Comus'), Douglas Bush observes that the poem is relatively unusual in having a serious subject. Thus whereas 'Comus' discourses earnestly on the virtues of chastity, the genre was 'mainly an excuse for an abundance of spectacle, music, and dancing', court productions in particular being 'lavish and expensive'.[27] The point of the masque, that is, was to foreground background, a generic convention made all the more salient in Ashbery's poem not only because the poem delights in its settings but because in 'Description of a Masque' setting is community. This is why there are so many changes of scene towards the end of the poem:

> Scenes from movies, plays, operas, television; decisive or little known episodes from history; prenatal and other early memories from our own solitary, separate pasts; events yet to come from life or art; calamities or moments of relaxation; universal or personal tragedies; or little vignettes from daily life that you just had to stop and laugh at, they were so funny, like the dog chasing its tail on the living-room rug. (W, 27)

Partly, then, the poem encourages understanding by observing the multiplicity of scenes (and so communities) that any individual inhabits. More importantly, the poem itself is a setting, its articulation of contemporary questions of community constituting the background against which the gay community and the wider community can come to understand one another.

The sequence of prose poems 'Haibun' to 'Haibun 6' is as tragically beautiful as 'Description of a Masque' is camp.[28] A 'Haibun' is a prose passage followed by a haiku, Ashbery's use of the form in *A Wave* being typical of a volume which is as formally various as *Shadow Train* was uniform, and in which the poet's haibuns sit happily alongside '37 Haiku', the rhyming doggerel of 'The Songs We Know Best', the prose of 'Whatever It Is, Wherever You Are', the lyric pathos of 'Down By the Station, Early in the Morning', the surging cadences of the long title poem, and the lavish settings of Ashbery's 'Masque'. But if they are formally and tonally diverse, in their central concerns the haibun poems and 'Description of a Masque' are directly comparable, the poet identifying, and identifying with, the gay community in the first poem of the sequence.

Opening with an opaque meditation on the difficulties of communication (on the 'dismal space between us'), the poem moves to the consolidating declaration that

> I'm hoping that homosexuals not yet born get to inquire about it, inspect the whole random collection as though it were a sphere. Isn't the point of pain the possibility it brings of being able to get along without pain, for awhile, of manipulating our marionette-like limbs in the strait-jacket of air, and so to have written something? (W, 39)

It is very rare for Ashbery to specify a readership like this, and his decision to do so here betrays his anxiety that he will go unread (or at least unrecognised) by gay readers. This is a real anxiety because, in so far as the sequence has, as it suggests, a 'lesson' for that readership, the lesson concerns the dangers of restrictive identification. This is, by definition, a hard lesson to teach, because if, in presenting it, the poet identifies too closely with a gay readership he risks reenforcing a limited sense of community, while if he does not identify closely enough he risks losing that readership, and the opportunity to affect it. The sequence is a negotiation of this dilemma.

'Haibun 2' and 'Haibun 3' detach themselves from the gay readership identified in the first poem, addressing themselves instead to the seemingly abstract questions of aesthetic scale. 'Haibun 2' contemplates an unnamed 'affair of some enormity', of 'superhuman scale' and tries to reassure itself that the situation has not exceeded human capacity for articulation. 'Haibun 3' turns its attention to more intricate matters, such as the 'grapefruit (spelled "grapfruit" on the small, painstakingly lettered card)', thus grounding itself in the details of things. Such meditations are not entirely unrelated to a concern with communities, addressing the dangers of restrictive identification by seeking to develop a sensibility which is alert to the competing demands of what Emerson calls 'Each and All'. But necessary as such a sensibility might be, there are ways and ways of fostering it, and in their abstraction 'Haibun 2' and 'Haibun 3', like Mercury's lecture to the gay bar, lack the 'personal touch' necessary if they are to win the readers whose thinking they mean to affect.

The second half of the sequence corrects this misjudgement, 'Haibun 4' beginning with just such a personal touch:

> Dark at four again. Sadly I negotiate the almost identical streets as little by little they are obliterated under a rain of drips and squiggles of light. Their message of universal brotherhood through suffering is taken from the top, the pedal held down so that the first note echoes throughout the piece without becoming exactly audible. (W, 42)

This is an altogether more appropriate expression in the circumstances, the poet situating himself in the midst of a city in crisis, and arriving, as he does so, at a much more precise formulation of his relation to that crisis. Thus, without making it 'exactly audible', without, that is, 'exactly' identifying with the gay community, it is none the less apparent from the images of obliteration and 'universal brotherhood through suffering' that the poem is addressing the situation the gay community finds itself in. In fact the poem stays only just this side of inaudibility, proceeding to identify

> a man with the conscience of a woman, always coming out of something, turning to look at you, wondering about a possible reward. How sweet to my sorrow is this man's knowledge in his way of coming, the brotherhood that will surely result under now darkened skies.
>
> The pressing, pressing urgent whispers, pushing on, seeing directly. (W, 42)

This hardly takes much decoding, Ashbery's concern with and for the gay community being audible to anyone who cares to listen. Slightly less audible, perhaps, are the echoes here of other gay poets writing from a state of crisis: the sweetly pressing eroticism recalling Whitman's efforts in the 'Calamus' poems to solve his crisis of identity by constructing a gay community; the 'darkened skies' over New York recalling 'September 1st 1939', and Auden's contemplation, from his 52nd Street bar, of the implications for ordinary lives of the looming crisis of the Second World War. Ashbery's response to his own crisis, and to the questions of identity and community it poses, lies in the sceptical handling of these differing voices with which his sequence concludes.

'Haibun 5' is a conversation with Whitman, Ashbery first questioning then adopting the imagery of 'Calamus'. Its opening is tensely argumentative: 'Bring them all back to life, with white gloves on, out of dream in which they are still alive. Loosen the adhesive bonds that tie them to the stereotypes of the dead, clichés like the sound of running water' (W, 43). The object here is not to forge a gay community, as Whitman sought to in 'Calamus' through his term 'adhesion'. The intention, rather, is to loosen those bonds which, while they consolidate it serve also to marginalise it, such a clearly defined community being prone to stereotyping and thereby, as the lines suggests, death. What the situation calls for, therefore, is not the over-identifying rhetoric of martyrdom Whitman went in for in 'Calamus' – the poet engaging in an act of self-sacrifice in the interests of his 'comrades' – but the detachment signalled by the clinical white gloves. Acting according to this impulse, 'Haibun 5' does detach itself, proceeding through a series of scattered observations which have to do with the gay scene only in so far as they show a world outside its concerns. But as before such a universalising gesture is not in itself an adequate response, the poem's record of the flow of events obscuring the gay community even as it lifts it out of itself, and so, after plunging back into an audibly homoerotic setting – into 'Broadway nights of notoriety and the warm syrup of embarrassed and insistent proclamations of all kinds of tidings that made you what you were in the world' – the poem concludes with a visual reference to Whitman's most potent symbol: 'A terminus, pole fringed with seaweed at its base, a cracked memory' (W, 43). This is the calamus root by any other name. To call it a terminus is to recognise with Whitman that it serves as a symbol around which a readership can group and define itself. But it is also a terminus in the sense of an ending, such an act of self-definition carrying all the risks Ashbery has already indicated.

In reaction to the transcendental tone he identifies and argues with in Whitman, in the final poem of the Haibun series Ashbery turns to Auden. In 'September 1st, 1939' Auden's response to the distortions of idealism which one way or another, as he saw it, had led to the Second World War, was to re-evaluate ordinariness; to bathe the ordinary in 'an affirming flame', so that people might better resist the blandishments of totalitarian politics. It is a humane response to a catastrophic situation which threatens to collapse into conservatism, but to which, poised on the verge of a crisis engineered by anti-individualistic politics, Auden could see little alternative. 'Haibun 6' tries a similar line, dropping away from the urgencies of Whitman to notice a frog hopping from his lily pad, and people coping (empty pails in hand) with an extended period of rainfall. And like Auden, Ashbery looks to affirm such scenes. Remarking that 'nobody seems eager to accord ideal status to this situation, and I, for one, would love to know why', he concludes the prose section of the poem with just such an article of faith: 'Meanwhile I lift my glass to these black-and-silver striped nights. I believe that the rain never drowned sweeter, more prosaic things than those we have here, now, and I believe this is going to have to be enough' (W, 44). The differences of the emergencies in which they find themselves writing notwithstanding, Auden's warning is not inappropriate to Ashbery's concerns. His detailed commitment to the prosaic things we have here now signals a commitment to individuality and individuals which does not reduce them to the groups they happen to identify with; and to a sense of community which has its basis in a shared present. Only such concern for the ordinariness of lives, the poem implies, guarantees that ordinary lives will not be disregarded; that, as it puts it, 'true standards of judgement' will be applied. This takes us to the ethical centre of Ashbery's poetic of the occasion, the point of which is to permit understanding and judgement of the present in the present by affording as capacious an articulation of the given occasion as the poet can muster. Arguably also, however, what we run up against here is the conservative limit of Ashbery's poetry which, while it is constantly propelled by the need to accept a changing situation, precludes the possibility of effecting change by its preoccupation with the here and now. But this is to conclude the argument without reading to the end of the poem, and so without taking account of 'Silver hair, inquisitive gloves, a face, some woman named Ernestine / Throckmorton, white opera glasses and more' (W, 44). Just at the point at which Ashbery's image of sweet prosaic things might fade in the reader's mind into a case for the status quo, Ashbery provides a figure extraordinarily camp enough to challenge it. Thus if the adhesive bonds of the gay scene have to be loosened for marginal lives to seem more ordinary, so also, always, ordinariness has to be affronted in the interests of heterogeneity. 'And', as the poem puts it, 'more'.

The 'Haibun' sequence addresses the complex of problems which, between them, Jones and Edelman argued, engage, or should engage, writing concerned with AIDS: addressing while not naming a crisis, identifying and not identifying with a given community, defining oneself while resisting definition. It does so by shuttling between the alternative poetic responses to crisis Ashbery finds in Whitman and Auden, in the hope and expectation that by having the argument, the tensions which inform the argument will lessen. It is a brilliantly supple but, by the harshest critical light, an ultimately limited poetic strategy, the poem's negative capability never quite lifting decisively clear of stalemate. But how could the poem conceivably go further, achieve the 'and more' it calls for in conclusion? How can it be possible for differing identities to be formulated in such a way that does not single them out? How can the many coincide with the one? What these questions point to, and what the crisis, at least as Jones and Edelman understand it, would seem to call into being, is what in 'A Wave' Ashbery terms 'unimaginable diplomacy'; and it is in 'A Wave' that he comes closest to that impossibly tactful conception of human relations.

The problem for the critic of this magnificent long poem is that precisely because it calls such 'unimaginable diplomacy into being', it is exceedingly difficult to talk about.[29] So to be clear, the suggestion here is not that 'A Wave' is a poem about AIDS. To define it as such would be altogether to overlook the breathtakingly supple handling of the question of definition which is central to its purpose.[30] The suggestion rather is that if one were to try to imagine a poem which really took seriously the deeply intractable questions of definition implicit in the problems of community and identity that Jones and Edelman argue surface as a result of the AIDS crisis, then one might imagine a poem so appropriate to the situation as to be difficult to recognise as such. A poem so 'right', as Ashbery and Schuyler put it in *A Nest of Ninnies*, 'one cannot see it until its time is past' (NN, 181). Arguably 'A Wave' is such a poem. In a significant sense it is the consummate Ashbery long poem, providing the poetic summation the history of whose making is told by the shorter poems in the collection. As such it is deeply concerned with questions of community and identity. These concerns, and the relation between them, are faintly audible behind the title itself: a wave both threatening inundation and defying definition.

The poem opens with an image of suffering:

To pass through pain and not know it,
A car door slamming in the night.
To emerge on an invisible terrain. (W, 68)

What largely consumes 'A Wave', however, is not the extreme circumstance of pain, but the business of ordinary life; its extended sentences wrapped up in the events, memories, meetings, reflections, thoughts, speculations and desires which make up a life. We have encountered all this before in Ashbery, watched his writing 'mope and thrash [its] way though time' this way. There is a renewed vividness to the writing, 'the thing / *Is* there in all its interested variegatedness'. But this is, as the poem puts it, 'business as usual'. We have read it, or something like it, before in Ashbery.

Gradually, however, as history happens, and while the living is getting done, audibly urgent concerns begin to impinge on the poet's thinking. Some five pages into the poem an issue emerges which partially distracts him from the business of living. 'I am prepared', the poet tells us,

to deal with this
While putting together notes related to the question of love
For the many, for two people at once, and for myself
In a time of need unlike those that have arisen so far.

(W, 73)

Love is one of the urgencies in the poem. Exclusion is another:

No, the
Divine tolerance we seem to feel is actually in short supply,
And those moving forward toward us from the other end of the bridge
Are defending, not welcoming us to, the place of power,
A hill ringed with low, ridgelike fortifications.

(W, 74)

A sense of helplessness in the midst of fear – of 'Being alone at the center of a moan that did not issue from me' – is another. These are aspects of a crisis, which, as it develops, comes increasingly to preoccupy the poem, until it can no longer absorb itself in the business of living, but must concern itself instead with both the

business of living and dying, the orderly
Ceremonials and handling of estates,
Checking what does not appear normal and drawing together
All the rest into the report that will finally be made

(W, 80)

The gathering sense of crisis – marked here by the funereal language – culminates in two passages around which the energy and imagery of the poem appear to coalesce. The first has to do with a community in crisis, in that it contemplates

The cimmerian moment in which all lives, all destinies
And incompleted destinies were swamped
As though by a giant wave that picks itself up
Out of a calm sea and retreats again into nowhere
Once its damage is done.

(W, 81)

According to Greek mythology the Cimmerians were a people who lived in darkness at the edge of the world. They are, accordingly, the archetype of the marginal community. Except that here, in their moment of crisis, they appear less marginal than ever, the giant wave which inundates them simultaneously overwhelming 'all lives, all destinies'. The second passage has to do with definition, the speaker exploring the question at length when he observes that

Being tall and shy, you can still stand up more clearly
To the definition of what you are. You are not a sadist
But must only trust in the dismantling of that definition
Some day when names are being removed from things, when all attributes
Are sinking in the maelstrom of de-definition like spars.
You must then come up with something to say,
Anything as long as it's no more than five minutes long,
And in the interval you shall have been washed. It's that easy.
But meanwhile, I know, stone tenements are still hoarding
The shadow that is mine; there is nothing to admit to,
No one to confess to. This period goes on for quite a few years
But as though along a low fence by a sidewalk. Then brandishes

[203]

New definitions in its fists, but these are evidently false
And get thrown out of court. Next you're on your own
In an old film about two guys walking across the United States.
The love that comes after will be richly satisfying,
Like rain on the desert, calling unimaginable diplomacy into being
Until you thought you should get off here, maybe this stop
Was yours.

(W, 84)

This is the history of a defining process, the speaker coming to terms with a definition of himself, dismantling it, abandoning himself to the 'maelstrom of de-definition', finding himself at the mercy of an aggressive re-definition, and finally, in a fond moment, seeming to imagine a scene 'two guys walking across the United States' in which definition was no longer an issue. This optimistic scene recalls the end of 'Palace Days', Ashbery, like White, offering an image of men comfortably identifying both with one another and also with 'we, yes, *we* Americans'.

Though it reaches for its setting into the past, the old movie suggesting, perhaps, a less troubled because more naive period, Ashbery's image looks forward to a period beyond definition made possible by an as yet 'unimaginable diplomacy'. The great achievement of 'A Wave' is in pointing us towards such a supple sensibility. It does so by developing two ideas from Auden: that 'suffering' takes place '[w]hile someone else is eating or opening a window or just walking dully along', and that 'We must love one another or die'. Ashbery builds the first idea into his the poem's shifting form. Line by line the poem resists definition because while it is sometimes concerned with an unnamed crisis, it is often taken up with eating, opening windows, or just walking dully along. The poem thus identifies a marginal community at risk, while always also being identifiable with the wider community of everyday life. Everyday life in Auden stands for indifference, whether as callousness as in 'Musée des Beaux Arts' or as universality as in 'September 1st 1939'. Ashbery's poem tends to move from the former meaning to the latter. Thus while, at the beginning of the poem, an image of suffering is offered only quickly to be disregarded in favour of more ordinary things and activities, the ending is an audible plea for human understanding:

Please, it almost
Seems to say, take me with you, I'm old enough. Exactly.
And so each of us has to remain alone, conscious of each other
Until the day when war absolves us of our differences. We'll
Stay in touch. So they have it, all the time. But all was strange.

(W, 89)

Crises such as wars absolve differences either because, in the face of the crisis, people mingle who would not ordinarily have contact with one another or because death is the great leveller. To avoid the cimmerian moment, this poem

appears to argue, it is necessary to overcome the divisions which are a conse-
quence of restrictive definitions. An unimaginable diplomacy is called into being.

April Galleons doesn't add substantially to Ashbery's achievement in this period.
The overwhelming urgency of *A Wave* has dissipated. In its place are a number
of poems which, in addressing the poet's followers, bring to the fore an issue
which preoccupies the poet at times in *A Wave* and which has been the defining
concern of his poetry since *Flow Chart*, namely his own poetic survival. Its sense
of its own fragility communicated in its titles – in 'Morning Jitters', 'A Mood of
Quiet Beauty', 'Posture of Unease', 'The Mouse', 'Sighs and Inhibitions',
'Becalmed on Strange Waters' and 'Bilking the Statues' – *April Galleons* contem-
plates the possibility of poetic survival in intriguingly delicate detail. It offers no
single poem, however, likely, in its own right, to stand the test of time. The Ash-
bery poem of this phase of his career that will survive is 'A Wave', its durabilty
ensured by the supple power of its handling of questions of identity, identifica-
tion, definition and community, and so by the timeliness of its appeal.

NOTES

1 Peter Stitt, 'The art of poetry XXXIII: John Ashbery', p. 394.
2 Susan M. Schultz, *The Tribe of John,* p. 1.
3 John Koethe, 'The absence of a noble presence', pp. 23, 25.
4 Ian Gregson, *Contemporary Poetry and Postmodernism*, p. 214.
5 David Lehman, *An Alternative to Speech*, p. 7.
6 Ibid., pp. 7–8.
7 That 'Soonest Mended' is one of the Ashbery poems that has most impressed Lehman
   would seem to be confirmed by his later poem, 'One Size Fits All: A Critical Essay',
   the title of which alludes to Ashbery's description in interview of 'Soonest Mended'.
8 The degree to which Ashbery's style has become an orthodoxy is dramatised in
   Lehman's collection by 'The Last Day of July', which opens on a New England high-
   way with the 'feeling of speeding / at seventy miles per hour', and closes in the poet's
   dormitory in Cambridge, England, and so quite literally, but again quite inadvertently,
   enacts the institutionalisation of a poetic which originally emerged in contradistinc-
   tion to the confines of the academic poem.
9 Paul Muldoon, '"A cat to catch a mouse": an Interview with Paul Muldoon', p. 14.
   Muldoon quotes Louis MacNeice.
10 Stitt, 'The art of poetry, p. 410.
11 Ashbery's impact on contemporary poetry has, it should be acknowledged, begun to
   diversify of late. American poets like John Yau, Donald Revell and Anne Lauterbach,
   and British poets like Denise Riley, Peter Didsbury and Mark Ford, offer increasingly
   deft responses to his presence, while poets, like Lehman himself and John Ash, who
   had previously been heavily under the influence, have come increasingly to establish
   their own territories. For extensive coverage of Ashbery's influence on contemporary
   poetry see Susan Schultz's collection of essays *The Tribe of John: Ashbery and Contempo-
   rary Poetry*.

12 Walt Whitman, *Collected Poetry and Collected Prose*, p. 270.

13 Anthony Howell has illuminating things to say on the problems Ashbery's imitators have caused him in 'Ashbery in perspective', p. 56. Shoptaw also mentions the 'claustrophobic' effect of Ashbery's followers. See *On the Outside Looking Out*, p. 281.

14 William James, *Pragmatism*, p. 50.

15 Howell, 'Ashbery in perspective', p. 56.

16 Piotr Sommer, 'An interview in Warsaw,' p. 306.

17 Gerrit Henry, *The Mirrored Clubs of Hell*, p. 1

18 Ibid., p. 81.

19 Shoptaw remarks on Ashbery's 'disturbing letters and phone calls'. See *On the Outside Looking Out*, p. 265.

20 Adam Mars-Jones and Edmund White, *The Darker Proof*, p. 199.

21 Suzanne Poirier, 'On writing AIDS: introduction', p. 8.

22 Joseph Cody, 'Immersive and counterimmersive writing about AIDS', pp. 245, 246.

23 James W. Jones, 'Refusing the name: the absence of AIDS in recent American gay male fiction', in Timothy F. Murphy and Suzanne Poiter (eds), *Writing AIDS*, pp. 229, 232.

24 Mars-Jones and White, *The Darker Proof*, pp. 232–4.

25 Lee Edelman, 'The mirror and the tank', pp. 14, 12, 28.

26 *A Wave* was mostly written between 1980 and 1983. White dates consciousness of AIDS in *Palace Days* by observing that Mark and Ned had met in 'late "81 when the official line had been, 'Limit the number of your partners. Know their names.'"

27 Milton, *Poetical Works*, p. 109.

28 The 'Haibun' sequence was written in late 1981, 'Haibun 4', as Shoptaw notes, being written in November 1981.

29 Shoptaw has an appendix charting the history of the poem's writing. The poem, which was begun in November 1982 and completed in 1983, went through six revisions, and in the process three titles: 'Landscape with Tobias and the Angel', 'Long Periods of Silence' and 'A Wave'. *On the Outside Looking Out*, pp. 343–351.

30 Shoptaw remarks that the 'ill-defined poem overwhelms its subjects'. *On the Outside Looking Out*, p. 277.

CHAPTER EIGHT

'And later, after the twister': the sense of an ending in recent Ashbery

Between late 1989 and early 1990, Ashbery delivered the Charles Eliot Norton lectures at Harvard University. Speaking under the title 'An other tradition', part of Ashbery's purpose in his lectures was, he told his audience, to 'shed some light on my own writing for those who feel the need of it' by discussing a group of poets who had 'probably' influenced him.[1] With this in mind he opened his first lecture by presenting a list of writers all of whom, one way or another, had had an impact on his poetry. Dividing the writers into three categories, 'major', 'minor' and the 'jump-start variety', Ashbery mentioned among the first group Auden, Stevens, Marianne Moore, Bishop, Pasternak and Mandel'shtam; among the second F.T. Prince, William Empson, Nicholas Moore, Jean Garrigue and Samuel Greenberg; while among the third group – of writers he reads to get his own poetry started – were Hölderlin, Pasternak, Mandel'shtam, Nicholas Moore, John Clare, Thomas Lovell Beddoes, John Wheelwright, Laura Riding and David Schubert. It was to these last five, Clare, Beddoes, Wheelwright, Riding and Schubert, together with Raymond Roussel, that Ashbery devoted his lectures.

The point of discussing this particular, and noticeably eclectic group of poets – as opposed to those more major influences who would, one might have thought, shed more light on Ashbery's poetry – was twofold. First, the fact of their being relatively little known, Ashbery told his audience, meant that he could discourse on them freely without fear of qualification. The occasions being what they were, and his audience being a hall full of academics, better, he thought, to speak on a group of poets two of whom – Wheelwright and Schubert – many in the room will not have heard of, and all of whom, with the possible exception of Clare, do not figure on university syllabuses. The ironic upshot of this was a certain, and no doubt carefully directed, irreverence, the Charles Eliot Norton lectures, in all their augustness, being taken up with poets so minor as to be all but entirely unheard of. But Ashbery's decision to speak about poets who do not, on the whole, figure on the syllabus was also, serious, the theme of his lectures being literary neglect.

These days literary neglect is a function, very largely, of institutionalised reading habits, and in various ways the point of Ashbery's lectures was to unsettle those habits by complicating the stories that conventionally get told within the academy both about literary history and about poetic influence. Thus, in his lecture on David Schubert, Ashbery assured his audience that Schubert is a more important poet than either Eliot or Pound. There is no way of knowing how seriously he meant this, but what he clearly meant to do was prompt a re-evaluation of the story that usually gets told about Modernism: a re-evaluation that would benefit Schubert certainly, but that would also, because it would require them to be read from a different perspective, benefit Eliot and Pound. Likewise, by presenting the eclectic list of writers that he does, all of whom, one way or another, have indeed been absorbed into his writing, Ashbery calls for a re-evaluation – *pace* Harold Bloom – of the story critics tend to tell about influence. He would himself, of course, benefit from such a re-telling, his poetry being refreshed by the different perspectives a sense of his multiple influences would bring. But so too would those major poets (Stevens in particular) who are always connected with him – liberated from a history of literary progression which only catches part of their meaning.

It was not, however, only by the eclectic nature of his list that Ashbery served to complicate prevailing ideas of literary of influence. He did so, also, by deciding to make his subjects those poets, as he says, whom he reads to 'jump-start' his own poetry. Clare, Beddoes, Roussel, Wheelwright, Riding and Schubert do not, by the poet's own account, brood competitively over Ashbery's poetry. Rather they give rise to it. His relation to their poems is not, as he describes it, antagonistic. Instead they inspire him, help him to get started. The effect Clare's poetry has on him, for instance, is, he says, 'always the same, that of re-inserting me in my present of re-establishing now'. Raymond Roussel 'is a poet who is about to be a poet. He is always bringing us face to face with the very latest moment in our thinking, the now where everything can and must happen, the locus solus where writing begins.' To take Ashbery at his word here is, some might argue, to be sold a pass; to fall for one of those decoys which are a not insignificant feature of his rhetorical repertoire. To believe this, however, is to be in danger of missing the point of Ashbery's 'other tradition'. Thus, where Bloomian theorising tends to tell a fatal story – of poets locked in mortal struggle with great figures from the past – Ashbery's 'other' tradition tells a lively one – of poets reading predecessors in the interests of the present. A lively story, moreover, which recalls another one, and which perhaps, in turn leads one to the influence prompting Ashbery's lectures themselves. A discussion not only of his reading, but of the act of reading, Ashbery's lectures variously argue against a fetishised relation with historic texts. As such, and for all their differences of tone and address, Ashbery's lectures to an assembly of American scholars recall Emerson's, 'An other tradition' being above all an argument for creative reading.

Ashbery's poetry has long tried to foster the kind of relation with the reader that his subversive stories of literary history and poetic influence imply, and so, as promised, the lectures shed a general light on his writing. They are, however, more especially illuminating of the poetry he was writing as he prepared them.

The flipside of Ashbery's discussion of critical neglect is poetic endurance, all of his six poets having struggled, for whatever reason, to survive the ravages of time; and two of them – Wheelwright and Schubert – still likely to endure only by virtue of his own creative reading. It is in this sense that Ashbery's lectures speak to the poetry he was writing around the time of their preparation: the question of endurance, of how his own poetry would survive the test of time, having become a pressing, not to say urgent, issue for Ashbery by the time he embarked on *Flow Chart*.

Ashbery wrote *Flow Chart* between December 1987 and July 1988. He wrote the lectures, Shoptaw informs us, while revising the poem, and the two projects are thus of the same moment.[2] Ashbery started the poem aged sixty, only a few years after he had suffered a near-fatal spine infection. One apparent, and hardly surprising effect, of this illness was that the prospect of death had for sometime figured quite large in his poetry. As he had put it in *A Wave*, in 'Around the Rough and Rugged Rocks the Ragged Rascal Rudely Ran':

> I think a lot about it,
> Think quite a lot about it –
> The omnipresent possibility of being interrupted
> While what I stand for is still almost a bare canvas

(W, 15)

Usually happy to be interrupted – a visitor or a telephone call diverting the course of a poem – by the late 1980s Ashbery had for some time been increasingly aware of the interruption that would end all interruptions. It was a preoccupation that became central in *Flow Chart*.

Almost all poets worry about death. They worry about it for the obvious reasons but they worry about it also because they fear the effects of the ravages of time on the work to which they have given their life. In this respect, in theory at least, Ashbery might have more reason to worry than most. Partly this is because, as 'Around the Rough and Rugged Rocks' has it, his poetry has met with much misunderstanding. It will not survive, the poet seems to fear, because what it stands for has not been made clear. It is still, as the poem puts it, almost a bare canvas. This is a problem, but not a devastating one. The meaning of Ashbery's poetry is becoming clearer. The background is being filled in. It is no longer the bare canvas it once was. Except, of course, and in a strict and much more troubling sense, it is – Ashbery's poetry standing precisely for an almost bare canvas. Written for the moment, unplanned, altered as the occasion requires it, what Ashbery stands for is a form of utterance fit for the particular situation in which it finds itself. What results, as this book has endeavoured to argue, is a life-enhancing poetry, but possibly also, and certainly in theory at least, a poetry which – like one of those mayflies that frequently flicker through it – will have all too short a life. How can poetry which aims so centrally to speak to the moment – and which originated, after all, partly in contradistinction to the self-consciously durable poetry of Lowell, Berryman and co. – survive the passing of that moment?

This fear can seem misplaced. It is unlikely, after all, that the poet who gave the Charles Eliot Norton lectures will slip into the kind of oblivion that has met David Schubert – unlikely but not, of course, impossible. It is, however, a very serious fear if one takes the poetry's meaning seriously. If the meaning of the poetry is to address the present, then with the passing of its present the poetry is in danger of ceasing to mean in the way it has always intended to. How, the question goes, can Ashbery's poetry survive in anything like its present form? This is a question the poet is increasingly posing himself, deeply worried, as he is, that, as he puts it in *Flow Chart*,

it seems

> desolation and solitude were the point we had set out for, the times of mirth
> forgotten now, recorded in disappearing ink that doesn't outlast winter
> and its holidays, its occasions.

(FC, 104)

Because the poet is keen, desperate even (so it seems at times) somehow to ensure that his poetry will outlast him, *Flow Chart* can often be heard straining against itself: testing and hoping to overcome the limits and possibly devastating implications of its occasional poetic approach. And nowhere is the strain more clearly felt than in its vast form (the poem running, in the British edition, to 208 pages). Formally speaking the poem was couched, uncharacteristically, between two important occasions. The whole project was prompted by the artist Trevor Winkfield's suggestion that Ashbery should write a one-hundred page poem about his mother, who had died the previous January. Though he acted on Winkfield's idea – the poem was, in typescript, a hundred pages long – Ashbery is keen to insist that "'of course, it's not about my mother'".[3] This is true in so far as Ashbery's poetry is rarely 'about' anything. But it is equally true that death in general, and his mother's death in particular, have a shaping effect on the poem. And sometimes very directly, as in an extended, and deeply poignant sentence on page 72:

> The stationary
> saraband of our considering it but deciding not to put it to a vote absorbs any
> hint of the disorder that highmindedness sometimes trails in its wake like a wisp of
> something in the sky, and in any case, our hands, our faces are clean, our plates empty
> and brimming with moonlight, a pious reminder to the unwashed and unready
>   that we will come
> again someday and make sense of this arbitrary and tangled forest of misplaced
> motives and other shades of imperfect sympathies that do no compromise us
>   perhaps
> as yet, yet I feel their aura, Mother, like a water table ascending,
> and I haven't the answer, don't know if I'll ever have it, yet it looks so young,
> pitiful and hopeless in morning light that one tries to suppress the intuition that to go
> forward will be to do battle with some angry titan, sooner or later, and all one's
> bad reactions will confront at every one of the house's apertures: slay me and then

leave me here, if that's going to help; just don't stand around
looking at me that way, that's all. Am I some kind of freak? No.

(FC, 72)

Syntactically this sentence is familiar, its twists and turns making the kinds
of demands on the reader Ashbery's poetry has been making since *Rivers and
Mountains*. Tonally, however, it is different, Ashbery introducing the kind of
confessional note that typically he has tended to deny himself. Contemplating his
mother's death, and faced with the prospect of his own, *Flow Chart* is in part a set-
tling of accounts, its occasion prompting him, and its vast scale permitting him, to
say things which haven't before belonged in his poetry. 'Am I some kind of freak?'

The other important occasion framing this poem was the poet's sixty-first
birthday, Ashbery setting out to write a page a day for the hundred days between
his date of commencement (on 8 December 1987) and his birthday (28 July
1988). This occasion informs the writing also, which, if it is not infrequently to
be found in the slough of despond, is at others desperately cheerful: the poet
seemingly at pains to remind himself that he has been successful and so surely
will continue to be so.

Well I see I've
not outstayed my welcome, that on the contrary quite a few people are waiting
in the anteroom to shake my hand. And with this reassurance, nothing ever
    quite seems
complete again. Yet it isn't exasperating. No furniture-bashing please.
And as we congregate this way, the actual lists of heaven seem roseate
anew. Flames lick the pulpit. This is the way to go – here. This the place
to be.

(FC, 102)

'This', the situation in which you are now, is always the place to be in Ashbery –
to think otherwise being not, as the poetry sees, to make the best of the present.
But 'this', here, is also the poetry, which is still receiving plaudits, and is more
than happy to do so.

But, if the poem is couched between significant occasions, it is still, primar-
ily a work of the ordinary. Indeed *Flow Chart* is more than ever a poetic diary:
more than ever a record of the events, thoughts and memories which are the
bunch of circumstances out of which the writing emerges. Even now, then, with
big thoughts on his mind – and even as he wishes, because it might help his
poetry to endure, that for once he had 'something more sizeable to say' – even
now nothing is too small for the poet's attention:

You see
how fond of him she was, and he, well he just took it,
like most things, change, pretzels.

(FC, 16)

What emerges from all this – from the playing of the big events of the poem's
frame against the daily events that are its substance, from the continuing

[211]

commitment to the small things of life and the desire to say the kind of big thing that helps ensure poetry's survival – is that most unlikely, and unquestionably strained of poetic genres, the occasional epic. Without actually departing from the poet's commitment to the casual, the ordinary and the neglected, *Flow Chart* is a work made likely to endure because of its sheer, undeniable size. Against all the odds, Ashbery has made a monument to the everyday.

Nor is the poet's straining against the implications, the possibly devastating limitations, of his poetic only to be felt in the poem's form. Stylistically, also, the poet swings dramatically between the monumental and the slight. Thus, one of the pure pleasures of reading late Ashbery is the frequency with which he produces monumental lines. Witness, with its allusion to Rilke's 'Archaic Torso':

> A bridge erects itself into the sky, all trumpets and
> twisted steel,
> but like the torso of a god, too proud to see itself, or lap up
> the saving grace of small talk.

(FC, 84–5)

But the other pure pleasure of late Ashbery is bathos, the small talk that always counters the large. The concluding section of *Flow Chart*, with its promise of the great summation, is as much marked by the ridiculous as the sublime. 'Excuse me while I fart. There, that's better. I actually feel relieved.' Or better still, though less relieving, from *Hotel Lautréamont*:

> In the casual track of a zipper my penis
> once got stuck, and it's been like that ever since

(HL, 44)

The cadence of the first clause is familiar. But so is the problem of the second. Rarely were the monumental ambitions of poetry so successfully pricked. But rarely, by the same token, was the prick so monumental. Ashbery's late poetry, it would seem, is feeling the strain.

It is strained, also, at times, discursively, Ashbery addressing himself to elements of his thought which his poetry has long held dear, but which now look rather different as he approaches his end. On page 10 of *Flow Chart*, for instance, Ashbery recalls Dr Zhivago's words to Anna as she lay on what seemed likely to be her death bed. 'You in others are yourself, your soul', Zhivago promised Anna, a sense of self Ashbery has often reached for, and which might now seem to offer consolation. *Flow Chart* sees things slightly differently:

> So it seems we must
> stay in an uneasy relationship, not quite fitting
> together, not precisely friends or lovers though certainly not enemies, if
> the buoyancy of the spongy terrain on which we exist is be experienced
> as an ichor, not a commentary on all that is missing from the reflection
> in the mirror. *Did I say that? Can this be me?*

(FC, 10)

He did say this certainly, 'Self-Portrait in a Convex Mirror' arguing at length that there's more to the self than one sees in the mirror. Now, though, while he's not exactly recanting on his spongy aesthetic here – he still has the sense that the self is largely to be found in the people and things that surround one – it now seems to him a distinctly metaphysical not physical truth. One's presence in others, and their presence in you, does not amount to an 'ichor'. It is not the liquid that flows through the veins of the god's. It does not make you immortal.

Similarly, Ashbery can sometimes be heard debating his ideas of influence. Influence is one of the means by of which a poet can endeavour to secure his or her survival. Thus when, in 'The Tower', Yeats sits down to make his poetic will, he chooses upstanding men to continue his legacy. It is partly because of the work of such upstanding men as Lowell and Heaney that the Yeatsian line continues to look so strong: poets drawn to Yeats being keen to differentiate themselves from him, of course, but keen also to be seen continuing his tradition, and not least in their charisma. Ashbery has not sought to influence in this way, arguing, at times, against the very idea of influence. As he told Piotr Sommer, 'The more you like a poet, the less you ought to write like him, because what you were liking in him is a uniqueness'. There is something admirably democratic about this, Ashbery abjuring influence in favour of, so he hopes, prompting others into their own fresh way of looking at the world. It is an attitude, however, which has implications for the poetry. Thus, on page 107 of *Flow Chart* the poet is to be found in conversation with a group of follower figures, keen to carry his word forward. Casting the followers as disciples, the poet himself momentarily assumes a prophetic status:

> You are my
> business in any case and it behooves me not to be in the shadow of you
> while I wait. And then one who came from a great distance said, why does it suit you
> to be ornery, if others cannot join the general purgative exodus, to which that
>   one inside
> said, and so it becomes you, if it become you. And then in the shade they put
>   their heads
> together, and one comes back, the others being a little way off, and says, who
> do you think taught you to disobey in the first place? And he says, my father.
>
> (FC, 107)

Ornery in his commitment to disobedience, Ashbery's stubborn conversation with his disciples is an argument against the possibility of discipleship. To spread his word they must spread their own, a model of influence, or anti-influence which, if it conforms to the democratic impulses of the poetry, tends to weaken its likelihood of survival; Ashbery's line, unlike Yeats's, not perpetuating itself by holding sway. But if he is faithfully reiterating an argument he has made at various moment in his career, at this late moment he is also straining against its limitations. He doesn't want disciples, but even to imagine he might have some is to cast himself in the most charismatic role possible, a role the Biblical tones of his argument serve only to underscore – 'And at that they were all struck dumb'. At various times, and in various forms, *Flow Chart* can be heard wanting it both ways.

For all this, however – for all that, in *Flow Chart*, Ashbery can be heard debating, and straining against, the implications of his writing – he is not about to renege on his commitments. Indeed the signs of strain are as tangible and audible as they are because, in the same breath, now, more than ever perhaps, Ashbery is insistent on the occasional quality of his poetry. Indeed, whether he is reminding himself or his reader, *Flow Chart* is forever remarking on its occasional character. On page 16 we learn that

> Everybody gets such ideas on occasion, but here was the little shot-glass
> of night, all ready to drink, and you spread out in it
> even before it radiates in you.

On page 17 (in an image that takes another side swipe at the followers) we are told rather disspiritingly, that

> no men heard of it,
> only teen-age girls and male adolescents with fruited complexions and scalps
> who were going to make it difficult for one should an occasion arise.

On page 26 we are forcefully reminded of the poetry's social ambitions:

> oh come off it, no
> one wants to be alone. And even, you know, accept the occasional invitation
> but also slog on unshod, solitary, except for casual greetings from
> even more casual acquaintances.

While later, and still with socializing in mind, the poem ask a rhetorical question:

> Why then, should people swing
> toward people
> in groups, and when some collide and others keep on going, misstate the occasion?
> Either it's a social event or it isn't.
>
> (FC, 89)

Nor does the poet's insistence on the occasional quality of his writing only take the form of an obsessive tic (a sign of anxiety in itself, perhaps, the poet returning time and again to the fragile quality of the work he is even now undertaking). At times, also, he engages in full and lucid explanations of what his sense of occasion means to him. Thus on page 113 and so at more or less the heart of the poem, a section is opened with an important announcement:

> There is no truth, saith the judge, and one is obliged to concur,
> if by truth one means that an occasion has been fitted to an event, and it all came
> about just so. If, however, one accepts a broader definition along the lines of
> something being more or less appropriate to its time and place, then, by gosh, one is
> pretty darn sure of having to own up to the fact that, yes, it does exist
> here and there, if only in the gaudy hues of the diaphanous wings
> of some passing insect.
>
> (FC, 113)

[214]

An 'occasion fitted to an event' is something like a wedding; everything coming about just so – everything proceeding felicitously – because everybody knows what is expected of them, everybody knows what is going on. Ashbery, this book has argued, and as the poet himself asserts here, has a broader definition of 'occasion', taking it to mean not the ordered event which is the exception not the rule in life but the 'tangled, muddy, painful and perplexed' situations in which most people find themselves most of the time. Much critical opinion to the contrary then, Ashbery's poetry, so the narrative voice tells us here, does embody an idea of truth: the true utterance being, according to this broader definition of occasion, that which is 'more or less appropriate to its time and place'.

One has to work hard to get to this moment of truth in *Flow Chart*, the poet's clarifying words a reward for over a hundred pages of readerly attention. But Ashbery has of late given considerable energy to drawing the reader's attention to the origins and fundamentals of his writing, and such passages are by no means always hidden. In 'My Philosophy of Life' (from *Can You Hear, Bird*), a poem which advertises itself to the uncertain reader, and does not prove to be a decoy, Ashbery makes the mild tricksy observation that

> Not a single idea emerges from it. It's enough
> to disgust you with thought. But then you remember something
>   William James
> wrote in some book of his you never read – it was fine, it had the
>   fineness,
> the powder of life dusted over it, by chance, of course, yet still looking
> for evidence of fingerprints. Someone had handled it
> even before he formulated it, though the thought was his and his alone.
>
> (CB, 73–4)

'*Refinement*,' William James said in *Pragmatism*, 'is what characterizes our intellectualist philosophies.':

> Refinement has its place in things, true enough. But a philosophy that breathes out nothing but refinement will never satisfy the empiricist temper of mind. It will seem rather a monument of artificiality. So we find men of science preferring to turn their backs on metaphysics as on something altogether cloistered and spectral, and practical men shaking philosophy's dust off their feet and following the call of the wild.[4]

'Pragmatism', by contrast, as James observes (in that book of his 'you never read'), muddies its fingers, colours its prose with the 'sweat and dirt' of ordinary life. 'My Philosophy of Life' means the reader to get this, to appreciate that this is what is meant by living in 'the gaps between ideas' (CB, 75). His almost blank canvas still an almost blank canvas, Ashbery is keener than ever that readers should do the research that will enable them to understand him.

'Safe Conduct' (from the same volume) points the reader in a different direction, the poet casting back briefly back over his fluctuating career, and singling out the early poem in which he is most readily located:

That was the other thing about him: how many times
he avoided using the word 'eclipse.' It was as though
he bore his personal darkness with him, furled
like an umbrella, but ready to snap to attention
at the fall of a wombat's tear.

(CB, 96)

The poem in which he didn't avoid using the word '"eclipse"' was 'The Picture of Little J.A. in a Prospect of Flowers', the poem in which the poet caught his rolled-up future in a childhood snap of himself accepting everything. The photo caught Ashbery at his spongiest, and thus, as its epigraph insisted, and as the title of this late poem reminds us again here, at his most Pasternakian.

The fact that, of late, Ashbery has been keener than ever to re-state the fundamentals and origins of his occasional aesthetic has partly to do with poetic survival, the poetry being more likely to survive if people understand what it means to do. But what such remarks signal also is that for all that the prospect of death places a great strain on the temporary implications of his writing, so also the temporary has never been so important. He has fewer moments ahead of him now; they are all that much more precious: all the more reason, then, at this late stage in his career, to savour those occasions that are left him. In *Flow Chart* one feels this need to relish each passing occasion in a series of what one might call temporal puns, the poet's apocalyptic sense of his own end bringing a kind of desperate clarity to the present situation. At the end of the first section of the poem, we catch a poignant glimpse of the poet at play:

Who could have expected a dream like this to go away for there are some
that are the web on which our waking life is painstakingly elaborated:
there are real, bustling things there and the burgomaster of success
stalks back and forth, directing everything
with a small motion of a finger. But when it did come,
the denouement, we were off drinking in some restaurant,
too absorbed, too eternally, expectantly, happy to be there or care.

(FC, 8)

Fondly imagining he could avoid the inevitable by being in the wrong place at the right time, the poet knows that the only way really to cope with it is to attend more closely then ever to the moment at hand. He is not, as of course he knows, eternally happy in any restaurant, but the prospect of eternity, of being without time, appears to focus his mind on the time that is left.

There are many such lines and scenes in *Flow Chart*, the prospect, or the absence of a prospect, of divine time, giving new dimension to Ashbery's sense of the moment. It is, however, in *And the Stars Were Shining* that the passage of time is made really luminous. One way to think of *And the Stars Were Shining* is as the book that develops *Flow Chart*. This is odd in that the book Ashbery published next after *Flow Chart* was *Hotel Lautréamont*. But *Hotel Lautréamont* collects together the short poems Ashbery wrote while writing *Flow Chart*, and so while there are differences of emphasis certainly – *Hotel Lautréamont* contrasting the glorious sprawl of *Flow Chart* by its repeated resort to the strictures of the pantoum – the two books are of the same moment. It is in *And the Stars Were Shining*, published in 1994, that Ashbery moves on from *Flow Chart*. It moves on most noticeably in that, while *And the Stars Were Shining* is still sharply personal poetry – this is still, very acutely, the writing of a poet nearing the end of life – the poetic 'I' here is not a diaristic 'I', and is, as a consequence, more general in its scope. The most striking effect of this is that in *And the Stars Were Shining* the sense of lateness with which the poet is everywhere concerned ('I have … rollicked in the texture of a late / unfinished sonata') is not only the poet's. The lateness, now, is the culture's also: a condition he addresses through his feeling for time.

Ashbery's poetry has always had time on its mind, his writing, at least since 'Clepsydra' (the water clock), making every effort to keep up with the flow. He has rarely, however, been quite as alert to the way time actually feels as he is in *And the Stars Were Shining*, rarely quite so alive to its sheer tick tock. What Ashbery seems, not unnaturally, especially alive to here is the imminence of his ending, the effect of which imminence, as the poet writes, is to generate a sense immanent crisis. Every poem in *And the Stars Were Shining* has an apocalyptic edge to it, every moment carries the potential for catastrophe. In the shorter poems this plays out in a series of crises, disasters hitting then passing as if nothing had happened. 'In a Waltz Dream' for instance, we are told how,

> And later, after the twister, slowly
> we mixed drinks of the sort
> that may be slopped only on script girls, like lemonade.
>
> (ATS, 20)

In 'Local Time' we hear

> the flames' roar, beaker of scotch, the old way
> things were probably supposed to be all along anyway.
>
> (ATS, 31)

In 'The Love Scenes' we learn that people are getting on

> famously – like
>
> 'houses on fire', I believe the expression
> is
>
> (ATS, 9)

Which sounds harmlessly enough except that later in the poem the '"houses on fire"' become

> a grand purgatorial
> romance of kittens in a basket

The end, this suggests, is not nigh, but now, here and always. Or at least so those appalling, omnipresent kittens would imply.

The whole volume continues like this, poem after poem meeting with disaster after disaster, and the lines, as a consequence, aflame with apocalyptic language. It is a language, perhaps, that comes naturally to the poet, his imminent ending making it an appropriate form of expression. But is a language, also, enhanced by his reading, for as he tells us in 'About to Move':

> I have read many prophetic books and I can tell you
> now to listen and endure

(ATS, 6)

In *The Sense of an Ending* Frank Kermode argued that with the widespread loss of faith in apocalyptic narratives – stories of human history with a beginning and an end – and given also society's recently acquired capacity for self-annihilation, thinking in the West was no longer marked by a sense of an imminent end but by an immanent end, each passing moment having the potential for catastrophe. The absence of an imminent end, and the presence of an immanent one, had two main effects as Kermode saw it. In the first place, life acquired a certain meaninglessness: the loss of faith in a final reckoning – in a final accounting – making human actions less consequential and so, in general, less meaningful. In addition to this, the sense of an immanent end had the effect that, in an age anyway characterised by 'ceaseless transition', a phrase he borrowed from Harold Rosenberg, people were more likely than ever to live life in a state of emergency – the frantic pace of things adding to the feeling of meaningless to produce a state of overall uncertainty. And the point of *The Sense of an Ending* was to work out what writers could do to ease such uncertainty, how they could help people cope. As Kermode saw it, 'Those that continue to interest us move through time to an end, an end we must sense even if we cannot know it; they live in change, until, which is never, *as* and *is* are one.'[5] The way this difficult Stevens-like formulation worked out in practice for Kermode was in something like a faith in the epiphany: the epiphany, the moment disclosing order, preserving the sense of, if not exactly a faith in, the imminent ending. Thus, 'The hiding places of power for Wordsworth or for Proust, are the agents of time's defeat ... sempiternal moments that transcend the giddy successiveness of world-time.'[6] *The Sense of an Ending* did not go beyond these hiding places in the search for order. It was, as Kermode knew, an unsatisfactory response, an age of ceaseless transition making the image of the still point or spot of time – the moment of harmony, the opportunity for reflection – considerably less seductive. There was, however, as he saw it, no alternative but confusion, and so he advocated the sempiternal moment as the still supreme fiction.

'And The Stars Were Shining' opens with such a moment of order:

> It was the solstice, and it was jumping on you like a friendly dog.
> The stars were still out in the field,

[218]

and the child prostitutes plied their trade,
the only happy ones, having learned how unhappiness sticks
and will not risk being traded in for a song or a balloon.
Christmas decorations were getting crumpled in offices
by staffers slumped at their video terminals,
and dismay articulated otherness in orphan asylums
where the coffee percolates eternally, and God is not light
but God, as mysterious to Himself as we are to Him.

(ATS, 76)

If this were a poem by Eliot, everything would now stand still – pause, reflect, draw strength from the moment – proceeding finally with its sense of an imminent ending still intact. But this is an Ashbery poem and so everything moves on. Dogs still jump. Prostitutes still solicit. The staffers, it is true, might seem momentarily to have stopped, but only because they are working so hard – the age of ceaseless transition tying them to their video terminals.

In a way we have been here before in Ashbery, 'The System' contemplating but dismissing the moment of calm, preferring instead to glean an order from the tangle of everyday life. 'And the Stars Were Shining' compares with 'The System' in being explicitly unseduced by the idea of order offered by a still point, but its response to the problem of how to live without the solace of such moments of grace is rather different, and perhaps yet more compelling. The poem has thirteen sections, and as in Stevens the point of the different sections is to present the multiple ways one might regard the poem's given object: the blackbird in Stevens's poem; time, extraordinarily, in Ashbery's.

The poem proceeds by giving a series of precisely felt images of the forms time takes, the way it feels. In section six it moves relentlessly on, as

> the bread-and-butter machine continues to churn out
> faxes, each grisette has something different
> about her forehead

(ATS, 83)

Likewise in section eight, we hear that

> Winter wasn't clear yet
> but all the days of the year were tumbling out of its crevices,
> the chic ones and the special-interest ones,
> and those with no name upon them.
> Everything looked slight,
> which was all right.

(ATS, 90)

In section six, in a luminously exact expression of the precise forms in which we mark the differences between times, we are told that

> time will be as a precise
> as a small table with a cordless telephone on it, next to a television.

(ATS, 84)

In section four, we are told how

> they grow up and have problems same as us –
> kind of puts us out into the middle of the golf course
> of the universe, where not too much ever happens

(ATS, 80)

Again the image is precisely rendered. Even the age of ceaseless transition, the age of faxes and cordless phones, is not without its periods of relative rest. These are not however, still points, pregnant with meaning, but the barren spaces of directed leisure. Chiefly, though, in this poem, people don't have time for the golf course, and the prevailing image is of ceaseless transition, as at the beginning of section nine, where

> New technology approaches the bridge.
> The weir, ah the weir, combing the falls,
> like the beautiful white hair of a princess.

(ATS, 92)

Ashbery's object in 'And the Stars Were Shining', like Stevens's in 'Thirteen Ways to Look at a Blackbird', is to trick the invisible subject of his poem into being. In Stevens the trick is twofold, the beauty of inflections (of different representations and forms of emphasis) bringing one closer to the poem's object by their careful expression. In turn, however, this leads to the beauty of innuendoes, one's attention to the various forms of expression serving, in the end to heighten one's awareness of what they are not capable of saying. There, in that moment of negative awareness, the thing is made real by language: the various errors of the careful inflections making one aware of what they've not said.

Ashbery's poem works the same way. Late in life as he is, and so aware, so it seems, of his imminent end that it has come to feel immanent to him, the passage of time has never seemed quite so luminously clear. And as it does, so he gives it precise expression, the various sharp-edged forms of modern technology, and technology in general, representing the age of ceaseless transition. Except that while it is ceaseless – and certainly nothing stops in this poem – things have somehow slowed down just a little. One feels it in the image of the princess over the weir, the comparison of the water with her long hair slowing the flow just enough to make it more visible. The beauty of Ashbery's precise inflections is that, as in Stevens, the attention they require calls the reader's attention to that which they express but which fundamentally they cannot say, and nowhere more so than when he observes,

> We sure live in a bizarre and furious
> galaxy, but now it's up to us to make it
> into an environment for maps to sidle up to,
> as trustingly as leeches. Heck, put *us*
> on the map, while you're at it.

[220]

That way we can smoke a cigarette, and stay and sway,
shooting the breeze with night and her swift promontories.

(ATS, 94)

The galaxy is no less furious than ever, but the poet, so it seems, is more than ever up to speed, and, as he is, so it feels, momentarily at least, that time *has* been mapped: that somehow it *is* possible to stay, even as one sways with the breeze that the poet shoots with us. As sublime a moment as any in Ashbery, this is no longer only the poetry of our time. 'And the Stars Were Shining' is the poetry of the time of our time.

Probably the decisive and, in some respects, insurmountable paradox of Ashbery's writing is the one he articulates at the end of *And the Stars Were Shining*, the poet inviting us, like Whitman at the end of 'Song of Myself', to join him, but acknowledging that in our busy lives, in our age of ceaseless transition, we very likely don't have the time to do so.

So – if you want to come with me,
or just pull at my sleeve, let them make that discovery.
Summer won't end in your lap,
nor are the stars more casual than usual.
Peace, quiet, a dictionary – it was so important,
yet at the end nobody had any time for any of it.
It was as if all of it had never happened,
my shoelaces were untied, and – am I forgetting anything?

(ATS, 100)

Sad to say, not really. As the poet strives ever harder to keep up with events, so late Ashbery is emerging at a seemingly ever increasing rate of knots: *Flow Chart*, *Hotel Lautréamont*, *And the Stars Were Shining*, *Can You Hear, Bird*, and *Wakefulness* all in the last ten years. It's a lot to take account of, but undoubtedly we ought to try, for, as the poet reminds us in the first poem of *Wakefulness*:

An immodest little white wine, some scattered seraphs,
recollections of the Fall – tell me,
has anyone made a spongier representation, chased
fewer demons out of the parking lot
where we all held hands?

This is, it will be appreciated, a rhetorical question.

NOTES

1 Rec. of 'John Clare's Inquisitive Eye', Lamont Library, Harvard University.
2 Shoptaw supplies much information about the composition of *Flow Chart*. See *On the Outside Looking Out*, pp. 301–41. For other insightful accounts of *Flow Chart* see especially: Helen Verdler, 'A steady glitter chasing shadows'; Keith Silver, '*Flow Chart*', *PN*

Review, 99, 42–3; Fred Moramarco, 'Coming full circle: John Ashbery's later poetry', Susan Schultz (ed.), *The Tribe of John*, pp. 38–59; Andrew Lawson, 'Review of John Ashbery, *Flow Chart*, and Stephen Roedefer, *Passing Duration*', *Fragremente: a Magazine of Contemporary Poetics*, 4 (Autumn/Winter 1991), 104.

3 Shoptaw, *On the Outside Looking Out*, p. 302.

4 William James, *Pragmatism*, p. 9.

5 Frank Kermode, *The Sense of an Ending*, p. 179.

6 Ibid., p. 169.

Bibliography

Aldan, Daisy (ed.), *A New Folder*, New York, Folder Editions 1959.

Allen, Donald (ed.), *The New American Poetry*, New York, Grove Press, 1960.

Altieri, Charles, 'Ashbery as love poet', *Verse*, 8:1 (Spring 1991), 8–15

Altieri, Charles, *Enlarging the Temple: New Directions in American Poetry During the 1960s*, Lewisburg, Bucknell University Press, 1979.

Altieri, Charles, *Self and Sensibility in Contemporary American Poetry*, Cambridge, Cambridge University Press, 1984.

Andrews, Bruce, 'Misrepresentation', Ron Silliman (ed.), *In the American Tree*, Orono, Maine, National Poetry Foundation, 1986.

Applethwaite, James, 'Painting, poetry, abstraction and Ashbery', *The Southern Review*, 24:2 (Spring 1988), 272–90.

Appleyard, Brian, 'Ecclesiast', *P.N. Review,* 21:1 (September–October 1994), 75–6.

Art and Literature: An International Review, nos 1–12 (March 1964–Spring 1967).

Ash, John, 'John Ashbery in conversation with John Ash', *PN Review*, 46, 12:2, 31–4.

Ashbery, John, *And the Stars were Shining*, Manchester, Carcanet Press, 1994.

Ashbery, John, *April Galleons*, London, Paladin Books, [1987] 1990.

Ashbery, John, *As We Know*, Manchester, Carcanet New Press, [1979] 1981.

Ashbery, John, 'Brooms and prisms', *ArtNews*, 65:1 (March 1966), 58–9, 82–4.

Ashbery, John, *Can You Hear, Bird*, Manchester, Carcanet Press, 1996.

Ashbery, John, 'The decline of the verbs', *Book Week*, 4:15 (18 December 1966), 5.

Ashbery, John, *The Double Dream of Spring*, New York, The Ecco Press, [1970] 1976.

Ashbery, John, *Flow Chart*, Manchester, Carcanet Press Ltd, 1991.

Ashbery, John, 'Frank O'Hara's question', *Bookweek* (25 September 1966), 23–35.

Ashbery, John, 'A game with shifting mirrors', *New York Times Book Review* (16 April 1967), 4.

Ashbery, John, 'Growing up surreal', *ArtNews*, 67:3 (May 1968), 41.

Ashbery, John, *The Heavy Bear: Delmore Schwartz's Life Versus his Art*. The English Literary Society of Japan, 1996.

Ashbery, John, *Hotel Lautréamont*, Manchester, Carcanet Press, 1992.

Ashbery, John, *Houseboat Days*, New York, The Viking Press, 1977.

Ashbery, John, 'The impossible', *Poetry*, 90:4 (July 1957), 250–4.

Ashbery, John, 'In darkest language', Raymond Roussel, *How I Wrote Certain of My Books*, ed. Trevor Winkfield, New York, Sun, 1977, pp. 59–64.

Ashbery, John, 'In the American Grain', *New York Review of Books* (22 February 1973), 3–6.

Ashbery, John, 'Introduction', Frank O'Hara, *The Collected Poems of Frank O'Hara*, ed.

Donald Allen, New York, Alfred Knopf, 1971, vii–xi.

Ashbery, John, 'Introduction', Gerrit Henry, *The Mirrored Clubs of Hell, Poems by Gerrit Henry*, New York, Little Brown and Company, 1991, xiii–xiv.

Ashbery, John, 'Introduction', Pierre Martory, *The Landscape Is Behind the Door*, tr. by John Ashbery, Riverdale-on-Hudson, New York, The Sheep Meadow Press, 1994, ix–xii.

Ashbery, John, 'Jerboas, pelicans, and Peewee Peese', *Bookweek*, 4:8 (30 October 1966), 1, 8.

Ashbery, John, 'John Ashbery interviewing Harry Mathews', *Review of Contemporary Fiction*, 7:3 (Fall 1987), 36–48.

Ashbery, John, 'Letter to the editor', *The Nation* (8 May 1967), 5, 78.

Ashbery, John, 'Letter to the editor', *The Nation* (29 May 1967), 674, 692.

Ashbery, John, 'On Raymond Roussel', Raymond Roussel *How I Wrote Certain of My Books*, ed. Trevor Winkfield, New York, Sun, 1977, pp. 45–55.

Ashbery, John, 'The poetic medium of W.H. Auden', senior thesis, Harvard College, 1949.

Ashbery, John, 'A reminiscence', Bill Berkson and Joe Le Sueur (eds), *A Homage to Frank O'Hara*, Berkeley, Creative Arts Company, 1980.

Ashbery, John, *Reported Sightings: Art Chronicles, 1957–1987*, ed. David Bergman, Cambridge, Mass., Harvard University Press, [1989] 1991.

Ashbery, John, 'Reverdy en Amérique', *Mercure de France*, 344 (January/April 1962), 109–12.

Ashbery, John, Review of Eliabeth Bishop, *The Complete Poems*, Lloyd Schwartz and Sybil P. Estess, *Elizabeth Bishop and Her Art*, Ann Arbor, Michigan University Press, 1983, pp. 201–5.

Ashbery, John, *Rivers and Mountains*, New York, The Ecco Press, [1966] 1977.

Ashbery, John, 'The romance of reality', *ArtNews*, 15 (1966), 28–30, 56.

Ashbery, John, 'Second presentation of Elizabeth Bishop', *World Literature Today*, 51:1 (Winter 1977), 9–11.

Ashbery, John, *Selected Poems*, London, Jonathan Cape, 1967.

Ashbery, John, *Selected Poems*, London, Paladin Books, [1985],1987.

Ashbery, John, *Self-Portrait in a Convex Mirror*, Manchester, Carcanet New Press, [1975] 1977.

Ashbery, John, *Self-Portrait in a Convex Mirror*, San Francisco, Arion Press, 1984.

Ashbery, John, *Shadow Train*, New York, The Viking Press/Penguin, 1981.

Ashbery, John, *Some Trees*, New York, The Ecco Press, [1956] 1978.

Ashbery, John, *The Tennis Court Oath*, Middletown, Wesleyan University Press, 1962.

Ashbery, John, *Three Madrigals*, New York, Poet's Press, 1968.

Ashbery, John, *Three Plays*, Manchester, Carcanet Press, [1978] 1988.

Ashbery, John, *Three Poems*, New York, The Ecco Press, [1972] 1989.

Ashbery, John, 'Tradition and talent', *Bookweek*, 3:52 (4 September 1966), 14–15.

Ashbery, John, *Turandot and Other Poems*, New York, Editions of the Tibor de Nagy Gallery, 1953.

Ashbery, John, *The Vermont Notebook*, with drawings by Joe Brainard, Los Angeles, Black Sparrow Press, 1975.

Ashbery, John, *Wakefulness*, Manchester, Carcanet Press, 1998.

Ashbery, John, *A Wave*, Manchester, Carcanet Press, 1984.

Ashbery, John (ed.), *Penguin Modern Poets 24: Kenward Elmslie, Kenneth Koch, James Schuyler*, Harmondsworth, Middlesex, Penguin Books, 1974.

Ashbery, John and Hess, Thomas, B., *Avant-Garde Art*, London, Collier-Macmillan, 1968.

Ashbery, John and Koch, Kenneth, *John Ashbery and Kenneth Koch (A Conversation)*, Tucson, Arizona, Interview Press, 1965.

Ashbery, John and Schuyler, James, *A Nest of Ninnies*, Manchester, Carcanet Press, 1987.

Auden, W.H. *Collected Poems* London, Faber and Faber, 1976.

Auslander, Philip, *The New York School of Poets as Playwrights: O'Hara, Ashbery, Koch, Schuyler and The Visual Arts*, New York, Peter Lang, 1989.

Austin, J.L. *How To Do Things With Words*, Oxford, Oxford University Press, 1962.

Bachinger, Katrina, 'Setting allegory adrift in John Ashbery's 'Rivers and Mountains', James Joyce's *Portrait of the Artist as a Young Man*, and Vincent O'Sullivan's *Let the River Stand*', Sabine Coelsch-Foisner, Wolfgang Gortschacher, and M. Klein-Holger, *Trends in English and American Studies: Literature and the Imagination*, Lewiston, NY, Mellen, 1996, pp. 285–93.

Bayley, John, 'Richly Flows Contingency', *New York Review of Books* (15 August 1991), 9.

Bayley, John, *Selected Essays*, Cambridge, Cambridge University Press, 1984.

Beaver, Harold, 'The dandy at play', *Parnassus*, 9:2 (Fall–Winter 1981), 54–61.

Bedient, Claude, 'The tactfully folded-over bill', *Parnassus*, 6 (1977), 161–9.

Bellamy, Joe David (ed.), *American Poetry Observed*, Urbana and Chicago, University of Illinois Press, 1984.

Berger, Charles. '"Vision in the form of a task": *The Double Dream of Spring*', David Lehman (ed.), *Beyond Amazement: New Essays on John Ashbery*, Ithaca and London, Cornell University Press, 1980, pp. 163–208.

Bergman, David, *Gaiety Transfigured: Gay Self-Representation in American Literature*, Madison, Wisconsin University Press, 1991.

Berkson, Bill and Le Sueur, Joe (eds), *Homage to Frank O'Hara*, Berkeley, Creative Arts Company, 1980.

Bernstein, Charles, *Content's Dream: Essays 1975–1984*, Los Angeles, Sun and Moon Press, 1986.

Bernstein, Charles, 'The influence of kinship patterns upon perception of an ambiguous stimulus', *Verse*, 8:1 (Spring 1991), 73–7.

Berryman, John, *Collected Poems*, London, Faber and Faber, 1991.

Berryman, John, *The Dream Songs*, London, Faber and Faber, 1991.

Berryman, John, *The Freedom of the Poet*, New York, Farrar, Straus & Giroux, 1976.

Berryman, John, 'Lowell, Thomas & Co.', *Partisan Review*, 14:1 (January–February 1947), 73–85.

Bhatt, Sujatta. 'Skinnydipping in History', *P.N. Review*, 21:1 (September–October 1994), 76.

Blasing, Mutlu Konuk, *American Poetry: The Rhetoric of Its Forms*, New Haven and London, Yale University Press, 1987.

Blasing, Mutlu Konuk, *Politics and Form in Postmodern Poetry: O'Hara, Bishop, Ashbery and Merrill*, Cambridge, Cambridge University Press, 1995.

Bleikasten, André, 'Entretien avec John Ashbery', *La Quinzaine Littéraire* (February 1993), 16–28.

Bloom, Clive and Doherty, Brian (eds), *American Poetry: The Modernist Ideal*, Basingstoke and London, Macmillan, 1995.

Bloom, Harold, *Agon: Towards a Theory of Revisionism*, New York and Oxford, Oxford University Press, 1982.

Bloom, Harold, *The Anxiety of Influence: A Theory of Poetry*, New York, Oxford University

Press, 1973.

Bloom, Harold, *Figures of Capable Imagination*, New York, Seabury Press, 1976.

Bloom, Harold, *A Map of Misreading*, New York, Oxford University Press, 1975.

Bloom, Harold (ed.), *Contemporary Poets*, New York, Chelsea House Publishers, 1986.

Bloom, Harold (ed.), *Deconstruction and Criticism*, London and Henley, Routledge and Kegan Paul, 1979.

Bloom, Harold (ed.), *Modern Critical Views: John Ashbery*, New York: Chelsea House Publishers, 1985.

Bloom, Janet and Losada, Robert, 'Craft interview with John Ashbery', *New York Quarterly*, 9 (Winter 1972), 11–33.

Bly, Robert, 'On political poetry', *The Nation*, (24 April 1967), 522–4.

Blythe, Caroline, 'Speaking in tongues: an interview with John Ashbery', *Oxford Poetry*, 6:2, 56–62.

Boland, Evan, 'Poetry the hard way', *P.N. Review* 21:1 (September–October 1994), 78–9.

Bourdieu, Pierre, *The Field of Cultural Production: Essays on Art and Literature*, ed. Randal Johnson, Cambridge, Polity Press, 1993.

Bowdan, Janet, '*April Galleons* and the taking of measure', *Verse*, 8:1 (Spring 1991), 42–7.

Bradley, George. 'A short article or poem in response to the work', *Verse*, 8:1 (Spring 1991), 4.

Breslin, James E.B., *From Modern to Contemporary: American Poetry 1945–65*, Chicago, University of Chicago Press, 1984.

Breslin, Paul, *The Psycho-Political Muse: American Poetry Since the Fifties*, Chicago and London, The University of Chicago Press, 1987.

Bromwich, David, 'John Ashbery: the self against its images', *Raritan*, 5:4 (Spring 1986), pp. 36–58.

Bromwich, David, 'Poetic invention and the self-unseeing', *Grand-Street*, 7:1 (Autumn 1987), 115–29.

Brooks, Van Wyck, 'Introduction', *Writers at Work: The Paris Review Interviews*, second series, ed. George Plimpton, Harmondsworth, Middlesex and New York, Penguin Books, 1977.

Bürger, Peter, *Theory of the Avant-Garde*, tr. Michael Shaw, Minneapolis, University of Minneapolis Press, 1984.

Burroughs, William S. and Gysin, Brion, *The Third Mind*, London, John Calder, 1979.

By many hands, *Three Hundred Things a Bright Boy Can Do*, London, Sampson, Low, Marson, 1911.

Cady, Joseph, 'Immersive and Counterimmersive writing about AIDS: the achievement of Paul Marette's Love Alone, Timothy F. Murphy and Suzanne Poirier (eds), *Writing AIDS: Cay Literature, Language and Analysis*, New York, Columbia University Press, 1993, pp. 244–63.

Carey, John, 'Grunts and groans', *The Sunday Times* (9 December 1979), 51.

Carroll, Paul, *The Poem in its Skin*, Chicago: Big Table Publishing Company, 1968.

Champion, Miles, 'Some thoughts on *The Tennis Court Oath*', *P.N. Review*, 21:1 (September–October 1994), 40–1.

Chiaromonte, Nicola, 'Pasternak's message', Donald Davie and Angela Livingstone (eds), *Modern Judgements: Pasternak*, London, Macmillan, 1969, 231–9.

Chui, Linda, 'Ode to a west wind', *P.N. Review*, 21:1 (September–October 1994), 76.

Clover, Joshua, 'In the act: John Ashbery's *And the Stars were Shining*', *The Iowa Review*, 25:1 (Winter 1995), 177–82.

Cohen, Keith, 'Ashbery's dismantling of bourgeois discourse', David Lehman (ed.), *Beyond Amazement: New Essays on John Ashbery*, Ithaca and London, Cornell University Press, 1980, 128–49.

Cohen, J.M., 'The Poetry of Pasternak', *Horizon* (July 1944), 23–4.

Connor, Steven, 'Points of departure: deconstruction and John Ashbery's "Sortes Vergilianae"', Antony Easthope and John Thompson (eds), *Contemporary Poetry Meets Modern Theory*, Hemel Hempstead, Harvester Wheatsheaf, 1991, pp. 5–18.

Conte, Joseph M., *Unending Design: The Forms of Postmodern Poetry*, Ithaca and London, Cornell University Press, 1991.

Cook, Albert, 'Expressionism not wholly abstract: John Ashbery', *American Poetry*, 2:2 (Winter 1985), 53–70.

Corn, Alfred, 'A magma of interiors', Harold Bloom (ed.), *Modern Critical Views: John Ashbery*, New York, Chelsea House Publishers, 1985.

Corn, Alfred, 'Nut-Brown Poet', *Verse*, 8:1 (Spring 1991), 5–7.

Costello, Bonnie, 'John Ashbery and the idea of the reader', *Contemporary Literature*, 23:4 (Fall 1982), 493–514.

Costello, Bonnie, 'John Ashbery's landscapes', Susan Schultz (ed.), *The Tribe of John: Ashbery in Contemporary Poetry*, Tucaloosa, Alabama, University of Alabama Press, 1995, pp. 60–80.

Cottom, Daniel, 'Ashbery's "Down by the station early in the morning"', *Explicator*, 52:4 (Summer 1994), 245–8.

Cottom, Daniel, '"Getting It": Ashbery and the avant-garde of everyday language', *SubStance*, 23:1 (1994), 3–23.

Cowley, Malcolm (ed.), *Writers at Work: The Paris Review Interviews*, first series, Harmondsworth, Middlesex and New York, Penguin Books, 1977.

Crase, Douglas, 'Justified times', *The Nation* (1 September 1984), 146–9.

Crase, Douglas, 'The prophetic Ashbery', David Lehman (ed.), *Beyond Amazement: New Essays on John Ashbery*, Ithaca and London, Cornell University Press, 1980, pp. 30–65.

Crawford, Robert, *Identifying Poets: Self and Territory in Twentieth-Century Poetry*, Edinburgh, Edinburgh University Press, 1993.

Crawford, Robert, 'Shallots', *Poetry Review*, 81:4, 11–13.

Crozier, Andrew, 'Thrills and frills: poetry as figures of empirical lyricism', Alan Sinfield (ed.), *Society and Literature 1945–1970*, London, Methuen, 1983, 199–233.

Culler, Jonathan, *Structuralist Poetics*, London: Routledge, 1975.

Davie, Donald, *Thomas Hardy and British Poetry*, London, Routledge and Kegan Paul, 1973.

Davie, Donald, *Under Briggflatts: A History of Poetry in Great Britain, 1960–1988*, Manchester, Carcanet, 1989.

Davie, Donald and Livingstone, Angela (eds), *Modern Judgements: Pasternak*, London, Macmillan, 1969.

Dayan, Joan, 'Finding what will suffice: John Ashbery's *A Wave*', *Modern Language Notes*, 100 (1985), 1045–79.

De Jongh, Nicholas, 'Waving not drowning: an interview with John Ashbery', *Guardian* (9 May 1987), 15.

Dembo, L.S., 'The "objectivist" poet: four interviews (George Oppen)', *Contemporary Literature*, 10, 159–77.

Dembo, L.S., 'Oppen on his poems', Burton Hatlen (ed.), *George Oppen: Man and Poet*, Orono, Maine, National Poetry Foundation, 1981, pp. 197–213.

Denby, Edwin, *Dance Writings,* London, Dance Books, 1986.

Derrida, Jacques, *Given Time: 1. Counterfeit Money*, tr. Peggy Kamuf, Chicago and London, University of Chicago Press, 1992.

Derrida, Jacques. 'Signature event context', *Between the Blinds: A Derrida Reader*, ed. Peggy Kamuf, Hemel Hempstead, Harvester Wheatsheaf, 1991, 82–111.

Deutscher, Isaac, 'Pasternak and the calendar of the revolution', Donald Davie and Angela Livingstone (eds), *Modern Judgements: Pasternak*, London, Macmillan, 1969, pp. 240–58.

Dewey, Anne, 'The relation between open form and collective voice: the social origin of processual form in John Ashbery's *Three Poems* and Ed Dorn's *Gunslinger*', *Sagetrieb*, 11:1–2 (Spring–Fall 1992), 47–66.

Dickstein, Morris, *Gates of Eden: American Culture in the Sixties*, New York, Basic Books, 1977.

Didsbury, Peter, Review of *Self-Portrait in a Convex Mirror*, *Poetry Review*, 68:1 (April 1978), 62–7.

Di Piero, W.S., 'John Ashbery: the romantic as problem solver', *American Poetry Review* (July/August 1973), 39–42.

Donoghue, Denis, *Reading America: Essays on American Literature*, Berkeley, University of California Press, 1987.

Duyn, Mona Van, 'Ways to meaning', *Poetry*, 100:6 (September 1962), 390–395.

Easthope, Antony and Thompson, John O. (eds), *Contemporary Poetry Meets Modern Theory*, Hemel Hempstead, Harvester Wheatsheaf, 1991.

Edelman, Lee, 'The mirror and the tank: 'AIDS', subjectivity and the rhetoric of activism', Timothy F. Murphy and Suzanne Poirier (eds), *Writing AIDS: Gay Literature, Language and Analysis*, New York, Columbia University Press, 1993, pp. 9–38.

Edelman, Lee, 'The pose of imposture: Ashbery's Self-Portrait in a Convex Mirror', *Twentieth Century Literature*, 32:1 (Spring 1986), 95–114.

Ehrenburg, Ilya, 'Boris Leonidovich Pasternak', Donald Davie and Angela Livingstone (eds), *Modern Judgements: Pasternak*, London, Macmillan, 1969, pp. 39–41.

Eichbauer, Mary, E., *Poetry's Self-Portrait: The Visual Arts as Mirror and Muse in René Char and John Ashbery*, New York, Peter Lang Publishing, 1992.

Emerson, Ralph Waldo, *Essays*, second series, being volume III of Emerson's *Complete Works*, Boston, Houghton, Mifflin and Company, 1894.

Emerson, Ralph Waldo, *The Journals and Miscellaneous Notebooks of Ralph Waldo Emerson*, vol. 14, 1854–1861, ed. Susan Sutton Smith and Harrison Hayford, Cambridge, Mass., The Belknap Press of Harvard University Press, 1978.

Ernst, John, 'Fossilized fish and the world of unknowing: John Ashbery and William Bronk', Susan M. Schultz (ed.), *The Tribe of John: Ashbery in Contemporary Poetry*, Tucaloosa, Alabama, University of Alabama Press, 1995, pp. 168–89.

Erwin, John W., 'The reader is the medium: Ashbery and Ammons ensphered', *Contemporary Literature*, 21:4, 588–610.

Everett, Nicholas, 'Ashbery's humour', *P.N. Review*, 21:1 (September–October 1994), 44–5.

Everett, Nicholas, 'Laughter and tears', *Times Literary Supplement* (7 February 1992), 27

Fenton, James, 'Getting rid of the burden of sense', *New York Times Book Review* (29 December 1985), 10.

Fink, Thomas, 'The comic thrust of Ashbery's poetry', *Twentieth-Century Literature*, 30:1 (Spring 1984), 1–14.

Fink, Thomas, '"Here and there": the locus of language in John Ashbery's "Self-Portrait in a Convex Mirror"', *Contemporary Poetry*, 4:3 (1982), 47–64.

Fink, Thomas, 'The poetry of David Shapiro and Anne Lauterbach: after Ashbery', *American Poetry Review*, 17:1 (January–February 1988), 27–32.

Finkelstein, Norman, '"Still Other Made-Up Countries": John Ashbery and Donald Revell', *Verse*, 8:1 (Spring 1991), 33–5.

Finkelstein, Norman, *The Utopian Moment in Contemporary Poetry*, London and Toronto, Associated University Presses, 1988.

Fite, David, 'John Ashbery: the effort to make sense', *Mississippi Review*, 2:2–3 (Spring 1979), 123–30.

Fite, David, 'On the virtues of modesty: John Ashbery's tactics against transcendence', *Modern Languages Quarterly*, 42:1 (March 1981), 65–84.

Five Young American Poets, Norfolk, Connecticut, New Directions, 1940.

Flint, R.W., 'Poetry chronicle', *Partisan Review*, 29:2 (Spring 1962), 290–4.

Ford, Mark, *A Critical Study of the Poetry of John Ashbery*, Ph.D. thesis, University of Oxford, 1991.

Ford, Mark, 'John Ashbery and Raymond Roussel', *Verse*, 3:1 (November 1986), 13–23.

Ford, Mark, 'A new kind of emptiness', *P.N. Review*, 21:1 (September–October 1994), 54–6.

Forrest-Thomson, Veronica, *Poetic Artifice: A Theory of Twentieth-Century Poetry*, Manchester, Manchester University Press, 1978.

Francis, Richard, 'Weather and turtles in John Ashbery's recent poetry', *P.N. Review*, 21:1 (September–October 1994), 45–7.

Fredman, Stephen, *Poet's Prose: The Crisis in American Verse*, Chicago, Cambridge University Press, 1983.

Freedberg, Sidney J., *Parmigianino: His Works in Painting*, Cambridge, Mass., Harvard University Press, 1950.

Fry, Paul, *A Defense of Poetry: Reflections on the Occasion of Writing*, Stanford, California, Stanford University Press, 1995.

Gangel, Sue. 'An interview with John Ashbery', Joe David Bellamy (ed.), *American Poetry Observed*, Urbana and Chicago, University of Illinois Press, 1984, pp. 9–20.

Gardener, Raymond, 'Interview with John Ashbery', *Guardian* (19 April 1975), 8.

Gardner, Thomas, 'Bishop and Ashbery: two ways out of Stevens', *The Wallace Stevens Journal*, 19:2 (Fall 1995), 201–18.

Gerould, G.H., *The Ballad of Tradition*, Oxford, The Clarendon Press, 1932.

Gery, John, 'The anxiety of affluence: poets after Ashbery', *Verse*, 8:1 (Spring 1991), 28–32.

Gilbert, Roger, *Walks in the World: Representation and Experience in Modern American Poetry*, Princeton, Princeton University Press, 1991.

Ginsberg, Allen and Koch, Kenneth, *Making It Up: Poetry Composed at St. Mark's Church on May 9, 1979*, New York, Catchword Papers, 1994.

Goethe, J.W., *Goethe's Literary Essays: A Selection in English*, ed. J.E.Springan, London, Oxford University Press, 1921.

Gooch, Brad, *City Poet: The Life and Times of Frank O'Hara*, New York, Alfred Knopf, 1993.

Goodman, Paul. 'Advance-guard writing 1900–1950', *The Kenyon Review*, 13:3 (Summer 1951), 357–80.

Goodman, Paul, *Speaking and Language: Defence of Poetry*, New York, Random House, 1971.

Gordon, Lyndall, *Eliot's Early Years*, Oxford, Oxford University Press, 1977.

Gray, Francine du Plessix, 'Introduction', George Plimpton (ed.), *Writers at Work: The Paris Review Interviews*, fifth series, Harmondsworth, Middlesex, Penguin Books, 1983.

Gray, Jeffrey, 'Ashbery's 'The Instruction Manual'', *Explicator*, 54:2 (Winter 1996), 117–20.

Gregson, Ian, *Contemporary Poetry and Postmodernism: Dialogue and Estrangement*, Basingstoke, Macmillan, 1996.

Gregson, Ian, 'Epigraphs for epigones: John Ashbery's influence in England', *Bête Noire*, 4 (Winter 1987), 89–94.

Gregson, Ian, 'The influence of John Ashbery in Britain', *P.N. Review*, 21:1 (September–October 1994), 52–3.

Guillbaut, Serge, *How New York Stole the Idea of Modern Art: Abstract Expressionism, Freedom and the Cold War*, Chicago and London: University of Chicago Press, 1983.

Guillory, Daniel L., '"Leaving the Atocha Station": contemporary poetry and technology', *Triquarterly*, 52 (Fall 1981), 165–82.

Habermas, Jürgen, *Legitimation Crisis*, tr. Thomas McCarthy, London, Heineman, 1976.

Habermas, Jürgen, *The Theory of Communicative Action, Volume 1. Reason and the Rationalization of Society,* tr. Thomas McCarthy, Cambridge, Polity Press, 1997.

Habermas, Jürgen, *The Theory of Communicative Action, Volume 2. Lifeworld and System: A Critique of Functionalist Reason,* tr. Thomas McCarthy, Cambridge, Polity Press, 1997.

Haffenden, John, *John Berryman: A Critical Commentary*, Basingstoke, Macmillan, 1980.

Hall, Donald, 'Introduction', *Poets at Work: The Paris Review Interviews*, Harmondsworth, Penguin, 1989.

Hampshire, Stuart, '*Doctor Zhivago*: As from a lost culture', *Encounter* 62 (1958), 3–5.

Heffernan, James A.W., *Museum of Words: The Poetics of Ekphrasis from Homer to Ashbery*, Chicago and London, University of Chicago Press, 1993.

Henry, Gerrit, 'In progress', *The Spectator* (31 July, 1979), 1.

Henry, Gerrit, *The Mirrored Clubs of Hell, Poems by Gerrit Henry*, with an introduction by John Ashbery, New York, Little Brown and Company, 1991.

Herbert, W.N., 'Ashbery and O'Hara: their respective selves', *Verse*, 3:3, 24–32.

Herbert, W.N., 'Variable coins', *P.N. Review*, 83:3, 15–16.

Herd, David, 'John Ashbery in conversation with David Herd', *P.N. Review*, 21:1 (September–October 1994), 32–37.

Herd, David, 'Kenneth Koch in conversation with David Herd', *P.N. Review* 22:2 (November–December 1995), 27–31.

Herd, David, 'Occasions for solidarity: Ashbery, Riley and the tradition of the new', *Yearbook of English Studies*, 30 (2000), 234–49.

Herd, David, 'What the poet does not leave out', *Times Literary Supplement* (8 March 1996), 28.

Herd, David, '"When time shall force a gift on each": Ashbery, Pasternak and avant-garde expression', *Critical Quarterly*, 40:4 (1998), 47–64.

Hilringhouse, Mark, 'A conversation with John Ashbery', *Soho News* (December 1981), 15–16.

Hoeppner, Edward Haworth, *Echoes and Moving Fields: Structure and Subjectivity in the Poetry of W.S. Merwin and John Ashbery*, Lewisburg, Bucknell University Press, 1994.

Holden, Jonathan, 'Syntax and the poetry of John Ashbery', *American Poetry Review*, 8:4 (July/August, 1979), 37–40.

Hollander, John, 'A poetry of restitution', *The Yale Review*, 70:2 (Winter 1981), 161–86.

Hollander, John, 'Soonest Mended', Harold Bloom (ed.), *Modern Critical Views: John Ashbery*, New York, Chelsea House Publishers, 1985, pp. 207–15.

Horvath, Brooke, 'Dwelling persuasion: John Ashbery's dream of life', *Ball State University Forum*, 25:4 (Autumn 1984), 55–62.

Howard, Richard, *Alone with America: Essays on the Art of Poetry in the United States Since 1950*, New York, Atheneum, 1980.

Howe, Irving, 'Freedom and the ash can of history', Donald Davie and Angela Livingstone (eds), *Modern Judgements: Pasternak*, London, Macmillan, 1969, 259–68.

Howell, Anthony, 'Ashbery in perspective', *P.N. Review*, 21:1 (September–October 1994), 56–7.

Hulse, Michael, 'John Ashbery', *P.N. Review*, 21:1 (September–October 1994), 58–9.

Imbriglio, Catherine, '"Our days put on such reticence": the rhetoric of the closet in John Ashbery's *Some Trees*', *Contemporary Literature*, 36:2 (Summer 1995), 249–88.

Jackson, Richard, 'The imminence of a revelation (John Ashbery)', Richard Jackson (ed.), *Acts of Mind: Conversations with Contemporary Poets*, Alabama, University of Alabama Press, 1983, 69–76.

Jackson, Richard, 'Writing as transgression: Ashbery's archeology of the moment – a review essay', *Southern Humanities Review*, 12 (1978), 271–84.

Jakobson, Roman, 'The prose of the poet Pasternak', Donald Davie and Angela Livingstone (eds), *Modern Judgements: Pasternak*, London, Macmillan, 1969, pp. 135–51.

James, William, *Pragmatism*, New York, Dover Publications, 1995.

Jameson, Fredric, *Postmodernism, or, The Cultural Logic of Late Capitalism*, London and New York, Verso, 1991.

Jarman, Mark, 'The curse of discursiveness', *Hudson Review*, 45:1 (Spring 1992), 158–66.

Jarrell, Randall, *Kipling, Auden and Co.: Essays and Reviews, 1935–1964*, New York, Farrar, Straus, and Giroux, 1981.

Jarrell, Randall, *Poetry and the Age*, London, Faber and Faber, 1973.

Jarvis, Simon, 'Soteriology and reciprocity', *Parataxis: Modernism and Modern Writing*, 5 (Winter 1993–4), 30–9.

Jenkins, Alan, 'Late-flowering dandy', *Sunday Times* (27 April 1986), 32.

Jones, James W., 'Refusing the name: the absence of AIDS in recent American gay male fiction', Timothy F. Murphy and Suzanne Poinier (eds), *Writing AIDS: Gay Literature, Language and Analysis*, New York, Columbia University Press, 1973, pp. 225–43.

Joyce, James, *A Portrait of the Artist as a Young Man*, London, Paladin Books, 1988.

Jumonville, Neil, *Critical Crossings: The New York Intellectuals in Postwar America*, Berkeley, University of California Press, 1991.

Kalstone, David, *Five Temperaments: Elizabeth Bishop, Robert Lowell, James Merrill, Adrienne Rich, John Ashbery*, New York, Oxford University Press, 1977.

Katz, Alex and Koch, Kenneth, *Interlocking Lives*, New York, Kulchur Press, 1970.

Kazin, Alfred, 'Introduction', George Plimpton (ed.), *Writers at Work: The Paris Review Interviews*, third series, Harmondsworth, and New York, Penguin Books Ltd, 1977.

Keeling, John, 'The moment unravels: reading John Ashbery's "Litany"', *Twentieth-Century Literature*, 38:2 (Summer 1992), 125–51.

Keller, Lynn, *Re-making it New: Contemporary American Poetry and the Modernist Tradition*, Cambridge, Cambridge University Press, 1987.

Kendall, Tim, 'Uh oh, no last words', rev. of John Ashbery, *Wakefulness*, *TLS* (21 August 1998), 23.

Kennedy, David, *New Relations: The Refashioning of British Poetry 1980–1994*, Bridgend, Seren, 1996.

Kermani, David, *John Ashbery: A Comprehensive Bibliography (Including his Art Criticism, and with Selected Notes from Unpublished Materials)*, foreword by John Ashbery, New York and London, Garland Publishing, 1976.

Kermode, Frank, *The Sense of an Ending: Studies in the Theory of Fiction*, Oxford, Oxford University Press, 1967.

Kervorikan, Martin, 'John Ashbery's *Flow Chart*: John Ashbery and the theorists on John Ashbery against the critics against John Ashbery', *New Literary History*, 25:2 (Spring 1994), 459–76.

Kimberley, Nick, 'An interview with John Ashbery', *City Limits* (16 May 1986), 29.

Kinzie, Mary, *The Cure of Poetry in an Age of Prose: Moral Essays on the Poet's Calling*, Chicago, Chicago University Press, 1993.

Koch, Kenneth, *The Art of Poetry: Poems, Parodies, Interviews, Essays, and Other Work*, Ann Arbor, The University of Michigan Press, 1996.

Koch, Kenneth, *Collaborations with Artists: Essay and Poems by Kenneth Koch*, intro. Paul Violi, Ipswich, Ipswich Borough Council, 1993.

Koch, Kenneth, *One Train*, New York. Alfred A. Knopf, Manchester, Carcanet 1997.

Koch, Kenneth, *Selected Poems*, Manchester, Carcanet, 1991.

Koestenbaum, Wayne, *Double Talk: The Erotics of Male Literary Collaboration*, London, Routledge, 1989.

Koethe, John, 'The absence of a noble presence', *Verse*, 8:1 (Spring 1991), 23–7.

Koethe, John, 'An interview with John Ashbery', *SubStance*, 9:4/10:1, 178–86.

Koethe, John, 'The metaphysical subject of John Ashbery's poetry', David Lehman (ed.), *Beyond Amazement: New Essays on John Ashbery*, Ithaca and London, Cornell University Press, 1980, pp. 87–100.

Kostelanetz, Richard. 'How to be a difficult poet', Richard Kostelanetz, *The Old Poetries and the New*, Ann Arbor, The University of Michigan Press, 1981, pp. 87–110.

Kramer, Lawrence, '"Syringa": John Ashbery and Eliott Carter', David Lehman (ed.), *Beyond Amazement: New Essays on John Ashbery*, Ithaca and London, Cornell University Press, 1980, 255–71.

Kramer, Lawrence, 'The Wodwo watches the water clock: language in Postmodern British and American Poetry', *Contemporary Literature*, 18:3 (Summer 1977), 311–42.

Kunow, Rudiger, '"You have it but you don't have it": John Ashbery's guarded affirmations of life', Gerhard Hoffman and Alfred Hornung (eds), *Affirmation and Negation in Contemporary American Culture*, Heidelberg, Carl Winter Universitätsverlag, 1994, 251–71.

Labrie, Ross, 'John Ashbery: an interview with Ross Labrie', *American Poetry Review*, 13:13 (May–June 1984), 29–33.

Larkin, Philip, *Collected Poems*, London, The Marvell Press, and Faber and Faber, 1990.

Larrissy, Edward, *Reading Twentieth-Century Poetry: The Language of Gender and Objects*, Oxford, Basil Blackwell, 1990.

Lawson, Andrew, 'Review of John Ashbery, *Flow Chart* and Stephen Roedefer, *Passing Duration*', *Fragmente: A Magazine of Contemporary Poetics*, 4 (Autumn/Winter 1991), 102–12.

Leckie, Ross, 'Art, mimesis, and John Ashbery's "Self-Portrait in a Convex Mirror"', *Essays in Literature,* 19:1 (Spring 1992), 114–31.

Lehman, David, *An Alternative to Speech*, New Jersey, Princeton University Press, 1986.

Lehman, David, 'John Ashbery: the pleasures of poetry', *New York Times Magazine* (16 November, 1984), 84–9.

Lehman, David, *The Last Avant-Garde: The Making of the New York School of Poets*, New York, Doubleday, 1998.

Lehman, David, 'The shield of a greeting: the function of irony in John Ashbery's

Poetry', David Lehman (ed.), *Beyond Amazement: New Essays on John Ashbery*, Ithaca and London, Cornell University Press, 1980, pp. 101–27.

Lehman, David (ed.), *Beyond Amazement: New Essays on John Ashbery*, Ithaca and London, Cornell University Press, 1980.

Lepkowski, Frank J., 'John Ashbery's revision of the post-romantic quest: meaning, evasion, and allusion in "Grand Galop"', *Twentieth-Century Literature*, 39:3 (Fall 1993), 251–65.

Le Queux, William, *Beryl of the Biplane: Being The Romance of an Air Woman of Today*, London, C. Arthur Pearson, 1917.

Lieberman, Laurence, *Unassigned Frequencies: American Poetry in Review, 1964–1977*, Urbana, Chicago, London, University of Illinois Press, 1977.

Lilly, Mark, *Gay Men's Literature in the Twentieth Century*, Basingstoke, Macmillan, 1993

Locus Solus, 1–5 (Winter 1961–Summer 1962), Lans-en-Vercors (Isère), France.

Logan, William, 'Late Callings', *Parnassus*, 18:2/19:1, 317–27.

Longenbach, James, *Modern Poetry After Modernism*, New York, Oxford University Press, 1991.

Lopes, Rodrigo Garcia, 'Notes about the process: an interview with John Ashbery', *Hayden's Ferry Review*, 12 (1993), 27–33.

Lowell, Robert, *Poems 1938–1949*, London, Faber and Faber, 1950.

Lowell, Robert, 'For John Berryman', *New York Review of Books* (6 April 1972), 3.

Lundquist, Sara L., 'Légèreté et richesse: John Ashbery's English "French poems"', *Contemporary Literature*, 32:3 (Fall 1991), 403–21.

Machiz, Herbert, *Artist's Theatre. Four Plays. Try! Try!, by Frank O'Hara. The Heroes, by John Ashbery. The Bait, by James Merrill. Absalom, by Lionel Abel*, New York, Grove Press, 1960.

Mandel'shtam, Osip (ed.), 'Notes on poetry', Donald Davie and Angela Livingstone (eds), *Modern Judgements: Pasternak*, London, Macmillan, 1969, pp. 67–72.

Mars-Jones, Adam and White, Edmund, *The Darker Proof: Stories From a Crisis*, London and Boston: Faber and Faber, 1988.

Martory, Pierre, *The Landscape Is Behind the Door*, tr. and intro. John Ashbery, Riverdale-on-Hudson, New York, The Sheep Meadow Press, 1994.

Mauss, Marcel, *The Gift: The Form and Reason for Exchange in the Archaic Societies*, tr. W.D. Hall, foreword by Mary Douglas, London, Routledge, 1990.

McCabe, Cynthia Jaffee (ed.), *Artistic Collaboration in the Twentieth Century*, Washington, D.C., Smithsonian Institute Press, 1984.

McCabe, Cynthia Jaffee, 'Artistic collaboration in the twentieth century: the period between the two wars', Cynthia Jaffee McCabe (ed.), *Artistic Collaboration in the Twentieth Century*, Washington, D.C., Smithsonian Institute Press, 1984, 15–44.

McCarthy, Penny, 'About Ashbery', *P.N. Review*, 21:1 (September–October 1994), 63–4.

McClatchy, J.D., *White Paper: On Contemporary American Poetry*, New York, Columbia University Press, 1989.

McCorkle, James (ed.), *Conversant Essays: Contemporary Poets on Poetry*, Detroit, Wayne State University Press, 1990.

McCorkle, James, 'Nimbus of sensations: eros and reverie in the poetry of John Ashbery and Ann Lauterbach', Susan M. Schultz (ed.), *The Tribe of John: Ashbery in Contemporary Poetry*, Tucaloosa, Alabama, University of Alabama Press, 1995, 101–25.

McCorkle, James, *The Still Performance: Writing, Self and Interconnection*, Charlottesville, University of Virginia, 1989.

McGann, Jerome, J, *Social Values and Poetic Acts: The Historical Judgement of Literary Work*,

Cambridge, Mass., Harvard University Press, 1988.

McGuinnes, Patrick, 'Ashbery', *P.N. Review*, 21:1 (September–October 1994), 64–6.

McNeil, Helen, 'Between brass and silver', *Times Literary Supplement* (5 June 1981), 644.

Mead, Philip, 'Memoranda of our feelings: John Ashbery's *A Wave*', *Scripsi*, 4:1, 103–19.

Melville, Herman, *Moby Dick; or, The Whale*, ed. Harold Beaver, Harmondsworth, Penguin, 1986.

Mersmann, James F., *Out of the Vietnam Vortex: A Study of Poets and Poetry Against the War*, Lawrence, University of Kansas Press, 1974.

Meyer, Stephen, 'Ashbery: poet for all seasons', *Raritan*, 15:2 (Fall 1995), 144–61.

Middleton, Christopher, '*A Wave*', *P.N. Review*, 21:1 (September–October 1994), 41–2.

Middleton, Peter, 'Who am I to speak?: The politics of subjectivity in recent British poetry', Robert Hampson and Peter Barry (eds), *New British Poetries: The Scope of the Possible*, Manchester and New York, Manchester University Press, 1993.

Miklitsch, Robert, 'John Ashbery', *Contemporary Literature*, 21:1 (Winter 1980), 118–35.

Miller, Chris, 'Ashbery: "What's keeping us here?"' *P.N. Review*, 21:1 (September–October 1994), 67–8.

Miller, S.H., 'Psychic geometry: John Ashbery's prose poems', *American Poetry*, 3:1 (Fall 1985), 24–42.

Miller, Stephen Paul, 'Periodizing Ashbery and his influence', Susan M.Schultz (ed.), *The Tribe of John: Ashbery in Contemporary Poetry*, Tucaloosa, Alabama, University of Alabama Press, 1995, 146–67.

Mills, C. Wright, *Power, Politics and People: The Collected Essays of C. Wright Mills*, ed. Irving Louis Horowitz, New York, Oxford University Press, 1963.

Mills, C. Wright, *White Collar: The American Middle Classes*, New York, Oxford University Press, 1951.

Mills-Court, Karen, *Poetry as Epitaph: Representation and Poetic Language*, Baton Rouge and London, Louisiana State University Press, 1990.

Milton, John, *Milton: Poetical Works*, ed. Douglas Bush, Oxford, Oxford University Press, 1983.

Mohanty, S.P. and Monroe, Jonathan, 'John Ashbery and the articulation of the social', *diacritics*, 17:2 (Summer 1987), 37–63.

Molesworth, Charles, *The Fierce Embrace*, Columbia, University of Missouri Press, 1979.

Monroe, Jonathan, 'Idiom and cliché in T. S. Eliot and John Ashbery', *Contemporary Literature*, 31:1 (1989), 17–36.

Mooneyman, Laura, '"As new wak't": Wallace Stevens's "Chorocua to it neighbour" and John Ashbery's "Spring Day"', *South Atlantic Review*, 55:2 (May 1990), 117–29.

Moramarco, Fred, 'Coming full circle: John Ashbery's later poetry', Susan M. Schultz (ed.), *The Tribe of John: Ashbery in Contemporary Poetry*, Tucaloosa, Alabama, University of Alabama Press, 1995, pp. 38–59.

Moramarco, Fred, 'John Ashbery and Frank O'Hara: the painterly poets', *Journal of Modern Literature*, 5:3 (September 1976), 436–62.

Moramarco, Fred, 'The lonesomeness of words: a revaluation of *The Tennis Court Oath*', David Lehman (ed.), *Beyond Amazement: New Essays on John Ashbery*, Ithaca and London, Cornell University Press, 1980, 150–62.

Morse, Jonathan, 'Typical Ashbery', Susan M. Schultz (ed.), *The Tribe of John: Ashbery in Contemporary Poetry*, Tucaloosa, Alabama, University of Alabama Press, 1995, pp. 15–25.

Morse, Samuel French, 'A baker's dozen?', *The Virginia Quarterly*, 38:2 (Winter 1962), 324–30.

Mottram, Eric, 'John Ashbery: "All in the refined assimilable state"', *Poetry Information*, 20–1 (Winter 1979–80), 31–48.

Mueller, Robert, 'John Ashbery and the poetry of consciousness: "Self-Portrait in a Convex Mirror"', *The Centennial Review*, 40:3 (Fall 1996), 561–72.

Muldoon, Paul, 'A cat to catch a muse', *Observer* (15 November 1998), 14.

Munn, Paul, 'An interview with John Ashbery', *The New Orleans Review*, 17:2 (1970), 153–62.

Munn, Paul, 'Vestigial form in John Ashbery's "A Wave"', *New Orleans Review*, 19:1 (Spring 1992), 19–22.

Murphy, John, 'John Ashbery: an interview with John Murphy', *Poetry Review*, 75:2 (August 1985), 20–5.

Murphy, Margueritte S., *A Tradition of Subversion: The Prose Poem in English From Wilde to Ashbery*, Amherst, University of Massachusetts Press, 1992.

Murphy, Rosalie, *Contemporary Poets of the English Language*, Chicago, St James Press, 1970.

Murphy, Timothy F. and Poirier, Suzanne (eds), *Writing AIDS: Gay Literature, Language, and Anlaysis*, New York, Columbia University Press, 1993.

Myers, John Bernard (ed.), *The Poets of the New York School*, Philadelphia, Pennsylvania University Press, 1969.

Nason, Richard, W., *Boiled Grass and the Broth of Shoes: Reconstructing Literary Deconstruction*, London, McFarland, Jefferson, 1991.

Nelson, Cary, *Our Last First Poets: Vision and History in Contemporary American Poetry*, Urbana, Chicago, London, University of Illinois Press, 1981.

Nemerov, Howard, *Contemporary American Poetry*, Voice of America Forum Lectures, 1965.

Nicholls, Peter, 'Of being ethical: reflections on George Oppen', *Journal of American Studies*, 31:2 (1997), 153–70.

Norfolk, Lawrence, 'Forever coming closer', *Times Literary Supplement* (23 June 1988), 31.

Norton, Jody, '"Whispers out of time": the syntax of being in the poetry of John Ashbery', *Twentieth-Century Literature*, 41:3 (Fall 1996), 281–305.

O'Brien, Geoffrey, 'Mayakovsky of MacDougal Street', *New York Review of Books* (2 December 1993), 22–3.

O'Brien, Sean, 'Historical sicknotes', *Poetry Review*, 88:1 (Spring 1988), 36.

O'Driscoll, Denis, 'The Irish Ashbery', *P.N. Review*, 21:1 (September–October 1994), 32–7.

O'Hara, Frank, *Art Chronicles 1954–66*, New York, George Braziller, 1975.

O'Hara, Frank, *The Collected Poems of Frank O'Hara*, ed. Donald Allen, intro. John Ashbery, New York, Alfred A. Knopf, 1971.

O'Hara, Frank, *Standing Still and Walking in New York*, ed. Donald Allen, Bolinas, California, Grey Fox Press, 1971.

Olson, Charles, *Selected Poems*, ed. Robert Creeley, Berkeley, Los Angeles, University of California Press, 1997.

Opello, Olivia, 'John Ashbery: the reader's dilemma', *Publications of the Mississippi Philological Association*, (1987), 79–87.

Oppen, George, *Collected Poems*, London, Fulcrum Press, 1972.

Oppen, George, *The Selected Letters of George Oppen*, ed. Rachel Blau DuPlessis, Durham and London, Duke University Press, 1990.

Osti, Louis. 'The craft of John Ashbery', *Confrontations*, 9 (Fall 1974), 84–94.

'Our Country and Our Culture: A Symposium', *Partisan Review*, 19:3 (May–June 1952),

282–326; 19:4 (July–August), 420–50; 19:5 (September–October), 562–97.

Paddon, Seija, 'John Ashbery and Paavo Haaviko: architects of the postmodern space in mind and language', *Canadian Review of Comparative Literature/Revue Canadienne de Litterature Comparée*, 20:3–4 (1993), 409–16.

Pascal, Blaise, *The Pensées*, tr. J.M. Cohen, Harmondsworth, Penguin, 1961.

Pasternak, Boris, *Doctor Zhivago,* tr. Max Hayward and Manya Harari, London, Harvill, 1992.

Pasternak, Boris, *An Essay in Autobiography*, tr. Manya Harari, London, Collins and Harvill Press, 1959.

Pasternak, Boris, *My Sister – Life,* tr. Mark Rudman with Bohdan Boydunk, Evanston, Illinois, Northwestern University Press, 1983.

Pasternak, Boris, *Safe Conduct: An Early Autobiography and Other Works*, London, Elek Books, 1959.

Pater, Walter, *Plato and Platonism: A Series of Lectures*, London and New York, Macmillan and Co., 1893.

Paulin, Tom, 'A naked emperor', *Poetry Review*, 74:3 (September 1984), 32–3.

'Paying attention: an interview with John Ashbery', *Economist* (14 September 1991), 136.

Perloff, Marjorie, '"Fragments of a buried life": John Ashbery's dream songs', David Lehman (ed.), *Beyond Amazement: New Essays on John Ashbery*, Ithaca and London, Cornell University Press, 1980, pp. 66–86.

Perloff, Marjorie, *Frank O'Hara: Poet Among Painters*, New York, George Braziller, 1977.

Perloff, Marjorie, *The Futurist Moment: Avant-Garde, Avant Guerre, and the Language of Rupture*, Chicago and London, University of Chicago Press, 1986.

Perloff, Marjorie, *Poetic Licence: Essays on Modernist and Postmodernist Lyric*, Evanston, Illinois, Northwestern University Press, 1990.

Perloff, Marjorie, *The Poetics of Indeterminacy: Rimbaud to Cage*, Princeton, Princeton University Press, 1981.

Perloff, Marjorie, *Poetry On and Off the Page: Essays for Emergent Occasions*, Evanston, Illinois, Northwestern University Press, 1998.

Perloff, Marjorie, *Radical Artifice: Writing in the Age of Media*, Chicago and London, University of Chicago Press, 1991.

Perloff, Marjorie, '"Transparent selves": the poetry of John Ashbery and Frank O'Hara', *The Yearbook of English Studies*, 8 (1978), 171–96.

Perreault, John, *Camouflage*, intro. John Ashbery, New York, Alines Books, 1996.

Pilling, John, 'Secret sorcery: early Ashbery', *P.N. Review*, 21:1 (September–October 1994), 38–40.

Pinsky, Robert, *The Situation of Poetry: Contemporary Poetry and Its Traditions*, Princeton, Princeton University Press, 1978.

Plotz, John *et al.*, 'An interview with John Berryman', Harry Thomas (ed.), *Berryman's Understanding: Reflections on the Poetry of John Berryman*, Boston, Northeastern University Press, 1988, 3–17.

Poirier, Suzanne, 'On writing AIDS: introduction', Timothy F. Murphy and Suzanne Piorier (eds), *Writing AIDS: Gay Literature, Language and Analysis*, New York, Columbia University Press, 1993, 1–8.

Porter, Peter, 'The messiness of life', *P.N. Review*, 21:1 (September–October, 1994), 77–8.

Poulin Jnr, A, 'The experience of experience: a conversation with John Ashbery', *The Michigan Quarterly*, 22:3 (Summer 1981), 242–55.

Prince, F.T., 'In a glass darkly', *P.N. Review*, 21:1 (September–October 1994), 37–8.

Printz-Pahlson, Goran, 'Surface and accident: John Ashbery', *P.N. Review*, 46, 12:2, 34–36.

Prestiani, Vincent, 'John Ashbery: an analytic bibliography of bibliographies', *Sagetrieb*, 11: 1–2 (Spring–Fall 1992), 235–6.

Quiller-Couch, Sir Arthur (ed.), *The Oxford Book of the English Verse 1250–1918*, Oxford and New York, Oxford University Press,1984.

Quinn, Justin, 'John Ashbery, nature poet', *P.N. Review*, 21:1 (September–October 1994), 68–70.

Ramke, Bin, 'How French is it? Recent translations and poems by John Ashbery', *Denver Quarterly*, 29:3 (Winter 1995), 118–24.

Rand, Richard, 'Sortes Vergilianae', Antony Easthope and John Thompson (ed.), *Contemporary Poetry Meets Modern Theory*, Hemel Hempstead, Harvester Wheatsheaf, 1991, 19–33.

Rapaport, Herman, 'Deconstructing apocalyptic rhetoric: Ashbery, Derrida, Blanchot', *Criticism*, 27 (1985), 387–400.

Ratcliffe, Stephen and Scalapino, Leslie (eds), *Talking in Tranquility: Interviews with Ted Berrigan*, Bolinas and Oakland, California, Avenue B/O Books, 1991.

Rawson, Claude, 'Bards, boardrooms, and blackboards: John Ashbery, Wallace Stevens, and the academicization of poetry', *P.N. Review*, 21:1 (September–October 1994), 71–4.

Rawson, Claude, 'A poet in the postmodern playground', *Times Literary Supplement* (4 July 1986), 723–4.

Reed, Jeremy, *Blue Sonata: The Poetry of John Ashbery*, Privately Printed, 1994.

Revell, Donald, '"Purists will object": some meditations on influence', *Verse*, 8:1 (Spring 1991), 16–22.

Richman, Richard, 'Our "most important" living poet', *Commentary*, 74:1 (July 1982), 62–8.

Rigsbee, David, 'Against monuments: a reading of Ashbery's "These Lacustrine Cities"', David Lehman (ed.) *Beyond Amazement: New Essays on John Ashbery*, Ithaca and London, Cornell University Press, 1980, 209–23.

Robinson, Peter, '"As my way is": John Ashbery's gift', *P.N. Review*, 21:1 (September–October 1994), 71–4.

Rorty, Richard, *Contingency, Irony and Solidarity*, Cambridge, Cambridge University Press, 1989.

Rosen, Charles, 'Who's afraid of the avant-garde?', *New York Review of Books* (14 May 1998), 20–3.

Rosenberg, Harold, *The Tradition of the New*, London, Thames and Hudson, 1962.

Ross, Andrew, *The Failure of Modernism: Symptoms of American Poetry*, New York, Columbia University Press, 1986.

Ross, Andrew, 'Taking *The Tennis Court Oath*', Susan M. Schultz (ed.), *The Tribe of John: Ashbery in Contemporary Poetry*, Tucaloosa, Alabama, University of Alabama Press, 1995, 193–210.

Roussel, Raymond, *How I Wrote Certain of My Books*, tr. with notes and bibliography by Trevor Winkfield, with two essays on Roussel by John Ashbery, and a translation of canto II of *Nouvelles Impressions d'Afrique* by Kenneth Koch, New York, Sun, 1977.

Salusinsky, Imre, 'The genesis of Ashbery's "Europe"', *Notes on Modern American Literature*, 7:2 (Fall 1983), Item 12.

Scammell, William, 'Review of *April Galleons*', *Poetry Review*, 78:1 (Spring 1988), 48–9.

Schmidt, Michael, 'Editorial', *P.N. Review*, 21:1 (September–October 1994).

Schmidt, Michael, *Lives of the Poets*, London, Weidenfeld & Nicolson, 1998.

Schultz, Susan M., '"The lyric crash": the theater of subjectivity in John Ashbery's *Three Poems*', *Sagetrieb*, 12:2 (Fall 1993), 137–48.

Schultz, Susan M., '"Returning to Bloom": John Ashbery's critique of Harold Bloom', *Contemporary Literature*, 37:1 (Spring 1996), 96–120.

Schultz, Susan M. (ed.), *John Ashbery's Influence on Contemporary Poetry*, *Verse* [John Ashbery Special Number], 8:1 (Spring 1991).

Schultz, Susan M. (ed.), *The Tribe of John: Ashbery and Contemporary Poetry*, Tucaloosa, Alabama, University of Alabama Press, 1995.

Schuyler, James, *Selected Poems*, New York, Farrar Straus, Giroux, 1988.

Schuyler, James, *The Diary of James Schuyler*, ed. Nathan Kernan, Santa Rosa, Black Sparrow Press, 1987.

Schwartz, Delmore, *In Dreams Begin Responsibilities and Other Stories*, ed. James Atlas, London, Secker and Warburg, 1978.

Schwartz, Delmore, *Selected Essays of Delmore Schwartz*, ed. Donald A. Dike and David H. Zucker, Chicago and London, University of Chicago Press, 1970.

Searle, John R., *(On) Searle on Conversation*, by John Searle *et al.*, compiled by Herman Parret and Jef Verschwerer, Amsterdam, Philadelphia, John Benjamin's Publishing Company, 1992.

Sedgwick, Eve Kosofsky, *Between Men: English Literature and Male Homosocial Desire*, New York, Columbia University Press, 1985.

Sedgwick, Eve Kosofsky, *Tendencies*, London, Routledge, 1994.

Sexton, David, 'John Ashbery: poetry's Daffy Duck', *Sunday Times* (16 June 1985), 43.

Shapiro, David, 'Art as collaboration: towards a theory of pluralist aesthetics', Cynthia Jaffee McCabe (ed.), *Artistic Collaboration in the Twentieth Century*, Washington, D.C., Smithsonian Institute Press, 1984, 45–62.

Shapiro, David, *John Ashbery: An Introduction to the Poetry*, New York, Columbia University Press, 1979.

Shapiro, David, 'Urgent masks: an introduction to John Ashbery's poetry', Stuart Friebert, David Walker and David Young (eds), *A Field Guide to Contemporary Poetry and Poetics*, Oberlin, Ohio, Oberlin College, 1997, pp. 243–54.

Shapiro, Karl, *Essay on Rime*, New York, Reynal and Hitchcock, 1945.

Sheed, Wilfred, 'Introduction', George Plimpton (ed.), *Writers at Work: The Paris Review Interviews*, fourth series, Harmondsworth, Penguin Books, 1976.

Shelley, Percy Bysshe, 'A defence of poety', ed. H.F.B. Brett-Smith, *The Four Ages of Poetry*, Oxford, Blackwell, 1972.

Shetley, Vernon, *After the Death of Poetry: Poet and Audience in Contemporary America*, Durham and London, Duke University Press, 1993.

Shoptaw, John, 'Investigating *The Tennis Court Oath*', *Verse*, 8:1 (Spring 1991), 61–72.

Shoptaw, John, 'James Merrill and John Ashbery', Jay Parini and C. Brett Millier (eds), *The Columbia History of American Poetry*, New York: Columbia University Press, 1993.

Shoptaw, John, 'The music of construction: measure and polyphony in Ashbery and Bernstein', Susan M. Schultz (ed.), *The Tribe of John: Ashbery and Contemporary Poetry*, Tucaloosa, Alabama, University of Alabama Press, 1995, 211–57.

Shoptaw, John, *On the Outside Looking Out: John Ashbery's Poetry*, Cambridge, Mass. and London, Harvard University Press, 1994.

Silliman, Ron (ed.), *In The American Tree*, Orono, Maine, National Poetry Foundation,

1986.

Silver, Keith, 'Flow Chart', *P.N. Review*, 21:1 (September–October 1994), 42–3.

Silvester, Christopher (ed.), *The Penguin Book of Interviews: An Anthology from 1859 to the Present*, Harmondsworth, Viking, 1993.

Simon, John, 'More brass than enduring', *Hudson Review*, 15:3 (Autumn 1962), 458–68.

Simpson, Louis, 'Dead horses and live issues', *Nation* (24 April 1967), 520–2.

Sinyavsky, Andrei, 'Boris Pasternak', Donald Davie and Angela Livingstone (eds), *Modern Judgements: Pasternak*, London, Macmillan, 1969, pp. 154–219.

Sloan, Benjamin, 'Houseboat Days and "houses founded on the sea": an example of Emerson as source for Ashbery', *Notes on Contemporary Literature*, 23:5 (May 1993), 5–6.

Smith, Dinita, 'Poem Alone', *New York* (20 May 1991), 50.

Sokolsky, Anita, '"A commission that never materialized": narcissism and lucidity in Ashbery's "Self-Portrait in a Convex Mirror"', Harold Bloom (ed.), *Modern Critical Views: John Ashbery*, New York, Chelsea House Publishers, 1985, 233–50.

Sommer, Piotr, 'An interview in Warsaw', Michael Palmer (ed.), *Code of Signals: Recent Writings in Poetics*, Berkeley, North Atlantic Books, 1983, 294–313.

Sontag, Susan, *Against Interpretation*, New York, Farrar, Straus, 1966.

Sontag, Susan, *AIDS and Its Metaphors*, Harmondsworth, Allen Lane, The Penguin Press, 1989.

Spurr, David, 'John Ashbery's poetry of language', *Centenniel Review*, 25:2 (Spring 1981), 156–61.

Staiger, Jeff, 'The hitherside of history: tone, knowledge, and spirit in John Ashbery's "The System"', *Texas Studies in Literature and Language*, 39:1 (Spring 1997), 80–95.

Stamelman, Richard, 'Critical reflections: poetry and art criticism in Ashbery's "Self Portrait in a Convex Mirror"', *New Literary History*, 15:3 (Spring 1984), 607–30.

Stein, Gertrude, *Look at Me Now and Here I am: Writings and Lectures 1909–1945*, Harmondsworth, Penguin Books, Ltd, 1990.

Stevens, Wallace, *Collected Poems*, London, Faber and Faber, 1990.

Stitt, Peter, 'The art of poetry: an interview with John Berryman', Harry Thomas (ed.), *Berryman's Understanding: Reflections on the Poetry of John Berryman*, Boston, Northeastern University Press, 1988, 18–44.

Stitt, Peter, 'The art of poetry XXXIII: John Ashbery', George Plimpton (ed.), *Poets at Work: The Paris Review Interviews*, Harmondsworth and New York, Penguin Books, 1989, 387–412.

Thoreau, Henry David, *Walden*, Oxford, Oxford University Press, 1999.

Tranter, John, 'An interview with John Ashbery', *Scripsi*, 4:1 (July 1986), 93–102.

Trotter, David, *The Making of the Reader: Language and Subjectivity in Modern American, English and Irish Poetry*, Basingstoke, Macmillan, 1984.

Tsvetayeva, Marina, 'A downpour of light: poetry of eternal courage', Donald Davie and Angela Livingstone (eds), *Modern Judgements: Pasternak*, London, Macmillan, 1969, 42–66.

Turco, Lewis, 'John Ashbery's handbook forms', *New Orleans Review*, 19:1 (Spring 1992), 5–8.

Tynyanov, Yuri, 'Pasternak's mission', Donald Davie and Angela Livingstone (eds), *Modern Judgements: Pasternak*, London, Macmillan, 1969, 126–34.

Vasari, Giorgio, *Lives of the Most Eminent Painters, Sculptors, and Architechts*, vol. 3, tr. Mrs Jonathon Foster, London, Henry G. Bohn.

Vendler, Helen, *The Given and the Made: Recent American Poets*, London, Faber and Faber,

1995.

Vendler, Helen, *The Music of What Happens: Poems, Poets, Critics*, Cambridge, Mass. and London, Harvard University Press, 1988.

Vendler, Helen, *Soul Says: On Recent Poetry*, Cambridge, Mass., Harvard University Press, 1995.

Vendler, Helen, 'A steely glitter chasing shadows', *New Yorker* (3 August 1992), 73–6.

Vendler, Helen, 'Understanding Ashbery', *New Yorker* (16 March 1981), 114–36.

Von Hallberg, Robert, *American Poetry and Culture 1945–1980*, Cambridge, Mass. and London, Harvard University Press, 1985.

Ward, Geoff, *Statutes of Liberty: The New York School of Poets*, Basingstoke and London, Macmillan,1993.

Ward, Geoff, '"Why, it's right there in the procès verbal": the New York School of Poets', *The Cambridge Quarterly*, 21:3 (1992), 273–82.

Warren, Robert Penn, *Democracy and Poetry*, Cambridge, Mass. and London, Harvard University Press, 1975.

Wasserman, Rosanne, 'Marianne Moore and the New York School: O'Hara, Ashbery, Koch', *Sagetrieb*, 6:3 (Winter 1987), 67–77.

Watt, Tessa, *Cheap Print and Popular Piety 1550–1640*, Cambridge, Cambridge University Press, 1991

West, Cornel, *The American Evasion of Philosophy: A Genealogy of Pragmatism*, Wisconsin, University of Wisconsin Press, 1989.

Wheelwright, John, *Collected Poems of John Wheelwright*, New York, New Directions, 1983.

Whitman, Walt, *Complete Poetry and Collected Prose and Letters*, New York, The Library of American, 1982.

Williams, Ned B., 'Ashbery's "The Grapevine"', *Explicator*, 49:4 (Summer 1991), 251–4.

Williamson, Alan, *Introspection and Contemporary Poetry*, Cambridge, Mass. and London, Harvard University Press, 1984.

Wilson, Edmund, 'Legend and symbol in *Doctor Zhivago*', *Nation* (25 April 1959), 40–56.

Wilson, Rob, 'John Ashbery's post-industrial sublime', *Verse*, 8:1 (Spring 1991), 48–52.

Wolf, Leslie, 'The brushstroke's integrity: the poetry of John Ashbery and the art of painting', David Lehman (ed.), *Beyond Amazement: New Essays on John Ashbery*, Ithaca and London, Cornell University Press, 1980, 224–54.

Wordsworth, William and Coleridge, S.T., *Lyrical Ballads*, ed. R.C. Brett and A.R. Jones, London, Routledge, 1991.

Wordsworth, William, *The Oxford Authors: William Wordsworth*, ed. Stephen Gill, Oxford and New York, Oxford University Press, 1986.

Yeaton, Diane, 'Compliments of a friend: a review of John Asbhery's *As We Know*', *American Poetry Review*, 10:1 (January–February 1981), 34–6.

Index

Note: page numbers in **bold** refer to major discussions; 'n.' after a page reference indicates a note number on that page.